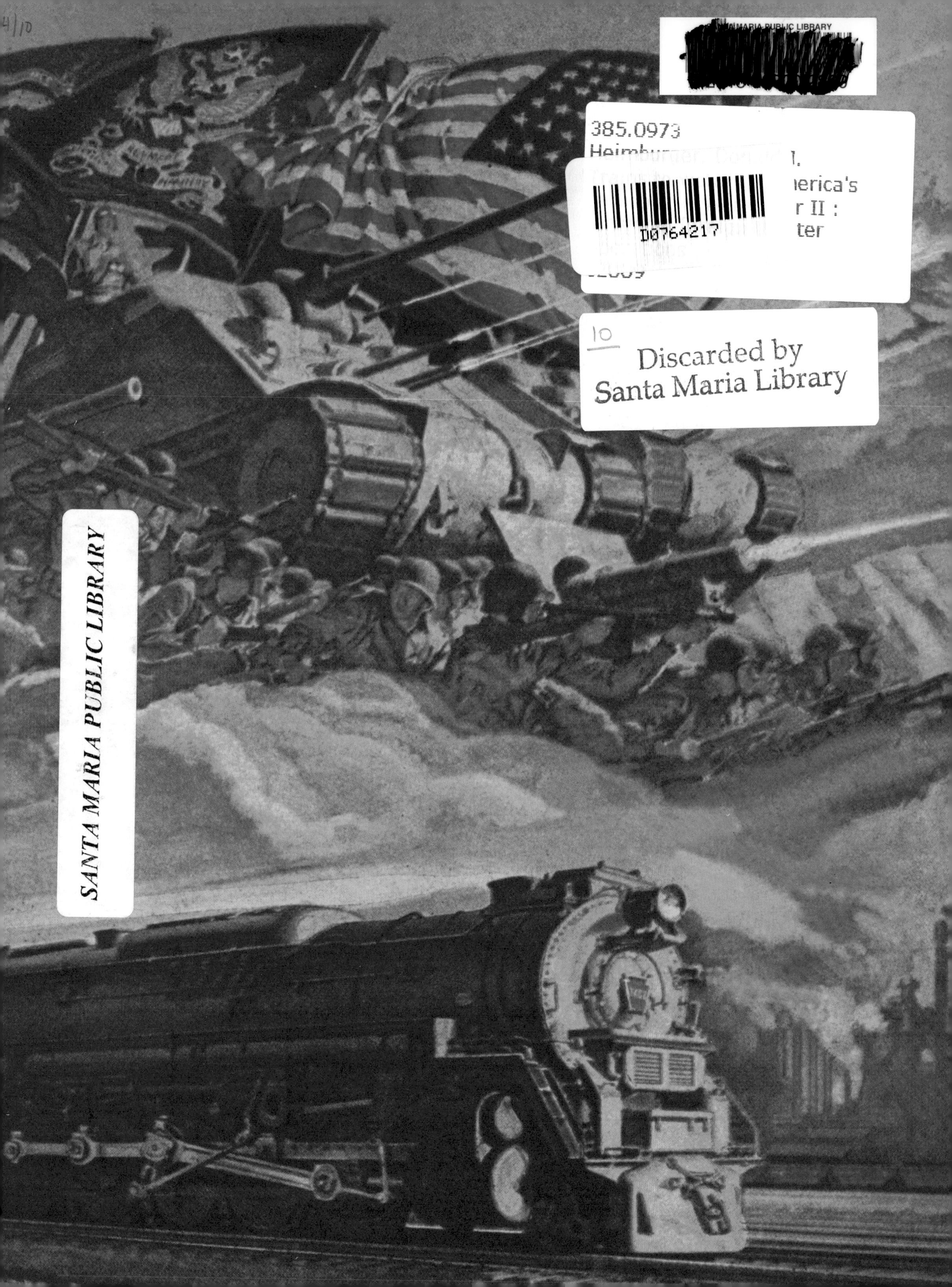

Trains to Victory
America's Railroads in World War II

A railroad conductor walks the train upon which Army tanks have been loaded. At times during World War II, the Army shipped as much as 12.5% of all the military freight carried by the rails. Not only did the military need equipment for current operations during the war, it had to project what it would need in the future, and have those materiels and supplies in the pipeline moving towards their final destination, whether it be in the U.S. or abroad. *David Myers collection*

Trains to Victory

America's Railroads in World War II

Including Foreign Theater Operations

By Donald J. Heimburger and John Kelly

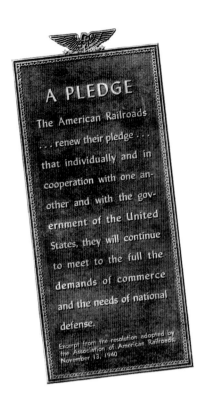

A PLEDGE

The American Railroads . . . renew their pledge . . . that individually and in cooperation with one another and with the government of the United States, they will continue to meet to the full the demands of commerce and the needs of national defense.

Excerpt from the resolution adopted by the Association of American Railroads, November 13, 1940

Dedication

This book is dedicated to freedom, and to all veteran and active duty members of the United States Armed Forces.

"This nation will remain the land of the free only so long as it is the home of the brave." —Elmer Davis

Library of Congress Catalog Card Number: 2008908451
ISBN-10: 0-911581-60-X
ISBN-13: 978-0-911581-60-7
First Edition
Printed in Hong Kong

Heimburger House Publishing Company
7236 West Madison Street
Forest Park, Illinois 60130 USA

Acknowledgements

This book was researched and written because the full and dramatic story of the United States railroads in World War II needed to be told.

Many books have been published that address certain aspects of U. S. railroads at war between 1941 and 1945, and other works have briefly touched on what happened in an overall sense. But to give a complete picture of what happened during the war years is a daunting task; thus, even this work could have been expanded, but the economics of such a book title would have been overwhelming.

In many projects, the more you learn, the more you realize there are other aspects of your subject that need more development. And so it is with this volume, despite the length and breath of this coverage.

The wealth of information and illustrations, and the number of sources for WWII information, is tremendous. We hope we have covered the subject as thoroughly as possible in this book. Some of the photos in this title are not to the standards of 21st century publishing, but they were included nevertheless, because many WWII-era original photos have been lost, damaged or have lost clarity with time, but these older photos still tell a relevant story about the war and railroading, and how they meshed between 1941 and 1945.

Publishing a book of this magnitude requires the assistance and cooperation of many people and organizations, along with a strong dose of perseverance and even a bit of luck. Besides the people and groups named here, many others helped direct the focus of this book. To you all, thank you for your support and your encouragement. We have been fortunate to have many friends who have helped us along the way, and to you, we tip our hats and salute you.

Special recognition goes to the Association of American Railroads, Nancy Bartol of Kalmbach Publishing Company, Bob's Photos, Thomas Burg, Chris Burritt, Hal Carstens from Carstens Publications, Clint Chamberlin, Chesapeake & Ohio Railroad Historical Society, Chicago & North Western Railway Historical Society, Stan Cohen from Pictorial Histories Publishing Company, Joe Collias, Regi Cordic, Dedman's Photo Shop, Brigadier General (Ret.) Kerry G. Denson of the Wisconsin Army National Guard, David Doyle, Charles Felstead collection, Mallory Hope Ferrell, James Griffin from the Lincoln County Historical Museum, J. Michael Gruber, Bob Hall, Doug Harley, Ursula Heinz, Dick Hillman of the Southern Museum of Civil War & Locomotive History, Donald Hofsommer, Sharon Weldon Hudgins, Mark Hughes and Robert L. Hundman of Hundman Publishing Company.

Others who have helped include Kalmbach Publishing Company, Patricia Kentner of Simmons-Boardman Publishing Co., Lisa Keys from the Kansas State Historical Society, Thomas Klinger, Owen Leander, Library of Virginia, McAlester Army Depot, M. D. McCarter, Louis Marre, Arthur H. Miller Jr. of Lake Forest College, Dr. Nathan Molldrem collection, David Myers, National Archives, Frank Nolte, John B. Norwood Jr., Northeast Rails, Harley Oswald who provided many wartime advertisements, Otto Perry collection at the Denver Public Library, Joe Piersen, Bill Raia, Gil Reid of Kalmbach Publishing Company, Robert W. Richardson, Dr. Richard C. Roberts, William Sabel, Linda Shult, Amit Shrestha of Lake Forest College, George Speir, Delbert Spencer, C. Douglas Sterner, Colonel (Ret.) Thomas W. Sweeney of the U.S. Army Transportation Corps, Donna Tabor of the 82nd Airborne Corps Division, *Trains* magazine, Robert Wayner, Thorton Waite, U. S. Army Signal Corps, William K. Walthers, Inc., Pat Wilder of the Prototype Encyclopedia Vol. 5, Jay Williams, Bob Withers, Lee Witten of Ogden Union Station, Jim Wrinn, and Carolyn Wright from the U.S. Army Transportation Museum. Many others also helped in our research and compilations, and we extend our grateful thanks to them.

Donald J. Heimburger and John Kelly

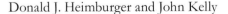

DOING DOUBLE DUTY
for the Duration

The rising tempo of America's war effort, coupled with requests for conservation of private motor vehicles, is creating an extraordinary demand for railroad transportation.

Since the imperative need for ships and armaments limits enlargement of railroad facilities at this time, maximum service must be exacted from every car and locomotive.

We are maintaining with existing facilities Burlington's traditionally high transportation standards, confident the patriotic cooperation of travelers and shippers will help America's railroads do double duty for the duration.

For counsel on how best to utilize the substantial part of the transportation facilities of the Burlington that are not yet required by war traffic, consult any Burlington representative or agent.

Burlington Route

Burlington Route timetable July-August, 1942

Table of Contents

Dedication 4

Acknowledgements 5

Preface 8

Introduction 10

Chapter 1   Magnitude of the Task 23

Chapter 2   Embarkation of Troops
             and Materiel 65

Chapter 3   The Military Railway Service
             Joins the Fight 91

Chapter 4   Crossroads of War 103

Chapter 5   Personal Glimpses of the War 179

Chapter 6   Built with Pride for the
             War Effort 193

Chapter 7   Military Camp Railroads 231

Chapter 8   Alaska's Railroads Weigh In 260

Color Gallery 265

Chapter 9   Women in War 299

Chapter 10   Foreign Theaters 306

Chapter 11   Returning Home from the War . . 338

Chapter 12   After the War 349

Chapter 13   They Succeeded Magnificently . . . 366

Bibliography 373

Index 374

Chris Burritt

Preface

From the earliest days of American railroading, the story of the Army and railroads has been intertwined. The U.S. Military Academy at West Point was founded in 1802 and served as the nation's only source of technical training for many years. Its engineers, surveyors and topographers helped to explore and open the nation to expansion and development.

When the Baltimore & Ohio Railroad was first chartered, two West Pointers—George Washington Whistler and William Gibbs McNeill—were detailed to serve as technical advisors to the new endeavor. For the first quarter century of railroad development, the Army was the principal source of civil engineers and managers for the burgeoning railroad network.

The Civil War demonstrated to the world that the railroad was an essential element of an industrialized war machine. The Union, particularly, used the railroads to support the massive requirements of modern warfare. The carefully orchestrated use of railroads managed by their owners, the employment of professional railroaders in the Lincoln administration to oversee military support operations, and the use of soldiers and civilian railroaders to operate the lines seized from the Confederacy, all helped to make war on a grand scale possible. Lessons learned from railroad operations in the Civil War would affect the whole concept of warfare evermore.

LESSONS FORGOTTEN

By the time of the Spanish-American War in 1898, the lessons of the Civil War had been forgotten by the Army and the federal government. Deployment ports such as Tampa were scenes of chaos. Rail traffic throughout the Southeast was at a standstill. Management by the Army and by the railroads was called into question. In Europe on the eve of World War I, however, the American lessons of the Civil War had not been forgotten. The Schlieffen Plan, the invasion of Belgium and France by the German Empire, was orchestrated with timetable precision, but then lapsed into a stalemate fed by industrial might on both sides.

America's entry into WWI came in 1917 and produced the greatest upheaval in industrial production, manpower demands and impact on civilian life ever experienced to that time. Managing this great upheaval proved to be too much

for many sectors of industry, resulting in the federal government stepping in to take control. The American railroad industry was taken over by the United States Railroad Administration (USRA) in 1918. It would attempt to rationalize the rail network, establish standardized designs for cars and locomotives and manage the railroad labor force. While producing some positive results, railroads were returned to their private owners in 1920, and the American railroad industry vowed that conditions would never be allowed to disintegrate to such a degree that government seizure would be required. Military and industrial planning in the 1920s and 1930s focused on keeping the railroads in private hands. The railroads themselves would plan, manage and operate in order to support the nation's war effort. That is precisely what happened in World War II, and it worked magnificently.

The overarching theme of any study of WWII is its magnitude. From the vast numbers of soldiers and civilians who participated, including the horrific worldwide death toll, to the incredible industrial activity, especially in the "Arsenal of Democracy," the breadth and scope of WWII is simply breathtaking. In examining any aspect of the war, the related numbers are amazing. For American railroads, the ton-miles produced, the number of people carried and the amount of materiel moved, all set marks that were thought impossible at the outbreak of the war.

The Second World War was also truly a worldwide conflict. Every continent felt some impact from the war. Europe, Asia and Africa experienced the pain and destruction of combat, but the Americas and Australia also labored to near exhaustion to arm, equip and feed military forces deployed around the world. Railroads were a key element of the support at home, and railway units of the U. S. Army were deployed to Alaska, North Africa, all of Western Europe, Iran, India, Burma and the Philippines to support combat operations of the Army and its allies.

DEMAND GROWS

At home the demand on the railroads grew at the same time the work force was being pressed into military service, either through voluntary enlistment or the draft. Working with the Army, individual railroads sponsored the creation of military railway units, ensuring that the units were filled with soldiers who had the proper railroad skills and that the companies themselves minimized the impact on continued operations at home. Women joined the railroad work force just as they entered virtually every field because of wartime demands. In the labor intensive maintenance-of-way work, thousands of Mexican laborers were brought in as "guest workers," initially in the Southwest, but gradually throughout the nation. Both women and foreign workers would have a profound impact on the labor scene from then until now.

Two agencies played key roles in managing the railroads during the war. The Office of Defense Transportation (ODT) oversaw the national allocation of transportation resources, balancing the needs of the military, the industrial base and the movement of raw materials and agricultural products. One of the significant decisions of the ODT was to order the elimination of all sleeping car service on routes of less than 450 miles. This meant that such important corridors as Chicago-Detroit, Chicago-Cleveland, New York-Washington, D.C., and New York-Boston were without sleeping car service. This freed up nearly 1,000 Pullman sleepers for more effective use on busy transcontinental lines and for troop movements. ODT also ordered the mothballing of lounge cars and cars with little passenger-carrying capacity. These measures served to wring extra capacity from an already overtaxed rail network.

The other agency, the War Production Board (WPB), was responsible for allocation of raw materials, industrial capacity and manufactured goods. It set priorities to meet the needs of the American war effort. Some of its decisions shaped the immediate wartime situation (1942-45), and some decisions had a huge impact on the post-war railroad industry. The WPB limited research, design and development of steam locomotives. If a railroad needed additional locomotives, it would have to make do with an existing design. For example, the Pennsylvania J-1 (2-10-4) was a copy of the Chesapeake & Ohio T-1. This caused a stagnation in steam design and development. In the postwar period no great strides like the prewar "super power" era were made in steam locomotive efficiency, sealing the fate of steam power on the railroads.

Another WPB decision had General Motors concentrating on the production of its FT road unit, giving it a manufacturing and marketing advantage in the postwar period when this style of locomotive would dominate every railroad's want list. The other locomotive builders were also restricted from significant development. The real aim of the War Production Board was to ensure maximum production of diesel power plants for the Navy to use in submarines and landing craft. Consequently, diesel locomotives for the railroads were a small part of diesel production.

IMPACTS RAILROADS

In the immediate postwar period, reconversion of industry to domestic, peacetime needs also had a great impact on the railroads. The pent-up demand for automobiles created an environment that created the American "love affair" with the automobile. The Army's worldwide experience with motorized operations using the basic 2½-ton truck also led to a burgeoning trucking industry. Airlines, too, benefited from steady development of bomber and cargo aircraft, opening the way for widespread air transportation. Despite massive investment by the railroads in new, streamlined, postwar equipment, the seeds had been sown for the decline of the railroad industry, particularly in passenger traffic.

For 180 years the American railroad industry has been in the forefront of technological innovation. Yet the basic element, the steel wheel on steel rail, has remained the underlying factor in its superb performance. From the Civil War to the war waged by "The Greatest Generation," railroads have been the lifelines of military might, industrial prowess and a free society. In this new age of globalization, a wave of activity and trade on a global scale never seen before, even in wartime, presents the railroads with a new set of challenges. As they have shown in the past, American railroads are equal to any challenge. *Colonel Thomas W. Sweeney, U.S. Army Transportation Corps (Ret.)*

Colonel Thomas W. Sweeney began his military service at Fort Bliss, Texas, serving in a missile unit in Key West, Florida, and an aviation unit in Vietnam. Army school assignments for Colonel Sweeney included the Army Transportation School, the Command and General Staff College and the Army War College. As an instructor he served at the U.S. Military Academy at West Point, the Combat Studies Institute at Fort Leavenworth, and was director of the Military History Institute at Carlisle Barracks, Pennsylvania. Upon his retirement from the Army, Sweeney served as professor of Strategic Logistics at the Army War College. Transportation assignments included duty as the Maintenance-of-Way Superintendent of the 714th Railway Operating Battalion at Fort Eustis. While assigned to U.S. Army-Europe, Sweeney represented the U.S. military in NATO transportation planning. He developed, in coordination with the Deutsche Bundesbahn, procedures which were used to deploy Army units in Germany to the ports for Operation Desert Shield. In the Pentagon for more than four years, Colonel Sweeney served as the Director of Logistics Plans and Operations on the Army Staff and as the Deputy Director of International Logistics on the Department of Defense staff. He has served as chairman of the Cumberland County (Pennsylvania) Transportation Authority and lectures annually at the Railroad Museum of Pennsylvania on the history of the Military Railway Service. He resides with his wife, Marilyn, in Mechanicsburg, Pennsylvania.

"Yesterday, December 7th, 1941—a date which will live in infamy—the United States of America
was suddenly and deliberately attacked by naval and air forces of the Empire of Japan."
—President Franklin D. Roosevelt

On December 7, 1941, Japanese forces attacked Pearl Harbor, Hawaii, inflicting heavy casualties and severe damage to the United States naval forces anchored there. Before a Joint Session of Congress on December 8, 1941, President Franklin D. Roosevelt called the attack "a date which will live in infamy."

Later that day, the United States formally declared a state of war between the United States and the Japanese Empire. Hitler's Nazi troops had invaded Poland on September 1, 1939, prompting Britain and France to officially declare war on Germany on September 2, 1939. America sided with Britain in the ensuing European conflict.

As a result of the Tripartite Pact between Germany, Italy and Japan (commonly known as the "Axis"), Germany and Italy declared war on the United States on December 11, 1941. The United States and its Allies would fight a two-front war in Europe and the South Pacific.

AMERICAN RAILROADS HELP IN WAR

In 1940, President Roosevelt had sought the railroads' help in the pending war effort. Roosevelt hoped to keep America out of combat, but he recognized that the government would need the railroads to mobilize American soldiers and equipment. In discussions with Ralph Budd,

The solid wheels of America's railroad war machine began to work overtime starting in 1940. Iron rails were America's link to victory.

president of the Chicago, Burlington & Quincy Railroad, Roosevelt suggested the federal government take control of the railroads as it did during World War I. Budd proposed that if the railroads remained private they would fully cooperate with the government. On May 28, 1940, President Roosevelt named Budd his Federal Transportation Commissioner. When America entered the war after the bombing of Pearl Harbor, Budd and the railroad industry began making major contributions to the war effort.

Within a few months the Office of Defense Transportation (ODT) was created to work with the railroads and the Pullman Company to expedite troop trains to ports of embarkation. Food, munitions and petroleum were shipped

Soldiers help unload halftrack trucks, a familiar scene throughout the United States in World War II. *David Myers collection*

10

From December 1941 to August 1945, American railroads carried 43 million military personnel, representing 97% of all troops moved during the war. By mid-1942, military troop trains were operating from the Atlantic Coast to the Pacific Coast 24 hours a day. Train stations were overflowing with men and women in uniform going to the battlefields of Europe, Asia and the South Pacific.

NORTH PLATTE CANTEEN

Many American soldiers, sailors and Marines rolled through tiny North Platte, Nebraska, on troop trains via Union Pacific to ports of embarkation. The town of North Platte, in cooperation with the Union Pacific, transformed its railroad depot into the North Platte Canteen. Every day of the year from 5 a.m. until midnight, local volunteers welcomed the troop trains with encouragement, friendship and baskets of homemade food for more than six million GI's until the war ended. America's streamliners went to war, too. Those proud monarchs of the rails, once devoted to luxury travel, were called to transport American soldiers. Most major streamliners added extra coaches to handle the overflow. Many railroads offered "travel tips for war-time trips" in their public timetables, suggesting passengers make advance reservations and travel mid-week to avoid peak weekend military troop movements.

Businesses and industries were asked to donate precious aluminum that could be melted down and used in war. The program was called "Metal for Victory," and Union Pacific answered the call by scrapping the *City of Salina* (M-10000), its first streamliner built by Pullman-Standard in 1933. Only eight years old, the train was already outmoded and could not accommodate wartime passenger traffic.

by rail from coast to coast, where they were loaded onto Liberty Ships for American troops and Allies overseas as part of the Lend-Lease Act. Lend-Lease legislation gave President Roosevelt the power to sell, transfer, exchange and lend equipment to any country to help defend themselves against the Axis powers.

In addition, the ODT ordered the Santa Fe Refrigerator Despatch cars and the Pacific Fruit Express fleet be made available to haul freight and other war supplies. Solid blocks of oil tank cars ran as freight extras in support of the war effort, and defense plants worked with the railroads to devise "just in time" delivery, long before anyone coined the phrase.

American railroads were the vital link to steel plants, weapons arsenals and other war industries across America. High above the roar and rumble of factories at work for war, you could hear the bells of freedom ringing on thousands of rushing railroad locomotives. Those bells symbolized the strength and determination of the United States of America, engaged in the largest war in its history.

Louisiana & Arkansas #806 4-6-2 powers a 10-car troop train extra northbound on July 16, 1944 at Sallisaw, Oklahoma. *Robert F. Collins, courtesy Louis Marre collection*

Another government agency, the War Production Board (WPB) authorized and controlled production of new locomotives, passenger and freight equipment for all railroads. The WPB approved some new FT freight locomotives to replace aging steam engines on the Santa Fe Railway in the Arizona desert, where water for the thirsty steamers was difficult to provide.

EFFECTS ON THE U.S.

World War II had many effects on the United States homefront, including increased factory production to complete the economic recovery started by President Roosevelt's New Deal. However, with millions of Americans, mostly men, entering the Armed Forces, a major gap in the labor force occurred, with serious implications for American industries that produced war materiels.

Women entered the work force to replace the men called to war. They worked in factories as riveters, welders and heavy machinery operators. The War Production Coordinating Committee printed posters featuring "Rosie the Riveter" proclaiming "We can do it." The posters were displayed in government buildings and train stations across America, as women were called to move men and materiels to victory. Railroading had traditionally been regarded as a man's job until World War II. But when war reached deeply into railroad ranks, taking skilled and experienced workers for the Armed Forces, women were employed to keep the trains rolling. Women filled positions as trainmen, ticket agents, passenger representatives, coach-sleeping car cleaners and baggage handlers; they even worked on track section crews. To help fund the huge war effort, the government and railroads rallied to promote the sale of war savings bonds. The Pennsylvania Railroad displayed the slogan "Buy War Bonds" on 500 of its boxcars.

SHORTAGE OF STEEL

"The fact that several very important industries, largely engaged in manufacture of munitions, were forced this past month by shortage of steel to drastically curtail production, and in some cases stop completely, came as a distinct shock to the whole country, particularly to those directly respon-

After soldiers completed basic training, they were generally offered specialized training at one or more military bases. Each of these moves required additional travel, often by rail. By the time a soldier reached a port of embarkation, he had made at least five Army-planned trips by railway or highway, and in most cases more. *Kalmbach Publishing Co. collection*

sible for keeping the war industries supplied with materiels," states an editorial in the August 1942 issue of *Railway Purchases and Stores.*

It continued: "The result of this has been that the Army and Navy Munitions Board has stepped into the picture in a much more prominent and dominating position—and this is as it should be, for the only thing that counts now is to win this war, and things are looking very dark for the Allied cause these days. It is all well enough to talk about ultimate victory, but time is outstandingly the essence of this great war, and we are now right at the crossroads of going all-out for the war program regardless of consequences, or of continuing on the old program of looking to self interest first.

NOTE OF WARNING

"Mr. Eastman (Joseph B. Eastman, Federal Coordinator of Transportation) recently sounded a note of warning as to the possibility of materiel supply for railroad transportation being largely cut off this fall, particularly of steel, in order to meet the demands of munitions production, Maritime Commission, Lend-Lease, etc. But transportation, particularly rail transport, is of such vital importance to every step of the war program, starting with the movement of war materiels and between every intermediate point of manufacture, on through to the delivery of finished munitions, as well as subsequent movement of those munitions and of troops, that it is simply unthinkable to risk the possibility of a falldown of our transportation system at this critical time.

"The railroads have performed so very splendidly in this war period in handling nearly a third more ton miles than a year ago, that they are being too much taken for granted, and therein lies the danger. Every element of railroad plant wears out practically in proportion to the ton miles handled and, if that plant is not adequately maintained, the rate of wear and tear will rapidly rise with lack of maintenance.

COUNTRY DEPENDS ON RAILROADS

Railway Purchases and Stores, July 1942

"Most certainly, we cannot take chances in deliberately planning to under maintain our railroad plant which is now being overworked as never before in the history of railroading and upon the unfailing performance of which, so much of the great war program of this country depends.

"It is most certainly to be hoped that in this new setup and realignment in the War Production Board, that transportation, and particularly railroad transportation, will continue to receive the favorable consideration which it has been receiving and which is so essential to providing it with adequate materiel supply, which is the 'sine qua non' of maintaining our good transportation service.

"Transportation is such a vital part of the whole war program that it should have special representation in the War Production Board through Mr. Eastman being definitely appointed as a member of it, and this would be no reflection on the excellent performance of the present staff of the Transportation Branch of WPB, but merely an assurance for the future that our transportation system will continue to be adequately provided for," the article concluded.

OVERSEAS OPERATIONS

Overseas railway operations near the battlefront were performed by soldier-railroaders who comprised units of the Military Railway Service under jurisdiction of the Army Transportation Corps. These men came from the operating departments of many American sponsoring railroads including the 713th Railway Operating Battalion (Santa Fe Railway), 727th Railway Operating Battalion (Southern Railway), 729th Railway Operating Battalion (New Ha-

The **RAILROADS CAN TAKE IT**

Since December 7th, and months before, American Railroads have gone all out to meet successfully every demand of our constantly increasing war program. More than five million soldiers have been transported an average of 1500 miles, new millions of civilians are riding the trains, over fifty billion ton-miles of freight hauled every month, with 7,000 fewer freight locomotives and one-half million fewer freight cars than were used in 1929. From coast to coast the railroads are speeding supplies to the fighting fronts.

STANDARD STOKER COMPANY, INC.
NEW YORK · CHICAGO · ERIE

STANDARD STOKERS

KEEP 'EM ROLLING AT TOP SPEED

STANDARD STOKER COMPANY, INC.
NEW YORK · CHICAGO · ERIE

Railway Purchases and Stores, 1942

Army sentries stand guard on a trainload of light tanks at Camp Erwin, California in April of 1942 bound for coastal ports of embarkation. *Kansas State Historical Society, Santa Fe collection*

ven Railroad) and the 730th Railway Operating Battalion (Pennsylvania Railroad).

The Military Railway Service sent more than 43,500 officers and enlisted men to transport soldiers and equipment, often under heavy fire, in North Africa (1943-1944), Iran (1942-1945), Philippines and Japan (1942-1945), Sicily and France (1943-1945) and Belgium and Germany (1944-1946). These highly trained railroaders played a substantial role in helping defeat the Axis powers. They used specially designed locomotives and rolling stock manufactured by American locomotive builders and sent overseas by cargo ships. In addition to hauling troops, armor and munitions to the battlefront, the Military Railway Service evacuated more than 48,000 wounded troops from the front lines during the North African campaign. They also helped clear mines, rebuilt antiquated steam engines and built hospital trains from junked box cars.

On August 14, 1944, General George S. Patton sent word he could reach Paris if 31 trains of ammunition, gas, oil and other supplies reached his troops at Le Mans, France, in 14 days. The soldier-railroaders of the 740th Railway Operating Battalion took the job, working day and night to implement Patton's orders. Five days later, instead of the 14 days requested, the 740th delivered 36 trainloads of supplies to Patton's troops.

One of the worst and bloodiest campaigns for the Military Railway Service advance section was the Battle of the Bulge beginning December 16, 1944. Hitler had sent a quarter million troops across an 85-mile stretch of Allied front, from southern Belgium to Luxembourg. In the cold of winter, German troops advanced 50 miles into Allied lines, creating a deadly "bulge" into Allied defenses. Military Railway Service troops, along with regular fighting troops, were heavily bombed and strafed by the German Luftwaffe. By January 15, 1945, the Allies regained the territory, but 78,000 Allied troops were either killed, wounded, missing in action or prisoners of war after the Battle of the Bulge.

WOODEN HORSE AT TROY

It was a wooden horse that supposedly caused the fall of ancient Troy, but during World War II another kind of horse, the Iron Horse, helped conquer the German war machine. On May 8, 1945, Victory in Europe (V-E Day), the Allies celebrated the defeat of Nazi Germany. World War II officially ended with victory over Japan (V-J Day), August 14, 1945 (August 15 in North America), after the United States dropped the first atomic bomb on Hiroshima, August 6, 1945, followed by another on Nagasaki, August 9, 1945.

"HIGH IRON"

"High Iron" is one of America's not-so-secret weapons. It is a railroadman's term for the 230,000 miles of mainline track — built, paid for and kept up by the railroads — which knit America together. • Over these strong highways of steel moves America's might — three quarters of all intercity transportation, 90% of all war freight. • In this mass movement of freight — a movement that far exceeds anything moved before by any means of transport — lies a vital lesson. • The lesson is this: America needs and must have — for success in war, for prosperity in peace — the low-priced, mass transportation which only railroads can deliver.

The time period from 1941 to 1945 has been regarded as the pinnacle of American railroading. Everyone acknowledged the railroads' outstanding work of moving troops and supplies during the biggest transportation job in history.

After World War II, the major carriers realized most of their passenger equipment was outdated from heavy wartime travel, and planned to expand with new, colorful streamlined passenger trains. Soon fleets of luxury streamliners like Santa Fe *Chiefs*, Southern Pacific *Daylights* and Burlington *Zephyrs* were carrying passengers in modern, air-conditioned coaches and sleepers. The future indeed looked bright for American railroads and postwar train travel.

American railroads had gained valuable experience during World War II, and the outgrowth of this challenge provided them with new technology. Oil tank trains progressed into the unit train concept; armored tanks and jeeps transported on flatcars pioneered piggyback trailer trains; and open hopper cars of wheat gave way to grain shipments in covered hoppers. Train dispatching on heavily-used single-track helped introduce Centralized Traffic Control (CTC). Today's freight railroads owe much of their continued growth and state-of-the-art technology to the gallant efforts of their predecessors during wartime railroading.

Here then, is the dramatic and compelling story of America's railroads in World War II.

U.S. Army troops transfer equipment from a Milwaukee Road troop train, with a Hiawatha engine in the lead, to army trucks during 1940 maneuvers at Camp McCoy, Wisconsin. Note the early-style military uniforms. *Milwaukee Road, Don Heimburger collection*

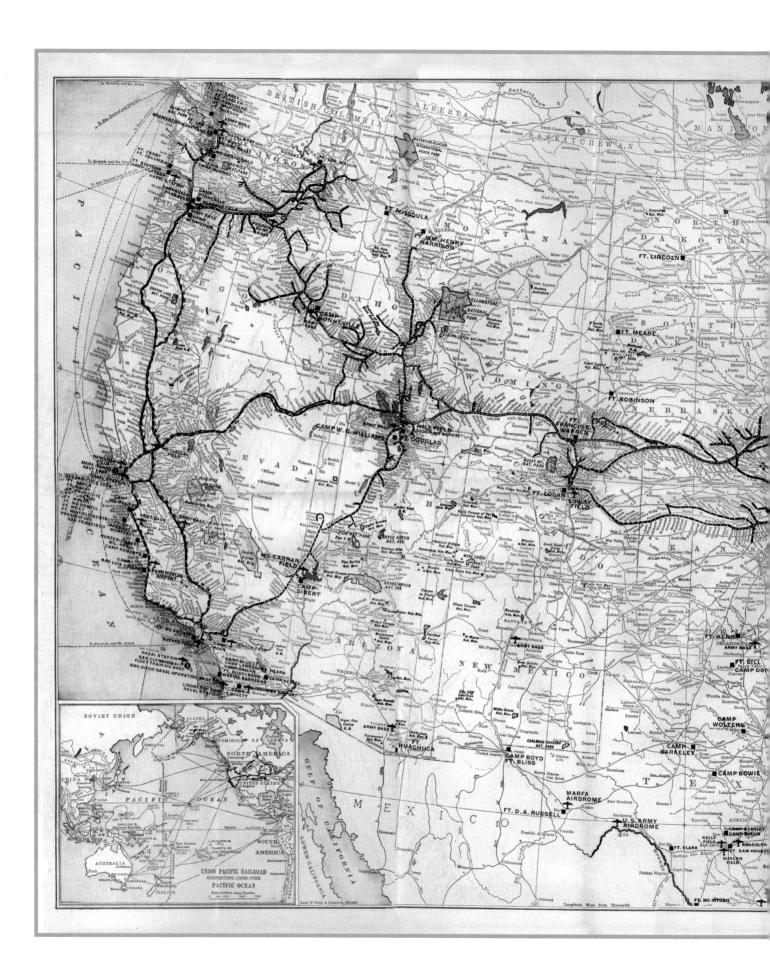

16

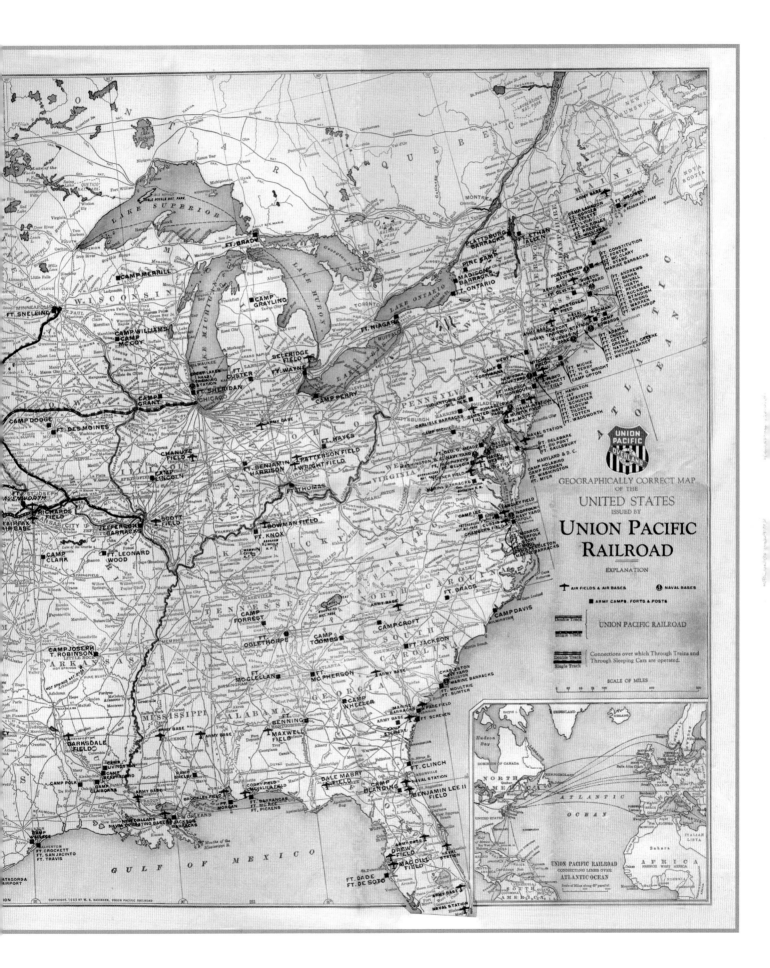

GEOGRAPHICALLY CORRECT MAP
OF THE
UNITED STATES
ISSUED BY

UNION PACIFIC
RAILROAD

EXPLANATION

AIR FIELDS & AIR BASES   NAVAL BASES

ARMY CAMPS, FORTS & POSTS

UNION PACIFIC RAILROAD

Connections over which Through Trains and
Through Sleeping Cars are operated.

SCALE OF MILES

UNION PACIFIC RAILROAD
CONNECTING LINES OVER
ATLANTIC OCEAN

17

U. S. Military Bases
with railroad stations and post office addresses

In addition to the points specially indicated on the map, the following list includes many other military posts. The points not shown on the map are marked with this character (*). Prefix (+) indicates post office address. *Map of the United States Showing Military Posts, Union Pacific Railroad, August 1, 1941*

A	RAILROAD STATION
*Aberdeen Proving Ground, Md.	Aberdeen, Md.
*Alcatraz Island, Calif.	San Francisco, Calif. (+Alcatraz, Calif.)
*Arlington Cantonment, Va.	Arlington, Va.
Army Air Base, Ariz.	Tucson, Ariz.
Army Air Base, Calif.	Fresno, Calif.
Army Air Base, Calif.	Salinas, Calif.
Army Air Base, Conn.	Windsor Locks, Conn.
Army Air Base, Fla.	Orlando, Fla.
Army Air Base, Fla.	West Palm Beach, Fla.
Army Air Base, Ga.	Augusta, Ga.
Army Air Base, Ga.	Savannah, Ga.
Army Air Base, Ind.	Fort Wayne, Ind.
Army Air Base, Ky.	Louisville, Ky.
Army Air Base, La.	Baton Rouge, La.
Army Air Base, Maine	Bangor, Maine
Army Air Base, Miss.	Jackson, Miss.
Army Air Base, Miss.	Meridian, Miss.
Army Air Base, N. H.	Manchester, N. H.
Army Air Base, N. Mex.	Albuquerque, N. Mex.
*Army Air Base, N. Y.	Hempstead, N. Y.
Army Air Base, N. Car.	Charlotte, N. Car.
Army Air Base, Okla.	Oklahoma City, Okla.
Army Air Base, Ore.	Pendair, Ore. (for frt. and spl. psgr. trains) / Pendleton, Ore. (for individual passengers)
Army Air Base, Ore.	Fir, Ore. (for frt. and spl. psgr. trains) / Portland, Ore. (for individual passengers)
Army Air Base, Utah	Salt Lake City, Utah
Army Air Base, Va.	Hampton, Va.
Army Air Base, Wash.	Spokane, Wash.
Army Air Base, Wash.	Tacoma, Wash.
* Army Air Depot, Calif.	Sacramento, Calif.
Army Air Depot, Utah	Ogden, Utah
Army Airdrome, Texas	Sanderson, Texas
*Army Air Post, Fla.	Jacksonville, Fla.
*Army Medical Center, D. C.	Washington, D. C.
* Army Motor Supply Depot, Calif.	Emeryville, Calif.
*Army Ordnance Depot, Md.	Baltimore, Md. (+Curtis Bay, Md)
*Army Ordnance Depot, S. Car.	Charleston, S. Car. (+N. Charleston, S. Car.)
*Army War College, D. C.	Washington, D. C.
*Artillery Target Range, Pa.	Tobyhanna, Pa.
* Augusta Arsenal, Ga.	Augusta, Ga.

B	
Banana River Naval Air Station, Fla.	Cocoa-Rockledge, Fla. (+Cocoa, Fla.)
Barksdale Field, La	Shreveport, La.
*Baytown Ordnance Works, Texas	Baytown, Texas
*Benicia Ordnance Intermediate Depot and Arsenal, Calif.	Benicia, Calif.
Benjamin Lee II Field, Fla.	Green Cove Springs, Fla.
*Bethany Beach, Del.	Frankford, Del.
*Biggs Field, Texas	El Paso, Texas / Ft. Bliss, Texas
*Boeing Field, Wash.	Seattle, Wash.
Boise Barracks, Idaho	Boise, Idaho
Bolling Field, D. C.	Washington, D. C.
Bowman Field, Ky.	Louisville, Ky.
Bremerton Navy Yard, Wash.	Bremerton, Wash.
Brookley Field, Ala.	Mobile, Ala.
*Brooks Field, Texas	Bergs, Texas / San Antonio, Texas
*Burgess Field, Pa.	Uniontown, Pa.

C	
Camp Barkeley, Texas	View, Texas
Camp Beauregard, La.	Tioga, La. (+Alexandria, La.)
*Camp Bergs, Texas	San Antonio, Texas
*Camp Biern (Owen), Texas	El Paso, Texas
Camp Blanding, Fla.	Starke, Fla. / Theressa, Fla.
Camp Bonneville, Idaho	Boise, Idaho
Camp Bonneville, Wash.	Vancouver, Wash.
Camp Bowie, Texas	Brownwood, Texas
Camp Boyd, Texas	El Paso, Texas / Ft. Bliss, Texas
Camp BullIs, Texas	Beckmann, Texas (+San Antonio, Texas)
*Camp Chigas, Texas	El Paso, Texas
Camp Callan, Calif.	Linda Vista, Calif.
Camp Claiborne, La.	Bringhurst, La. (+Alexandria, La.) / Forest Hill, La.
Camp Clark, Mo.	Nevada, Mo.
Camp Clatsop, Ore.	Warrenton, Ore.
*Camp Clayton, Calif.	Monterey, Calif.
*Camp Conley, W. Va.	Point Pleasant, W. Va.
Camp Croft, S. Car.	Spartanburg, S. Car.
Camp Davis, N. Car.	Wilmington, N. Car.
*Camp Dawson, W. Va.	Kingwood, W. Va.
Camp Dodge, Iowa	Des Moines, Iowa
Camp Doniphan, Okla.	Fort Sill, Okla.
*Camp Douglas, Wis.	Camp Douglas, Wis.
*Camp Eagle Pass, Texas	Eagle Pass, Texas
Camp Edwards, Mass.	Falmouth, Mass.
Camp Elliott, Calif.	Linda Vista, Calif.
*Camp Fordyce (Sam), Texas	Sam Fordyce, Texas
Camp Forrest, Tenn.	Tullahoma, Tenn.
*Camp Furlong, N. Mex.	Columbus, N. Mex.
Camp Grant, Ill.	Rockford, Ill.
*Camp Grayling, Mich.	Grayling, Mich.
*Camp Guernsey, Wyo.	Guernsey, Wyo.
*Camp Guild (Curtis), Mass.	Wakefield, Mass.
Camp Haan, Calif.	Riverside, Calif.
Camp Hearn (Lawrence J.), Calif.	Palm Beach, Calif.
Camp Holabird, Md.	Baltimore, Md.
Camp Hulen, Texas	Palacios, Texas
*Camp Jones (Harry J.), Ariz.	Douglas, Ariz.
*Camp Lake View, Minn.	Lake City, Minn.
Camp Langdon, Me.	Portland, Me.
Camp Lee, Va.	Petersburg, Va.
Camp Lincoln, Ill.	Springfield, Ill.
Camp Livingston, La.	Simms, La. (+Alexandria, La.)
*Camp Little (Stephen D.), Ariz.	Nogales, Ariz.
Camp Lockett, Calif.	Campo, Calif.
*Camp Luna, N. M.	Las Vegas, N. M.
*Camp Mabry, Texas	Austin, Texas
*Camp McAllen, Texas	McAllen, Texas
Camp McCoy, Wis.	Camp McCoy, Wis.
Camp McQuaide, Calif.	Watsonville, Calif.
*Camp Mercedes, Texas	Mercedes, Texas
Camp Merrill, Wis.	Phillips, Wis.
*Camp Michie (Robert E. L.), Texas	Del Rio, Texas
Camp Murray, Wash.	Fort Lewis, Wash.
*Camp Normoyle, Texas	San Antonio, Texas
Camp Pendleton, Va.	Virginia Beach, Va.
Camp Perry, Ohio	Port Clinton, Ohio / Lacarne, Ohio
Camp Pine, N. Y., see Pine Camp	
Camp Polk, La.	Leesville, La.
*Camp Rapid, S. Dak.	Rapid City, S. Dak.
Camp Richie, Md.	Cascade, Md.
*Camp Ripley, Minn.	Little Falls, Minn.
Camp Roberts, Calif.	San Miguel, Calif. (+Paso Robles, Calif.)
Camp Robinson (Joseph T.), Ark.	Little Rock, Ark.
Camp Rodman, Md.	Aberdeen, Md.

Camp San Luis Obispo, Calif. ... San Luis Obispo, Calif.
*Camp Savannah, Ga. ... Savannah, Ga.
*Camp Seale, Texas ... Camp Seale, Texas
Camp Seeley, Calif. ... Seeley, Calif.
*Camp Shannon, N. Mex. ... Hachita, N. Mex.
Camp Shelby, Miss. ... Hattiesburg, Miss.
*Camp Sherman, Ohio ... Chillicothe, Ohio
Camp Sibert, Nev. ... Boulder City, Nev.
*Camp Stafford, La. ... Alexandria, La.
Camp Stanley, Texas ... Leon Springs, Texas (+San Antonio, Texas)
Camp Stewart, Ga. ... Walthourville, Ga. (+McIntosh, Ga.)
Camp Tobyhanna, Pa. ... Tobyhanna, Pa.
Camp Toombs, Ga. ... Toccoa, Ga.
Camp Upton, N. Y. ... Yaphank, N. Y. (+Riverhead, N. Y.)
Camp Wallace, Texas ... Hitchcock, Texas
Camp Wheeler, Ga. ... Franklinton, Ga.
Camp Williams, Wis. ... Sparta, Wis.
Camp Williams (W. G.), Utah ... Salt Lake City, Utah
Camp Withycomb, Ore. ... Clackamas, Ore.
Camp Wolters, Texas ... Mineral Wells, Texas
Carlisle Barracks, Pa. ... Carlisle, Pa.
Chambers Field, Va. ... Norfolk, Ya.
Chanute Field, Ill. ... Rantoul, Ill.
*Chapman Field, Fla. ... Miami, Fla.
*Charleston Army Ordnance Depot, S. Car. ... North Charleston, S. Car.
Chevalier Field, Fla. ... Pensacola, Fla.
*Chollas Heights, Calif. ... San Diego, Calif.
*Clackamas Rifle Range, Ore. ... Clackamas, Ore.
*Clover Field, Calif. ... Santa Monica, Calif.
*Coast Artillery Firing Range, Calif. ... Barstow, Calif.
*Cochran Field, Ga. ... Avondale, Ga.
*Connellsville Airport, Pa. ... Connellsville, Pa.
Corry Field, Fla. ... Pensacola, Fla.
*Curtis Bay Army Ordnance Depot, Md. ... Baltimore, Md. (+Curtis Bay, Md.)

D

*Daniel Field, Ga. ... Augusta, Ga.
*Daugherty Field, Calif. ... Long Beach, Calif.
*Davis Monthan Field, Ariz. ... Tucson, Ariz.
*Delaware Army Ordnance Depot, Del. ... Pedricktown, N. J.
*Destroyer Base, Calif. ... San Diego, Calif.
Drew Field, Fla. ... Tampa, Fla.
Duncan Field, Texas ... San Antonio, Texas

E

*Edgewood Arsenal, Md. ... Edgewood, Md.
*Eglin Field, Fla. ... Crestview, Fla. (+Valpariso, Fla.)
*Ellington Field, Texas ... Genoa, Texas
*English Field, Texas ... Amarillo, Texas
*Erie Ordnance Depot, Ohio ... Lacarne, Ohio

F

Fairfax Air Base, Kan. ... Kansas City, Kan.
*Fairfield Air Depot, Ohio ... Fairfield, Ohio
*Fisherman's Island Military Post, Va. ... Old Point Comfort, Va. (+Kiptopeke, Va.)
Fitzsimons General Hospital, Colo. ... Bunell, Colo. (for frt. and spl. psgr. trains); Denver, Colo. (for individual passengers)
Fleet Training Base, Calif. ... San Diego, Calif.
*Flexible Gunnery School ... Las Vegas, Nev.
Floyd Bennett Field, N. Y. ... Brooklyn, N. Y.
Fort Adams, R. I. ... Newport, R. I.
Fort Allen (Ethan), Vt. ... Fort Ethan Allen, Vt.
Fort Andrews, Mass. ... Boston, Mass.
Fort Baker, Calif. ... San Francisco, Calif.
Fort Banks, Mass. ... Boston, Mass.
Fort Barrancas, Fla. ... Pensacola, Fla.
Fort Barry, Calif. ... San Francisco, Calif.
*Fort Bayard, N. Mex. ... Bayard, N. Mex.
Fort Belvoir, Va. ... Accotink, Va.
Fort Benning, Ga. ... Columbus. Ga.
Fort Bliss, Texas ... El Paso, Texas
Fort Brady, Mich. ... Sault Ste. Marie, Mich.
Fort Bragg, N. Car. ... Fayetteville, N. Car.
*Fort Brown, Texas ... Brownsville, Texas
Fort Canby, Wash. ... Warrenton, Ore
Fort Casey, Wash. ... Seattle, Wash. (+Port Townsend, Wash.)
*Fort Caswell, N. Car. ... Wilmington, N. Car. (+Southport, N. Car.)
Fort Church, R. I. ... Little Compton, R. I.
Fort Clark, Texas ... Spofford, Texas
Fort Clinch, Fla. ... Fernandina, Fla.
Fort Columbia, Wash ... Warrenton, Ore.
Fort Constitution, N. Hamp. ... Portsmouth, N. Hamp.
Fort Crockett, Texas ... Galveston, Texas
Fort Cronkhite, Calif. ... San Francisco, Calif.
Fort Crook, Nebr. ... Omaha, Nebr.
Fort Custer, Mich. ... Battle Creek, Mich.
Fort Dade, Fla. ... St. Petersburg, Fla.
*Fort Dawes, Mass. ... Boston, Mass.
Fort Delaware, Del. ... Delaware City, Del.
Fort Des Moines, Iowa ... Des Moines, Iowa
Fort De Soto, Fla. ... St. Petersburg, Fla.
Fort Devens, Mass. ... Ayer, Mass.
Fort Dix, N. J. ... Fort Dix, N. J.
Fort Douglas, Utah ... Salt Lake City, Utah
Fort Du Pont, Del. ... Delaware City, Del.
Fort Duvall, Mass. ... Boston, Mass.
Fort Eustis, Va. ... Lee Hall, Va.
Fort Flagler, Wash. ... Port Townsend, Wash.
Fort Foster, Maine ... Portsmouth, N. Hamp.
Fort Funston, Calif. ... San Francisco, Calif.
*Fort Gaines, Ala. ... Mobile, Ala.
Fort Getty, R. I. ... Newport, R. I.
Fort Gorges, Maine ... Portland, Maine
Fort Greble, R. I. ... Newport, R. I.
Fort Greene (Nathaniel), R. I. ... Narragansett Pier, R. I.
Fort Hamilton, N. Y. ... Brooklyn, N. Y.
Fort Hancock, N. J. ... Highland Beach, N. J.; New York, N. Y.
Fort Harrison (Benjamin), Ind. ... Lawrence, Ind.
Fort Harrison (William Henry), Mont. ... Helena, Mont.
Fort Hayes, Ohio ... Columbus, Ohio
Fort Heath, Mass. ... Boston, Mass.
Fort Houston (Sam), Texas ... San Antonio, Texas
*Fort Howard, Md. ... Baltimore, Md.
*Fort Hoyle, N. J., see Edgewood Arsenal
Fort Huachuca, Ariz. ... Fort Huachuca, Ariz.
Fort Humphreys, Va. ... Washington, D. C. (+Ft. Belvoir, Va.)
*Fort Hunt, Va. ... Washington, D. C.
Fort Jackson, S. Car. ... Columbia, S. Car.
Fort Jay, N. Y. ... New York, N. Y.
Fort Kearney (Philip), R. I. ... Narragansett Pier, R. I.
*Fort Keogh, Mont. ... Miles City, Mont.
Fort Knox, Ky. ... Fort Knox, Ky.
Fort Lafayette, N. Y. ... New York, N. Y.
Fort Lawton, Wash. ... Seattle, Wash. (+Interbay, Wash.)
Fort Leavenworth, Kan. ... Leavenworth, Kan.
Fort Levett, Maine ... Portland, Maine
Fort Lewis, Wash. ... Ft. Lewis, Wash.
Fort Lincoln, N. Dak. ... Bismarck, N. Dak.
Fort Logan, Colo. ... Denver, Colo.
Fort Lyon, Maine ... Portland, Maine
Fort MacArthur, Calif. ... San Pedro, Calif.
Fort McClary, N. H. ... Portsmouth, N. H.
Fort McClellan, Ala. ... Anniston, Ala.
Fort McDowell, Calif. ... San Francisco, Calif. (+Angel Island, Calif.)
*Fort McHenry, Md. ... Baltimore, Md.
Fort McIntosh, Texas ... Laredo, Texas
*Fort MacKenzie, Wyo. ... Sheridan, Wyo.
Fort McKinley, Maine ... Portland, Maine
Fort McPherson, Ga. ... Atlanta, Ga.
Fort McRee, Fla. ... Pensacola, Fla.
Fort Madison, Maine ... Castine, Maine
Fort Mason, Calif. ... San Francisco, Calif.
Fort Meade, S. Dak. ... Sturgis, S. Dak.
Fort Meade (George G.), Md. ... Ft. George G. Meade, Md.
Fort Michie, N. Y. ... New London, Conn.
*Fort Mifflin, Pa. ... Philadelphia, Pa.
Fort Miley, Calif. ... San Francisco, Calif.
Fort Missoula, Mont. ... Missoula, Mont.
Fort Monmouth, N. J. ... Little Silver, N. J. (+Red Bank, N. J.)
Fort Monroe, Va. ... Old Point Comfort, Va. (+Fortress Monroe, Va.)
Fort Morgan, Ala. ... Mobile, Ala.
Fort Mott, N. J. ... Salem, N. J.
Fort Moultrie, S. Car. ... Charleston, S. Car. (+Moultrieville, S. Car.)
Fort Myer, Va. ... Washington, D. C.

Fort Niagra, N. Y.	Niagara Falls, N. Y. (+Youngstown, N. Y.)
Fort Norfolk, Va.	Norfolk, Va.
Fort Oglethorpe, Ga.	Chattanooga, Tenn.
Fort Omaha, Nebr.	Omaha, Nebr.
Fort Ontario, N. Y.	Oswego, N. Y.
Fort Ord, Calif.	Salinas, Calif. (+Monterey, Calif.)
Fort Pickens, Fla.	Pensacola, Fla.
*Fort Pillow, Tenn.	Henning, Tenn.
*Fort Porter, N. Y.	Buffalo, N. Y.
Fort Preble, Maine	Portland, Maine
Fort Reno, Okla.	El Reno, Okla.
Fort Revere, Mass.	Boston, Mass. (+ Hull, Mass.)
Fort Riley, Kan.	Fort Riley, Kan.
*Fort Ringgold, Texas	Rio Grande City, Texas
Fort Robinson, Nebr.	Crawford, Nebr.
Fort Rodman, Mass.	New Bedford, Mass.
*Fort Roots (Logan H.), Ark.	Little Rock, Ark.
Fort Rosecrans, Calif.	San Diego, Calif.
Fort Ruckman, Mass.	Lynn, Mass.
Fort Ruckman, Mass.	Nahant, Mass.
Fort Russell (D. A.), Texas	Marfa, Texas
Fort San Jacinto, Texas	Galveston, Texas
Fort Saulsbury, Del.	Milford, Del.
Fort Schuyler, N. Y.	New York, N. Y.
Fort Scott (Winfield), Calif.	San Francisco, Calif.
Fort Screven, Ga.	Savannah, Ga.
Fort Sheridan, Ill.	Fort Sheridan, Ill.
Fort Sill, Okla.	Fort Sill, Okla.
Fort Slocum, N. Y.	New Rochelle, N. Y.
*Fort Smallwood, Md.	Baltimore, Md.
Fort Snelling, Minn.	Ft. Snelling, Minn.
Fort Standish, Mass.	Boston, Mass.
*Fort Stanton, N. Mex.	Capitan, N. Mex.
Fort Stark, N. Hamp.	Portsmouth, N. H.
*Fort Steilacoom, Wash.	Steilacoom, Wash.
Fort Stevens, Ore.	Warrenton, Ore.
Fort Story, Va.	Cape Henry, Va. (+Virginia Beach, Va.)
Fort Strong, Mass.	Boston, Mass.
Fort Sumter, S. Car.	Charleston, S. Car.
*Fort Taylor, Fla.	Key West, Fla.
Fort Terry, N. Y.	New London, Conn.
Fort Thomas, Ky.	Cincinnati, Ohio (+Covington, Ky.)
Fort Tilden, N. Y.	Rockaway Park, N. Y.
Fort Totten, N. Y.	Bayside, N. Y.
Fort Townsend, Wash.	Port Townsend, Wash.
Fort Travis, Texas	Galveston, Texas
*Fort Tuthill, Ariz.	Flagstaff, Ariz.
Fort Wadsworth, N. Y.	New York, N. Y.
Fort Ward, Wash.	Seattle, Wash.
Fort Warren, Mass.	Boston, Mass.
Fort Warren (Francis E.), Wyo.	{ Cheyenne, Wyo. / Russell, Wyo.
Fort Washington, Md.	Washington, D. C.
Fort Wayne, Mich.	Detroit, Mich.
Fort Wetherill, R.I.	Narragansett Pier, R. I. (+Newport, R. I.)
Fort Whitman, Wash.	Mt. Vernon, Wash. (+La Conner, Wash.)
Fort Williams, Maine	Portland, Maine
*Fort Wingate, N. Mex.	Wingate, N. Mex.
Fort Winthrop, Mass.	Boston, Mass.
*Fort Wood, N. Y.	New York, N. Y.
Fort Wood (Leonard), Mo.	Newburg, Mo.
Fort Wool, Va.	Norfolk, Va.
Fort Worden, Wash.	Port Townsend, Wash.
Fort Wright (George), Wash.	Spokane, Wash.
Fort Wright (H. G.), N. Y.	New London, Conn. (+Fishers Island, N. Y.)
*Frankford Arsenal, Pa.	Bridesburg, Pa.
*Front Royal Quartermaster Depot, Va.	Front Royal, Va.

G

*Godman Field, Ky.	Fort Knox, Ky.
*Governors Island, N. Y.	New York, N. Y.
Gowen Field, Ida.	Boise, Ida.
Great Lakes Naval Training Station, Ill.	Great Lakes, Ill.
*Gunter Field. Ala.	Montgomery, Ala.

H

Hamilton Field, Calif.	De Witt, Calif. (+San Rafael, Calif.)
*Hampton Roads Naval Operating Base, Va.	Norfolk, Va.
*Hat Box Field, Okla.	Muskogee, Okla.
*Hawthorne Naval Ammunition Depot, Nev.	Hawthorne, Nev.
Hensley Held, Texas	Grand Prairie, Texas
*Hicks Field, Texas	Fort Worth, Texas
Hill Field, Utah	Arsenal, Utah (+Ogden, Utah)
*Hingham Naval Ammunition Depot, Mass.	Hingham, Mass.
Hunter Ligget Training Area, Calif.	King City, Calif. (+Jolon, Calif.)
*Hunters Point Naval Dry Docks, Calif.	San Francisco, Calif.

I

*Indiana Ordnance Works, Ind.	Charlestown, Ind.
Indiantown Gap Military Reservation, Pa.	Indiantown Gap, Pa. (+Annville, Pa.)
*Iona Island Naval Ammunition Depot, N. Y.	Iona Island, N. Y.
*Iowa Ordnance Works, Iowa	Burlington, Iowa

J

*Jackson Airport, Miss.	Jackson, Miss.
Jackson Barracks, La.	New Orleans, La.
Jacumba Airport, Calif.	Jacumba Hot Springs, Calif.
Jefferson Barracks, Mo.	Jefferson Barracks, Mo.
*Jeffersonville Quartermaster Depot, Ind.	Jeffersonville, Ind.
*Jesup Quartermaster Depot, Ga.	{ Atlanta, Ga. / Ft. McPherson, Ga.

K

*Kankakee Ordnance Works, Ill.	Elwood, Ill.
Kelly Field, Texas	San Antonio, Texas
*Key Field, Miss.	Meridian, Miss.
*Keyport Torpedo Station, Wash.	Keyport, Wash.
*Kingsbury Ordnance Plant, Ind.	Kingsbury, Ind.

L

*Lake Denmark Naval Ammunition Depot, N. J.	Dover, N. J.
Lakehurst Air Station, N. J.	Lakehurst, N. J.
Langley Field, Va.	Hampton, Va.
*Lawson Field, Ga.	Ochillee, Ga. (+Fort Benning, Ga.)
*League Island Navy Yard, Pa.	Philadelphia, Pa.
Lindbergh Field, Calif.	San Diego, Calif.
*Logan Field, Md.	Baltimore, Md.
*Love Field, Texas	Dallas, Texas
Lowry, Colo.	{ Bunell, Colo. (for frt. and spl. psgr. trains) / Denver, Colo. (for individual passengers)
*Luke Field, Ariz.	Phoenix, Ariz.
*Lunken Airport, Ohio	Cininnati, Ohio

M

Mabry Air Base, Fla.	Tallahassee, Fla.
McCarran Field, Nev.	Las Vegas, Nev.
McChord Field, Wash.	Tacoma, Wash.
McClelland Field, Calif.	Sacramento, Calif.
MacDill Field, Fla.	Tampa, Fla.
Madison Barracks, N. Y.	Sackets Harbor, N. Y.
March Field, Calif.	Riverside, Calif.
Mare Island Navy Yard, Calif.	Napa Junction, Calif. (+Vallejo, Calif.)
Marfa Airdrome, Texas	Marfa, Texas
*Marine Air Station, Calif.	San Diego, Calif.
*Marine Air Station, Ga.	Savannah, Ga.
Marine Air Station, N. H.	Manchester, N.H.
Marine Air Station, Va.	Quantico, Va.
Marine Barracks, Calif.	San Diego, Calif.
Marine Barracks, Ga.	Savannah, Ga.
Marine Barracks, N. H.	Portsmouth, N. H.
Marine Barracks, S. Car.	Parris Island, S. Car.
Marine Barrack, Va.	Quantico, Va.
Matagorda Airport, Texas	Matagorda, Texas
*Mather Field, Calif.	Sacramento, Calif.
Maxwell Field, Ala.	Montgomery, Ala.
*Mesa Del Rey Flying Field, Calif.	King City, Calif.
Mitchell Field, N. Y.	Garden City, N. Y.
Mobile Air Depot, Ala.	Mobile, Ala.
*Moffett Field, Calif.	Mountain View, Calif.
*Mojave Anti-Aircraft Range, Calif.	Baker, Calif.
*Morrison Field, Fla.	West Palm Beach, Fla.
*Muroc Lake Bombing Range, Calif.	Muroc, Calif.
Mustin Field, Pa.	Philadelphia, Pa.

N

*Nansemond Ordnance Depot, Va. .... Portsmouth, Va.
Naval Air Station, Calif. .... Alameda, Calif.
Naval Air Station, Calif. .... San Diego, Calif.
*Naval Air Station, Calif. .... San Pedro, Calif.
Naval Air Station, D. C. .... Washington, D. C.
Naval Air Station, Fla. .... Jacksonville, Fla.
*Naval Air Station, Fla. .... Key West, Fla.
Naval Air Station, Fla. .... Opa Locka, Fla.
*Naval Air Station, Fla. .... Pensacola, Fla.
Naval Air Station, N. J. .... Cape May, N. J.
Naval Air Station, N. J. .... Lakehurst, N. J.
*Naval Air Station, R. I. .... East Greenwich, R. I.
Naval Air Station, R. I. .... Newport, R. I.
Naval Air Station, Texas .... Corpus Christi, Texas
*Naval Air Station, Va. .... Norfolk, Va.
*Naval Air Station, Va. .... Quantico, Va.
Naval Air Station, Wash. .... Seattle, Wash.
*Naval Ammunition Depot, Mass. .... Hingham, Mass.
*Naval Ammunition Depot, Nevada .... Hawthorne, Nevada
*Naval Ammunition Depot, N. Y. .... Iona Island, N. Y.
*Naval Ammunition Depot, S. Car. .... Charleston, S. Car.
*Naval Ammunition Depot, Va. .... Portsmouth, Va.
*Naval Mine Depot, Va. .... Lee Hall, Va.
Naval Operating Base, Calif. .... San Diego, Calif.
*Naval Operating Base, Calif. .... San Francisco, Calif.
*Naval Operating Base, Fla. .... Key West, Fla.
Naval Operating Base, La. .... Algiers, La. (+New Orleans, La.)
Naval Operating Base, Va. .... Norfolk, Va. (+Portsmouth, Va.)
*Naval Ordnance Plant, W. Va. .... South Charleston, W. Va.
*Naval Powder Factory, Md. .... Indian Head, Md.
*Naval Station, Fla. .... Key West, Fla.
*Naval Submarine Base, Calif. .... San Diego, Calif.
Naval Submarine Base, Conn. .... New London, Conn.
*Naval Torpedo Station, Wash. .... Keyport, Wash.
*Naval Training Station, Calif. .... San Diego, Calif.
*Naval Training Station, Calif. .... San Francisco, Calif.
Naval Training Station, Ill. .... Great Lakes, Ill.
Naval Training Station, R. I. .... Newport, R. I.
*Naval Training Station, Texas .... Corpus Christi, Texas
*Naval Training Station, Va. .... Norfolk, Va.
*Naval Torpedo Station, R. I. .... Newport, R. I.
Navy Yard, Mare Island, Calif. .... Napa Junction, Calif. (+Vallejo, Calif.)
Navy Yard, D. C. .... Washington, D. C.
Navy Yard, Mass. .... Boston, Mass.
Navy Yard, N. H. .... Portsmouth, N. H.
Navy Yard, N. Y. .... Brooklyn, N. Y.
Navy Yard, League Island, Pa. .... Philadelphia, Pa.
Navy Yard, S. Car. .... Charleston, S. Car.
Navy Yard, Va. .... Norfolk, Va. (+Portsmouth, Va.)
*New Cumberland General Depot, Pa. .... New Cumberland, Pa.
New Orleans Air Base, La. .... New Orleans, La.
*New Post, Okla.. .... Fort Sill, Okla.
*Normoyle Quartermaster Depot, Texas .... San Antonio, Texas
*Norton Field, Ohio .... Columbus, Ohio

O

*Ogden Army Ordnance Depot, Utah .... Arsenal, Utah (+Ogden, Utah)
*Old Hickory Ordnance Depot, Tenn. .... Nashville, Tenn.
Olmstead Field, Pa. .... Middletown, Pa.

P

*Parks Airport, Ill. .... East St. Louis, Ill.
Paso Robles Airport, Calif. .... Paso Robles, Calif.
Patterson Field, Ohio .... Osborn, Ohio (+Dayton, Ohio)
Pearson Field, Wash. .... Vancouver, Wash.
Pendair Army Base .... { Pendair, Ore. (for frt. and spl. psgr. trains)
                                 { Pendleton, Ore. (for individual passengers)
*Phillips Field, Md. .... Aberdeen, Md.
*Picatinny Arsenal, N. J. .... Picatinny, N. J. (+Dover, N. J.)
*Pig Point Ordnance Depot, Va. .... Norfolk, Va. (+Portsmouth, Va.)
Pine Camp, N. Y. .... Great Bend, N. Y.

Plattsburg Barracks, N. Y. .... Plattsburg, N. Y.
*Pope Field, N. Car. .... Fort Bragg, N. Car.
*Portland Columbia Aiport, Oregon .... { Fir, Ore.
                                           { (for frt. and spl. psgr. trains)
                                           { Portland, Ore.
                                           { (for individual passengers)
*Post Field, Okla. .... Fort Silt, Okla.
Presidio of Monterey, Calif. .... Monterey, Calif.
Presidio of San Francisco, Calif. .... San Francisco, Calif.
*Puget Sound Naval Ammunition Depot, Wash. .... Bremerton, Wash.

Q

Quantico Marine Barracks, Va. .... Quantico, Va.
*Quonset Point Naval Air Station, R. I. .... East Greenwich, R. I.

R

*Radford Ordnance Works, Va. .... Radford, Va.
Randolph Field, Texas .... Randolph Field, Texas
*Raritan Arsenal, N. J. .... Metuchen, N. J.(+New Brunswick, N. J.)
*Ravenna Ordnance Plant, Ohio .... Ravenna, Ohio
Reeves Field, Calif. .... San Pedro, Calif.
*Reilly Field, Ala. .... Fort McClellan, Ala.
Richards Field, Kan. .... Kansas City, Kan.
*Rock Island Arsenal, Ill. .... Rock Island, Ill.
*Roosevelt Field, N. Y. .... Mineola, N. Y.

S

*St. Juliens Creek Naval Ammunition Depot, Va. .... Portsmouth, Va.
*San Antonio Arsenal, Texas .... San Antonio, Texas
Sand Point Naval Air Station, Wash. .... Seattle, Wash.
*Savanna Ordnance Depot, Ill.. .... Proving Ground, Ill. (+Savanna, Ill.)
*Schenectady General Depot, N. Y. .... Schenectady, N. Y.
Scott Field, Ill. .... Belleville, Ill.
Selfridge Field, Mich. .... Mount Clemens, Mich.
*Selma Air Base, Ala. .... Selma, Ala.
*Sheppard Field, Texas .... Wichita Falls, Texas
Snohomish Air Field, Wash. .... Everett, Wash.
Southeast Air Depot, Ala. .... Mobile, Ala.
*Souther Field, Ga. .... Arles, Ga.
*Springfield Armory, Mass. .... Springfield, Mass.
*Stackhouse Field, Wis. .... Camp McCoy, Wis.
*Stockton Field, Calif. .... Stockton, Calif.
Sunset Field, Wash. .... Spokane, Wash.

T

*Torpedo Testing Barge Branch, Md. .... Piney Point, Md.
Turner Field, D. C. .... Washington, D. C.

U

*Umatilla Ordnance Depot, Ore. .... Ordnance, Ore.
U. S. Military Academy, N. Y. .... West Point, N. Y.
U. S. Naval Academy, Md. .... Annapolis, Md.
*U. S. Nitrate Plants, Ala. .... Sheffield, Ala.
*Utah General Depot, Utah .... Ogden, Utah

V

Vancouver Barracks, Wash. .... Vancouver, Wash.

W

Washington Navy Yard, D. C. .... Washington, D. C.
*Watertown Arsenal, Mass. .... Boston, Mass. (+Watertown, Mass.)
*Watervliet Arsenal, N. Y. .... Watervliet, N. Y.
*Weldon Springs Ordnance Works, Mo. .... Weldon Springs, Mo.
*Wendover Field, Utah .... Wendover, Utah
Westover Field, Mass. .... Chicopee Falls, Mass.
*Wingate Ordnance Depot, N. Mex. . .Gallup, N. Mex. (+Fort Wingate, N. Mex.)
Wright Field, Ohio .... Dayton, Ohio

Y

*Yerba Buena Is. Naval Training Station, Calif. .... San Francisco, Calif.
*Yorktown Naval Mine Depot, Va. .... Lee Hall, Va.

This U.S. Army photo of halftracks on flatcars was taken at bustling wartime San Luis Obispo, California in 1941. America's railroads were already meeting one of their greatest challenges. *Don Hofsommer collection*

Magnitude of the Task

"They have given their sons to the military services. They have stoked the furnaces and hurried the factory wheels. They have made the planes and welded the tanks, riveted the ships and rolled the shells." —President Franklin D. Roosevelt

The burden imposed upon transportation in the United States in World War II far exceeded that in any previous war.

First, there was the size of the military establishment. It was unprecedented in the nation's history. From November 1940 to the conclusion of hostilities in August 1945, the Army inducted more than 10 million men and women, as compared with 3,832,000 during WWI. In the United States, these personnel had to be transported to induction stations, reception centers and training centers. After completion of basic training, a large portion of the troops were given specialized training and put through field maneuvers, all of which involved further travel.

By the time soldiers had reached a port of embarkation ready for service overseas, they had made at least five Army-planned trips by railway or highway, and in most cases more. In addition, soldiers probably had made several furlough trips at their own expense.

ARMY MOVES MILLIONS

More than 7.29 million passengers were moved by the Army from United States ports to overseas destinations between December 1941 and August 1945, as compared

Troops assigned to loading detail lined up motorized tanks at the rear of the train, and each tank proceeded up a portable ramp "circus style," moving ahead to an assigned flatcar. *Kansas State Historical Society, Santa Fe collection*

with about 2,059,000 in 1917-18. American soldiers were stationed on every continent and on a multitude of large and small islands. Some of them were transported relatively short distances to nearby bases, but more than 4 million were sent to North Africa and Europe over routes averaging about 3,500 nautical miles, more than 2 million were moved to the Pacific where the shipping lanes ranged up

Military troops block and tie down heavy tanks on flatcars under the watchful eye of an Army transportation officer. *Kansas State Historical Society, Santa Fe collection*

With military equipment loaded, troops are ordered to board their Santa Fe troop train for departure. Some of the soldiers have holstered pistols. *Kansas State Historical Society, Santa Fe collection*

to 6,300 miles, and substantial numbers were transported much greater distances to India and Iran.

In addition to the long routes over which troops and supporting supplies had to be moved before contact with the enemy could be made, there was the perpetual problem of overseas discharge ports. During the war, vessels under Army control delivered men and freight at 330 different ports and beaches throughout the world. Many of the ports were small and their facilities wholly inadequate. Others had been badly damaged before U.S. forces gained control of them. Often the operations at ports and beachheads were carried on under enemy artillery fire and aerial attack. Frequently the available native labor was insufficient in quantity and inefficient in quality. The swiftly developing tactical situation sometimes rendered it inadvisable for

ships to discharge at the ports for which they had been loaded.

These working conditions added to the great distances which had to be covered, meant long turn-arounds for the vessels, and limited the amount of traffic which they could handle in a given period.

The maintenance of so large a fighting force involved a tremendous amount of construction work. In the zone of interior there were cantonments, depots, fortifications, airfields and many other types of military installations that had to be built.

The same was true overseas, and in addition, the Army constructed or reconstructed many ports, railways and high-

(Continued on page 33)

Troops block and tie down an M2 light Howitzer artillery piece and a Caterpillar tractor. *Kansas State Historical Society, Santa Fe collection*

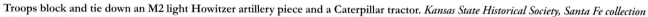

Expand...
the railroads' capacity

WITH LIMA SUPER-POWER LOCOMOTIVES

Freight traffic conditions today call for hauling heavier loads at passenger speeds. Modern power expands the capacity of the railroad by producing more ton-miles per locomotive hour.

On many roads throughout the country Lima Super-Power Steam Locomotives, like the famous 2-6-6-6 "Allegheny Type" freight locomotive shown above, are keeping 'em rolling ... fast ... with few interruptions in traffic.

LIMA LOCOMOTIVE WORKS, INCORPORATED, LIMA.

"The railroad freight car is truly a weapon of war because it is the freight car, together with the locomotive which pulls it and the track on which it runs, that make possible all the other instruments of war. Without them, the whole war effort would collapse."

JOHN J. PELLEY,
President,
Association of American Railroads

WAR DEPARTMENT COMMUNIQUE NO. 2
★ ★ ★
"4. Steps to augment the defenses of both the East and West coasts commenced Sunday night when the War Department placed plans in effect which have materially strengthened the forces already stationed in those areas. The railroads aided greatly in the movement of troops and material, operating through trains to destinations on emergency schedules. In addition ... the ground troops moved, the ... ... redistrib...

KATY FLYER FREIGHT!

★ THE KATY KOMET

Southbound from St. Louis and Kansas City ... Fastest service ever on the Katy Lines ... Merchandise, livestock and packing house products, second morning delivery at Houston and San Antonio.

★ THE BULLET

Additional southbound service from St. Louis and Kansas City to Dallas, Fort Worth, Waco, Austin, San Antonio, Houston and Galveston.

★ THE KATY PACKER

Northbound with livestock and perishables to Kansas City and St. Louis ... Close connections for eastern and northern markets ... 18½ hours Fort Worth to Kansas City ... and 25¾ hours to St. Louis.

★ THE KATY KLIPPER

Southbound from St. Louis — supplementary fast freight service to Parsons, Muskogee, Denison, Dallas and Fort Worth.

★ THE ROCKET

Northbound from Fort Worth and from Dallas, via Denton — Hours slashed from schedules mean more efficient service.

HELPFUL HINTS FOR THE WARTIME TRAVELER

TRAVEL LIGHT

Civilian passengers are urged to take with them as little luggage as possible —thus contributing to the travel comfort of all during this war emergency period.

LABEL IT RIGHT

Don't risk losing some of your luggage in the rush! Label each bag or parcel with your name, address and destination station. Use a tie-on and stick-on label on each piece.

Atlantic Coast 'Dimout' May Hit Yard Floodlights

Floodlighting of railway yards and terminals along the Atlantic coast may be severely restricted as a result of recent Army orders requiring the elimination of sky glow in that region. This measure is a part of a general "dimout" program put into effect all along the shore in a zone some fifteen miles deep.

Aimed particularly at large cities, as well as shore resorts, the order effects a virtual elimination of lighted outdoor advertising signs, blacks out high buildings and materially cuts down street and highway lighting within the affected area. All lights visible from the sea must be shielded or hooded, and floodlights and high power arcs must either be cut out or effectively dimmed or screened, because the glow from such sources silhouettes ships off shore and makes them easy targets for enemy submarines.

No satisfactory means has been found as yet to eliminate reflection from the concentrated illumination at industrial plants, shipyards, piers, railway yards and other locations where outdoor work essential to the war effort is in progress around the clock. It is reported that military authorities are determined to reduce this glow, particularly in the area surrounding New York harbor, where its intensity is greatest, even though they recognize the effect that policy may have on the efficient operation of many facilites. Pending a clarification of military policy, essential lighting of railway facilities continues, though shields and screens have been employed in many instances in an effort to reduce the reflection. *Railway Age, courtesy Lake Forest College*

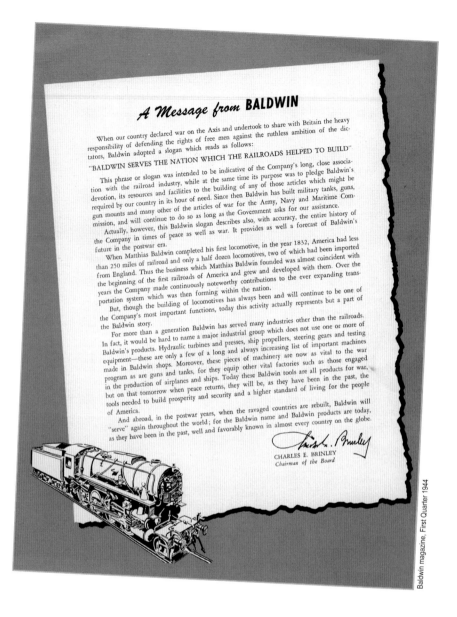

A Message from BALDWIN

When our country declared war on the Axis and undertook to share with Britain the heavy responsibility of defending the rights of free men against the ruthless ambition of the dictators, Baldwin adopted a slogan which reads as follows:

"BALDWIN SERVES THE NATION WHICH THE RAILROADS HELPED TO BUILD"

This phrase or slogan was intended to be indicative of the Company's long, close association with the railroad industry, while at the same time its purpose was to pledge Baldwin's devotion, its resources and facilities to the building of any of those articles which might be required by our country in its hour of need. Since then Baldwin has built military tanks, guns, gun mounts and many other of the articles of war for the Army, Navy and Maritime Commission, and will continue to do so as long as the Government asks for our assistance.

Actually, however, this Baldwin slogan describes also, with accuracy, the entire history of the Company in times of peace as well as war. It provides as well a forecast of Baldwin's future in the postwar era.

When Matthias Baldwin completed his first locomotive, in the year 1832, America had less than 250 miles of railroad and only a half dozen locomotives, two of which had been imported from England. Thus the business which Matthias Baldwin founded was almost coincident with the beginning of the first railroads of America and grew and developed with them. Over the years the Company made continuously noteworthy contributions to the ever expanding transportation system which was then forming within the nation.

But, though the building of locomotives has always been and will continue to be one of the Company's most important functions, today this activity actually represents but a part of the Baldwin story.

For more than a generation Baldwin has served many industries other than the railroads. In fact, it would be hard to name a major industrial group which does not use one or more of Baldwin's products. Hydraulic turbines and presses, ship propellers, steering gears and testing equipment—these are only a few of a long and always increasing list of important machines made in Baldwin shops. Moreover, these pieces of machinery are now as vital to the war program as are guns and tanks, for they equip other vital factories such as those engaged in the production of airplanes and ships. Today these Baldwin tools are all products for war, but on that tomorrow when peace returns, they will be, as they have been in the past, the tools needed to build prosperity and security and a higher standard of living for the people of America.

And abroad, in the postwar years, when the ravaged countries are rebuilt, Baldwin will "serve" again throughout the world; for the Baldwin name and Baldwin products are today, as they have been in the past, well and favorably known in almost every country on the globe.

CHARLES E. BRINLEY
Chairman of the Board

Baldwin magazine, First Quarter 1944

Wartime in the South meant that small roads like the 175-mile-long Columbus & Greenville, which started construction in 1878, pulled longer and heavier trains to keep materials moving to aid the military effort. Beautifully-styled Mikado #505 is westbound clawing up Blue Cut Hill just outside Columbus, Mississippi on March 10, 1944. *C.W. Witbeck, Don Heimburger collection*

Railroad Purchases Need Priorities Now

Large 112-foot-long bolted sectional steel barge panels for military operations are loaded on railroad gondolas during the war. Many odd-sized loads were carried and special movements were made between 1941 and 1945 on U.S. rails. *Louis Marre*

CONSERVING RUBBER ON THE RAILROADS

Rubber was a valuable wartime commodity that U. S. railroads tried desperately to conserve. Many railroads' and industries' supplies were depleted. *Railway Purchases and Stores, September 1942*

United Kingdom Crusader tanks sit on a Pennsylvania Railroad flatcar awaiting movement in 1944. Used between spring 1941 and the winter of 1942-1943, some were built in Toronto for the British and then shipped through U. S. ports. *M.D. McCarter*

Transportation is the very bloodstream flow of industry in bringing together from the far corners of our land the vast quantities of materials of every sort which are needed for the defense program. Transportation, as Ralph Budd recently said, is "as important as battleships," and the railroads still handle about two-thirds of all inter-city transport.

So the railroads cannot be permitted to fail in handling this rapidly expanding defense program, and their needs for materials and supplies and new equipment must be met fully and without delay. In some ways there will be less change in the functioning of the material supply for railroad use than there will be in industry generally. But as demands of the doubled and quadrupled defense program double up on the same sources of supply from which the railroads draw, the procurement of those materials is going to become more and more difficult.

PRIORITIES

In fact, priorities for railroad cars will have to come at once, for already four large car-building plants are shut down or delayed on car construction because of a shortage of steel. Up to the end of May a production loss of 3,200 cars has been experienced in these four plants. Another plant reports that on June 15 it will have to shut down because of lack of steel, and a further loss of 50 cars per day will be experienced thereafter in that plant alone due to the shortage of steel.

The railroads have given ample evidence of their ability and desire to serve efficiently. They are most certainly entitled to better support in the way of priorities in steel to meet their needs for new equipment than this present situation would indicate. Freight car production lost today cannot be made up tomorrow or next fall when the peak load of traffic comes and when car shortages are upon us. Authorities are now giving steel priorities for cargo ship construction, but how can those ships load if there are not adequate freight cars to bring their traffic to the coastal points? Priorities, to be of real value in this unlimited national emergency, must be intelligently administered. The very authorities in Washington who are dealing out the priorities would probably be among the first to place complete blame upon the railroads for a transportation failure due to car shortages. So under the circumstances it certainly behooves railroad officers and the supply industry to keep pressing for the priorities needed. *Railway Purchases and Stores editorial, June 1941*

Mighty and massive 67"-drivered Union Pacific #9059 (#9000-9087), a rare 4-12-2 with a Vanderbilt tender, was the largest steam locomotive built with a rigid wheelbase. The "Nines" were constructed by the Alco Brooks plant, with the first delivered in April of 1926. Intended for use mainly on Sherman Hill between Cheyenne and Ogden, and over the desert of Wyoming and into Weber Canyon, the Nines delivered war freight—fast. On the African war front, Axis troops began to arrive in Tunisia in early November, 1942, and were reinforced the following fortnight until they numbered about 20,000 combat troops (which were subsequently heavily reinforced by air). UP #9059's tonnage would all be part of the Allied buildup to defeat the Axis wherever they were. The #9059 rolls near Meneken, Kansas in November of 1942. *Don Heimburger collection*

World War II military flatcar loads on the Santa Fe Railway in southern California included two-axle military trucks with canvas tops. Strings of these shipments were made week after week. *Kansas State Historical Society, Santa Fe collection*

Young U. S. troops on board a Norfolk & Western troop train wave as they leave the station headed for their port of embarkation on May 9, 1943. These twelve-wheel clerestory roof coaches had windows that opened. *U. S. Army Signal Corps, Library of Virginia*

An Army troop train sits in Sparks, Nevada on September 30, 1942 before it continues on its wartime journey. *Bob's Photos*

America's Roads to Victory
are boulevards of steel and stamina

"FASTER, faster," is wartime America's cry to the railroads. Speed the troop trains! Speed the supply and munitions trains! Speed the critical materials to the factories!

It's a challenge the railroads are taking in stride. They're coming through on every assignment, even though their need today is more new equipment than is available under existing priorities.

The railroads are mastering war traffic problems because they were ready with a modern plant that, in recent years, had been utilized to only half its capacity.

The Milwaukee Road, for example, prepared with new power as well as new freight and passenger cars, in the decade before war struck. It improved more than 2,000 miles of track with heavier rail and new ballast. It rebuilt over 80,000 lineal feet of bridges. It reduced curvatures to permit faster schedules...and 500 grade crossings were eliminated or provided with automatic protection.

These improvements, plus heavier tonnage on both cars and trains, account for The Milwaukee Road's present ability to double its load. Aided by the co-operation of business and government shippers, its 35,000 loyal, determined employees are ably handling their tremendous responsibilities.

The Milwaukee Road and the other railroads constitute one of our vital war industries.

CHICAGO
MILWAUKEE
ST. PAUL
AND PACIFIC

THE MILWAUKEE ROAD
11,000-MILE SUPPLY LINE FOR WAR AND HOME FRONTS

Sometimes military equipment could be piggybacked such as these wagons placed in the bed of Army trucks loaded on flatcars. "The need for the utmost economy in the employment of transportation equipment was recognized well in advance of our entry into the war," read a military booklet. *David Myers collection*

Soldiers unload M3 Grant medium tanks at Camp Polk, Louisiana in August of 1942 using wooden ramps. A total of 6,258 were built in 1941 and 1942. Between December 1941 and August 1945, freight—such as these tanks—moving on War Department bills of lading totaled 324,891,000 short tons. *David Myers collection*

A unit train of U.S. Army MTL tugboats, about 47 feet long each, arrives at New Orleans 8th Transportation Zone in 1943. As many as 40 boatyards constructed more than 1,200 of these vessels during the war. *David Myers collection*

Note "Central War Time" printed on cover of this North Shore Line timetable of December 1, 1942.

(Continued from page 24)

ways to facilitate the movement of U.S. forces and their supplies into and through foreign countries. The transportation of the necessary materials and building equipment was in itself a sizable task. This was especially true in regards to overseas construction, and it is worth noting that while in some areas it was possible to obtain building materials locally, in many instances most or all of those materials had to be supplied from the U.S.

Whether at home or abroad, whether training or fighting, whether in the mountains or the desert, the Arctic or the tropics, U.S. forces had to be supported with a constant stream of military equipment and supplies suitable to the operation in which they were engaged.

American soldiers were provided with the best fighting tools, the best food and clothing, the best living conditions and the best medical care that scientific and employment would allow.

Morale was considered as important as physical condition, and so books and magazines, athletic and recreational equipment, ice cream, soft drinks and many other things to which American youth was accustomed at home, were provided at training camps and overseas stations—even though they added considerably to the tightness of an already tight transportation situation.

TRANSPORTATION LOGISTICS

The strategy of the war, involving so many amphibious assaults upon enemy-held territory, had large transportation implications. In only a few instances were these assaults launched from American ports. Generally they were mounted at overseas bases where U.S. troops, military supplies and construction materials had been assembled in advance. This involved the employment of large numbers of ships within the various war theaters and necessitated repeated loadings and unloadings. It also necessitated the construction of port facilities, depots and airfields at many rear bases which later were abandoned for more advanced bases. It meant that more men and supplies had to be kept in the pipeline between America's shores and the combat areas, involving a proportionately greater amount of transportation.

This global conflict saw many significant developments in the art of warfare. Prominent among them were the more complete mechanization of ground forces and the great advance in air power. Each of these had direct transportation implications. The machines themselves—the motor vehicles, armored tanks and airplanes—were bulky and required a great amount of space when shipped by railway, highway or water. They consumed large quantities of gasoline and oil, a large part of which moved from point of origin to point of consumption in tank cars, tank trucks and tank vessels.

The intricate mechanisms also required constant maintenance, so that repair shops and replacement parts had to be shipped wherever they were needed. Animals and forage were considered space-consuming freight, but they did not approach the requirements of the motor-propelled machines which characterized WWII as the first great mechanized war.

At times during the war, the Army utilized as much as 50% of the sleeping cars and 30% of the coaches in service on American railroads, shipped as high as 12.5% of the freight carried by the railroads, and had in its service more than 48% of the ocean-going shipping, other than tankers, under American control.

The heavy transportation requirements of the Army by land and sea naturally constituted only part of the load placed

Railway crews shove portable loading ramp in place to unload tanks, with large white U.S. stars stencilled on the turrets, which have just been carried on an expedited Santa Fe military train. *Santa Fe Railway, Mallory Hope Ferrell collection*

A trainload of 28-ton M-3 tanks rolls away from a large Midwestern tank arsenal to be delivered to the U.S. Army. The M-3s featured a 37 mm anti-aircraft gun, machine guns and a 75 mm main gun. *Office of War Information, Mallory Hope Ferrell collection*

On America's railroads, military traffic came first during the war years. Civilians and civilian goods were delayed because the movement of equipment, such as these half-tracked personnel carriers called *Trac Scouts*, had priority over other materials not directly related to the war effort. *Mallory Hope Ferrell collection*

When Santa Fe military trains stopped enroute, the conductor and brakeman made hurried inspections of the cars, while the soldier-guard in the M-3 tank turret kept watch. *Kansas State Historical Society, Santa Fe collection*

A farewell kiss on tiptoe is received by this pretty miss from a young man reporting for military duty aboard a Santa Fe troop train at Los Angeles Union Passenger Terminal. *Kansas State Historical Society, Santa Fe collection.*

Wartime tonnage was often doubleheaded to speed the shipment of men and materiel. Union Pacific #2866 and #3119 with Vanderbilt tenders pull this 17-car heavyweight passenger consist, leaving a bellowing trail of white smoke in its path at Riview, Wyoming in 1941. *Otto Perry, Denver Public Library, Western History Section*

a "31" order

The wires hum. It's a "31" order—important instructions for a train soon to arrive and for which the conductor must sign. The station agent sets the semaphore. The red light flashes its warning. The train arrives and rumbles to a stop.

This is just one of many safety measures established by Union Pacific to assure reliable transportation of passengers and freight. War resulted in a tremendous increase in rail traffic. As might be expected, a large part of that traffic has been directed over Union Pacific's "strategic middle route" uniting the East with the Pacific Coast.

Through constant vigilance and tireless effort on the part of employes, thousands of men and trainloads of materials have been moved efficiently and quickly to aid the Allied cause.

* * * *

The constant improvements in railroading—resulting in safe, efficient transportation—are due in large measure to the American system of encouraging workers to seek advancement through personal enterprise and initiative. We're fighting and working to maintain that spirit of equal opportunity for all.

★ Listen to "YOUR AMERICA" radio program on Mutual nationwide network every Sunday afternoon. Consult your local newspaper for the time and station.

THE PROGRESSIVE
UNION PACIFIC
RAILROAD

THE STRATEGIC MIDDLE ROUTE UNITING THE EAST WITH THE PACIFIC COAST

Railway Performance in Handling Passengers

	July 1920	July 1940	July 1942	July 1943	July 1944
Number of passenger locomotives	13,562	7,306	7,017	6,823	6,794
Number of passenger-carrying cars	41,564	27,592	27,706	27,902	28,545*
Passengers carried one mile (thousands), average daily	154,871	72,374	153,693	269,958	280,830
Passenger train-miles, average daily	1,568,000	1,082,000	1,159,000	1,282,000	1,297,000
Pass. train-miles per locomotive, average daily	116	148	165	188	191
Passenger-carrying car-miles, average daily	7,008,000	4,892,000	6,271,000	7,967,000	8,272,000
Average miles per pass. car daily	168	177	226	285	290
Average pass.-carrying cars per train	4.5	4.5	5.4	6.2	6.4
Average passengers per car	22.1	14.8	24.5	33.9	33.9
Average passengers per train	98.7	66.9	133.0	210.5	216.4
Average trip per passenger (individual railway)	41.9	57.2	79.2	98.6	102.4
Passengers carried one mile per locomotive, average daily	11,419	9,906	21,903	39,566	41,335
Passengers carried one mile per pass. car, average daily	3,726	2,623	5,547	9,675	9,819

* Estimated.

Statistics given in the accompanying table from Railway Age show how the railways have accomplished what a few years ago would have been regarded as the impossible task of handling with fewer locomotives and cars a passenger traffic which this year is four and one-third times as large as in 1940.

Like Father, Like Sons

THIS IS NORTH WESTERN'S
"PAL" HOLLAND
HIS FIGHTING SONS ARE **ALL** "NORTH WESTERN" MEN, TOO!

CHICAGO NORTH WESTERN SYSTEM

On a 5½-mile stretch of double track, just outside of Norway, Iowa, Section Foreman Arthur M. (Pal) Holland keeps himself and his crew mighty busy. Theirs is one of the important jobs of railroading. For this piece of main line, like all other "North Western" track, must be kept in perfect condition.

Significantly, "Pal" Holland has five sons who went into service, *all five former "North Western" employes*. And a grand lot they are! There's Cyril, in the Field Artillery, now in the Southwest Pacific. And Sergeants Leon and Arthur, both fighting in France — Leon with the Engineers, Arthur in a Gun Battalion. Creighton, too, is in France, with the Infantry.

Finally, there's Blaine, who enlisted in the Navy. A medical discharge brought him back to Norway, so once again he's a member of the "North Western" family, working as a section laborer.

★   ★   ★

When a "North Western" man steps out of his working clothes and into Uncle Sam's uniform, we admire him for it. But when five of them, all from the same family, don fighting garb, it's a story well worth telling. Naturally, we're proud of the Hollands. They're typical of legions of Americans, each fighting in his way to speed the day of total victory.

CHICAGO and NORTH WESTERN SYSTEM
SERVING AMERICA IN WAR AND PEACE FOR ALMOST A CENTURY

Soldiers get settled after boarding Pullman troop train at Camp Haan, California. Pullman heavyweight sleepers accommodated 39 soldiers in each car. Two men shared a wide, lower berth and one man occupied a single, upper berth. *Kansas State Historical Society, Santa Fe collection.*

FOR
• • • ▬
BUY
UNITED STATES
WAR BONDS
& STAMPS

Pennsylvania Railroad timetable, September 27, 1942

Troops on their way to the front in October of 1942 hang their uniform tops on the luggage racks above their seats, light up a cigarette or cigar, and settle in for a long trip over the rails to a port of embarkation. Their final destination was sometimes unknown even to them until later. *Bob's Photos*

BOTH MAY BE FOUND ON THE RAILROADS

Thousands of jobs are open in the railroad industry. They are open because thousands of railroad employees are in military service; because there is a greater volume of freight and passengers to be moved than ever before in the history of the Nation; and because those two circumstances converge to create an urgent need for more men and women to help move this peak volume of traffic.

Here is an opportunity to make a real contribution to the war and an opportunity to make a place for yourself in a permanent industry that will move forward with the Nation's future progress and development. When victory has been won and American industry is again able to devote its ingenuity and productive capacity to the needs of peace, the American railroads will uphold their reputation for vision and progress and will be a pillar of strength in maintaining a high level of employment in the Nation.

Take a job with the railroads! Take a job with an American industry that has a tradition of fair treatment and steady jobs!

Any railroad officer will be glad to discuss the subject with you, or you may apply direct to any office of the Railroad Retirement Board or United States Employment Service.

Atlantic Coast Line Railroad timetable, April 1945

To meet the emergency demands of the Armed Forces and others engaged in war activities, it may be necessary to temporarily discontinue or divert certain Pullman car lines on short notice. Therefore, the Pullman equipment shown in this folder is subject to change. We are confident you will understand the necessity for such action.

New York Central timetable, February 20, 1944

Denver & Rio Grande Western #3706, a mighty 4-6-6-4, leads a long 14-car eastbound loaded troop train with three headend cars at Grand Junction, Colorado on June 18, 1944. *Otto Perry, Denver Public Library, Western History Section*

upon the carriers. The shipping program of the Navy also was large. The huge quantities of equipment and foodstuffs which were sent to the Allies under the Lend-Lease Act competed for car and ship space with the supplies which were transported to U.S. forces.

Whereas in 1917-18 the American Expeditionary Forces obtained about half of their supplies and equipment from European sources, in WWII the U.S. assumed the role of the Arsenal of Democracy. The home civilian economy, though curtailed in some respects, suffered no serious encroachments and continued to make heavy demands upon the carriers.

The difficulties which the American transportation industries encountered as a result of the war were great, and the way they were overcome was remarkable. The problems and accomplishments of the Army Transportation Corps were divided into two phases—that of domestic transportation and that of ocean shipping. Success in both fields was necessary to win the war. Both experienced periods of crisis. The most critical stage in ocean shipping came in the early months of American participation; that in domestic transportation came toward the close of the war.

During WWI, particularly the first year of U.S. participation, the transportation situation in the zone of interior was confused and constituted a detriment to the military effort. No such situation was permitted to develop in WWII.

Although the rail carriers were hard pressed at times to handle the unprecedented traffic, they were able to do so in a manner that involved no impairment of military effectiveness and only a limited curtailment of civilian privileges.

Several factors operated to make the load that fell to domestic rail carriers a heavy one. The war followed a period of general business depression, during which the position of the transportation industries in regard to equipment had undergone some recession.

After the U.S. entered the war, the possibility of procuring additional equipment to meet the rising demand for transportation was severely restricted by the prior claims of strictly military supplies upon the available materials and manufacturing facilities of the country. The neccessity of withdrawing ships from coastal and intercoastal services to use them on the strategically more important overseas routes, put an additional heavy burden on the railways and highways. The rationing of gasoline and tires, and the scarcity of replacement parts, forced many private automobiles off the roads, with the result that the large intercity passenger traffic which they normally handled had to be absorbed by the common carriers. These conditions are reflected in Table I.

Table I.

Percentages of intercity passenger and freight traffic handled by railroads during WWII.

Passenger traffic (passenger-miles)

	1941	1942	1943	1944
Railroads	9.6%	22.5%	34.7%	41.4%

Freight traffic (ton-miles)

	1941	1942	1943	1944
Railroads	63.62%	70.23%	71.97%	68.78%

The need for the utmost economy in the employment of transportation equipment was recognized well in advance of the entry into the war, and the creation of the Office of Defense Transportation to deal with this problem followed entrance into the war soon after.

Possessed of broad authority to regulate operations and eliminate waste due to overlapping services and inefficient practices, the ODT introduced regulations which squeezed the most work from the available transportation resources.

Unlike in a mess hall, Army sergeants enjoy a relaxed dining car meal during the war years. *Don Hofsommer collection*

Troops in a rounded roof passenger coach ride an Army Liberty Special train during the war years. Note the roof vents and lights located in the middle of the car. *Don Hofsommer collection*

Under the ODT mandate, it was possible to set up a system for the overall control of port-bound traffic, covering commercial shipments as well as those of the Government, which kept the ports free of congestion and permitted a smooth flow of military supplies to overseas forces.

This control system, which leaned heavily on machinery already created by the Army for the regulation of its own traffic, and was supervised by a committee for which the Chief of Transportation provided the executive staff, was an outstanding success.

RAILROADS BETTER ORGANIZED

Although American railroads had less equipment in 1941 than in 1917, it was better equipment. The railroad's physical plant generally was greatly improved, and as an industry they were much better organized to meet the emergency. In particular, the establishment of a strong central organization, the Association of American Railroads, was a noteworthy improvement. This organization, which had broad authority to act for its members, maintained headquarters in Washington so that cooperation between the Army Transportation Corps and the railroads was greatly simplified. In fact, the Association's Military Transportation Section was located in the Pentagon and functioned as much as an agent of the Army as of the railroads. This same close coordination existed between representatives of the AAR and the Transportation Corps.

The pressure of wartime operations was felt by the railroads first in the passenger field. To the heavy demand upon passenger equipment created by the mobilization of large military forces, there was added the neccessity for increased business travel and the tendency of the civilian population to spend a portion of its mounting income on pleasure trips.

Since military traffic had priority, some curtailment of regular train service was necessary beginning in 1942 to insure sufficient sleeping cars and coaches for troop trains. More drastic action in that area was required after the end of the war to handle the heavy movement of repatriated troops.

In the freight area, strain upon the railways developed gradually as the war progressed. There were temporary local shortages of certain types of equipment, but through a free interchange of rolling stock between carriers, and persistent efforts to avoid waste through backhauls, empty hauls, part loads, and other uneconomical practices which characterized peacetime operations, nonmilitary shipments were effected without serious delays, and military traffic was handled promptly.

The most serious situation developed during the severe winter of 1944-45. Exceptionally bad snow and ice conditions in the Northeast immobilized large blocks of equipment or slowed down operations to the extent that it was

41

Chart A

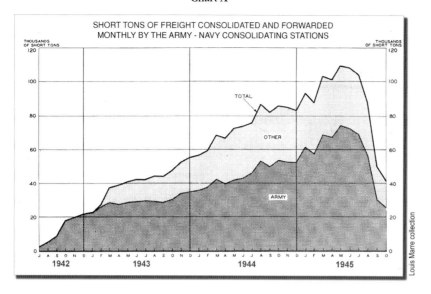

SHORT TONS OF FREIGHT CONSOLIDATED AND FORWARDED
MONTHLY BY THE ARMY - NAVY CONSOLIDATING STATIONS

TOTAL

OTHER

ARMY

Louis Marre collection

Chart B

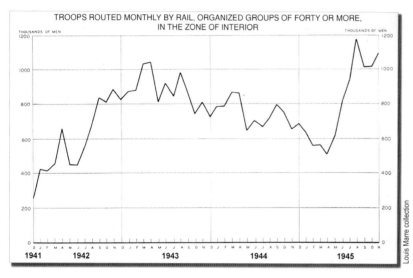

TROOPS ROUTED MONTHLY BY RAIL, ORGANIZED GROUPS OF FORTY OR MORE,
IN THE ZONE OF INTERIOR

Louis Marre collection

This scene shows a busy Santa Fe rail yard during the war. Three steamers, and a diesel at middle right, switch the yard tracks. War supplies to factories and plants were expedited. *Railway Purchases and Stores, 1942*

This faded, early photo depicts WWII paratroopers from Camp Hoffman (later named Camp Mackall), North Carolina lining up prior to boarding troop trains. These soldiers are from the 11th, 13th and 17th Airborne. *82nd Airborne Corps Office of the Command Historian, courtesy Donna Tabor*

neccessary to place several brief embargoes against non-military shipments into that territory. The effect of this situation was felt throughout the country, and it was not cleared up until well into the spring. However, except for some restrictions on the movement of less urgently needed types of supplies, which the Army voluntarily placed in effect, shipments destined to the forces at home and overseas moved without delay.

From the end of 1939 to the end of 1944 the number of passenger cars on American railroads increased from 29,685 to 30,997, but between those years the number of passengers carried per car increased from 13.36 to 31.87, and the total revenue passenger miles increased from 22.651 billion to 95.549 billion.

NET RAIL TONS INCREASE

During this period the number of freight cars of all types increased only from 1,931,217 to 2,040,514, but the average net tons per loaded car increased from 26.9 to 32.7, while revenue ton miles advanced from 333.438 billion to 737.246 billion. The number of railroad-owned locomotives increased from 42,511 to 43,612, but the average miles traveled per day increased from 184.2 to 222.9 for active passenger locomotives, and from 104.0 to 122.8 for active freight locomotives.

These figures reflect the increased efficiency which enabled railroads to cope with the tremendous traffic of the war. This increased efficiency was the result of wholehearted cooperation between government agencies, the carriers and shippers.

The danger that railway equipment might fall short of requirements in the event of involvement in the war was foreseen in some quarters at least a year before Pearl Harbor, but no effective steps were taken then to prepare for the contingency. The railroads, which for a number of years had experienced a surplus of rolling stock, were disinclined to invest in additional equipment merely on the chance that

it might be needed. With somewhat the same point of view, and in line with its policy to rely entirely on the common carriers for transportation in the zone of interior, the Army was not disposed to procure such equipment.

LIMITED NEW ROLLING STOCK

After entry into the war by the U.S., the number of new cars and locomotives that could be built without encroaching upon the supply of weapons and other strictly military equipment was severely limited. The railroads were able to procure a small amount of new rolling stock, and Government orders were placed for 2,400 troop sleepers, 800 troop kitchen cars and 380 hospital cars.

An integrated transportation service did not come into existence until three months after the U.S. entered the war; its transition into the Transportation Corps did not take place until several months more had passed; and the final substantial addition to the Corps' responsibilities came almost a year after Pearl Harbor. Thus the new transportation service was under the necessity of building up its organization and establishing procedures, while also coping with unprecedented operating problems during the most critical phase of the war.

During the peace period the movement of troops and supplies by common carriers in the zone of interior, and by Army transports and commercial vessels between the U.S. and overseas bases, was the responsibility of The Quartermaster General.

The Chief of Engineers was responsible for the construction of military and utility railroads, the procurement of all railroad equipment required by the Army, the training of railroad troop units, and the operation and maintenance of military railroads. The Quartermaster General was responsible for the operation and maintenance of utility railroads, except at installations which were under the exclusive control of other supply services.

The commanders of ports of embarkation reported directly to the War Department General Staff, and the line of demarcation between their duties with regard to Army transports and those of The Quartermaster General was

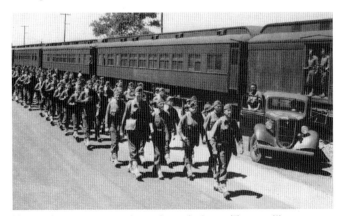

Troops leave a troop train on its arrival at a Texas military camp. The wooden car with the two soldiers standing in the doorway is the kitchen car. *U.S. Army, David Myers collection*

Military personnel spent countless hours on troop trains that rolled from coast to coast. Radios provided some entertainment on board. *Santa Fe Railway, Mallory Hope Ferrell collection*

not clearly drawn. As matters developed in the fall of 1941, commanders of the two holding and reconsignment points which were being built to aid in the regulation of the flow of traffic to the ports, also were to be responsible directly to the General Staff. Overall supervision of these activities was exercised by the Supply Division (G-4) of the General Staff.

As the size of the Army increased under the Selective Service Act of September 1940, and the extension and strengthening of U.S. overseas bases progressed, the Army's transportation problems grew in both size and complexity.

ARMY REORGANIZATION

The first step in solving these problems was taken in connection with the Army reorganization which became effective March 9, 1942. A Transportation Division (soon renamed Transportation Service) was established as one of the components of the newly-created Services of Supply (predecessor to the Army Service Forces). Because the Transportation Service needed a huge increase in trained personnel, it was recommended that a special replacement training center and officer candidate school be established, rather than depend on officers detailed from other branches of the Army. A proposal was made to the Chief of Staff of the Army, General George C. Marshall, that a separate corps paralleling the Corps of Engineers or the Quartermaster Corps be established. On July 31, 1942 the new Transportation Corps was activated, with responsibility for traffic management, ports of embarkation and port units, harbor craft and railhead companies.

The operation, maintenance-of-way and the equipping of military railways was transferred from the Corps of Engineers to the Transportation Corps in September 1942, and the operation and maintenance of equipment of utility railroads was transferred from The Quarter-

master Corps at the same time. The design, procurement, storage and issue of all railway equipment, the training of railway troop organizations, and the entire Military Railway Service was transferred from the Corps of Engineers to the Transportation Corps in November of 1942.

BALDWIN
Number 70,000

Baldwin magazine, First Quarter, 1944

Saturday, December 4, 1943, started off very much like any other work day in the Baldwin Erecting Shop at Eddystone. The usual number of locomotives were scheduled for completion and, one by one, they moved out of the shop as the day progressed.

Preoccupied with production problems, nobody paid much attention to the fact that one of the engines nearing completion bore the Baldwin Construction Number 70,000. To a nation at war it was just another locomotive for the United States Army, but to Baldwin it marked a milestone in the life of America's oldest locomotive builder.

This sturdy little 2-8-0 type locomotive is one of a large number being built for the United States Army and is a down-to-earth "irondough-boy" without frills or trimming. Modern prototype of the famous "Pershing" locomotives which Baldwin built in such great numbers during World War I, these newest Baldwins are already playing an active part in many of our military operations abroad. *(See pages 171, 323)*

The dining car on a railroad passenger train was often a big step up from a meal in a mess hall on a military base. Here troops are served by a waiter and taken care of by a steward. *Bob Withers collection*

Loaded for War

Take a good look at this picture. It shows a Santa Fe train loaded for war.

That war train is ready to roll. It is *going through!*

In railroad language, it has the right-of-way over everything else on the line.

So it must be with *all* American transportation until this war job is done.

Victory Rides on Wheels

This is essentially a war of rolling wheels.

Millions of men and tens of millions of tons of vital foods, raw materials, and finished products must be moved swiftly and surely, where and when they are needed.

Stop the wheels that move them, and we stop all that floats and flies as well.

That is why, on the Santa Fe, movements essential to the war effort are topping the greatest transportation job in all our history. They *must* come first, beyond argument or selfish interest.

★ During 1942, *with 26% fewer locomotives,* Santa Fe moved 122% *more* freight ton-miles and 79% *more* military and civilian passenger-miles than in 1918, during the First World War. The Army and Navy, the ODT, and civilian shippers and travelers everywhere are cooperating 100% with the railroads of America in making records like this possible.

SERVING THE SOUTHWEST FOR 70 YEARS

Santa Fe

Saturday Evening Post, 1943

First Step toward the fighting front

It leads him to a good night's rest in a soft, sleep-inviting bed.

And that's the least that anyone can wish him—although the demand for so many sleeping cars to move troops results in occasional inconvenience to civilians traveling Pullman in wartime.

We are grateful for the tolerance with which you accept the situation—for your understanding attitude that says as plain as words:

"He comes first with all of us!"

AN AVERAGE OF ALMOST 30,000 TROOPS A NIGHT NOW

Go Pullman

★ Buy United States War Bonds and Stamps Regularly! ★

Copyright 1944, The Pullman Company

"Maybe you're the guy I'm grateful to!"

"**Tough day!** Assembly line got all snarled up. Didn't finish till seven o'clock.

"Then came a phone call from Plant 5. They need an engineer. Tomorrow morning. 300 miles away. So it's up to me to climb on my horse—my iron horse.

"I tried for a Pullman bed, of course, as soon as I knew I had to go, because a fellow sure does need sleep going to keep going on a job like mine. But everything was sold. Which didn't surprise me, either, for I know that half the Pullman fleet is busy moving troops. And that the other half is carrying more passengers than the whole fleet did in peacetime.

"Anyway, there I was—dead tired—and no bed. I saw myself sitting up all night and getting to that essential job too fagged out to tell a blueprint from a blueprint.

"But somebody cancelled a reservation just in time for me to get this space. Maybe it was you! If it was, thanks a million. Boy, will I sleep tonight! And will that sleep pay dividends tomorrow!"

* * *

You never know how important the Pullman bed that you can't use may be to someone else. So please cancel promptly when plans change.

That is one of the most helpful contributions you can make to wartime travel, because sleeping cars are loaded to a higher percentage of capacity than ever before. Yet practically every train carrying Pullmans still goes out with wasted space due to people who either just don't show up or who cancel too late for the space to be assigned to others.

And only your cooperation can prevent this waste of needed accommodations!

★ LET'S ALL BACK THE ATTACK WITH WAR BONDS! ★

PULLMAN

● For more than 80 years, the greatest name in passenger transportation—your assurance of comfort and safety as you go and certainty that you'll get there

Husky Pennsylvania #6904 4-8-2 Baldwin-built Mountain tugs a very long heavyweight troop train along at Englewood, Illinois. Pennsy ran a total of 301 Mountain-type locomotives. Note the single-dome tank car trailing the engine. *Paul Eilenberger, Bill Raia collection*

KEEPING IN STEP WITH OUR COUNTRY'S NEEDS

In full cooperation with our Nation's war effort, travelers can aid immeasurably by following these few suggestions whenever they must travel.

● **PLAN YOUR TRIP IN ADVANCE**

During wartime, train schedules are subject to change on short notice. See your agent about accommodations and connecting service as early as possible. Buy round-trip tickets. This will save you money and time.

● **MAKE RESERVATIONS EARLY**

Avoid congestion and last-minute crowds at ticket counters by reserving your accommodations as soon as you can. Also, please take whatever Pullman space is available instead of postponing your trip until your favorite accommodation is available.

● **CANCEL RESERVATIONS PROMPTLY**

If plans change and you must postpone your trip, please notify your agent immediately so your space may be used by some one else.

● **TRAVEL MIDWEEK**

(Tuesday, Wednesday, Thursday) Leave week ends open for use by furloughed men and women and for war workers who can travel at no other time. Accommodations are better and your trip will be more enjoyable when these rush periods are avoided.

● **TRAVEL LIGHT**

Extra baggage takes up room and results in discomfort to all passengers on crowded trains. Please try to get along on one small bag. If you must take larger pieces — send them in the baggage car.

THE ALTON is proud to be a member of America's Great Transportation System *United for Victory*

Bad Luck for the Axis

"Bad Luck for the Axis" was the headline over this photograph when it was published in the Baldwin magazine for June of 1942. These 13 M-3 Baldwin-built riveted tanks were ready for shipment by rail.

BY DIVISIONS, FORWARD MARCH!

There are more than 11,000 men in an armored division. When they move, everything they need to fight with goes along. So when the railroads get a call to move one division it means that 75 trains are needed. That is only 11,000 men, and the railroads have been moving an average of one and one-half million troops a month.

Baldwin magazine, Second Quarter 1944

'Mikado' Becomes 'MacArthur'

All of the "Mikado" type locomotives of the Central of Georgia Railway, many of which were built by Baldwin, have been changed to "MacArthur" types in honor of the hero of the Philippines. The former designation MK has been removed from the sides of the locomotive cabs and the letters MacA have been substituted.

The name "Mikado," now so generally applied to locomotives of the 2-8-2 type, traces its origin to the first locomotives of this design which were built by Baldwin in 1897 for the Nippon Railway of Japan. Therefore, the substitution of the name "MacArthur" is particularly appropriate at this time and for all time to come.

Baldwin magazine, June 1942

Soldiers, with weapons strapped to their backs and gear in strong canvas bags, board a troop train during WWII and wave as they leave; they likely don't know where they will end up as yet, because security was very tight, and soldiers weren't told much. "Without transportation our soldiers and our guns, tanks and other weapons of war would be useless," reads a booklet issued by the Association of American Railroads, Washington, D.C. entitled *Railroads in Two Wars*, comparing statistical data between the two great battles. It continued, "The railroads are doing a bigger and better job today because of years of preparation for emergency, beginning as long ago as 1923, when they embarked upon their $10 billion dollar program of rehabilitation and modernization." *U.S. Army Signal Corp*

Railroads in Two Wars, Association of American Railroads

RAILROADS IN TWO WARS

★ ★ ★ ★ ★ ★ ★ ★ ★ ★ ★ ★ ★

IN THE FIRST WORLD WAR, as in the present World War, the railroads played an essential — indeed, a vital — part in the fighting power of the nation.

Railway performance in this war, however, differs tremendously from that of the First World War.

A few of the many changes and contrasts between railroading today and railroading in the period of the First World War are here shown in graphic form.

The graphs are based upon two three-year periods. The first starts with 1916, when the United States undertook its program of preparedness, and extends through 1917 and 1918, when the United States was an active belligerent in the First World War. The second period starts with 1940, when the United States entered upon its national defense and lend-lease program, and extends through 1941 and 1942, when the United States was an active belligerent.

One great difference — perhaps the greatest of all — cannot be shown by so simple a presentation. This is the difference in the smoothness and dependability of the flow and movement of freight. In the First World War there was almost constant congestion. In the present war, a far heavier load has been moved freely and without delay or congestion of consequence.

The railroads are doing a bigger and better job today because of years of preparation for emergency, beginning as long ago as 1923, when they embarked upon their ten-billion-dollar program of rehabilitation and modernization. They have built increased capacity and efficiency into their plant. They have improved their methods of operation and their organization for cooperation among themselves.

But what the railroads have done in this war has been accomplished, not by the railroads alone, but by the joint work of railroads and shippers and receivers of freight. This cooperation was first organized nearly twenty years ago through the Shippers Advisory Boards, collaborating with the *Car Service Division* of the *Association of American Railroads*. With the beginning of the defense program, this cooperative organization was expanded by the addition of more than 500 local car efficiency, or "vigilance," committees of shippers, set up to assist in the prompt loading, unloading and release of freight cars.

The Association of American Railroads has added to its Car Service Division a *Military Transportation Section*, to work in closest cooperation with the armed forces; a *Port Traffic Section*, to deal with the flow of export traffic through American ports; a *Passenger Car Section*, to deal with the greatly increased problems of the joint use of passenger cars; and a *Tank Car Section*, to deal with the special problems created by the vastly multiplied demand for rail transportation of oil.

From government agencies, notably the *Office of Defense Transportation* and the *Interstate Commerce Commission*, charged with special responsibilities for transportation matters, there has been a most effective and helpful cooperation. The government agencies using transportation also have assisted in its efficient production.

This is especially effective in the case of the government departments which are the largest users of transportation—the *Transportation Division, Bureau of Supplies and Accounts of the Navy Department*, and the *Army Transportation Corps*, which has become by far the greatest shipper the world has ever known.

To show the various changes and contrasts on a uniform scale, the figures for 1918, the peak traffic year of the First World War period, have been shown as an index of 100, with figures for other years shown to scale above or below this index.

A massive Duluth, Missabe & Iron Range 2-8-8-4 Yellowstone, built in 1943, helped move iron ore tonnage from the Mesabi Range for the war effort. These locomotives featured unique 4-10-0 pedestal-type coal tenders. When delivered the turntables and roundhouses couldn't accommodate the engines without alteration. In 1941, the first year these locomotives were produced, DM&IR tonnage increased to 37 million tons. *Don Heimburger collection*

Advertisement from Cramp Brass & Iron Foundries, a subsidiary of Baldwin Locomotive Works. *Baldwin magazine, June 1942*

A U.S. Army tank, along with crated equipment, is loaded on an International-Great Northern (Missouri Pacific subsidiary railroad) flatcar in 1945 for shipment from a military base to another location. *U.S. Army Transportation Museum*

4211

Boiler mounted on front locomotive bed.

New Passenger and Freight Pow

The Southern Pacific was one of the early users of Mallet locomotives and, in 1928, they rebuilt one of them as a single-expansion engine. In the same year they ordered ten single-expansion, articulated locomotives of the 4-8-8-2 type from Baldwin. These were followed by 16 locomotives in 1929, 25 in 1930, 26 in 1936 and 28 in 1939.

Baldwin is now delivering 40 of these locomotives and 30 additional duplicates are on order. With the completion of this new order, the Southern Pacific will have a total of 175 of these giants of the rails engaged in transporting the men and materials so vital to a nation at war.

Completed boiler ready for the erecting shop.   *Firebox and combustion chamber.*   *Interior view of the outer firebox shell.*

the Southern Pacific

Helping with America's War Effort

The 4-8-8-2 locomotives are used in both freight and passenger service on the heavy grades of the Sierra Nevada and other mountainous parts of Southern Pacific Lines. East bound, over the Sierras, three of these locomotives handle trains of 100 refrigerator cars, at high speeds and on regular schedules. In passenger service one such locomotive can handle the heaviest overland passenger trains over the 2.5 per cent ruling grade.

The locomotives have 4 cylinders 24 in. by 32 in., steam pressure 250 lb per sq in., driving wheels 63½ in. diameter, engine weight 657,900 lb, total weight of engine and tender 1,051,200 lb, tractive force 124,300 lb.

Set of connecting rods for one side of one unit.

Cast-steel locomotive bed for the front unit.

Cast-steel locomotive bed for the rear unit.

Tender under construction showing dash plates.

Baldwin magazine, June 1942

Thousands of civilian and military passengers crowded rail terminals as they await their train departures during the war. Note the sea of military uniforms from several branches. *Association of American Railroads, Washington, D.C.*

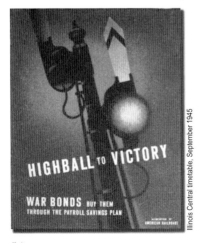

HIGHBALL TO VICTORY

WAR BONDS BUY THEM
THROUGH THE PAYROLL SAVINGS PLAN

Illinois Central timetable, September 1945

INDISPENSABLE!

*"The importance of the railroad transportation system of the country in its relation to the national defense can, I think, be summed up in one word—Indispensable."

Because railroads <u>are</u> indispensable to the national defense, is another reason why you should support every effort to bring about a Square Deal in Transportation—to give your railroads a chance to prepare for the peak loads of peace—or of war.

* Col. James L. Fink, Chief of the War Plans and Training Branch, Office of the Quartermaster General, War Department, in 1936.

ASSOCIATION OF AMERICAN RAILROADS
WASHINGTON, D. C.

Association of American Railroads, Washington, D.C.

LET FREEDOM RING!

HIGH ABOVE the roar and rumble of America's factories at work for war, you hear the bells of freedom ringing on tens of thousands of rushing railway locomotives.

Those bells dramatically symbolize the strength and resourcefulness and determined will of this land of free men to whom freedom of initiative and freedom of opportunity have never been denied.

America's railroads, planned by free men, financed and operated by free men, managed by men with a strict sense of responsibility towards those who patronize them and to-

wards their government, have done more perhaps than any other one activity to make this a nation united and indivisible.

One truly representative American railroad is the far-flung, 11,000-mile Milwaukee Road—with bands of shining steel linking the industrial ports of the Great Lakes to the world ports of the Pacific North Coast. This railroad is proud of the productive region it serves and proud to be a part of America's free railroad system.

Untrammeled transportation facilities are vital to victory! LET FREEDOM RING!

THE MILWAUKEE ROAD

SERVING THE SERVICES AND YOU

CHICAGO MILWAUKEE ST. PAUL AND PACIFIC

BUY MORE WAR BONDS

RIGHT. Santa Fe's efforts during the war were extraordinary. When WWII came, the Southern Pacific and Santa Fe's Tehachapi Line was deluged with tonnage for three-shift war plants. The roads made a valiant attempt to maintain their usual schedules, and they did that by utilizing the equipment and motive power they had in a carefully planned maintenance program that kept the cars and engines rolling. *Joe Collias*

The St. Louis Union Station concourse is busy in August of 1942 with military soldiers trying to catch their assigned trains. By the end of the summer of 1942, German U-boats were sinking 700,000 tons of British-American tonnage a month in the Atlantic, more than could be replaced in the booming shipyards of the U.S., Canada and Scotland. By the end of September, 1942 Hitler's conquests were staggering. German troops were stationed from the Norwegian North Cape on the Arctic Ocean to Egypt, from the Atlantic at Brest to the southern parts of the Volga River on the border of Central Asia. *Three photos, Joe Collias*

A lot was happening in the war in the fall of 1944. The Warsaw, Poland Resistance Army surrendered to the Germans after two months of heavy fighting. On October 21, 1944, the first German city—Aachen—fell to the 1st and 9th American armies. The Allies were also heavily bombing German oil centers by day, and the biggest naval battle of the war took place at Leyete Gulf on October 23. To keep pace with the activity, American railroads were busily hauling troops and supplies across the country on iron rails to supply the war needs. Two Union Pacific 4-8-2's—#7019 and #7852—tug at an Extra West of troop cars at Cajon Pass, California in October, 1944. *William J. Barham, Joe Collias collection*

> "The railroads have more than justified the confidence reposed in them by Army men."
> — *Major General C. P. Gross, Chief of Army Transportaion Corps*

World War I versus World War II Comparisons

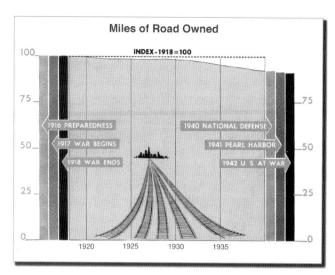

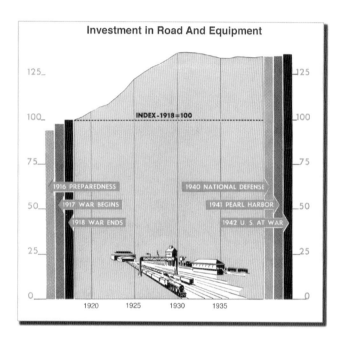

A large wheeled artillary piece has been loaded on a railroad flatcar for shipment overseas.

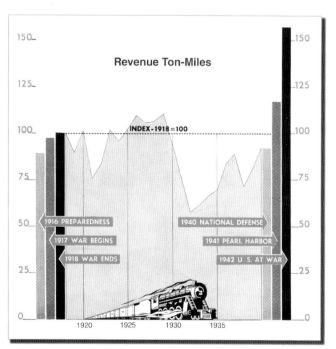

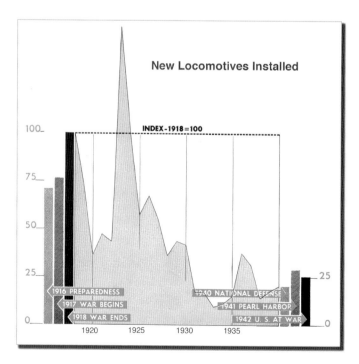

A familiar sight on America's railroads during WWII are these flatcars loaded with halftracks going to war. "If more cars are needed," read an ad by the Pullman-Standard Car Manufacturing Co. in the August, 1942 issue of *Railway Purchases and Stores*, "then a start should be made now to provide material and to recall dispersed organizations." This is in response to reports the railroads would need more cars to carry war supplies.

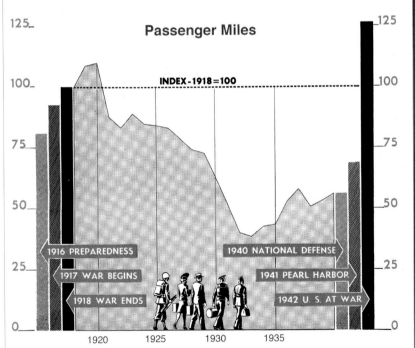

Charts and photo, Railroads in Two Wars, Association of American Railroads, Washington, D.C.

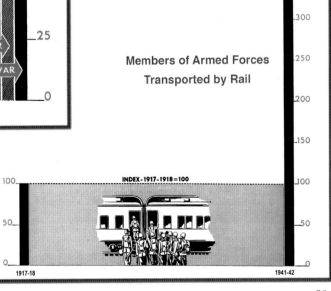

Herr Goebbels Was Wrong

The American railroads did the impossible by successfully carrying fabulous wartime traffic

By Elmer T. Howson, *Trains magazine, July 1944*

Shortly after Pearl Harbor, Paul Goebbles, Germany's minister of propaganda, directed attention to the fact that American railways were entering the present war with 10,000 fewer locomotives and 500,000 fewer freight cars than they had at the beginning of the First World War and drew the not-illogical conclusion that such a shortage in facilities would prove an insuperable handicap to our nation's war effort. Transportation, and particularly rail transportation, he declared, would prove the Achilles' heel of America's war effort.

And Dr. Goebbels was not alone in his dire forebodings, for there were those among our own numbers who gave expression to similar views. One such authority stated in the fall of 1941 that "this country is now teetering on the edge of a transportation shortage. We face a critical situation in all modes of transport—a railroad car shortage of as high as 40,000 cars a week may develop in October." Another spokesman predicted a shortage of 80,000 cars and stated that the railroads would need 370,000 new cars by the fall of 1942. Still another "author-

ity" placed the anticipated shortage at 49,978 cars; why he did not add 22 more cars to bring the total to 50,000 is unexplained. So much for Dr. Goebbels' prediction and for others of similar vein. What of their accuracy?

FREIGHT TRAFFIC

In 1918, the peak traffic year of World War I, the railways sagged under a load of 405 billion ton-miles of freight traffic. In 1929, the year of heaviest traffic during the boom period of the '20's, the total reached 447 billion ton-miles. Yet, in 1941, the railroads produced 475 billion ton-miles; in 1942 this was raised to 638 billion ton-miles and last year they produced 725 billion ton-miles. In other words, they produced 8 per cent more freight service last year than in 1918; in fact, they produced more than in the years 1918 and 1939 combined. And they did this with 500,000 fewer freight cars and 20,000 fewer locomotives than they had in 1918. In this spectacular performance they proved Dr. Goebbels was wrong in his forecast with regard to the rail-

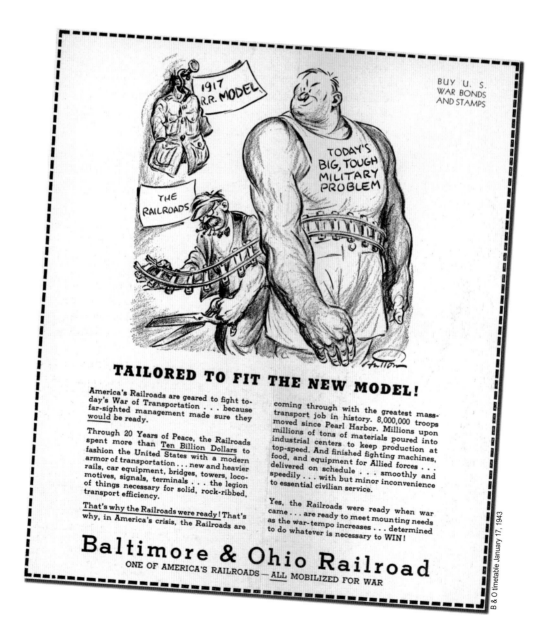

TAILORED TO FIT THE NEW MODEL!

America's Railroads are geared to fight today's War of Transportation . . . because far-sighted management made sure they would be ready.

Through 20 Years of Peace, the Railroads spent more than Ten Billion Dollars to fashion the United States with a modern armor of transportation . . . new and heavier rails, car equipment, bridges, towers, locomotives, signals, terminals . . . the legion of things necessary for solid, rock-ribbed, transport efficiency.

That's why the Railroads were ready! That's why, in America's crisis, the Railroads are coming through with the greatest mass-transport job in history. 8,000,000 troops moved since Pearl Harbor. Millions upon millions of tons of materials poured into industrial centers to keep production at top-speed. And finished fighting machines, food, and equipment for Allied forces . . . delivered on schedule . . . smoothly and speedily . . . with but minor inconvenience to essential civilian service.

Yes, the Railroads were ready when war came . . . are ready to meet mounting needs as the war-tempo increases . . . determined to do whatever is necessary to WIN!

Baltimore & Ohio Railroad
ONE OF AMERICA'S RAILROADS — ALL MOBILIZED FOR WAR

BUY U. S. WAR BONDS AND STAMPS

B & O timetable January 17, 1943

60

ways of America just as realistically as our men in uniform will prove fallacious his more recent statements about the outcome of the war.

PASSENGER TRAFFIC

In passenger traffic, their performance has been even more spectacular. In 1918 they produced less than 43 billion passenger-miles; in 1920 this figure rose to a predepression peak of 46 billion. Yet in 1942, the output rose to the new high record of 54 billion passenger-miles and last year it approximated the prodigious figure of 85 billion, nearly four times that of as recent a year as 1939 and approximately twice that of 1918, the peak year of the previous war. And the railroads did this with 16,000 fewer passenger cars than they had in 1918.

This spectacular record is being achieved by the most outstanding display of efficiency ever witnessed in transportation. To mention only a few indices, in 1923 the railways set for themselves a goal of 30 miles per freight car per day; they reached it in only one month of that year and in only one month of the following year. Yet in 1943 they averaged 52.3 miles per car per day. Similarly, the average load carried per car rose from 27.9 tons in 1923 to 33.5 tons in 1943.

The average gross tons per freight train crossed 1,100 for the first time in 1943 to reach the record figure of 1,116, an increase of 403 tons over 1923. Prior to 1939 this figure never exceeded 804 tons. As a result of this increased train loading and of the hight speed at which these trains were operated, gross ton-miles per train-hour exceeded 36,000, or more than twice the 16,764 total for 1923.

Similarly, the average number of passengers carried per train-mile increased from 37.6 in 1939 and 60.3 in 1940 to 186.2 in 1943!

This remarkable contribution to the nation's war effort has been made at a time when other transportation agencies—on the water, on the highways and in the air—have been forced for one reason or another to curtail their activities. In fact, the tremendous load that has been thrust on the railways has resulted in part from the transfer to them of burdens heretofore carried by other agencies. The suspension of coastwise and intercostal shipping, the diversion of oil tankers from coastwise to other service, and limitations on highway and air transport have all increased the railroad load. This is shown by the fact that while, in normal times, the railways handle approximately 60 per cent of the total commercial traffic of the country, this ratio has now risen to 70 per cent.

WARTIME INCREASE
FALLS ON RAILWAYS

More than four-fifths of the wartime increase in the nation's freight traffic has fallen on the railways. They are moving more than 93 per cent of all the Army's freight and express and over 80 per cent of the armed personnel. During the first 20 months of the present war, the railways transported 2½ times as many troops in special trains and cars as in the 19 months of World War I —without counting the thousands upon thousands of service men and women who have traveled individually or on furlough. The magnitude of this accomplishment is realized only when the highly mechanized character of this war is appreciated, for it now requires as many as 65 trains and approximately 1,350 freight and passenger cars to transport a single division.

This, in brief, is the record the railways have made to date—a contribution to the nation's war effort that is not excelled by any other industry of comparable magnitude. And they are not yet through, for they still have not reached their ultimate capacity. In fact, to repeat a recent statement of a vice-president of the Association of American Railroads, the railways do not know what their real capacity is. Probably 1944 will reveal this figure, for recent estimates point to further increases of 6 per cent in ton-miles and 15 per cent in passenger-miles in 1944.

RECORD MADE POSSIBLE

How has this record been made possible? Several factors have contributed. Near the top is the expenditure of more than eight billion dollars since the last war for additions and betterments to railroad properties, to strengthen roadway and structures, to add new modern cars and locomotives and eliminate bottlenecks in the wide variety of signaling and other facilities that go to make up a modern railroad. Means have also been developed for coordinating the effort of individual railways, to a degree found in few other industries, into a unified program for all in order to utilize to the full the capacity of each unit. And to this should be added a degree of shipper cooperation that is unique in industry, a cooperation that cannot be overemphasized because of the importance of its contribution to the present performance of the railways.

Such is the record of 1943—a record of contribution to the nation's objectives that is unsurpassed by that of any other industry.

61

Fixing 'em on the Fly for Victory

How Santa Fe Is Speeding Up the Servicing Time of War-Vital Freight Cars

Another chapter in the story "Working for Victory on the Santa Fe"

War can't wait. The load on a freight car might win a battle . . . and save the lives of thousands of our fighting men.

There's a battle-winning spirit in the way Santa Fe crews are keeping freight cars rolling these days. They are actually repairing loaded cars without unloading them!

When an inspector reports a flat wheel, a splintered side, or a shifted load on a Santa Fe freight, the car is cut out of the train . . . fixed "on the fly" on a repair track . . . and switched back on the same train, or the one immediately following.

Ready to Roll Again

A Santa Fe gondola has pulled up with a flat wheel. The car and its war load are lifted by pneumatic jacks. Within a few minutes a complete new truck of four wheels is in place, and the car is again ready to roll.

SANTA FE SYSTEM LINES

Serving the Southwest and California

ONE OF AMERICA'S RAILROADS—ALL UNITED FOR VICTORY

March 1944

RIGHT OF WAY FOR THE U.S.A.

Plan your trip to fit AMERICA'S WARTIME TRAVEL PROGRAM

★ Plan your trips as far ahead as possible.

★ Make arrangements for Pullman space early.

★ Cancel those arrangements promptly if travel plans are changed.

★ Buy tickets in advance to relieve congestion at station ticket windows.

★ Go and return in mid-week to avoid peak travel over weekends.

★ Take along as little baggage as possible.

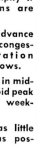

Alton Railroad timetable, August 1943

SOLDIERS AT CAMP...

Send all your gifts to your favorite soldier by quick, economical RAILWAY EXPRESS. Low rates. Passenger-train speed. For service, just phone

RAILWAY EXPRESS
AGENCY INC.

Wabash timetable, October 26, 1941

NOTICE
Due to the war time emergency schedules and consist of trains are subject to change.

Chicago & North-Western timetable, September 15, 1942

Multiply him by *1,458,912—*

MULTIPLY him by 1,458,912 and you have the number of passengers who rode The Milwaukee Road's Hiawathas during 1943 — as many people as the population of Milwaukee, St. Paul, Minneapolis and Tacoma combined — the equivalent of the personnel in 97 infantry divisions!

Many of those Hiawatha passengers were men and women in uniform—traveling under orders or on furlough. Many others were civilians on missions vital to war production. And to the credit of Americans, let it be said that trips "just for pleasure" were few and far between.

The nearly a million and a half that the Hiawatha fleet carried last year were swelled by millions of others who rode the Olympian, the Pioneer Limited, the Arrow, the Southwest Limited, the Chippewa, the Marquette, the Sioux and other Milwaukee Road trains.

In addition, hundreds of thousands of men in the armed forces were transported to camps, maneuvers and embarkation ports on special trains via The Milwaukee Road and its connections. Altogether, America's railroads carried over four times as many passengers during 1943 as they did in recent pre-war years.

What form of transportation, other than the railroads, could keep the nation's passenger traffic moving so smoothly under existing war conditions? What other form of transportation could provide such swift, dependable, economical service for the mass movement of a nation of 133,000,000 people?

THE MILWAUKEE ROAD

SERVING THE SERVICES AND YOU

March 1944

GREAT NORTHERN RAILWAY
BETWEEN GREAT LAKES AND PACIFIC

Route of the Empire Builder

GREAT NORTHERN'S IRON ORE HAUL IS "SPECIAL DELIVERY" OPERATION

Precision Handling, Efficient Equipment Speed Flow from Mines to Docks

For nearly eight months of every year—from April through late November—Great Northern transports iron ore from Minnesota's sprawling mines to the railway's docks on Lake Superior. More than 23½ million long tons in 1944; and at least that much this year!

Moving mountains of Victory-vital iron ore is a *Special Delivery* assignment, requiring operating skill and efficient use of equipment. When the shipping season is on, Great Northern has in service 7,300 ore cars and a fleet of super-husky locomotives —power built for heavy duty.

In addition, the railway maintains two vast yards. Trainloads of ore are assembled in one; in the other loaded cars are weighed "on the move" and classified as to types of ore before delivery to the docks.

Great Northern's Allouez docks in Superior, Wis., are the world's largest, and designed to speed the loading of vessels which transport iron ore down the Great Lakes to steel mills.

"*Special Delivery*" handling of iron ore is one of the many things which make Great Northern great.

World's largest open pit mine is on the Minnesota iron range. The pit is nearly 4 miles long, over a mile wide and 600 feet deep.

It requires only five "bites" of this giant power shovel to fill a 75-ton G. N. iron ore car.

A section of G. N.'s classification yards where ore trains deliver cars for weighing and sorting.

Allouez docks rise 80 feet above water. During the 1944 ore season a total of 2,184 Great Lakes boats were loaded here.

A troop train arrives from Camp Patrick Henry, Virginia, at Hampton Roads Port of Embarkation, Newport News, Virginia, on May 9, 1943. Primed and readied with training, equipment and supplies, troops board Naval transport P77 for overseas deployment. In a 45-month period from 1941 to 1945, the Transportation Corps embarked 7.29 million passengers for overseas destinations. *Library of Virginia collection*

CHAPTER TWO

Embarkation of Troops and Materiel

"You are about to embark upon the great crusade toward which we have striven these many months. The eyes of the world are upon you. I have full confidence in your courage, devotion to duty and skill in battle." —D-Day, June 6, 1944, Army General Dwight D. Eisenhower

The movement of troops and cargo to and from oversea destinations was a tremendous operation. At its peak in July, 1945 the ocean-going fleet in Army service totaled 1,706 vessels amounting to 15,940,000 deadweight tons, of which 261 were classified as troop or hospital ships and 1,445 as cargo ships. In addition, troops and military supplies were shipped on vessels under the control of the Navy.

To keep so many vessels fully employed on routes reaching to all parts of the globe, and to obtain the greatest possible amount of transportation service from them, required a large staff of shipping experts, huge port installations for the handling of ships, passengers and cargo, and a complete system of intelligence and control.

The utmost care was employed to insure that all phases of each operation were thoroughly coordinated in the planning stage and executed with the best results possible under wartime circumstances.

OUTWARD TROOP TRAFFIC

During the 45-month period, December 1941 through August 1945, the Transportation Corps sent 7,293,354 passengers to overseas destinations. Of these, 6,902,717 (over 94%) were Army personnel. The remainder consisted of Navy and Allied military personnel, civilians and prisoners of war. Civilians traveling in the national interest, and approved by the State Department, were accommodated on troop transports when space could be spared from strictly military uses.

Total embarkations showed a general upward trend until the late months of the war, as the total troop lift was increased by the addition of new vessels and the conversion of old ones. The embarkation figures varied considerably from month to month, due in part to the spacing of convoys and in part to changing strategical requirements, which called for exceptional efforts to place more troops in a particular theater during a specific period, or a permanent shift of emphasis from one theater to another.

Thus there were unusually heavy outward movements during the months before and just after the invasion of France, and as a result of the German counteroffensive in December 1944 and January 1945. During the spring of 1945,

The 6,461-mile Illinois Central Railroad joined the war effort in a major way with employee and corporate support.

SEPTEMBER 1944

Cover of Illinois Central Railroad magazine, September 1944

WESTERN UNION telegram

CLASS OF SERVICE
This is a full-rate Telegram or Cablegram unless its deferred character is indicated by a suitable symbol above or preceding the address.

1299

A. N. WILLIAMS
PRESIDENT

NEWCOMB CARLTON
CHAIRMAN OF THE BOARD

J. C. WILLEVER
FIRST VICE-PRESIDENT

SYMBOLS
DL = Day Letter
NL = Night Letter
LC = Deferred Cable
NLT = Cable Night Letter
Ship Radiogram

The filing time as shown in the date line on telegrams and day letters is STANDARD TIME at point of origin. Time of receipt is STANDARD TIME at point of destination

CD383UC (WA736) GOVT NL

1944 JUL 18 PM 9 20

WASHINGTON DC JULY 18 1944

TO THE MEN AND WOMEN OF ILLINOIS CENTRAL RR CO

ATTN MR J L BEVEN PRES 135 EAST ELEVENTH PL CHGO

THE SUCCESS OF THE ALLIED LANDINGS ON WESTERN EUROPE — IN FACT, THE SUCCESS OF EVERY CAMPAIGN UNDERTAKEN BY AMERICAN SHIPS AND MEN IN EVER WAR THEATER — HAS DEPENDED HEAVILY UPON THE EFFICIENT TRANSPORTATION FACILITIES WHICH THE RAILROADS OF THE UNITED STATES HAVE MADE AVAILABLE TO THE ARMED FORCES AND TO THE WAR PLANTS PRODUCING FOR THEM MATERIALS MUST ARRIVE AT FACTORIES AND SHIPYARDS ON TIME IF PRODUCTION SCHEDULES ARE TO BE MET. MEN AND EQUIPMENT MUST ARRIVE AT EMBARKATION DOCKS ON TIME IF INVASION SCHEDULES ARE TO BE MET. IT IS TO THE LASTING CREDIT OF THE MEN AND WOMEN WHO STAFF AND OPERATE OUR RAILROADS THAT THEY HAVE NEVER FAILED TO MEET THESE GRAVE RESPONSIBILITIES. EVERY ONE OF YOU MAY BE PROUD OF YOUR INDIVIDUAL PART IN HELPING THE NAVY TO GAIN COMMAND OF THE SEAS AND CARRY THE FIGHT RELENTLESSLY TOWARD THE INNER CITADELS OF THE ENEMY

W B YOUNG REAR ADMIRAL (SC) USN CHIEF OF THE BUREAU OF SUPPLIES AND ACCOUNTS

Transferring equipment to ships for a final European destination was a time-consuming and tedious job. Here a small U.S. Army Transportation Corps diesel is lifted off a cargo ship and onto foreign rails. Plenty of soldiers have turned out for the unloading. *Bob's Photos*

A 2-8-0 80-ton Consolidation steam locomotive is hoisted with a large crane onto a cargo ship at Hampton Roads Port of Embarkation on November 2, 1943. This same scene was re-enacted many times over as millions of tons of equipment and supplies were brought by rail to various ports for eventual transfer overseas. After the invasion, all European units were to leave the U. S. fully equipped and convoy-loaded. *Library of Virginia collection*

when the fighting in Europe was drawing to a close and measures were being taken to increase the flow of troops to the Pacific, the total embarkations decidedly declined.

Because of the wide distribution of U.S. forces and the changing designations applied to certain theaters, a complete analysis of overseas troop traffic by destinations is difficult to ascertain. However, the following breakdown of embarkations at United States ports (officers and enlisted men only) during the 45 war months, is indicative of what happened:

Area of Destination	U.S. Troops Embarked
Atlantic:	
North and South America	167,851
Africa, Mediterranean and Middle East	1,036,137
United Kingdom and European Continent	3,273,418
Total Atlantic	4,477,406
Pacific:	
North America	205,581
Central and South Pacific	965,145
Southwest Pacific	1,007,118
Asia	247,467
Total Pacific	2,425,311
Grand Total	6,902,717

COORDINATION OF TROOPS

Overseas troop movements, starting from home stations in the zone of interior and ending at discharge ports in the theaters, required a vast amount of coordination to make the various stages of the journey mesh perfectly, and to insure that troops and their equipment arrived overseas according to plan.

Overall coordinating responsibility rested with the Movements Division in the Office of the Chief of Transportation. It worked with the Operations Division of the War Department General Staff and the Mobilization Division of the Army Service Forces to make sure that movements were planned and orders written in accordance with the capabilities of the available troop ships. It worked with other elements of the Transportation Corps to make sure that transportation of men and their equipment to the ports was properly executed, and that the complex machinery of the Army ports of embarkation was geared to handle the load.

The problems differed according to the types of troops that were moved. Units, because of their organizational equipment, and because of the fact that both personnel and equipment often required extensive processing at the ports, placed the greatest responsibility on the Transportation Corps.

The heavy movement of divisions to Europe, which took place during the last half of 1944, put the machinery to the supreme test. During the early part of 1945, when the demand from Europe was for replacements to keep the units on hand at full strength, rather than for additional units, the troop movement problem was considerably eased, for those troops carried only individual equipment, and they had been so well screened at the replacement depots that they required little attention at the port staging areas. The traffic resulting from the policy of rotating troops who had seen long service in active theaters, was in the same category as replacements.

HANDLING OF EQUIPMENT

The handling of organizational equipment was a matter of continual study and experimentation. It was desirable that this equipment be in the theater by the time the units themselves arrived. The conventional way of meeting this requirement was to have the equipment move overseas in the same convoys with the troops.

Since the equipment came from various origins—the units' home stations, technical service depots and manufacturers—bringing it to the port at the proper time and stowing it in ships in the manner that would make it most readily available on arrival overseas was a complicated task.

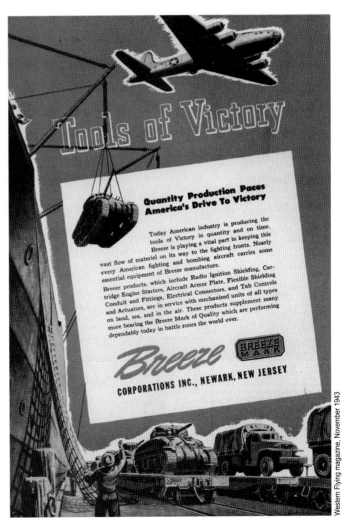

Western Flying magazine, November 1943

REPORT OF PERSONNEL NEEDS

The Illinois Central System needs the following employes, according to the report issued by C. R. Young, manager of personnel, on September 1:

OCCUPATION	Chicago Terminal	Illinois Division	Springfield Division	St. Louis Division	Iowa Division	Kentucky Division	Mississippi Division	E. St. Louis Terminal	Louisville Division	Vicksburg Division	Memphis Division	New Orleans Terminal	*—D. & E.	Burnside Shop	Paducah Shop	Dining Car Service	Accounting Dept.	Tel. and Signal	Purchases and Stores	TOTAL
Accountants																	11			11
Agent Operators				5					4											9
Auditor-Traveling		1																3		3
Baggagemen-Station																				1
Boilermakers	4			5	3				1	4	9			1	2	6				35
Brakemen and Flagmen		17							16	6	10									56
Bridgeman	15																			15
Car Cleaners	23															6	20			49
Carmen & Upholsterers	17			2	2									2		13				36
Carpenters—Cabinetmakers	21	15		12	18									5		2				73
Carpenter Helpers		12																		12
Clerk—Stenographers	1	1							4											6
Cooks																6				6
Draftsmen																		1		1
Electricians	8			3						3		6								20
Firemen-Locomotives	12								10	4	5									31
Firemen—Stationary	3																			3
Frt. Hse. Clks. & Laborers	220	1						10												231
Investigator—Frt. Claim																	5			5
Laborers—Mechanical	22	4	15	4	5				9	6		5	15	4						89
Laborers—Sect. & B&B	125	85	40	75	188	90		30	95	64	30	15								837
Laborers Storehouse																			38	38
Laundry Helpers																8				8
Linemen																		6		6
Linemen Helpers																		3		3
Machinists	9		2	8	3				1	7	18	2	5	38				3	2	95
Mechanical Apprentices	30		7	28					8				10							83
Mechanical Helpers	26		19	2	10							10	6						2	75
Painters B&B	20	8		6	6															40
Painters—Car														3	3					6
Pipefitters	2			3							1									6
Porters—Tr. & Baggage	3	5																		8
Signalmen	6				17															23
Signalmen Helpers	10		5	5																20
Sheet Metal Workers																		3		3
Sheet Metal Work. Apprt.																		5		5
Sheet Metal Work. Help.																		2		2
Specialists—Clerks																	42			42
Statisticians																	2			2
Steamfitters	2																			2
Stockmen																			2	2
Supervisors I.B.M.																	1			1
Switchmen-Switchtenders	11	3	3		2				5	5	6	32	5							72
Telegraph Operators		5	7		14															26
Teletype Maintainer	1																	1		1
Tinner																				1
Train Dispatchers			2																	2
Truckers		7																		7
Yard Clerks	3	4	4		1	1					8	5							1	26
Washer Assistant	3																			1
Water Testers	3																			3
Waterworks Repairers	5										3									8
Waterworks Helpers	5			5																10
Welder Machinists									3											3
Welder Oxy-Acetylene				1																1
TOTALS	607	168	104	135	305	91			45	152	98	114	53	70	40	44	6	64	11	53 2160

*Diesel & Electric

In 1944 the Illinois Central Railroad, the largest north-south railroad in the U.S., was short employees because of the war. In its employee magazine, it listed personnel needs, likely hoping current employees could persuade their sons, daughters, friends and relatives to join the IC's workforce.

The war called for a steady hand on the throttle, making sure that war materiel and troops got through to their destinations. This 1944 photo was used in a vitamin ad directed to railroaders to help them gain "split-second efficiency" while on the job.

Trains, August 1944

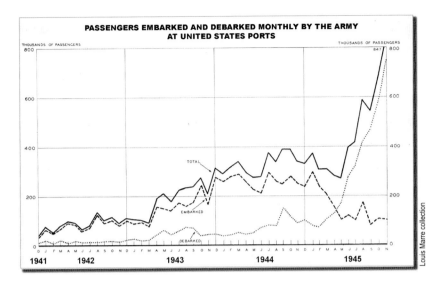

**PASSENGERS EMBARKED AND DEBARKED MONTHLY BY THE ARMY
AT UNITED STATES PORTS**

THOUSANDS OF PASSENGERS

THOUSANDS OF PASSENGERS

TOTAL

EMBARKED

DEBARKED

1941 1942 1943 1944 1945

Louis Marre collection

Lugging their heavy backpacks, which likely include a small tent, troops destined for overseas entrain at Camp Myles Standish, staging area of the Boston Port of Embarkation. *Louis Marre*

A deck load of railway tank cars are destined for England and will later be moved to continental Europe. *Louis Marre*

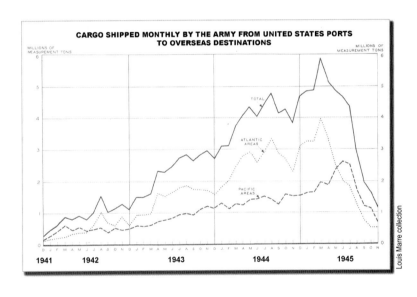

**CARGO SHIPPED MONTHLY BY THE ARMY FROM UNITED STATES PORTS
TO OVERSEAS DESTINATIONS**

MILLIONS OF MEASUREMENT TONS

MILLIONS OF MEASUREMENT TONS

TOTAL

ATLANTIC AREAS

PACIFIC AREAS

1941 1942 1943 1944 1945

Louis Marre collection

M-18 tank destroyer "Hellcats" with powerful Wright R-975 400-hp engines are ready to be loaded on Liberty Ship *Thomas Nelson* in July of 1944 at Hampton Roads, Virginia. With a road speed of 45 mph and a highly effective 76 mm gun, this tank was an excellent weapon against most Axis armor. *David Myers collection*

VICTORY
HANDLE WITH CARE

New York Central timetable, February 1944

STILL TODAY'S MOST IMPORTANT TRAVELER

He may be leaving for a training camp, a port of embarkation, or on a well-earned furlough. Perhaps he's fought in grim battles already won, or will soon risk all for victories yet to come. He's still America's most important traveler . . . *his trip can't wait!*

Today's most important traveler still deserves first consideration, and others can help to see that he receives such consideration by traveling only when it is really necessary.

The railroads of the Nation every day are still handling thousands upon thousands of the members of our armed forces in special troop trains, as well as in regular trains; thousands upon thousands of men and women still travel daily on urgent military and civilian business; and there is still insufficient equipment for the railroads to give all of their passengers the comfort they might otherwise enjoy.

Until travel conditions become more favorable, those whose trips are not of vital importance may find it more comfortable to postpone their journeys, or, certainly, to plan their trips in midweek and avoid the larger weekend crowds.

ATLANTIC
COAST LINE
RAILROAD

THE RAILROADS ARE COOPERATING—COOPERATE WITH THE RAILROADS

Atlantic Coast Line Railroad timetable, April 1, 1945

Soldiers offer a goodbye wave from their Pullman troop train as they leave for their embarkation point, which could be on either coast.

PLEASE!

Buy Tickets Before Boarding Trains

Your cooperation will be a big help to busy trainmen these wartime days.

To save time, please buy Round-Trip Tickets.

In purchasing Pullman tickets

–it is necessary to present your railroad tickets at the same time.

Pennsylvania Railroad timetable, Nov. 26, 1944

BATTLES WON'T WAIT
for the
TRAIN THAT'S LATE!

Railway Purchases and Stores, July 1942

Soldiers, just de-trained, wait for their ship at a port of embarkment.
Louis Marre

The big hook wraps around the boiler of a 2-8-0 steam locomotive on board the *Texas* as it is placed on the pier at Cherbourg, France on August 13, 1944. *Louis Marre*

Illinois Central timetable, September 26, 1943

The New York Port of Embarkation

The New York Port of Embarkation, being the largest, aptly symbolizes the most important of our activities. Here, both men and materiel are concentrated for movement to the fronts. Troops rarely proceed immediately to ship side. Instead, they are brought forward from the interior in advance of the scheduled shipping date, in accordance with plan and on the call of the Port Commander, and are received at staging areas near the Port, which are in reality huge posts under the command of the Port Commander, for final processing prior to embarkation. Each staging area is so located that troops may be moved to ship side by alternate routes, providing for any tactical emergency. Four staging areas for troops now serve the New York Port. Each must be equipped to provide shelter and food. In the few days or weeks that the men are there, they must be given final physical checkups, units must be brought to full strength, personnel records must be completed, shortages in equipment must be made up and training deficiencies must be corrected. When the men leave for ship side, they must be ready for immediate action.

STAGING AREAS

There are staging areas for supplies as well. Nearly six and one-half million square feet of storage space and a total of 14 piers provide facilities for handling most of the ordinary cargo. In addition to the great number of lighters that serve our ships, a vast amount of specialized equipment is required, such as switching engines, tugs and other harbor craft, tractors, lift trucks and other handling and loading equipment, and miles of holding track.

AMMUNITION

Ammunition requires the use of two distinct but integrated facilities. The first is located back of the port and provides safe standing for 400 cars of ammunition. The second is at the piers, to which the cars are moved for loading, where 8 working berths are available. Trackage is sufficient to accommodate the current day's loading capacity, to which the number of loaded cars on hand at the terminal is strictly limited.

EQUIPMENT AND ARTILLERY

Wheeled equipment and artillery are prepared for shipment at a large processing plant, complete with lighterage facilities and having an open storage capacity of 6,000 vehicles. Vehicles must be serviced, repaired, prepared to resist ocean weather, then lightered to ship side, stowed, blocked and braced. The magnitude of this job, which was almost non-existent in the First World War, is revealed by the fact that there is one vehicle for every six men in a motorized triangular division and one for every four men in an armored division. *Railway Age, June 12, 1943*

This can be readily understood in light of the fact that between August 1944 and February 1945, a total of 36 divisions, including nine armored and two airborne divisions, were sent to Europe. The personnel of these divisions were moved in 126 troop ships, and their organizational equipment was sufficient to fill 266 Liberty Ships. Many smaller units as well as replacements also moved during the same period.

Two methods of dealing with this problem were introduced during the war, and both were comparatively successful. During the buildup of U.S. forces in the United Kingdom, large quantities of organizational equipment were shipped in advance of the troops.

This eased the problem of coordinating the movements to the ports of embarkation, and it enabled equipment to be assigned to the units promptly upon their arrival at their destination, ready for service. This plan, which presupposed the existence of well-organized bases for the handling of the equipment after its arrival overseas, was utilized for other theaters also.

FULLY EQUIPPED AND READY

After the invasion of Europe, the War Department directed that from D-Day plus 90 all units destined to the European Theater of Operations leave the U.S. fully equipped and convoy-loaded. To meet this requirement, and to lighten the burden on the ports of embarkation at New York and Boston as much as possible, an equipment staging area was set up in the Elmira Holding and Reconsignment Point to receive and sort the materiel, and hold it until it was called for by the ports.

In the beginning, many complaints were received from the theaters because trucks, tanks and other automotive equipment, particularly that shipped on deck, had arrived in poor condition. Sometimes the equipment had not been in good order at the time of shipment, but frequently it had suffered from corrosion caused by salt water and salt air.

To counter this, the ports of embarkation established processing plants where unboxed equipment was inspected before it was forwarded to the loading piers, motors drained and cleaned, repairs made when necessary, spare parts replaced if found missing, and all openings and crevices sealed with sealing compound and tape.

The situation was especially acute in the Pacific in 1942 because the discharge ports did not have adequate repair or assembly facilities. Consequently, the vehicle processing plant of the San Francisco Port of Embarkation, located at Emeryville, California, was the first to be fully developed on assembly line principles, and it was the prototype for similar plants at other ports. During 1944 the processing plant of the New York Port of Embarkation located at Port Johnston, New Jersey, handled a total of almost 90,000 units of equipment.

The many branches and installations of the War Department which were concerned with troop movements, and the many details which had to be carried out in connection with each phase, left many opportunities for errors of

Coastal artillery troops, with full gear, detrain from passenger cars for assignment. *David Myers collection*

This is an aerial view of the Army base at Oakland, California, a facility of the San Francisco Port of Embarkation, soon after it was built. Note the long railroad storage tracks and the numerous structures in the immense complex. World War II put heavy pressure on the San Francisco Port of Embarkation and soon was overwhelmed, expanding onto land across San Francisco Bay in Oakland, where it built a subsidiary called the Oakland Army Terminal, which was much larger than its headquarters. The port and its subsidiary, served by three transcontinental railroads, handled more than 350,000 freight car loads and employed 30,000 military and civilian employees, not counting the longshoremen who loaded and unloaded railcars and ships. *Louis Marre*

The 8,108-ton *Seatrain Texas*, built in 1940 by the Sun Shipbuilding & Drydock Company of Chester, Pennsylvania to transport loaded railway cars on the Havana-Gulf ports, moved thousands of tanks and vehicles during the war. Here it is at a port of embarkation. *Louis Marre*

omission, as well as commission, in preparing the units and forwarding them to the ports.

EARLY STEPS TAKEN

Early in the war steps were taken to formulate standard procedures, which would clearly establish and define all responsibilities. This led to the publication of a pamphlet entitled *Preparation for Overseas Movement* (POM), and additional instructions regarding the preparation of Army Air Forces, units AIR-POM, and a complementary pamphlet entitled *Identification of Organizational Impedimenta* (IOI). These instructions appreciably reduced the task that fell on port commanders with regard to troops passing through their installations, but the responsibility remained a heavy one.

At the staging areas troops were under the command of the port commander, who took steps to insure that they were ready for overseas duty. Units were brought up to full strength. Individuals who were physically or mentally unfit

to move with their units were detained and replacements made. Clothing and other individual equipment was inspected and replaced if found not up to overseas standards. And unit records were brought up to date.

Personal matters, such as family allotments, insurance and wills, were taken care of. Pay due up to the time of sailing was disbursed. Deficiencies in practice with weapons were made up. In the early stages of the war, the frequent failure of home stations to complete the processing of troops left much work to be done at the staging areas. Preparations at home stations were much more complete, with a large burden lifted from port commanders.

Every possible means was used to protect the morale of the men while they were at the staging areas. For many this was a critical point in the transformation from trainee to soldier. The messes were important from a morale standpoint, and in January 1944 the Chief of Transportation employed an expert mess advisor who gave this matter his special attention. Entertainment and recreation within the station was made available for the soldiers, and larger staging areas published newspapers which dealt with the lighter, as well as the more serious side, of Army life.

PERFECT PRECISION

During the staging period, instructions were given regarding the routine of the forthcoming embarkation and ocean voyage. Instructions, and frequently training, was given in abandon-ship tactics and other safety measures.

For reasons of security, embarkations generally took place at night, and the movement from staging area to ship was accomplished quickly. The schedule for these movements was worked out in detail between the embarkation officer and the staging area, and it had to be executed with precision. The men carried their complete individual equipment on them when they arrived at the piers for embarkation.

Throughout the journey from the staging area and on the pier they were often required to stay in formation, and generally consecutive numbers

A soldier-guard uses the seat of a jeep as his accommodations on a military train during WWII. He was assigned to protect the load. *David Doyle*

A steam locomotive tender with "U.S.A." stenciled on the sides is loaded by crane aboard a ship at the New York Port of Embarkation (Brooklyn) during the war. Note the locomotive boiler at right which belongs to USA #1752. *David Myers collection*

A long string of tracked military vehicles with canvas coverings, and supported and braced so that they won't move enroute, await disposition on a railroad siding during the war. *David Doyle*

were chalked on their helmets. As each man passed the embarkation desk, his last name was called, and he responded with his first name. An officer of the unit was stationed at the desk to identify each individual.

On board, the men were conducted to their assigned compartments, and they were required to remain there until the embarkation was complete.

The ports and port commanders controlled the arrival of troops at the staging areas to insure their proper reception and accommodation. At busy ports, each incoming movement had to be synchronized with the departure of other troops.

The Army deemed it unwise to have soldiers arrive at staging areas unnecessarily far in advance of sailing, since they had to be kept under some restraint for security reasons, and it naturally was a period of emotional strain for the inexperienced and the men with strong family ties. The time spent at the staging areas prior to embarkation varied according to circumstances, but it generally was less than one week.

ARMY PORTS OF EMBARKATION

An Army Port of Embarkation (POE) was a large and complicated institution—a complex of installations and subordinate commands. Roughly speaking, it presented a cross-section of all Army activities in the zone of interior, since it embraced not only transportation, but also housing, training and equipping of troops, the procurement, storage and issue of supplies and many subsidiary functions.

Since all traffic to the overseas theaters flowed through the ports, and since the line of communication was no stronger than the weakest segment, it was necessary in a global war

This rail yard is crowded with war loads, ready to help fight the Axis powers. The iron warpath was abuzz with activity, and the railroads rushed to meet the daunting challenge. By June of 1942, Class I railroads employed 1,292,595 workers, an increase of 11.83% compared with the same month of 1941. *Louis Marre*

that the ports of embarkation have adequate facilities—including rail—and be operated efficiently.

Fortunately, many good facilities, which had been started by the Army during WWI and finished after the Armistice, were still available and in reasonably good condition when the U.S. rearmament program began in 1940. Some of these facilities were the Army bases at Boston, New York (Brooklyn), Philadelphia, Norfolk, Charleston and New Orleans.

All of these facilities, except a portion of the Brooklyn base, had been leased to other operators during peacetime, but with "recapture" clauses, and one by one they were brought back under Army control. As the result of a survey made during the summer of 1941, it was concluded that, so far as the Army's general cargo operations on the Atlantic and Gulf coasts were concerned, the privately owned facilities that might be leased, would suffice. Terminal facilities were also leased at Searsport, Baltimore and Mobile.

The situation on the Pacific Coast was not the same. The only Army-owned port installation was at Fort Mason, California, and it was not only small but unfavorably situated for expansion.

ESTABLISHED BASES

The first move was to acquire facilities in Seattle to serve as a terminal for the Army's steamship service to Alaska, and this was completed in January 1941. Plans had been under discussion for the establishment of an Army base at Oakland, California, and action to that end was taken during the early months of 1941 by the acquisition of a site which included limited facilities and provided space for considerable expansion. The Army built additional general cargo piers and warehouses at both Seattle and Oakland before entering the war, and added further facilities afterwards.

The Army also built new facilities at Prince Rupert, Juneau and Excursion Inlet, where subports to the Seattle Port of Embarkation were established. Existing facilities were leased at Los Angeles and Portland.

During World War II, Pasco, Washington was home to an Army Depot with 745 acres of land, 31 miles of railroad track and 1.7 million square feet of buildings and warehouses. *Louis Marre*

These general cargo terminals had to be supplemented by special facilities for handling ammunition and explosives, located in more isolated areas. During peacetime when the quantities were small, these shipments were handled over regular piers or were loaded at anchorages. The increase of both Army and Lend-Lease shipments of explosives during 1941 made it clear that numerous special facilities would be required. As a result, before the U.S. entered the war, construction work had begun on explosives piers at New York Harbor; Charleston, South Carolina; San Jacinto, Texas; and Benicia, California. Proposals also had been made for construction of piers at or near Boston, Philadelphia, Baltimore, Newport News, Mobile, Los Angeles, Portland and Seattle.

The proposals included special explosives storage facilities to back up such piers that were not located near existing ordnance depots. This program was approved immediately following Pearl Harbor. Soon it was augmented by construction of a pier and a storage facility at Prince Rupert, and in 1944 by construction of a pier at Earle, New Jersey, just outside New York Harbor.

The war also called for extensive new facilities for staging troops. Prior to Pearl Harbor, the ports of embarkation which were then active had so-called overseas discharge and replacement depots, where embarking and debarking troops were accommodated.

Although they had been expanded somewhat in 1941, the capacities of such depots were small. With the war, it was necessary to utilize Army camps near the ports and to improvise facilities in public buildings and on piers. The space at the camps was needed for other purposes, and the improvised facilities were unsatisfactory, so that the construction of new staging areas was necessary.

The 11 new staging areas, as originally planned, had a capacity of about 170,000 gross, and 140,000 net square feet, that is, after deducting space for station complements. Later, additional barracks were built, but a considerable amount of space was taken for troops in training. During the early part of 1945 the aggregate net capacity for in-transit troops, on the basis of 60 square feet per enlisted man, was about 140,000. This could be increased, if the situation required, by reducing the space allotment per man.

OPERATION AND EMBARKMENT

In addition to pier and staging facilities, the ports of embarkation controlled large warehouses, open storage spaces, railway storage yards, equipment processing plants, marine repair shops, post offices for handling the great volume of overseas Army mail, training ships for seafaring personnel, wet storage for small boats awaiting shipment overseas, and housing for troop units stationed at the ports.

The operation, maintenance and guarding of these facilities constituted a large task, which the ports had to assume as auxiliary to their strictly transportation functions. The

fact that at the larger ports these facilities were scattered over many miles of waterfront added to the challenges.

In July 1940 there were two Army ports of embarkation—at New York and San Francisco. At the end of the war there were eight ports of embarkation, three subports and three cargo ports. During this period the personnel of the port organizations increased from approximately 3,000 to 180,000. Of the latter figure, 10,000 were officers, 63,600 were enlisted men, 77,400 were civilian employees, 18,000 were civilians engaged under stevedoring and other contracts, and 11,000 were captured Italians and Germans prisoners.

Under the control of the Port Transportation Division, cargo for export arrived at the terminals of the ports of embarkation by many means. The percentages of the total delivery handled by the respective carriers varied widely between the ports. At New York, for example, a large percentage was delivered by railroad lighter, which was not true elsewhere. At Seattle and New York there were substantial deliveries by coastal ships and barges. During 1944 the percentage of the total cargo delivered to the eight ports of embarkation by each type of transportation was as follows:

Type of Transportation	Percentage of Cargo
Railroad, carload	78.6
Railroad, lighter	7.2
Railroad, L.C.L. (less-than-carload)	1.0
Railway express	.2
Motor truck	7.4
Coastal ship and barge	5.1
Miscellaneous	.5
Total	100.0

ONE MORE TON PER CAR CAN MEAN VICTORY!

This USOX was an ammunition car used only by the Coast Artillary Corps for supplying 8" railway guns defending the U. S. coastline. *David Doyle*

St. Louis Car Company

Military contracts dominated the St. Louis Car Company's wartime activities, with the first contract a $744,600 order from the War Department for all-steel ammunition cars. The firm built gliders, Fairchild PT-23s, railed mobile power stations, tanks, landing craft and more. Sales of the company in 1942 were more than $6.2 million, with sales the next year of $18 million. St. Louis Car Company built special purpose railroad cars as well.

St. Louis Car Company, St. Louis, Missouri, made self-contained mobile power stations such as this one being loaded onto a ship at Portland, Oregon in 1944 for shipment to Russia as part of a Lend-Lease agreement. The units were built on trucks of Russian gauge and were intended for quick transfer to a war area that had lost its power supply. The units came in sizes from 300 KW to 800 KW. *The History of the St. Louis Car Company*

USOX #8703 was one of a handful of the #8700 series built in November of 1942 as tool cars for maintenance-of-way trains at a few major Army bases. *David Doyle*

The St. Louis Car Company, makers of everything from street cars to fare boxes, interurbans, standard gauge railroad cars, automobiles and even airplanes, manufactured these antenna mounts (on flatcars) for the war effort. *The History of the St. Louis Car Company*

The first Russian mobile power station was constructed in 1943 by the St. Louis Car Company.

Pacific War Ports' Record Is Revealed

Army moved 44 million tons of cargo and 2½ million men West in 45 months

The first detailed report of the performance of the various Pacific Coast ports in the movement of troops and supplies to the Pacific theater has been released by the War Department, covering the 45-month period from December, 1941, through August, 1945, and accounting for the transfer overseas of nearly 2½ million men and of more than 44 million ship tons of cargo.

The bulk of the outgoing movement, both of men and materiel, was handled through the San Francisco Port of Embarkation, where 1,655,000 troops and 22,751,000 ship tons of cargo were dispatched. The second port in importance in this service was the Seattle Port of Embarkation, which handled 524,000 men and 10,219,000 ship tons of freight. Sub-ports, administered so far as the Army organization is concerned through Seattle, were Portland, which handled 53,000 troops and 1,731,000 ship tons of cargo, and Prince Rupert, B. C., where 31,000 men and 940,000 ship tons of supplies were loaded. *Railway Age, September 22, 1945*

ABOVE. Rails embedded in wharf allowed both freight and passenger cars to roll right up to ships for loading and unloading during the war. *Louis Marre* **NEXT PAGE, UPPER RIGHT.** Lend-Lease Decapods are re-assembled at a West Coast port and loaded on board ship for the long trip across the Pacific to Russia. They are partially dismantled before leaving the plant. *Baldwin magazine, First Quarter 1945* **NEXT PAGE, LOWER RIGHT.** Depressed center flatcars bear the weight of M-3 tanks; soon this equipment will be on the battlefront. *David Doyle collection*

Demand for flatcars during the war to move military equipment was heavy; War Department freight transported by railroads was 5.1% of total freight in 1942, increasing to 12.5% in June of 1945. *Louis Marre*

Newspapers, magazines and military and government authorities have paid the railroads some mighty fine compliments for the smooth, efficient job they are doing in the transportation of our fighting men. These pats on the back are genuinely appreciated, and spur railroaders on to doing a better and better job.

And now, the Norfolk and Western wants to pay a compliment and express sincere appreciation to the folks in civilian life—who know and accept the fact that Uncle Sam's fighters come first with the railroads; who give the right-of-way to the men in uniform; who do not fuss or criticize when they have to take the best they can get in train travel.

It is this teamwork, this spirit of cooperation between civilian travelers, the railroads, and military authorities, that makes America invincible . . . that gives our fighting men the confidence and courage—to go places and do things!

Norfolk & Western timetable, October 15, 1942

Sixteen quarter-ton trucks double-decked on a flatcar take full advantage of car capacity and railway clearances. Military expediency was given precedence over freight rates when necessary to move the goods. *Louis Marre*

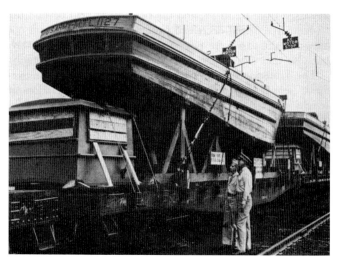

With cabins removed, these motor towing military launches were moved across the U.S. Note this train is in electrified territory. *Louis Marre*

Shore Patrol examines liberty papers of naval personnel at the Rock Island Railroad station in Memphis, Tennessee. *U. S. Navy*

LEFT. In this dated photo, troops line up in formation prior to boarding a troop train which will take them to a port for overseas duty. There were a total of 261 Army troop and/or hospital ships available for such movements in mid-1945; the Navy also moved troops on their vessels.

Among their other duties, the Military Police were to examine transportation and passes of Army personnel going on furlough. *U. S. Navy*

These two views show how U.S. Army trucks were secured on flatcars. *David Doyle*

"Pamphlet No. MD-5," Association of American Railroads-Operations and Maintenance Department

LIMA-BUILT for Service Abroad

Several hundred

of these Lima-built loco-motives are already in serv-ice in — or on their way to —the British Isles. Built to conform to the British track gauge, all decorative work and superfluous metal has been discarded. Their some-what severe, but workman-like, appearance has led the British to refer to them as "Austerity" locomotives.

LIMA
LOCOMOTIVE WORKS
INCORPORATED

LIMA **OHIO**

Trains magazine, January 1945

They Come First!

Trains are needed constantly for troop movements. Equipment temporarily withdrawn for military use means less available for the public.

Please accept this situation as one of "the fortunes of war." Meanwhile, the Pennsylvania will do its level best to provide the best possible service under wartime conditions.

PENNSYLVANIA RAILROAD

Pennsylvania Railroad timetable, September 27, 1942

Honoring Reduced Rate Tickets and Free Transportation on Certain Trains

Trains	The reduced rate tickets and free transportation indicated below will *NOT* be honored on trains shown in first column. *Pass Holders* to be governed by restrictions shown on passes held.	
1, 2, 101, 102, 103, 104,	Banana Messengers Blind and Attendant Blind and (Seeing eye) Dog Caretakers Charity Clergy C. C. C. C. C. C. C. Drovers	Disabled Volunteer Soldiers Employes (half rate) Furlough Homeseekers Livestock Contracts Show Scrip Books Veterans Army Hospitals Week-End Coach Excursion
111, 112	Furlough	
27, 28,	Banana Messengers C. C. C. C. C. C. C. *Will be honored between Chicago and De Witt, Stanwood, Mount Vernon, Ia. and California points.	*Caretakers *Drovers *Livestock Contracts
7, 8. 87, 88,	Blind (unaccompanied) Blind and (Seeing eye) Dog	

Chicago & NorthWestern timetable, September 15, 1942

Fifty three Lend-Lease steam locomotives, off their chassis and resting on the ground, await shipment to Russia at Pasco, Washington in June of 1944. *National Archives*

Young sailors, with their heavy duffel bags and suitcases, walk along a Southern Pacific heavyweight passenger train that will take them to a port of embarkation. *Kalmbach Publishing Company Library*

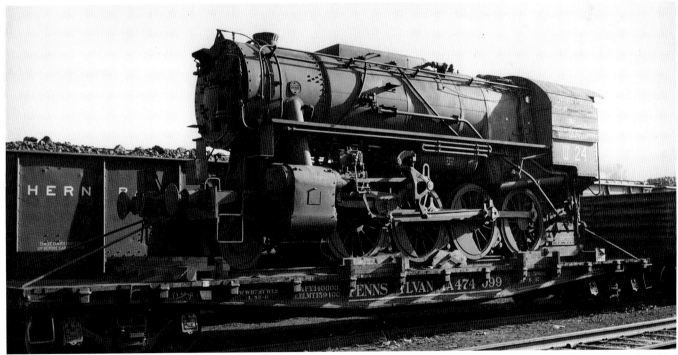

A beefy 2-8-0 Consolidation destined for Russia rests securely on a Pennsylvania flatcar on Northern Pacific rails. The flatcar locomotive shipment was required in the United States as the Russian track gauge is wider than the American 4' 8" gauge. *U.S. Army Signal Corps, Bob Hall collection*

Passenger lines were long during the war even to obtain a seat ticket. *Kalmbach Publishing Company Library*

Soldiers chat with the conductor on board a troop train headed for war. *Kalmbach Publishing Company Library*

Over land and sea, twenty-four hours a day, history's greatest relay race is being run to deliver the men and materiel to the world's fighting fronts.
Baltimore & Ohio magazine, March 1944

B&O LINKING 13 GREAT STATES WITH THE NATION **BALTIMORE & OHIO RAILROAD**
One of America's Railroads-All United for Victory

A three-axle Army truck with three military trailers is secured and waiting on Pennsylvania Railroad flatcar #473296 at Ft. Bragg, North Carolina for disposition. *Bob's Photos*

Small military trucks are positioned on a Nashville, Chattanooga & St. Louis flatcar at Ft. Bragg, North Carolina. Note the large crawler on the flatcar to the left. *Bob's Photos*

NEXT PAGE, TOP. Chesapeake & Ohio car float #2 is loaded with military vehicles and equipment at Newport News, Virginia in 1943. The C&O operated car ferries on Lake Michigan as well as car ferries on the East Coast. *Chesapeake & Ohio Railroad Historical Society collection*

Hampton Roads Port of Embarkation, Norfolk, Virginia, is the scene as 500-pound bombs are transferred from a wooden outside-braced Burlington Railroad box car by forklift. An officer stands at right to oversee the operation. *Library of Virginia collection*

NEXT PAGE, BOTTOM. Covered military tanks present a ghostly image. *M.D. McCarter*

These **Military Railway Service** troops operate a steam locomotive on the **Claiborne-Polk Military Railway** in 1941. *U.S. Army Transportation Museum*

The Military Railway Service Joins the Fight

"As never before, America needs its railroads to transport military equipment and men." —Baldwin Locomotive Works

When measures were taken to strengthen the Military Railway Service prior to entry of the U.S. into the war, the establishment of Army Reserve units sponsored by American railroads was the basis of the plan. The sponsoring railroads provided the officers and enlisted personnel from among their own employees and also provided technical training. The arrangement offered the Army high-caliber railway troops.

When all sponsored units had been called to active duty, and more railway troops were needed, contracts were made with the railroads to provide technical training. This arrangement also worked out very satisfactorily. Not only did the men receive excellent instruction and real experience, but the railroads supplied the necessary equipment and shops, which it would have been difficult for the Army to secure quickly because of wartime shortages. In most cases the units were housed at Army camps near the railroads which were training them.

When enlisted men with railway experience were called from the reserve to active duty, or were inducted into the Army through Selective Service, they were sent from the reception centers directly to the Military Railway Service training center at Camp Plauche near New Orleans, or, after September 1944, to Ft. Francis E. Warren, Wyoming. There they received basic military training in a provisonal unit until it had attained full strength and was activated and sent to a railroad for technical training. Up to 1944 the units were composed almost entirely of experienced rail-

Railroaders from the 716th Railway Operating Battalion operated steam locomotive #974 at the Southern Pacific Railway yards in San Antonio, Texas on May 11, 1944. This railroad-military service arrangement worked well. *U.S. Army Transportation Museum*

A railway battalion soldier sits in the engineer's seat of a steam locomotive on a training exercise. *Courtesy Dick Hillman, Southern Museum of Civil War & Locomotive History Archives*

In 1942, Colonel Carl R. Gray, Jr. (fifth from right), general manager of the Military Railway Service, visits Camp Shelby, Mississippi along with Clark Hungerford (third from right), Southern Railway general manager of the Western Lines, and officers of the 727th Railway Operating Battalion. *Courtesy Dick Hillman, Southern Museum of Civil War & Locomotive History Archives*

ABOVE AND BELOW. Experience taught military officers that any railroad taken over by American troops under combat conditions would most likely have suffered catastrophic damage. Thus, getting track rebuilt quickly was the first objective of a military railroad unit, and training for this task was rigorous. *Courtesy Dick Hillman, Southern Museum of Civil War & Locomotive History Archives*

road men. Thereafter it was necessary to utilize some inexperienced personnel, but the proportion of experienced men did not fall below about 85%.

Because of the limited facilities which it possessed, and the unusual advantages gained during wartime by having troops trained on commercial railroads, only a small proportion of the railway units activated during the war received their technical training on the Claiborne-Polk Railway.

Nevertheless, this 50-mile stretch of track which was built by the Army during 1941-42 for training exercises, served a very useful purpose. Problems in track and bridge repair work, and in dealing with derailed rolling stock, could be worked out on this training line, which could not be introduced on railroads actively engaged in handling traffic.

TYPES OF RAILWAY ORGANIZATIONS

There were four major types of railway organizations. The headquarters, Military Railway Service, was required only where the operation was large, and in fact only three such organizations were established—in the North African (Mediterranean) Theater, the European Theater and the Persian Gulf Command. The headquarters, Railway Grand Division, was organized to supervise two to six operating battalions and one or two shop battalions.

The Railway Operating Battalion included a transportation company with two platoons of 25 train crews each, a maintenance-of-way company, a maintenance of equipment company, and when needed, a diesel section and an electric power transmission company. The Railway Shop Battalion included an erecting and machine shop company, a boiler and smith shop company and a car repair company.

A soldier-conductor signals that his train is ready to depart as military troops learn railroad procedures. This wood-sided center cupola caboose was assigned to military training operations on the Southern Railway. *Courtesy Dick Hillman, Southern Museum of Civil War & Locomotive History Archives*

The Southern Railway furnished a private office car and 21 camp cars for use in the training of railway battalion personnel. Shown are Clark Hungerford (center); and two unidentified companions. *Courtesy Dick Hillman, Southern Museum of Civil War & Locomotive History Archives*

In addition to these major units, there were hospital train maintenance platoons, mobile workshop platoons and track maintenance platoons. The Military Railway Service was prepared to handle any kind of work that might be required, except new construction of tracks and structures, which was a Corps of Engineers function. It handled many repair jobs, however, which were tantamount to new construction.

Since most of the officers and enlisted men had railroad experience, and in order that the period of unit training might be as long as possible, the Army Service Forces requirement that troops receive basic technical training before being assigned to units, was waived in the case of railway units, which were activated immediately after completion of basic military training

LONGER TRAINING

Railway troops, therefore, received longer training as units than other Transportation Corps organizations. Headquarters, Military Railway Service, and headquarters, Railway Grand Division, received 11 weeks of unit training, operating battalions 17 weeks, and shop battalions 19 weeks.

During the greater part of the war, supervision of such training was under a Director of Railway Training, who was stationed at Camp Plauche MRS Training Center, but functioned under the general supervision of the Director of Military Training in the Office of the Chief of Transportaion. By December 1944, however, the training program was so far completed that the Office of the Director of Railway Training was discontinued.

Trains magazine, February 1945

93

Many of the recruits undergoing training at the Southern Railway facility at Meridian, Mississippi were experienced railroaders, but everyone had to learn the new requirements of railroading under combat conditions. Here students quickly learn how to rebuild a damaged car and ready it for another military load. *Courtesy Dick Hillman, Southern Museum of Civil War & Locomotive History Archives*

A sergeant "oils around" a steam locomotive to keep it operating properly and in good condition. Soldier-railroaders were an important part of the overall military effort during WWII. *Courtesy Dick Hillman, Southern Museum of Civil War & Locomotive History Archives*

Military recruits had to clean out journal boxes as part of their training. *Courtesy Dick Hillman, Southern Museum of Civil War & Locomotive History Archives*

Soldiers work in the smokebox of a steam engine; they needed to know how to assemble and disassemble a locomotive. *Courtesy Dick Hillman, Southern Museum of Civil War & Locomotive History Archives*

Personnel of the 727th Railway Operating Battalion go through the procedure of loading water into a steam locomotive tender in this WWII scene on American soil. *Courtesy Dick Hillman, Southern Museum of Civil War & Locomotive History Archives*

BELOW AND RIGHT. Troops lay track and build railway trestles at Camp Claiborne, Louisiana in 1941. *U.S. Army Transportation Museum*

Its training completed, the 727th Railway Operating Battalion prepares to leave Hattiesburg, Mississippi, for the theater of operations overseas. E. M. Tolleson, Southern Railway superintendent, tells Lt. Col. Fred W. Okie "good-bye and good luck." *Courtesy Dick Hillman, Southern Museum of Civil War & Locomotive History Archives*

Some of the men of the 727th Railway Operating Battalion, now a well-trained group of combat railroaders, gather at the Hattiesburg, Mississippi, depot ready to head off to war. *Courtesy Dick Hillman, Southern Museum of Civil War & Locomotive History Archives*

The 727th Railway Operating Battalion leaves Hattiesburg, Mississippi. The train continued on to Fort Dix, New Jersey, where the men were moved into a tent camp in preparation for their overseas departure. By December 12, the battalion was loaded on three ships and left the Port of New York for service in North Africa. *Courtesy Dick Hillman, Southern Museum of Civil War & Locomotive History Archives*

Men of the 727th Railway Operating Battalion ride a train headed for Fort Dix, New Jersey, on November 20, 1942. By December 26, 1942, the men would be docking at Mers El Kebir, near Oran, Algeria. By January 19, 1943, the 727th had assumed operation of the meter gauge railroad lines in eastern Algeria and Tunisia. *Courtesy Dick Hillman, Southern Museum of Civil War & Locomotive History Archives*

Trains magazine, April 1944

Close cooperation was maintained between the Military Training Division and the Rail Division in all matters affecting railway troop organizations. When the Office of the Director of Railway Training was closed, the Rail Division assumed responsibility for inspection of railway units in training and established a branch to carry out that activity. Reports of inspections were received by both the Military Training Division and the Rail Division, and corrective actions were taken.

SUMMARY OF TROOP UNITS

A summary of railway troop units activated up to the end of the war, including the few which were activated abroad, with authorized strength, is given here:

Type of unit	Number of units	Officers and warrant officers	Enlisted men
Hq. Military Ry. Service	3	96	526
Hq. Ry. Grand Division	12	311	810
Ry. Operating Battalion	38	970	31,668
Ry. Shop Battalion	12	312	7,660
Other Railway Units	33	59	2,633
Total	98	1,748	43,297

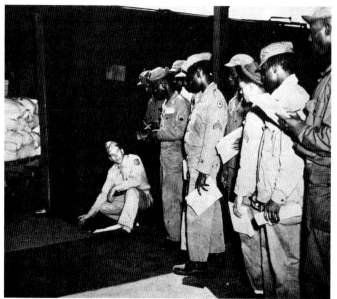

U.S. Military Railway troops assigned to transferring freight in the Army are shown the hazards involved and the safety measures to apply. *Louis Marre*

Traffic regulation groups were required in theaters of operation to insure the prompt and orderly movement of supplies and the efficient use of transportation equipment in the communications zone. They consisted of teams which were specifically trained to deal with railway, highway, inland waterway and air traffic.

Generally, they were assigned for operation to base, intermediate or advance sections, and the types of teams comprising a group depended on the nature of the traffic in the section where it served. Fifteen such groups were activated in the zone of interior and received their training at Camp Plauche, and 15 were activated overseas. One traffic regulation battalion was activated overseas. The total authorized personnel of these organizations was 1,405 officers and 7,771 enlisted men.

Base depot companies handled Transportation Corps supplies in the theaters. In the beginning, they were organized to deal primarily with railway supplies and were trained by railroads in the United States, as were units of the Military Railway Service.

Later, their organization was revised and their training broadened, so that they were prepared to handle all Transportation Corps supplies. The units then received technical training in the handling of railway supplies at the Marietta Holding and Reconsignment Point, and in the handling of port and marine supplies at the Voorheesville Holding and Reconsignment Point. Ten such units were activated in the zone of interior and nine overseas, with an aggregate authorized strength of 95 officers and 2,396 enlisted men.

The 727th Railway Operating Battalion was placed on alert on November 2 and again on November 9, 1942. On November 20 the battalion left on three trains, two from Camp Shelby and one from Key Field near Meridian, Mississippi. Southern Railway engine #727, a Ks-2 2-8-0, handled the first train, manned by personnel of the battalion from Hattiesburg, Mississippi. *Courtesy Dick Hillman, Southern Museum of Civil War & Locomotive History Archives*

BELOW. The first 400 men of the 727th Battalion received basic military training as shown here in May of 1942; the men of Company A are engaged in a weapons inspection. Weapons training on the rifle range began in August of that same year. *Courtesy Dick Hillman, Southern Museum of Civil War & Locomotive History Archives*

Organization of the
Military Railway Service

The plan of the chief of engineers developed an organization in the Military Railway Service of the General Manager's Headquarters. Known as Engineers Headquarters, it consisted of railroads with 10 Railroad Division Headquarters, 42 operating railway battalions and six railway shop battalions. The operating battalion was composed of 24 officers and 847 enlisted men, divided into four companies: one Headquarters Service Company; a Maintenance-of-Way-Constructors Company; a Maintenance-of-Way Equipment Company; and a Transportation Company. The Railway Shop Battalion was composed of 23 officers and 657 enlisted men.

An ingenious way was conceived by the chief of engineers prior to the start of the war to obtain the personnel from the railroads for these units. It was an affiliation by which American railroads said, "We will accept affiliation of this unit, and agree to supply, insofar as we have the manpower, the officers and as many of the enlisted men as we can give you."

So there was set up some four or five years ago these units accredited to, affiliated with, and sponsored by the American railroad industry. Then as war seemed more sure, we wondered how we were going to train these men, how we were going to make a military unit out of railroad men, so we went again to America's railroads and asked if they would accept back on their properties these battalions after they were organized, train them on their own railroads, and use their officers and civilian employees as instructors of and demonstrators to the military personnel.

UNITS IN ACTIVE SERVICE

As of today there has been called into active service, and are now under training, the 702nd Railway Grand Division Headquarters, affiliated with the Union Pacific, and commanded by Colonel Stoddard; the 703rd Railway Grand Division Headquarters, affiliated with the Atlantic Coast Line, and commanded by Colonel Burpe; my own headquarters, affiliated with the Omaha Railroad, the 711th, which was a voluntary group, called a year ago for the purpose of building the Claiborne-Polk Military Railroad, between Camp Claiborne and Camp Polk, 50 miles; the 713th Railway Division, affiliated with the Santa Fe Railroad, in training at Camp Reed, in New Mexico; the 714th Operating Battalion affiliated with the Omaha, being activated Oct. 31; the 715th, being activated on the 31st of this month, and affiliated with the Illinois Central; the 727th, the first units called into service, affiliated with the Southern Railroad, and in training since last April at Hattiesburg on the Southern Railroad; the 730th, affiliated with the Pennsylvania Railroad, in training at Fort Wayne since May 15; the 759th, affiliated with the Missouri Pacific, going into training at Van Buren, Ark.; the 753rd Shop Battalion, affiliated with the New York Central and Big Four, in training since May 15 at shops of the New York Central at Bucyrus, Ohio; the 754th, affiliated with the Southern Pacific Railroad, and just going into active training now; the 760th, a Railway Shop Battalion, Diesel; and the 761st Railway Shop Battalion, Diesel.

How many men are in the Armed Forces of the United States today? I should say, on the best calculations I have been able to make, between 75,000 and 100,000. But, un-

fortunately for the Military Railway Service, at least, they are not all in that service. I have no brief with the Tank Corps, the Air Corps, and other branches of the Army. They know good men when they see them, and once they get ahold of one of these good railroad men, it is rather difficult for us to get him transferred to us.

The Canadian National recently published a booklet which indicated that they had 6,562 of their men in Canadian war service.

ARMY OPERATING ALASKA RAILROAD

I am privileged to announce this regarding our latest activity of the Military Railway Service, and one, very frankly, that we did not anticipate at all. The War Department release reads today, as follows:

> The White Pass and Yukon Route, a short line railroad extending from Skagway, Alaska, to Whitehorse, Yukon Territory, has been leased by the United States Army for the duration of the war, it was announced by the War Department today. The line provides a rail connection between the Coast and the Alaska-Canadian Military Highway, which passes through Whitehorse, headquarters of the Northwest Service Command. The Alaska Highway, as previously announced, is under construction by the United States Corps of Engineers, and it is expected to be completed for military use about December 1, 1942. The Military Railway Service, of which Brigadier General Carl R. Gray, Jr., is Commanding General, with headquarters at St. Paul, Minn., is already operating the White Pass & Yukon Route, with Major John E. Ausland, Corps of Engineers, in command. Technical supervision is under Brigadier General Gray, who negotiated the lease for the War Department. The entire operation is under the jurisdiction of the Northwest Service Command, Brigadier General James A. O'Connor, Commanding General.

And if you think that this last four or five weeks has not been interesting, then you fail to realize that that little 111 miles of railroad runs through two countries, and three states, and that it has to be continued to be operated as a commercial railroad in addition to the war traffic that it must bear. I want to say to you that I have had an experience that I will long remember.

That force with which Major Ausland was sent up there contains snow-fighting men, because it goes down to 72 degrees below zero, with a gale of 35 miles an hour constantly blowing. So we sent a trainmaster from the Union Pacific from up in the mountains; a chief train dispatcher from the D.L.&W.; an assistant to a superintendent on the Great Northern from the Rockies; a general yardmaster from the snowbound top of the narrow gauge at Gunnison on the D.&R.G.; a road foreman of equipment from the Santa Fe; a construction superintendent, who had built many railroads in foreign lands; an assistant roadmaster off the Northern Pacific; and a general storekeeper off the Texas & Pacific. *Brig. General Carl R. Gray, Jr., General Manager, Military Railway Service. Railway Purchases and Stores, November 1942.*

ABOVE. Illinois Central's Railway Battalion photographs. *Illinois Central magazine, October 1944*

Troops from a railway battalion learn how to repair a trestle and also receive training in putting on a replacement steam locomotive siderod. *Louis Marre*

This group of officers of the 701st Railway Operating Battalion completed the Atlantic Coast Transportation Corps railway operating course at Fort Slocum, New York. *Railway Age 1943*

IN UNCLE SAM'S SERVICE

A large crowd gathers to board a Newark-Trenton-Philadelphia-Baltimore-Washington passenger train at busy Pennsylvania Station during the war years. Note the large number of military personnel in the crowd, and the Service Men's Lounge signs. The American flag hangs in the rear as a testament to what the overriding hope is for many of those traveling through this station: peace, freedom and prosperity. Pennsylvania Station, located at 8th Avenue and 31st Street in midtown Manhattan, was the largest through station in the world when it opened at a cost of $114 million in November of 1910. The pink Milford granite station structure covered two complete city blocks. There was stairway access to 21 platform tracks below the main station area. In the peak war year of 1945, nearly 110 million people used this facility. In the main lobby of the 30th Street Station in Philadelphia, Pennsylvania, the Pennsy RR erected a WWII memorial with the inscription: "In memory of the men and women of the Pennsylvania Railroad who laid down their lives for our country 1941-1945." On the back of the statue it reads: "That all travelers here may remember those of the Pennsylvania Railroad who did not return from the Second World War." *Don Heimburger collection*

Crossroads Of War

"It takes the full, three-way cooperation of those who ship goods, of the railroads which haul them, and of those who receive them. Such teamwork as this has enabled the railroads to handle the greatest transportation job in history." —Railway Age, May 23, 1942

The Transportation Corps was the operating agency of the War Department when it took control of American railroads on December 27, 1943. Because continued operation of the railroads was threatened by strikes scheduled to begin December 30, President Franklin D. Roosevelt, by Executive Order, empowered and directed the Secretary of War, Henry Stimson "to manage and operate or arrange for the management and operation of the carriers, in such manner as might be necessary to assure continous and uninterrupted transportation service."

Secretary Henry Stimson delegated his authority to the Commanding General, Army Service Forces, who in turn charged the Chief of Transportation with direct responsibility for operations. A comprehensive plan for the possession, control and operation of the railroads by the Army, which had been prepared in advance of the emergency, was immediately placed in effect. The president of a large railroad was appointed principal advisor to the War Department. Seven leading railroad executives were commissioned colonels and appointed regional directors. The field personnel of the Transportation Corps, augmented by staff officers provided by the service commands, was organized to operate under the supervision of the regional directors.

The plan contemplated that the Army would leave operations in the hands of railroad managements unless a different course should become necessary. This did not happen, and following settlement of the dispute between labor and management, the Army relinquished control of the railroads on January 18, 1944. An interruption or impairment of service at this critical juncture in the war would have had serious military implications.

During the period of U.S. participation in the war—a period of 45 months from December 1941 through August 1945—the Office of the Chief of Transportation routed 33,678,000 passengers in organized groups of 40 or more. Of this total, 32,881,000 (97.6%) were routed by rail, and 797,000 (2.4%) by motorbus. The best comparable data for WWI indicates that 5,046,000 passengers were moved by special trains during a period of 18 1/3 months, from May 1, 1917 through November 10, 1918.

ARMY REGULATIONS

Under Army regulations all organized groups of 40 or more traveling on War Department orders were routed by the Office of the Chief of Transportation. Smaller groups and individuals were routed by transportation officers at their points of origin.

In all cases when groups consisted of 15 or more and were traveling by railroad, the routings were worked out initially by the respective territorial passenger associations of the railroads. The War Department relied upon these associa-

The *Admiral* was a Pennsylvania streamliner born of wartime necessity, with coaches spun off the *General*. Here the wartime *Admiral* leaves Chicago, just passing a lift bridge over one of the city's canals, on May 5, 1942. *Jay Williams collection*

A fast New York Central westbound tripleheader roars through Hazelton, Ohio and past hard-working steel mill blast furnaces with 77 loaded cars of wartime goods and materiel. Note the solidly built ballast-tie-rail combination. *E. L Thompson, Jay Williams collection*

The first of two New York Central heavy coal trains, loaded with precious black gold for fuel during the war, and with #2770 4-8-2 leading the first section, powers through Vernon, Ohio in 1944. *Jay Williams collection*

Passing Oscawanna, New York on December 14, 1941, passengers on board the sleek, streamlined 622-passenger *Empire State Express*, billed as "The World's Finest Day Train," are likely thinking about and talking about the tragedy that befell their country just seven days before at Pearl Harbor. The inaugural run of this New York Central flagship train was scheduled for Sunday, December 7, and thus publicity and the trackside turnout to watch this new train on that day was low. It was the last pre-war passenger train inaugurated. *Jay Williams collection*

A smoky, steamy westbound NYC freight with ruggedly-built #2776 4-8-2 in the lead thunders over the cold iron rails in New York State on January 10, 1942, carrying essentials for the war effort. *Jay Williams collection*

A doubleheaded NYC eastbound mixed freight with #2982 and a second L-2 up front on the Belt Line in Cleveland, Ohio has the "all clear" to bring its cargo to waiting industry on June 8, 1945. These powerful Mohawks best symbolized the New York Central System; 300 L-2 and their subclasses were built. *D.V. Bearse, Jay Williams collection*

RIGHT. A vital wartime commodity, ore, is transported at Ashtabula, Ohio to waiting steel mills in this shot on the New York Central in August of 1942. The well-maintained roadbed and high-poundage rail speaks volumes about the daily traffic loads on this stretch of track between 1941 and 1945. *Ed Nowak, Jay Williams collection*

A Nickel Plate Road westbound manifest freight with Lima-built S-2 #752 2-8-4 in the lead, and a war emergency 40-foot boxcar the first car in the consist, makes haste at Bay Village, Ohio on July 27, 1944. Note the tender sans lettering. *D.V. Bearse, Jay Williams collection*

Mighty New York Central Mohawks churn up the ballast and dust as they control an unusually long freight laden with war supplies at East Syracuse, New York in May of 1942. Water scoops under the tenders keep these behemoths on precision schedules necessary to deliver raw materials to America's hungry factories and foundries. *Ed Nowak, Jay Williams collection*

FREIGHT CAR PERFORMANCE			
	World War I (1918)	World War II (1942)	CHANGE
NUMBER OF CARS OWNED	2,354,244	1,742,704	-26%
TOTAL CAR CAPACITY	96,766,585 TONS	88,032,655 TONS	-9%
AVERAGE CAR CAPACITY	41.1 TONS	50.5 TONS	+23%
AVERAGE REVENUE LOAD PER CAR	29.2 TONS	31.8 TONS	+9%
AVERAGE MILES PER CAR PER DAY	24.6 MILES	46.3 MILES	+88%

This *Railway Age* chart from 1943 shows freight car performance between World War I and II, featuring an 88% increase in mileage of freight cars and other changes.

tions to effect the proper distribution of traffic among the individual carriers, and look after other railroad interests.

When the routings proposed by the associations did not meet Army requirements, changes were requested. Representatives of the passenger associations were stationed in the Traffic Control Division of the Office of the Chief of Transportation, as well as at the larger Army installations, so that adjustments could be made quickly.

PROVIDING SLEEPING CARS

The objective during the war was to provide sleeping cars for troops en route over 12 hours, whose trips terminated after midnight. Due to the shortage of sleeping cars, it frequently was not possible to adhere to that plan, and it sometimes was necessary in order to carry out prescribed schedules, to require troops to travel in coaches one or more nights.

When traveling by tourist sleeper, two men were assigned to a lower berth and one to an upper. One of the 14 sec-

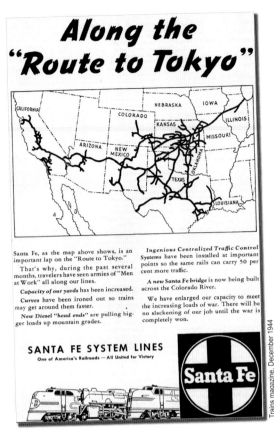

Along the "Route to Tokyo"

Santa Fe, as the map above shows, is an important lap on the "Route to Tokyo."

That's why, during the past several months, travelers have seen armies of "Men at Work" all along our lines.

Capacity of our yards has been increased.

Curves have been ironed out so trains may get around them faster.

New Diesel "head ends" are pulling bigger loads up mountain grades.

Ingenious Centralized Traffic Control Systems have been installed at important points so the same rails can carry 50 per cent more traffic.

A new Santa Fe bridge is now being built across the Colorado River.

We have enlarged our capacity to meet the increasing loads of war. There will be no slackening of our job until the war is completely won.

SANTA FE SYSTEM LINES
One of America's Railroads — All United for Victory

Santa Fe

Trains magazine, December 1944

tions was reserved for other than sleeping purposes, so that the usual complement was 39 men to a sleeping car. In normal coach travel, three men were assigned to two seats, but when coaches were used for overnight or very long trips, an effort was made to assign only one man to a seat.

When a sufficient number of troop cars moved over a given route, special troop trains were made up, since this greatly simplified control of the movement and the discipline of the men, as compared with troop cars attached to regular trains.

Each troop train had a troop train commander, and it was attended by a medical officer. The troop train commander appointed an assistant, a baggage officer, a mess officer, and a commander for each car to maintain discipline and enforce sanitary regulations.

A troop kitchen car was assigned to each train carrying 100 or more troops, and an additional kitchen car was added if the number exceeded 250.

Baggage cars were fitted by the Army to serve as kitchen cars, until specially-built kitchen cars were provided by the Government. Sometimes the trains included box cars and flatcars, the latter for heavy organizational equipment such as tanks and artillery.

"Buy War Bonds" was a constant mantra during the war, and railroads did everything possible to publicize this endeavor. On the Great Northern, this colorfully-decorated celestory roof diner was used as a rolling billboard to increase patronage of war bonds which were first called Defense Bonds, but after the U.S. entered the war were called "War or Victory Bonds" used to take money out of circulation to prevent inflation. The first war bond was sold to President Franklin D. Roosevelt on May 1, 1941 by Secretary of the Treasury Henry Morgenthau. *Donald Hofsommer collection*

A RAILROAD MAN'S FAMILY AT WAR
The LIGHTBURNS of Crestline, Ohio

Capt. James B. Lightburn. Formerly with the Freight Traffic Department of the Pennsylvania Railroad—now in Iran with a railroad battalion.

1st Lt. Robert A. Lightburn. Previously employed in the Pennsylvania Railroad's Crestline Shops—now in the Medical Corps, San Antonio, Texas.

Lt. Joseph G. Lightburn. On furlough from the Maintenance-of-way Department of the Pennsylvania Railroad—now with the Navy in the Pacific.

1st Lt. Willis Lightburn. Formerly a locomotive fireman on the Pennsylvania Railroad—now with the Air Force in North Africa.

Keeping the "Engines of War" rolling, **James G. Lightburn**, engineman and father of the family. He has been with the Pennsylvania Railroad 40 years.

Mrs. Blanch L. Lightburn, mother of eight fine children—four boys, four girls, all serving their Country.

This is the story of a fighting American family—a Pennsylvania Railroad family—the Lightburns of Crestline, Ohio.

On December 31, 1940, a year before Pearl Harbor, the Lightburns, father, mother, four girls, and four sons, held a family reunion in the pleasant home where the children were born and reared.

Today, this family group is scattered—all the boys officers in our Army or Navy while the girls, too, are playing vital roles.

An unusual family? Not according to "Jim" Lightburn. But a family reared in the tradition of service—ready when called to serve the cause of Freedom and their Country.

Pennsylvania Railroad salutes the Lightburns with pride and pleasure. A real railroad family, they are one of many railroad familiea who have given their sons and daughters to serve our Nation. Such families reflect the spirit and character of the manhood and womanhood which enablews this and all America's railroads to meet successfully the vital transportation needs of our Country at war.

Mrs. Helen Lightburn Boecher is a welfare nurse.

Mrs. Sara Lightburn Snyder serves the Pennsylvania Railroad at Crestline.

Virginia Lightburn, now a clerk in the Pennsylvania Railroad ticket office at Crestline.

Jacqueline Lightburn is a member of the U. S. Cadet Nurse Corps.

BUY UNITED STATES WAR BONDS AND STAMPS

Locomotive #916 on the MKT is at South Coffeyville, Oklahoma on August 30, 1944. Long stretches of the rails in the U.S. were in rural areas such as Oklahoma, but roads such as the MKT helped bring the all-important embarkation ports together. In the Midwest, MKT connected with other roads at St. Louis, and in the West and Southwest at Oklahoma City, San Antonio and other points. *Robert F. Collins, Louis Marre collection*

The *Katy Flyer* with #379 in the lead pulls a 16-car wartime passenger load through Wagoner, Oklahoma on July 23, 1944. *Louis Marre collection*

During the years 1943 and 1944 the railways assigned the following equipment to move troops and other passengers traveling in groups of 40 or more:

	1943	1944
Tourist sleepers	137,421	138,253
Coaches	97,635	55,987
Baggage cars	45,444	37,612
Flatcars	47,454	13,732
Standard sleepers	3,077	3,134
Boxcars and miscellaneous	4,759	25,330
Total	345,790	274,048

In the spring of 1943 when troop movements were especially heavy, the Armed Forces at times used as much as 50% of the sleeping car equipment available in the country and 30% of the coaches. Then it was decided to build 1,200 special troop sleepers, and also 400 special troop kitchen cars, with funds provided by the Defense Plant Corporation. The sleepers, although light and of very simple design, were well-equipped, and each provided 30 berths in tiers of three. They were turned over to the Pullman Company for operation. When it became evident that the redeployment and demobilization of forces from Europe required an unprecedented amount of sleeping car space, additional orders were placed for 1,200 troop sleepers and 400 kitchen cars. However, delivery of the sleepers was seriously delayed by strikes.

When troop movement orders involving considerable numbers were being drawn up by the Operations Division of the General Staff, representatives of the Traffic Control Division of the Office of the Chief of Transportation were consulted regarding any transportation or traffic factors which might affect the movement.

PEAKS AND VALLEYS

In this way peaks and valleys of troop travel were avoided, and it was possible to schedule movements so that railway equipment was released by one group in time for it to be used by another group leaving from the same general area.

Eventually it was arranged that departure times be left flexible and that the Office of the Chief of Transportation be permitted to adjust them within a limit of 72 hours. By doing this, it was possible to work out a much more economical utilization of railway equipment through a reduction in the deadheading of passenger cars.

An organized troop movement, whether it moved by special train or in special cars on a regular train, was under the control of the Office of the Chief of Transportation from the point of origin to its destination. Times of departure and arrival were reported by both unit commanders and the railroads. The carriers also gave passing reports at each junction point to the Association of American Railroads. This information was available to the Army when needed, and it was useful not only in forecasting train arrivals at destinations, but also in the arranging for diversions.

During the strenuous days following December 7, 1941, when many troop units were being moved to new stations within the country or to ports of embarkation, and when hastily prepared plans were subject to sudden change, this complete reporting system was of inestimable value.

Passenger troop fares paid by the War Department were in accordance with the Military Passenger Agreement which was negotiated annually with the railroads by the Army, Navy, Marine Corps, and Coast Guard, acting jointly. The agreement provided for reduced rates for military traffic. Advantage was taken also of land-grant rates, where applicable. There was no general rate agreement with bus operators, and bus service was obtained either under charter terms or at tariff fares. Although the motor carriers often could provide more satifactory service for smaller groups moving over shorter distances, generally speaking the railroads were preferred for military movements because of their ability to handle larger groups with better control, their sleeping car and kitchen car facilities, and their ability to transport bulky equipment with the troops.

The tremendous increase in railway passenger traffic, both military and civilian, made it progressively more difficult to obtain reservations on Pullman cars and reserved-seat coaches. As a result, Army officers and other employees traveling on official business frequently found it impossible to maintain their travel schedules, and personnel on leave of absence or furlough were often delayed.

To meet this situation in June 1942, the railroads arranged to hold blocks of space for use only by the Army, Navy and certain other Government agencies. Early in 1943 the War Department established Army reservation bureaus in convenient locations at principal railway centers. Eventually 92 such bureaus and branches were functioning.

Operated by the Chief of Transportation and staffed with trained personnel, these agencies greatly eased the problems of both travelers and railroads. Up to the end of hostilities, they had dealt with more than 5 million requests and had succeeded in making reservations as requested in all but 4.1% of cases. During 1943 the proportion of failures was 8.5%, but during the first six months of 1945 it was only 3.0%. Navy, Marine Corps and Coast Guard personnel were permitted to use the Army reservation bureaus in places where their own service did not provide a similar facility.

RETURNING TROOPS

In order to properly care for the sick and wounded returning to the U.S. from overseas theaters, and to reduce the number of Pullman cars required to handle patients, the Army built 320 hospital ward cars during the war, and also 60 hospital kitchen cars. Designed according to the most up-to-date standards of equipment, ventilation and safety, the cars were operated by the service commands, which assigned them to several ports in proportion to the volume of the traffic to be handled.

The Movements Division of the Office of the Chief of Transportation, in conjuction with The Surgeon General, indicated the number of cars required to meet each incoming hospital ship, or regular transport carrying patients. The ports maintained specially-trained troop units to move patients from ships to waiting trains.

Prisoners of war were moved in groups, generally by special trains and always in coaches. Exceptions to this general rule were made only in the case of patients. Special cars were provided by the railroads for the movement of such prisoners. All windows were blocked so that they could be opened only a few inches, and all emergency tools were sealed. Only cars allowing unobstructed views from one end to the other were utilized, and all interior doors were removed. The Provost Marshal General provided guards for the cars.

CAREFUL PLANS LAID

Before the German surrender, careful plans had been laid for handling the inland transportation of troops who began pouring into U.S. Atlantic Coast ports as soon as the fighting in Europe ceased. It was evident that these returning troops, each man making from two to six moves prior to separation from the service or embarkation to a new station in the Pacific, would impose a heavier burden on the railroads than they previously had encountered.

To keep traffic under control as much as possible and afford soldiers as good train accommodations as could be given, it was decided to move the men in organized parties whenever feasible, rather than permit them to travel individually. This applied not only to trips from the ports to personnel centers, but also to trips from personnel centers to homes, from home to assembly stations, and to whatever trips might follow. The plan proved highly satisfactory from the standpoint of orderliness of movement and economical use of railroad equipment.

Prior to the German capitulation, the peak month for troop traffic in the zone of interior was April 1943, when 1,059,000 men were routed in groups of 40 or more. Thereafter, with the number of troops remaining in the U.S. declining, this traffic diminished, and in April 1945 it was only 527,000. Then with the beginning of redeployment from Europe it began to mount, and in August 1945, a new high of 1,205,000 was reached. Of that number, 1,174,000 moved by rail and 31,000 by bus.

August of 1945 was the peak month for the entire war period, since after V-J Day, troop moves for training purposes and movements to the ports of embarkation were greatly reduced.

The heavy arrivals of Army and Navy personnel at Pacific Coast ports in November 1945 overtaxed the rail facilities, with the result that many men were detained at the port disposition centers several days beyond the normal period, because rail equipment could not be furnished for transporting them to personnel centers. The basic difficulty was availability of cars. A much larger number of men had to be moved from Pacific Coast ports to Eastern states than from the Eastern seaboard to the Western states, so that the number of cars leaving the West Coast was greater than the number arriving. The failure of rail car manufacturing plants to obtain scheduled deliveries of special troop sleepers because of strikes, which had been ordered in the spring of 1945, had a material bearing on the situation.

Various measures were taken to improve this condition. The Office of Defense Transportation and the railroads were asked to divert cars, both sleepers and coaches, from regular train service to handle troop traffic. A thousand additional cars were obtained this way, and several hundred

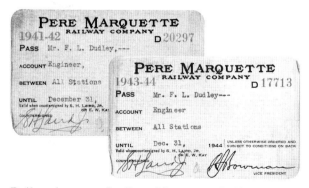

Railroad passes for Pere Marquette Railway Company between 1941-1944. *Don Heimburger collection*

During the war, many freight trains were run in sections because of the tremendous tonnage that accumulated in the railyards. Here, the third section of Frisco Train #344, with 61 cars, passes near Nichols, Missouri on September 3, 1944. *Louis Marre collection*

At Corsicana, Texas, St. Louis-Southwestern 4-8-4 #802 on Train #126 tugs at 27 cars on October 15, 1944. The big GS-7 Class was re-numbered to #4475 in June of 1953. When German U-boats threatened waterway movements of oil, the Cotton Belt reinforced its bridges to accommodate oil trains led by the big 800s of the railroad. *Robert F. Collins, Louis Marre collection*

The Pennsylvania Railroad operated 598 Decapods, a tremendous number of engines of the Class I1s 2-10-0 wheel arrangement. Husky-looking, powerful and rugged, by 1924 these locomotives were the heavy freight haulers on the railroad. The Decapods operated in the mountainous regions of Pennsylvania but also as far west as central Ohio, as this photo shows: #4578 is at Columbus in February of 1942. *Don Heimburger collection*

Date: 1944. Railroad: Santa Fe. Location: Top of Raton Pass, New Mexico. Two monster Santa Fe locomotives combine their tractive effort into one mean wartime pulling machine on this tough 7,834-foot-high pass, part of the old Santa Fe Trail on the east side of the Sangre de Cristo Mountains on the Colorado-New Mexico border. *Mallory Hope Ferrell collection*

were deadheaded to the Pacific Coast so that they could be used to move troops from disposition centers with the least possible delay.

The Transportation Corps arranged for Army cots to be converted and installed in 312 troop sleepers which had been completed except for the installation of berths—work which had been stopped because the manufacturer's plant was strikebound. As many Army hospital cars as could be spared from transporting patients were assigned to troop traffic.

The Office of Defense Transportation was requested to raise the minimum distance from 450 to 500 miles over which sleeping cars could be used in regular train service, in order to make more of the cars available for troops, but the request was not granted.

When the heavy return movement began in the summer of 1945, it was arranged that troops would be moved by air from both coasts. In October 32,000 troops were moved this way, approximately half from Atlantic and half from Pacific ports. In view of the situation which developed in November, and the even more difficult situation which was a prospect for December, arrangements were made for troops to use 10,000 additional airplane seats per month from the Pacific Coast. This additional allotment represented about 70% of the available eastbound space on commercial air lines.

Between December 1941 and August 1945, freight moving on War Department bills of lading totaled 324,891,000 short tons. This movement, which began with 1,600,000 tons in the first month of the war, reached a peak. Of 11,001,000 tons in March 1945, it then began to decline as the German resistance weakened, and the end of the war in Europe appeared to be near.

The heaviest monthly movement of War Department freight by rail during WWI was 1,105,000 tons in October 1918. The volume increased after the Armistice to a peak of 1,446,000 tons in March 1919.

All carload shipments, whether domestic or for export, were routed by the Office of the Chief of Transportation. As many as 40,000 route orders were issued in a single month. A substantial part of the less-than-carload shipments was handled by the consolidated car service which the Transportation Corps operated. Other LCL shipments were routed by transportation officers at points of origin. An analysis by carrier (except air) of freight moving on War Department bills of lading during the 45-month period, December 1941-August 1945, shows:

	Short tons	Percent
Rail-carload	288,142,000	88.7
Rail-LCL	4,880,000	1.5
Rail-express	1,099,000	.3
Motor carrier	26,534,000	8.2
Inland waterway	4,236,000	1.3
Total	324,891,000	100.0

On the basis of ton-miles, War Department freight transported by the railroads was 5.1% of their total freight in 1942, increasing to 12.5% of the total in June of 1945. Between the year 1942 and the first 11 months of 1945, the average distance covered by War Department shipments by rail increased from 700 to 780 miles.

The Santa Fe promoted its 1943 war efforts via billboards. These pictures were taken in Chicago by Paul Stringham. *William Raia collection*

In normal times the choice of routes for shipments was determined primarily on the basis of rates. During the war this requirement was relaxed, and military expediency was given precedence. However, the matter of rates was still considered, and in a large percentage of cases, it continued to be the governing factor. A complete file of tariffs was maintained in the Traffic Control Division in the Office of the Chief of Transportation, as well as a staff trained in the utilization of these tariffs and in the very intricate problems involved in the use of land-grant rates.

Very thorough studies were made with a view to saving freight charges for the War Department. Rate reductions were obtained by negotiation with the carriers, or, when necessary, by formal proceedings before regulatory bodies. Classification ratings as applied to War Department items were adjusted to make them more equitable, and numerous new ratings were worked out with the carriers on a fair basis.

With about a million items in use by the Army, classification ratings presented a large and intricate problem. Storage in transit privileges were made applicable to a large number of Army installations, resulting in reduced transportation costs. It's estimated that the savings in freight charges effected on that basis were about $60 million annually.

This wartime poster asking civilians to reduce train travel was distributed by the Association of American Railroads in cooperation with the Office of Defense Transportation. *Railway Age, 1943*

The Transportation Corps conducted a persistent campaign against wasteful detention of cars at Army installations. One feature of this campaign was a monthly report showing the speed with which cars were unloaded and released at more than 200 of the Army's largest freight handling points. The report was sent to the installations studied, and since it showed their relative standing, it created a spirit of competition.

As a result, between July 1944 and July 1945, the percentage of cars released before the expiration of 24 hours increased from 62 to 71, and the percentage held beyond the 48-hour free period decreased from 14 to 7. This meant not only that the cars were put back in circulation quicker, but also that demurrage charges were substantially reduced.

TRANSPORTATION CORPS SUPPORT

The Transportation Corps gave its full support to the movement, which was countrywide, for the full utilization of freight car space. Transportation officers in the field were constantly impressed with this neccessity and were coached in techniques.

As a result, the average weight of War Department freight loaded in a car increased from 28.9 short tons in April 1943 to 30.0 tons in June 1945. That the War Department average was less than the overall average was due to the fact that so large a part of Army freight was made up of types which were light in proportion to their bulk. Vehicles, for example, constituted more than 10% of the total Army freight moved by rail. Other types required special stowing, which consumed space.

Methods of stowing, blocking and bracing large pieces of Army equipment, such as vehicles, tanks and artillery, were greatly improved during the war. In the early stages these improvements generally were developed by the respective arms and services—notably the Ordnance Department and the Armored Force Board—in direct dealings with the

This former Norfolk & Western Y3 2-8-8-2 was sold to the Santa Fe in 1943 to help with moving the military overload of tonnage and troops. Later, seven of the Y3's were sold to the Virginian in 1948. Here #1793 and helper take *The Chief* up Raton Pass below Wooton, Colorado. *Mallory Hope Ferrell collection*

Already in February of 1941 railroads were aware of looming problems abroad and promoted the patriotism theme to their passenger customers. *Baltimore & Ohio Railroad timetable, February 2, 1941*

WARTIME
DINING CAR SERVICE

As you know, many dining cars are now serving the armed forces, and material to build new ones is not available. At the same time essential civilian travel is steadily increasing. All of which means that there are many more passengers to be served without extra equipment with which to do it. So if you're kept waiting for dinner, please be patient. And when you have finished, won't you kindly leave the diner promptly, so that others may be served as soon as possible.

To assist further in expediting dining car service, the sale of alcoholic beverages must necessarily be suspended during meal hours except with food service.

The sale of liquor on our trains is subject to the laws of the States through which we operate, and we are required to see that they are obeyed. This prohibits us from selling alcoholic beverages to anyone under the influence thereof or to minors. Your cooperation in the observance of the law is respectfully requested.

Like others, we too are strictly rationed by the Government on a number of items, particularly coffee, tea and sugar, and we must, therefore, restrict servings in order to provide for a greatly increased patronage.

May we ask your indulgence in these matters?

B. J. Bohlender, Manager Dining Service, New York

New York Central menu

117

These spiffy cars were colorful roving street billboards in Chicago for the war bond effort. *Photo by J. Diaz, Bill Raia collection*

loading rules committees of the railroads, and frequently without consultation with the Transportation Corps. Later the Transportation Corps itself initiated proposals and conducted experiments to test their practicability.

Early in 1945 the Chief of Transportation was specifically assigned staff supervision over all car loading procedures, with control over liaison between the Armed Services and the railroad loading rules committees.

Wastage through cross-hauling and back-hauling also received constant attention in the Office of the Chief of Transportation. The seriousness of these practices, in the light of the car shortage, was broadcast to all transportation officers.

By studying the route orders for specific commodities, it was possible for the Traffic Control Division to discover what seemed to be avoidable cross-hauls and back-hauls, and such cases were brought to the attention of the procuring services involved. It was then the responsibility of those services to work out changes in future shipping programs that were feasible.

NEXT PAGE, BOTTOM. Two Illinois terminal traction units grind through the Illinois landscape in the war years with a war bond slogan stenciled on the lead unit's nose. Locomotive #74 was rebuilt by the road's Decatur shops in September of 1942 from locomotive #1588. With WWII taxing all rail lines, the IT was inundated with tonnage from connecting steam roads, many smaller on-line plants engaged in the war effort, and from the large Illiopolis, Illinois munitions plant. The $35 million, 15,000-worker Sangamon Ordnance Plant, which opened in April of 1942, was operated by Remington Rand, Inc. for the U. S. Army and included 20,000 acres which were obtained through eminent domain. At one point, the U.S. War Production Board ordered the IT railroad to scrap 151 miles between Mackinaw Junction and Decatur, Illinois and even signed a contract with Metals Reserve Company to dismantle the track, but by 1943 the track was still operating and was never torn up. *Bill Raia*

Service
The SCENIC ROUTE
between the
NORTH and SOUTH

NEW YORK
PHILADELPHIA
BALTIMORE
WASHINGTON
LYNCHBURG
ROANOKE
BRISTOL
NASHVILLE   KNOXVILLE
MEMPHIS   CHATTANOOGA
SHREVEPORT   BIRMINGHAM
        MERIDIAN
    NEW ORLEANS

The TENNESSEAN

Washington to Memphis
Coach Seats on the Tennessean
are reserved in advance—no
extra charge.

The BIRMINGHAM
Special

The NEW YORK
CHATTANOOGA
and NEW ORLEANS
Limited

Norfolk *and* Western *Railway*

Norfolk & Western Railway timetable, October 15, 1942

"Fly for Navy" was the theme of this Chicago street car which featured a clever "wave" on the bottom portion of the car. "High School Grads 18 to 26. Apply at 141 W. Jackson Blvd.," reads the side slogan. *J. Diaz, Bill Raia collection*

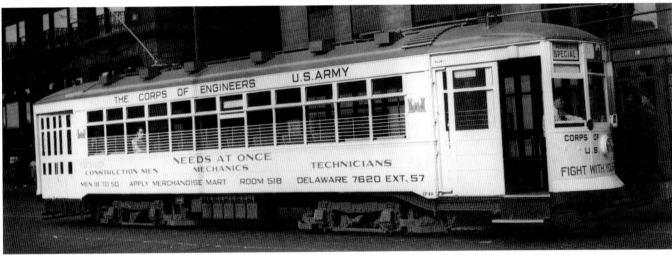

The U.S. Army Corps of Engineers used the Chicago street car line to advertise for construction workers, mechanics and technicians. Applicants were to apply at Chicago's Merchandise Mart. *J. Diaz, Bill Raia collection*

Edelstein Hill on the Santa Fe was a tough climb, but this twin-unit DL-109/DL-110 (#50 and #50A), built by the American Locomotive Company, developed 4,000 hp and thus made the grade. Note the elongated wartime headlight used to mask unnecessary light that could be observed from enemy warplanes. *Paul Stringham, William Raia collection*

RIGHT. This July 11, 1942 photo shows massive Rock Island motive power leading a string of refrigerator cars at Bureau, Illinois. Right before and during the war, the Rock Island modernized 18 M-50 Class 4000 series 4-8-2s (#4044-#4061) with roller bearings on all axles, lightweight main and side rods, Timken hollow piston rods and crossheads with aluminum shoes and block tin faces. Also modernized were 28 heavy 2-8-2s between #2680-2712. *Paul Stringham, William Raia collection*

Railroads and the War

The people of the United States owe a debt to the nation's railroads that will be most difficult to repay. After virtually relegating them to the status of a stepchild, they called upon the railroads immediately after the attack on Pearl Harbor to supply most of their transport needs. Accepting the task, the railroads last year did the greatest transportation job in the history of this or any nation.

Having emerged from a ten-year period of poor business, the railroads were not well prepared for such a gigantic job. After reporting net deficits for four of those years, many were in bankruptcy proceedings. The fact, however, that the volume of freight handled last year was one and one-half times that moved in the First World War year 1918 showed that, despite their lean period, they had maintained their fixed plant and equipment in excellent condition.

In their poverty of the Nineteen Thirties, the statement that the railroads were "through" as the mainstay of the nation's transport facilities generally was accepted as an accomplished fact. Interest was centered in the development of other transportation methods. The rubber-borne vehicle and the vast network of highways would be the nation's mainstay in a crisis. Inland waterways and coastwise and intercoastal water routes would be the other principal methods.

Under the impact of war these methods of transport did not meet the test. With the Japanese soon in posses-sion of the source of 90 per cent of the world's crude rubber, the effectiveness of the rubber-borne vehicle in meeting the increased transport needs was greatly reduced. Submarine sinkings and the diversion of ships to war services overseas soon resulted in coastwise shipping dropping to a fraction of its former importance. Inter-coastal freight traffic through the Panama Canal was suspended.

These traffic disruptions made the nation more dependent on rail transportation than at any other period. To the railroads fell the job of maintaining a steady flow of materials to war industries and then moving the weapons they produced to ports and training centers. Millions of men in the Armed Services had to be transported, and essential civilian transport needs had to be met. The railroads have handled this enormous volume of traffic with remarkable efficiency.

Billions of dollars are being spent by the Government to expand other industries, but the railroads have done their war job well without any outside assistance. Furthermore, they have contributed liberally, through taxes, to Government expenditures. John J. Pelley, president of the Association of American Railroads, recently estimated that railroad taxes in the twelve months ended with October amounted to the unprecedented sum of $1,077,000,000, the equivalent of revenues derived from fifty-six days of operation. *Editorial, New York Times, January 4, 1943*

A Santa Fe Mikado 2-8-2 #3192 drops down over Edelstein Hill near Galesburg, Illinois with vital war tonnage on July 28, 1942. All of the #3129 ATSF Class of engines were scrapped by 1954. *Paul Stringham, William Raia collection*

The NYC's Mohawks—which performed admirably during WWII—had the look of modern power with their long tenders with six-wheel trucks to carry more weight, their large boilers, and their 350,000 pounds of steel. *Ed Nowak, Jay William collection*

121

The *Grand Canyon Limited* rolls east of Galesburg, Illinois on the Santa Fe on June 2, 1942, a few days after the British sent 1,000 bombers on a raid to Cologne, Germany. Just a few months before, the first American forces arrived in Britain to begin training for D-Day. *Paul Stringham, William Raia collection*

This was the fire truck and equipment manned by the Stores Department to protect Union Pacific shops and stores at Omaha, Nebraska in the mid-1940s. Note female on the rear platform and the Union Pacific emblem on the truck. *Railway Age, September 21, 1946*

Burlington timetable, July-Aug. 1942

This odd-looking single-end, high-cab configuration Santa Fe diesel, rebuilt in 1938, was a one-of-a-kind locomotive on the railroad. The lead truck was exchanged for a drop-equalizer, and the trailing truck was later replaced as well. Here it is in charge of a passenger train gliding through Streator, Illinois on November 26, 1942. Wonder what military personnel might be on board? *Paul Stringham, William Raia collection*

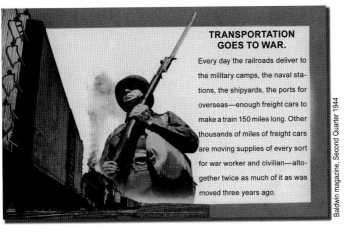

Baldwin magazine, Second Quarter 1944

Locomotives #5012 and #5001 team up to tug along a heavy tonnage load during the war in 1942 at Bureau, Illinois. During the spring of 1932, the Santa Fe carried five times the westbound traffic that it carried in 1938, and by 1945 it carried 10 times the 1938 volume. *Paul Stringham, William Raia collection*

Five months after the U.S. entered the war, Santa Fe's *Chief* with 11 streamlined passenger cars plies the iron near Wilburn, Illinois on May 8, 1942. *Paul Stringham, William Raia collection*

Baldwin magazine, Second Quarter 1944

Throughout the war specially expedited freight shipments were necessary to meet war theater requirements. Orders for such service were given only by the Transportation Corps. During the critical stages of the invasion of Germany, expedited shipments of ammunition were run directly from ordnance plants to ports to meet carefully phased convoy sailings.

SPECIAL TRACTOR SHIPMENT

Following the U.S. occupation of Attu and Kiska, a shipment of 169 sorely-needed tractors was rushed to the San Francisco Port of Embarkation from Peoria, Illinois by utilizing all high-speed box cars available in the vicinity and running them through to the port in two special trains. This is only one example of a procedure which became almost routine during the war.

When dealing with such movements, the Transportation Corps determined whether expedited regular train service or special train service was necessary. The Association of American Railroads then made the arrangements and assigned special symbols. Reports on the progress of shipments were received through the AAR, and final checks were made at the ports to determine whether the arrivals had been according to schedule.

Origin	Carloads	Percent
Industrial (vendor) plants	653,000	47.7
Army depots	363,000	26.5
Industrial (Army) plants	149,000	10.9
Posts, camps, stations, ports	114,000	8.3
Holding and reconsignment points	30,000	2.2
Commercial warehouses	28,000	2.0
Army-Navy consolidating stations	18,000	1.3
Miscellaneous	15,000	1.1
Total	1,370,000	100.0

Origins of War Department carload freight as disclosed by an analysis of bills of lading for the five-month period, August-December 1944.

The establishment of an Army consolidated car service was an innovation, but it was virtually a necessity. During the first year of the war, about 40% of the total number of War Department shipments were less-than-carloads. As such they were routed by transportation officers in the field and were consolidated into carload lots by the railroads. These shipments passed completely out of War Department control, and their delivery was additionally delayed by the consolidating and break-bulk operations.

After studying the situation, the Army decided that by establishing its own consolidated car service for shipments

Nickel Plate Road Class S 2-8-4 #714 turns on the Frankfort, Indiana turntable in 1943. During 1940-1945, NKP had to turn its engines as fast as they entered the terminals and get them back onto the road. Cramped, small backshops at Conneaut, Lima and Frankfort nevertheless kept the fleet rolling. NKP ran freights in sections rather than increase train lengths to meet wartime schedules. Note the white-striped tender in the stall which encourages people to "Buy War Bonds." *William Rittase, Jay Williams collection*

The B&O's *National Limited*, way behind schedule and seen without the usual EA and EB diesel units hauling it, is westbound at 6th Street in Parkersburg, West Virginia on September 1, 1940. B&O historian Bob Withers says the large volume of mail traffic on the railroad played havoc with passenger service, causing many delays. *Stephen P. Davidson, Bob Withers collection*

between certain areas, it could not only overcome these handicaps but would effect a large savings in freight charges by paying carload rather than LCL rates.

CONSOLIDATING STATION IN CHICAGO

The first Army Consolidating Station was established at Chicago in July 1942 for shipments to the State of California. The undertaking was so successful that additional consolidating stations were set up in New York, Philadelphia, St. Louis and Cleveland, and freight distributing agencies for their respective areas were installed at San Francisco, Oakland, Los Angeles, Portland, Tacoma, Seattle, Spokane, Ogden, El Paso, Fort Worth, San Antonio, Atlanta, Memphis, Chicago and Philadelphia.

Certain distributing agencies also did consolidating. When a full car could be consolidated for a single depot or other installation, it was consigned directly to that installation. In February 1943 the Navy began participating in the service, although the operation continued exclusively under the Army Chief of Transportation.

From July 1942 through August 1945, a total of 140,000 carloads were consolidated, of which approximately 65% represented Army freight and 35% Navy freight. This total included 45,782 refrigerator cars which otherwise probably would have been deadheaded to the Pacific Coast.

GERMAN STRATEGY

The strategy of defeating Germany before the full weight of the U.S. armed might was turned against Japan called for a complete plan for the readjustment of export traffic

movements when V-E Day came. The planning was begun in August 1943, and every contingency had been provided for when Germany surrendered. Since October 1944 all shipments destined to Europe had been marked either SHP (ship) or STO (stop) before leaving the depot or contractor's plant. So far as possible the two classes were shipped in separate cars. Upon notification from the War Department, it was a relatively simple matter for the railroads to hold STO cars, report them to the Office of the Chief of Transportation and await notice of disposition.

STO cargo at ports of embarkation and holding and reconsignment points also was to be reported to Washington by special courier. Representatives of the several procuring services were stationed in the Traffic Control Division to receive reports of stopped cargo and arrange for its disposition. This plan was placed in effect on May, 6 two days before the official V-E Day, and by May 10 disposition orders had been furnished on all STO cargo, representing 7,112 carloads. A similar plan was used at the time of the Japanese capitulation, and the 15,396 carloads stopped by the railroads or reported by the ports were all disposed of by September 1945.

CONTROL OF PORT-BOUND FREIGHT

Remembering the harmful effect of port congestion on the movement of military supplies to France in 1917-18, the Army took steps early in 1941 to control its own traffic.

The first measures were designed merely to keep the Office of The Quartermaster General fully informed regarding export freight on hand at the Army ports of embarkation and anticipated shipments to those installations. During

In July, 1942 the first Army Consolidating Station was established in Chicago for shipments to California. More such stations were eventually added in New York, Philadelphia, St. Louis and Cleveland. *Louis Marre*

1944 MINUTEMEN

Every mintue of the day and night, America's railroads move one and one-third million tons of freight a distance of one mile. Every mintue, fifteen new freight trains are made up and started on their runs. Right around the clock, railroad men—modern minutemen—are at work hauling military supplies, raw materials, fuel and food needed by a nation at war.

Baldwin magazine, Second Quarter 1944

When the war broke, all procuring agencies of the War Department were under heavy pressure to make deliveries at the ports with utmost speed, and large quantities of Lend-Lease supplies also were moving to the United Kingdom and Russia.

Steps were taken to tighten the enforcement of Army control over its own shipments, but it was evident that control was necessary also over the substantial shipments of Lend-Lease supplies which the Treasury Department and the Department of Agriculture were making. At a meeting held on December 11, 1941, those departments agreed to recognize any requests that the War Department made regarding the movement of their export shipments to avoid congestion and keep military supplies moving freely.

Ten such installations eventually were built to support Atlantic, Gulf and Pacific ports. In the fall of 1941 the War Department established agencies at New York and Boston to represent the Army's interests in keeping Lend-Lease supplies moving smoothly through the ports, and the number of such agencies was increased as the need grew.

Immediately following U.S. entry into the war, five regulating stations were set up on the transcontinental rail lines—at Spokane, Ogden, Salt Lake City, Albuquerque and El Paso—to stop or divert cars destined to the Pacific Coast as directed.

SERIOUS CONGESTION

Due to lack of effective control over port-bound shipments, and other conditions growing out of the sudden U.S. entry

(Continued on page 132)

the summer of that year, however, a system of release and routing was instituted which applied to all War Department shipments of one carload or more destined to the ports, whether for the Army itself or for Lend-Lease.

Release and routing orders were issued by the Transportation Division in the Office of The Quartermaster General, upon receipt of a request from shippers, and after consideration had been given to actual conditions at the respective ports, and the amount of Army cargo recently released for shipment to the ports.

RIGHT. Steam locomotives and the wartime products they delivered weaved America together in many ways. Santa Fe #2907 4-8-4, shown here delivering goods on a fast freight schedule, was one of the last steam locomotives built for the Santa Fe in 1944. These locomotives turned in exceptional mileage records, many running between Los Angeles and Kansas City with only intermediate servicing. All were scrapped by 1960 except #2921. *Mallory Hope Ferrell collection*

GANGWAY FOR A GOOD SOLDIER!

Trains, August 1944

A big Milwaukee Road 4-8-4 #136 pulls a National Guard Extra through Techny, Illinois, a part of unincorporated Cook County near Chicago. The Milwaukee Road pitched in to do its part: a red, white and blue bucket was hung on each side of Milwaukee Road switch locomotives at major terminals as catch-alls for scrap material found on the property. Also, the 1886 clock tower in Milwaukee's Everett Street Depot was removed for scrap. *William Raia, Owen Leander collection*

New York Central locomotives hiss and smoke as they simmer at West Detroit, Michigan in 1944, awaiting their assignments to move material for the military effort. The NYC was second in size only to the Pennsylvania Railroad, operated 11,000 miles of track, and at one point owned nearly 5,000 steam locomotives. *Robert Hadley, Jay Williams collection*

Milwaukee Road coach #457, built for the 1942 *Hiawatha*, was used as part of a railroad-sponsored promotion to boost war bond sales. It featured red window panels, blue letterboards and skirts, and the rest of the sides were white. The stars above and below the windows were gold. A formal dedication for the car occurred on October 1 at Chicago's Union Station, after which it traveled the system, finally being used on one of the *Afternoon Hiawatha* train sets. *Owen Leander collection*

Many railroads participated in the war effort by painting certain cars in their fleets with war-related messages. "Fly For Navy" was painted on a white background, and a large United States Navy emblem adorned the bottom half of this Chicago & NorthWestern lightweight coach #3420, which was delivered from Pullman-Standard to the railroad in December of 1941, as part of Lot 6658. In 1947 the car was remodeled into a coach-lounge, and in 1958 it was renumbered to #845. *Don Heimburger collection*

CONSERVE ★ DON'T WASTE

This 1942 view at Peru, Indiana shows Wabash O-1 Class Baldwin-built (1930) #2915 and a sister locomotive moving tonnage on this 2,500-mile rail line that served the heart of America. This "Follow the Flag" bridge railroad was a trustworthy WWII transportation company. *William Swartz, collection of M.D. McCarter*

The Milwaukee Road was responsible for at least 27 different pre-war WWII special troop trains which were the primary factor in the 1940 transportation of more than 32,000 National Guardsmen and regular Army troops to Wisconsin's military installations for training. *Association of American Railroads, Owen Leander collection*

The Wabash Railroad entered Chicago from Indiana as well as from the south through Illinois on a line that split at Bement. Here at 81st Street, an eastbound freight pulls out all the plugs to deliver war materiel: Chicago was second only to Detroit in war goods produced at $24 billion in value. Plants in Chicago made field rations, parachutes, electronics, torpedoes and more. Date: March, 1945. *Paul Eilenberger, collection of Don Heimburger*

Salute to the Railroads

No Army-Navy "E" pennant flies from the thousands of locomotives that, day and night, are hauling the greatest traffic in transportation history. Yet, no war production plant along the right-of-way is more important to the war effort than are the railroads of America.

Without great tonnage trains of coal and iron ore, the steel plants, tank arsenals and shipyards could not function. Likewise, tanks or pieces of artillery can win no wars at the factories at which they are made; they must be shipped to ports of embarkation and thence overseas.

Consider also the job of supplying the nation with coal, just one of the many items needed. In 1943, the railroads transported more than 10.5 million carloads of coal, using enough cars to form 26 solid trains reaching from New York to San Francisco.

Military men divide warfare into: Strategy, Tactics and Logistics. The first two we must leave to the soldiers, but Logistics—the science of transporting and supplying an army in war—is largely the province of the more than a million and a quarter railroad men in the United States.

The Wall Street Journal, in its issue of March 11, 1944, painted a portion of the picture as follows:

> "Newspapers recently reported the arrival in England of 'one of the greatest' contingents of troops ever to cross the Atlantic. They didn't tell the start of this story of mass movement of men and materiels—logistics—the military-minded like to call it.
>
> Months before the great convoy set out for England, the railroads had begun picking up trucks in Detroit, planes from Midwest factories and small ammunitions from New England mills and delivering them to the ports of embarkation on the Atlantic Coast. Later they did the same for the thousands of soldiers transported to England."

A COMPLICATED, STUPENDOUS TASK

In the years prior to 1939, some people had arrived at the conclusion that the day of the railroad was passing, and that we could afford to belittle the rail transportation system upon which America had been built. The advent of war changed that. These same people suddenly found the adequacy of the railroad system a source of concern as they realized how important mass transportation could be in time of war.

That the railroads have successfully met the huge task with which they were confronted is a matter of public knowledge and official record. Secretary of War Stimson, in a radio address delivered on December 28, 1943, said in part:

> "During the present emergency, the railroads have been bearing more than 90% of the burden of all transportation. They have carried more than five

times as much Army freight and express in the little more than two years of this war as they did in the entire 20 months of our participation in the conflict of 1917 and 1918."

Long before Pearl Harbor, the railroads had started to feel the impact of defense preparations. Looking at freight traffic statistics, in 1939 Class 1 railroads handled some 333 billion revenue miles of freight. In 1940 the figure was 373 billion, and in 1941 it was 475 billion. Then came December 7, 1941, and the railroads really went to work.

Twelve hours after the news of the Japanese attack was flashed to a startled world, the railroads started the preliminary movement of troops and materiels. The organzied movement of an army corps of two infantry divisions to the West Coast started on December 14, 1941 and was completed a few days later.

WHAT IS INVOLVED

To appreciate this task we must consider what is involved in such a troop movement. To transport one infantry division, which means about 15,000 men with their equipment, requires approximately 1,350 cars of all classes. This makes about 65 special trains. An armored division with its 3,000 tanks, half-tracks and wheeled vehicles, takes 75 trains from 28 to 45 cars each.

Beginning on December 7, 1941, the first five weeks of war involved a rail movement of approximately 600,000 troops with their vehicles, guns and equipment. Passenger traffic also went steadily upward from the 29 billion passenger-miles of 1941 to the total of 88 billion in 1943. This latter figure exceeded 1920, the previous peak year prior to the war, by about 88 percent. Likewise, Pearl Harbor Day set off the greatest movement of freight in railroad history.

From the 475 billion revenue-ton-miles of 1941, freight movement went steadily upward to 638 billion in 1942 and to the all-time high of 727 billion ton-miles in 1943. This figure represents 79% more freight traffic than in 1918, the peak year of WWI.

Much of the freight and passenger traffic of 1943 was direct service to the Armed Forces. During the year railroads carried more than 10 million troops in special trains and special cars. In addition to these organized movements, railroads last year transported millions of men traveling under orders in smaller groups. More millions of soldiers and sailors traveled singly on furloughs or weekend passes.

During 1943, the railroads handled nearly 83 million tons of Army freight and express, almost 4½ times as much as they moved during the entire period of WWI. But traffic increases alone do not measure the remarkable job that railroad management and men are doing. It involves also the question of available equipment.

Currently, the railroads are handling more than twice the freight traffic and nearly four times the passenger traffic of 1939, and doing it with very little more equipment than they had then.

In fact, the total locomotive ownership on October 1, 1943 was 871 locomotives less than it was on the same date in 1939. However, fine planning and hard work resulted in a reduction in the number of unserviceable units so that there were 5,178 more locomotives available for duty on October 1, 1943 than on the same date four years earlier.

Similarly, although total freight car ownership increased only 6.3% during this four-year period, the actual number of serviceable cars increased by 17.2%. More intensive use has been made of available locomotives and cars. The average daily movement of both freight and passenger locomotives in 1943 was the highest on record. Freight cars carried higher average loads and the average of passengers per car was the highest in history.

Cooperation between railroads and shippers has resulted in less idle time at the loading platform, which means more useful work out on the line.

To handle today's traffic the railroads are operating about 24,000 freight trains and 17,500 passenger trains per day. In other words, every time your watch ticks off two seconds, a train starts on its run somewhere in the U.S. This means that both men and equipment must give their best efforts, twenty-four hours a day.

In any consideration of the future of the railroads, one fact is basic. The U.S. is a mass production nation, and there can be no mass production without mass transportation—and mass transportation in America means transportation in trains on tracks. The only vehicle yet devised by man which combines the economy of mass movement with the flexibility of the separately and individually loaded and unloaded car, is the railroad train. *Baldwin magazine, Second Quarter 1944*

Western roads such as the Western Pacific were put to the wartime task of moving freight quickly over the mountains. Here four FTs with a combined 5,400 horsepower, built by EMD in 1944, growl through the Feather River Canyon in California. *Jay Williams collection*

(Continued from page 126)

into the war, the winter of 1941-42 brought the threat of serious congestion at a number of large ports. This was notably true at New York, Philadelphia and San Francisco.

Among the contributing causes was the unusual volume of freight for export, the detention of some Lend-Lease shipments at the ports pending a decision as to whether the supplies would be needed by the U. S. Army, the redistribution of shipping to meet new requirements, and the temporary withdrawal of vessels from service for arming and degaussing.

The Port of San Francisco was affected immediately. It was called upon to handle the bulk of shipments to the Pacific by both the Army and the Navy, and the rail facilities were inadequate for the load.

In an attempt to relieve New York of part of its heavy export traffic load, it was decided to utilize the Port of Philadelphia more. Due primarily to the uncontrolled movement of Lend-Lease freight into Philadelphia, and the failure of ships to become available as promptly as had been anticipated, congestion developed. The backlog of freight held in cars, on the docks, and in storage became so great that it handicapped operations.

The system eventually established embraced a dual control, exercised through the issuance of block releases and unit permits. The block releases were issued by a Transportation Control Committee, consisting of representatives of the Army, Navy, Office of Defense Transportation, War Shipping Administration and British Ministry of War Transport. The committee met daily in the Office of the Chief of Transportation, and its executive and staff were appointed by him.

The railroads, through the Port Traffic Office of the AAR, provided helpful analyses of carloads actually at the ports. The authority to control traffic was exercised not only to hold and divert shipments, but also to expedite those which were needed at the ports to complete ships then loading or to meet new military or Lend-Lease priorities.

Ceilings were established for each port, representing the maximum number of cars of export freight which could be held under load in the respective port areas without interference with operations.

Data prepared by the AAR indicates that between 1940 and the early months of 1945, the average number of carloads of export freight (excluding coal, grain and bulk liquids) unloaded daily at Atlantic Coast ports increased from 1,300 to 3,410, while at Pacific Coast ports the daily average increased from 203 to 1,847 carloads.

TRANSIT STORAGE OPERATIONS

The judicious utilization of transit storage was an important factor in the control of port-bound traffic. The facilities to handle this were two kinds—holding and reconsignment points (HARPS) and railroad open storage yards. In planning them, the basic idea was that there should always be covered and open storage space a short distance back from the ports, where supplies destined overseas could be held temporarily until the ports were ready to receive them.

This arrangement relieved the ports holding cargoes indefinitely, pending the availability of shipping. This procedure place a varied store of supplies near the ports, which could be called forward and received within 24 hours, if an emergency should arise. It also provided a convenient place for assembly of component parts and related items which could move overseas simultaneously.

The advantages of such facilities were recognized by the War Department early in 1941 when the scarcity of shipping began to be felt. Following the passage of the Lend-Lease Act in March 1941, and the establishment of a large program of Lend-Lease shipments to the United Kingdom, the matter was considered urgent. The first step, taken in May, was the leasing of an industrial plant at Shamokin, Pennsylvania for conversion into an in-transit depot. This plant was soon wholly inadequate in size, and not favorably located from the standpoint of rail connections with the Eastern seaboard.

Accordingly, in July two entirely new facilities were built, one at Voorheesville, New York, on the New York Central System, and another at Marietta, Pennsylvania, on the Pennsylvania Railroad. The original concept was that each should have about a million square feet of closed storage

Transit Journal, April 1942

space and about 2 million square feet of open storage space. To provide for expansion, if it became necessary, sites of at least 500 acres were sought.

During the autumn of 1941, with Russia receiving Lend-Lease supplies and the danger of trouble in the Pacific steadily growing, recommendations were prepared for the construction of six additional holding and reconsignment points, one to back up the southern Atlantic ports, two the Gulf ports, and three the Pacific ports. Promptly following the attack on Pearl Harbor, this program was approved. All were to have the same storage space as Marietta and Voorheesville, except one in the South, which was to be half the size. In the spring of 1942 an additional installation in New York State was approved, and in the summer of 1943, another was authorized in the State of Washington, making 10 in all.

Location of Installation	Closed storage space (sq. ft.)	Open storage space (sq. ft.)	Acreage of site
Voorheesville, NY	1,037,000	9,255,000	692
Elmira, NY	1,499,000	6,029,000	677
Marietta, PA	1,440,000	5,662,000	506
Richmond, VA	1,037,000	3,861,000	305
Montgomery, AL	1,042,000	4,025,000	865
Shreveport, LA	520,000	1,517,000	371
Yermo, CA	1,031,000	2,397,000	2,031
Lathrop, CA	1,522,000	4,677,000	720
Pasco, WA	1,038,000	3,871,000	745
Auburn, WA	1,498,000	1,500,000	598
Total	11,664,000	42,794,000	7,510

These were the holding and reconsignment points under control of the Chief of Transportation in January, 1944. Open space at the Voorheesville Holding and Reconsignment Point included 1,424,000 square feet of space located at Ravena, New York, which was leased and operated by the Point. After deducting space not available for actual storage, the total net usable space at the 10 holding and reconsignment points was 8,127,000 square feet closed, and 20,857,000 square feet open.

Some shipments had been sent to open storage at Marietta prior to entry of the U.S. into the war, and Voorheesville received its first freight in the early days of January 1942. The accumulation of cargo at the Eastern ports necessitated use of these in-transit storage facilities as rapidly as their space became available.

In January of 1944, with the last of the points nearing completion, total closed storage space was 11,664,000 square feet gross, and total open storage space was 42,794,000 square feet gross. Both closed and open capacities were increased at certain points beyond the original plans. The warehouses were single-story, approximately 180 feet by 960 feet.

When holding and reconsignment points were being planned, the Lend-Lease Administration agreed to share the expense, but wanted the installations to be operated solely by the War Department. For several months after freight began arriving at Marietta and Voorheesville, operations were under the general supervision of the Supply Branch of G-4, and technical supervision was given by the Depot Division of the Office of The Quartermaster General. It was argued, however, that since the function of the holding and reconsignment points was directly related to transportation, they should be operated by the transportation agency of the War Department. This view prevailed, and when a Chief of Transportation position was created in March of 1942, commanders of the points were made responsible to him. He promptly established a Transit Storage Division in his office to supervise this activity.

A fairly typical analysis of space occupancy at the holding and reconsignment points during latter stages of the war was made as December 27, 1944. On that date the Government procuring agencies had 30,566 carloads of freight in storage, which represented 41% of the available working space; there were advance bookings for 10,041 additional carloads, equaling 13% of the space; and 46% of the space which was unoccupied and uncommitted represented storage for 34,332 carloads. The Transportation Corps had the unusually large amount of 10,547 carloads on hand, mostly at Eastern points where it was being held pending shipment to the European Theater of Operations.

Agency	Carloads in closed storage	Carloads in open storage	Total carloads	Percent of total
Corps of Engineers	876	789	1,665	5.4
Quartermaster Corps	1,168	166	1,334	4.4
Signal Corps	174	96	270	.9
Medical Corps	790	35	825	2.7
Chemical Warfare Service	153	55	208	.7
Ordnance Department	1,149	2,336	3,485	11.4
Transportation Corps	2,000	8,547	10,547	34.5
Treasury Department	4,303	3,073	7,376	24.1
War Food Administration	347	-----	347	1.1
Miscellaneous	522	3,987	4,509	14.8
Total	11,482	19,084	30,566	100.0

Freight on hand at the 10 holding and reconsignment points on December 27, 1944, classified according to procuring agencies.

The Office of the Chief of Transportation saw to it that the best warehousing techniques were employed, and that both personnel and equipment were efficiently utilized at the holding and reconsignment points. Between October 1943 and July 1945 the average tons handled per man-day by the freight handlers increased from 10.5 to 20.7, and the average tons handled per man-day by the storage division increased from 6.0 to 11.2.

Since sites for the holding and reconsignment points were chosen with a view to avoiding congested areas, so that traffic in and out always could move freely, they were located near small communities and in some cases in isolated areas. This necessitated supplying Government housing at certain points for civil service labor. At five installations contract labor was utilized. The price per ton basis enabled the contractor to import workers from more advantageous labor markets. By careful supervision of operations, and close study of terms when the contracts came up for renewal, efficient and low-cost service was obtained.

In the beginning, each procuring agency that utilized the holding and reconsignment points had representatives stationed there to supervise handling of its supplies. This resulted in a lack of uniformity in methods of operation, and the attempt to maintain detailed property accountability slowed the handling of traffic, and in 1943 this system was discontinued. All such personnel then became responsible directly to Transportation Corps officers in command of the installations and accountability was placed on a simple carload basis. The results were greater orderliness in the functioning of the installations and a saving of manpower.

Aside from serving as reservoirs for regulating the day-to-day flow of freight to the ports, the holding and reconsignment points were utilized to protect the ports on many special occasions.

In April 1944, for example, because the number of ships assigned to load supplies for the European Theater of Operations had been reduced temporarily, 1,500 carloads of supplies which had been released for shipment to the ports were sent to holding and reconsignment points.

In October 1944, when the backlog of ships awaiting discharge in the European Theater necessitated a reduction of loadings at U.S. ports, more than 1,000 carloads of freight

were ordered into holding and reconsignment points. In April 1945, in anticipation of the collapse of Germany, action on requisitions for certain supplies was suspended by the theater, and about 600 carloads were sent to holding and reconsignment points to await disposition.

During 1944 and 1945, more than 5,000 carloads of Army freight alone were shipped back from Atlantic Coast ports to holding and reconsignment points, or diverted en route, at the request of Army port commanders.

RAILROAD OPEN STORAGE YARDS

The railroad open storage yards served the same general purpose as the holding and reconsignment points, and supplemented those installations. However, they were owned by the railroads, and operated by them under contract with the Army. These were excess or antiquated railyards, most of which were in remote locations. This made them secure from pilferage and spying eyes. The allocation of space was controlled by the Office of the Chief of Transportation, and it was responsible also for inspection of the yards to determine that proper operating techniques were being employed and adequate guarding and fire protection provided.

There were 48 such yards at the disposal of the Army, all but one of them situated east of the Mississippi River. At no time were all of them in active status, the number varying according to requirements, but usually being above 40.

The Transit Storage Division in the Office of the Chief of Transportation was responsible for technical supervision of the operation of the holding and reconsignment points and the railroad open storage yards, and controlled the utilization of the storage space. Part of the responsibility for supervision was delegated to Zone Transportation officers in whose territories the installations were located.

From the beginning of operation to V-J Day, holding and reconsignment points received and stored approximately 300,000 carloads of Army and Lend-Lease supplies. Dur-

ing the same period the railroads' open storage yards received and stored approximately 100,000 carloads.

UTILITY RAILROADS

From November 1942, the Transportation Corps was responsible for the design, procurement and assignment of railway equipment required by utility railways at Army posts and camps in the zone of interior. Such railways were in operation at 365 installations on June 30, 1945, and the following Army-owned equipment was assigned to them:

Locomotives	1,476 units
Auto railers	85 units
Locomotive cranes	322 units
Cars of all types	8,274 units
Maintenance-of-way	759 units
Total	**10,916 units**

The Transportation Corps was responsible also for the operation and maintenance of utility railway equipment, except where it was assigned to installations pertaining exclusively to another service. In the latter case, general supervision was given, and the Transportation Corps' trainmasters and master mechanics rendered technical service upon request. Checks were made to ascertain whether the equipment was being efficiently employed and effectively maintained. Shortcomings were analyzed and remedial measures prescribed. Methods of reducing crews were developed, with a resulting conservation of labor. Where assigned equipment was in excess of needs, transfers were made. These activities were carried on under the direct control of Zone

This float, built and operated by the Toronto Transportation Commission, tours Toronto streets to aid the sale of "Victory" bonds by the Canadian government. *Transit Journal, April 1942*

Transportation officers, and under the general direction of the Rail Division in the Office of the Chief of Transportation.

The Army's railroad repair shops were operated by the Transportation Corps after May 1, 1944. Prior to that the shops were operated by the commanders of the installations which they were attached. Initially the Transportation Corps assumed control of three such shops—at Holabird, Maryland (operated by the Holabird Quartermaster Depot); Ogden Arsenal, Utah; and Ft. Benning, Georgia. On June 1, 1944 a shop of the New York Central Railroad at Bucyrus, Ohio, which had been used as a training facility for military railway troops under control of the Fifth Service Command, was transferred to the Transportation Corps for use as a railroad repair shop, and also for training purposes.

The Transportation Corps decided whether repairs, not performable at the installations to which the equipment was

In 1944, the Norfolk & Western Railway operated a strategic war route between Cincinnati and the port at Norfolk, Virginia.

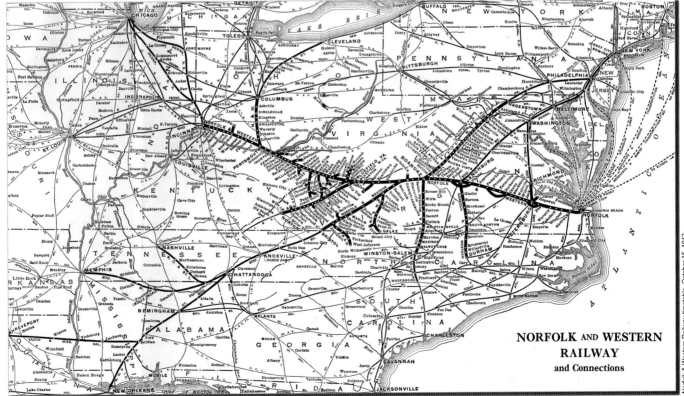

NORFOLK AND WESTERN RAILWAY and Connections

Norfolk & Western Railway timetable, October 15, 1942

assigned, should be obtained commercially or be effected at one of its own repair shops. The Transportation Corps shops peformed 239 repair jobs during the 12 months ending June 30, 1945.

TRACKAGE LAYOUT

The layout of trackage at Army installations, and the establishment of switching connections with common carrier lines, was given careful supervision by Transportation Corps technicians. Unfortunately, the larger part of the Army's new installations had been completed, or at least placed under construction, before the Transportation Corps came into existence. In those early days of the emergency, sites sometimes were chosen and trackage laid without due consideration of operating efficiency and economy. This oversight was attributed in part to the haste with which the projects were planned, but it also

was due in part to the absence of a permanent Transportation Corps to which other elements of the Army might have turned for advice in such matters.

The 320 hospital ward cars and 60 hospital kitchen cars which the War Department owned and operated in the zone of interior, were not strictly speaking, utility railway equipment. The Rail Division of the Office of the Chief of Transportation collaborated with the Office of The Surgeon General in the design of this equipment. The cars were assigned to the Service Commands in which were located the ports where sick and wounded soldiers from overseas were landed. The Service Commands had primary responsibility for their operation and maintenance. However, the Rail Division exercised technical supervision over their maintenance as railway rolling stock, and represented the War Department in all operating arrangements made with the Association of American Railroads.

At the end of the war, the Army owned approximately 4,000 tank cars which it employed for the transportation of petroleum products to installations where large quantities of gasoline and oil were used, and other liquids to ordnance and chemical manufacturing plants.

The Army undertook ownership of these cars because most of the equipment was not owned by the common carrier railroads, but by private concerns. Maintenance and repairs were subcontracted to various commercial companies. Their operation was under the management of the Traffic Control Division of the Office of the Chief of Transportation.

In 1942 young boys view the spectacle of a Santa Fe military train loaded with tanks carded for Ft. Erwin, California Desert Training Center. These young men will be in uniform soon themselves. *Mallory Hope Ferrell collection*

AUG. 4, 1944

Following his father's death in 1923, industrialist Harry Darby of Kansas City obtained a bank loan to buy his father's boiler firm to found Darby Steel Company which grew to be one of the largest steel plate manufacturing firms in the country. During WWII the corporation built war materiel, including bombs and amphibious landing craft. At one stage during the war, these were launched on the Kaw River at the rate of one per day. The company eventually floated 1,400 landing craft downriver to New Orleans for shipment overseas. The Darby Corporation became a major wartime producer of locomotives and 1,000-pound (450 kg) bombs. The Darby-built troop landing craft known as LCTs and LCMs were used in the invasions of Italy, occupied France and the Pacific Islands. The accompanying photos show Darby-built products on flatcars, and locomotive boilers being constructed in Darby shops. *Photos, Don Heimburger collection*

Indians on our Warpath

When the first transcontinental railroad tracks were under construction Indian raiders were a constant threat to workmen on the right of way.

But descendants of these first Americans today make common cause with all Americans. Indians are serving in the armed forces, buying war bonds —and helping to keep the war trains rolling!

As our locomotives come whistling around Kintner curve east of Yuma—and at other points along Southern Pacific lines in Arizona—bands of husky Indian braves wave greetings from beside the tracks.

Navajos, Hopis, Pimas and Apaches are working on our right of way—the railroad's warpath. These patriotic Redmen came from the reservations and from scattered hogans in answer to our wartime call for extra manpower.

Garbed in purple and scarlet shirts, wearing bright headbands, the Indians form America's most colorful and unique section gangs. Under the brilliant Arizona desert sky they swing picks and tamp ballast with the grace and endurance for which the Indian is famed.

During this wartime emergency Americans of varied backgrounds and skills have rallied to the railroad's aid. People know the trains must run, and they see that we are handicapped by shortage of help—that we badly need more workers, both men and women. In many communities all along our 15,000 miles of line,

Southern Pacific is the main war industry . . . often the only local industry directly engaged in war work.

So throughout the West and South, thousands who never did railroad work before have come to help out in our offices and machine shops, on our trains and in our yards. Women have stepped into hundreds of S.P. jobs formerly handled by men. Without this fine cooperation from the folks along our lines we could hardly hope to carry our war load successfully.

From New Orleans in the deep South, from the Pacific Northwest . . . from Chicago and the Midwest . . . S.P. lines converge at West Coast ports. To these "take off" points we haul a big share of all the troops and supplies needed for the war against Japan.

No railroad in the nation is more strategically situated to help win the war than our own.

And in the postwar world, when good railroad service will also be vital, we will be a stronger railroad. Stronger in facilities, and able to provide better transportation. *Stronger, too, in friendships gained through public understanding of our problems now.*

S·P
The friendly
Southern Pacific

One of America's railroads—ALL united for Victory!

Trains, July 1944

C. & E. I. has 184 Acres
of 'Victory Gardens'

A total of 184 acres of land on the right-of-way of the Chicago & Eastern Illinois has been planted for "victory gardens." The railroad has made unused land on its right-of-way available to employees and others who wish to turn the ground into useful production. Most of the land being worked is planted as truck gardens, although quite a few acres have been planted in corn. *Railway Age, 1942*

SEALED LIPS for VICTORY

Because railroad people are at the very center of the war effort—moving the armed forces and what they train and fight with; and

Because a casual remark might prove of benefit to enemy ears, B & O's 70,000 men and women are cautioned not to talk about their work to anyone—*even at home.*

With a smile for all—but gossip for none—these patriotic workers are supporting fully our country's drive to victory.

Battle Stations

America is at battle stations all over the world—in North Africa, in the South Pacific, in Northern Europe, in Burma and India, on the islands, on the sea, in the air.

And railroad trains are at battle stations right here at home—wherever one loads troops, or picks up raw materials, or hauls the finished goods of war, or does any one of a thousand necessary wartime tasks.

Railroad men and railroad trains are working harder today than ever before—carrying one - and - a - half times the tonnage of freight and more than double the volume of military passenger travel they carried in the first World War.

For America, waging war on the gigantic scale that spells eventual victory, depends now more than ever upon the mass transportation service of its railroads.

AMERICAN RAILROADS
ASSOCIATION OF
ALL UNITED FOR VICTORY

Listen to your conscience
before you take the train

A furlough is not much good to a soldier unless he can visit home. And vital war business may be delayed if war plant experts can't get on the train. All trains are full, so please don't make *unnecessary* trips. Before you plan a train trip, listen to your conscience!

S·P The friendly Southern Pacific

Advance reservations required for S. P. coach space

7-8-4—2 col. x 84 lines—Newspapers—August, 1943
7—50%   8—50%
FOOTE, CONE & BELDING

Victory speeds out of the night
ROCK ISLAND LINES
KEEP BUYING WAR BONDS

We Americans are embarked on our fourth year of war. Many victories are behind us; more are yet to be won.

As we look back, our railroads—with less equipment than in 1918—have achieved the greatest transportation job in history. We at the Illinois Central take pride in having done our share.

Now, we must carry forward into another year. Until final Victory comes, moving reinforcements to the battlefronts will continue to be the main concern of 42,000 Illinois Central war workers.

But working hard for Victory is also preparing us for peace. War has taught us much. Its necessities have mothered thousands of improvements. Since Pearl Harbor, alert Illinois Central workers have offered 72,210 suggestions for bettering our operations, and 12,910 have been adopted.

War has taught us closer co-operation, too. Today, more than ever, the Illinois Central is a family *united* along 6,600 miles of railroad in fourteen states.

When V-Day comes, all we have learned will be turned to account in improving Illinois Central service. When peace gives us the go-ahead—the "highball" in railroad language—we will be ready. We want to *keep on* earning your good will!

PRESIDENT

ILLINOIS CENTRAL SYSTEM

Calling All Railroaders!
By The Trackwalker

You all know me. I've spent most of my life patrolling the roadbed. The other morning you saw me picking cinders out of my brogans down by the switchman's shanty. Later you found me upstairs in an office, peeking at train sheets and listening to dispatchers' lingo. Maybe, next day, you wondered why I was hanging around a freight yard instead of counting ties on the main line. Well—it's no secret. This old trackwalker has a new job, and it's a honey! I'm looking for the inside stories about American railroaders at war.

You've heard how America's 250,000-mile railroad system is thundering day and night, making the mightiest transportation effort of all time? You've heard how 6,500,000 boys in service khaki have been shuttled back and forth across the continent by our railroads? And how 1,000,000 tons of war and civilian materiels are rolling over our steel rails every minute of every hour? Mister, those are tremendous facts and figures—but they don't tell the real story of railroading. It's something like seeing train smoke rising from behind a hill. You know that a locomotive is pulling a string of cars—but you can't see the engine, the cars, or the trainmen who keep their train moving.

The real story of American railroading is about fellows like you. More than 1,000,000 hard-working, quick-thinking, well-seasoned railroaders, doing your duty as daily "routine"—but performing miracles in transportation.

MY NEW JOB

So my new job is to patrol all the American railroads, getting smoke in my eyes, the smell of hot oil in my nose, the hiss of steam in my ears, and grease on my clothes. From men on the main line and sidetracks, at whistle stops, back shops and supers' desks, in signal towers and roundhouses I'm picking up your stories about what railroading really means to America. These stories will surprise some of you—but all of them will make all of you proud of the men and women who have made ours the world's greatest transportation system.

I've got the "all clear" signal, and you'll see stories about you and your fellow railroaders each month on this page. Slow down here next month and I'll tell you an inside story of how American railroaders are using their railroadin' experience to speed the defeat of the Axis. *Railway Purchases and Stores, November, 1942*

A refrigerator block rounds Cajon Pass in California on the veteran Santa Fe Railroad. Commercial and military goods were kept moving throughout the system during WWII so as not to choke yards and main lines. *Mallory Hope Ferrell collection*

CHICAGO'S PROVISO YARD
SPEEDS WAR-SWOLLEN FREIGHT

Wartime freight meant big-time railroading. The Chicago & NorthWestern's huge 1,250-acre classification yard 13 miles west of downtown Chicago was once the biggest and busiest railroad yard in the world.

Chicago & NorthWestern's 260 miles of classification yard handled 15,000 freight cars daily. *Photos by Jack Delano, courtesy Chicago & NorthWestern Railway Historical Society and Joe Piersen*

Smoke spirals upwards as a loaded wartime train departs busy Proviso Yard near Chicago on a cold winter day.

Carmen, like the one shown in the foreground, got their exercise at Proviso, hoping in and around and between trains. Track capacity at the yard was 26,000 cars. Note the bus on a flatcar in the middle right of the picture.

141

Wood-roof boxcars and stock cars crowd the yard carrying food, lumber, perishables, livestock and more to keep the U.S. not only in the war but ahead of the game. Proviso featured two fully-equipped repair yards.

Overview of yard with military vehicles on flatcars was a common site during the war years at Proviso Yard near Chicago.

ABOVE. Overall view of Proviso Yard which contained 260 miles of track. The 59-track hump yard and tower is at the western edge of the yard. Proviso was opened on October 1, 1927 and included a modern icing plant for perishable freight and even a passenger station next to the yard office building. Direct rail connections at the yard were with the B&O Chicago Terminal, Belt Railway of Chicago and the Indiana Harbor Belt Railroad.

LEFT. Amphibious landing craft called "Ducks" take a ride on a freight rolling through Proviso on their way to a port of embarkation and then on a ship for overseas duty. Proviso saw lots of military activity during 1941-1945.

This was the locomotive servicing tracks for Proviso Yard in 1944, with the coaling station in the background and facilities for handling sand and cinders at right. The yard was built at a cost of $16 million and included a transfer house for less-than-carload freight that had a capacity of 700 cars a day.

A number of C&NW Proviso Yard office employees hop motorized carts and wagons for a publicity photograph during the war.

Proviso Yard

"With the tremendous growth of Chicago and its importance as a transportation center and railroad terminus there came the necessity of greater transfer and interchange facilities not only for present needs but to take care of future growth, and in full realization of the situation, this vast project was conceived by this company."
Chicago & North Western Railway, 1927

The Santa Fe *Chief*, powered by gargantuan 4-8-4 Northern #3777, leaves Las Vegas with its wartime headlight visor applied. A mix of clerestory but mostly streamlined passenger cars is the order of the day. *Jay Williams collection*

Santa Fe 4-8-4 #3753 with a troop train in tow, powers its way along Western rails carrying soliders to their destination. Hundreds of troop trains ran over the Santa Fe, which stretched 13,050 miles throughout the United States from Chicago to Los Angeles and San Francisco, and as far south as Galveston, Texas. *Jay Williams collection*

OIL TRAINS SAVE THE DAY

With German U-boats prowling the waters off the coasts of the U.S., military officials thought it much safer to send their precious oil cargoes over land, rather than over water. Thus, railroads were asked to perform the vital work of oil transportation between refineries, storage depots and ports, thus averting a critical shortage of fuel in dangerous times. Again the railroads pulled their weight, transporting the critical commodity in a timely, safe and efficient manner.

ABOVE. A westbound New York Central empty oil train with muscular Lima-built (1930) A-1c #1445 in charge, rounds a long sweeping curve of high-poundage rail at Weston Park, Massachusetts west of Boston in October of 1942. *Jay Williams collection*

Missouri Pacific 2-8-2 #1514 with 10,000-gallon USRA-style water tender gallops along with oil tankers in its 65-car consist at Wagoner, Oklahoma on September 26, 1944. Another train is at left "in the hole." *Robert F. Collins, Louis Marre collection*

NEXT PAGE, TOP. A Nickel Plate Road S-1 2-8-4 #718, laden with oil tankers filled with crucial wartime petroleum, travels westbound arriving Frankfort, Indiana from Lima, Ohio on July 4, 1944. *R.A. LeMassena, Jay Williams collection*

NEXT PAGE, LOWER. Frisco's oil-fired 4-8-4 #4500 with six-wheel tender and "Meteor" inscribed in script on the tender as well, corrals a long string of 76 oil cars westbound through Nichols, Missouri. This second Train #33 also sports a white stripe on the boiler domes. *Louis Marre collection*

New Haven #1105 pushes its steel frame, with dozens of oil cars as added weight, against the cold atmosphere of a winter's day. Oil trains were a vital supply line in the war effort, and kept oil tankers off the waters near U. S. coasts, thus insuring safe arrival of this precious commodity. *Jay Williams collection*

With 44 cars southbound on September 26, 1944, a Kansas, Oklahoma & Gulf Railway (for freight service only, 328 miles) train carries a good number of oil tankers behind 2-10-0 #110 at Wagoner, Oklahoma. *Robert F. Collins, Louis Marre collection*

Paul Stringham captured this eastbound oil train with NKP 2-8-2 #615 in charge rolling through Deer Creek, Illinois on October 27, 1942. To reach Chicago proper, the NKP had eight miles of trackage rights over the New York Central. *Jay Williams collection*

Big, sleek 4-8-2 Wabash Mountain #2804 takes a spirited spring outing at Wabash, Indiana on April 3, 1942 with oil tankers destined for supplying the war's military machines. The Wabash Railroad turned in a fine performance during the war, then set about to modernize its motive power in 1946 with its first diesel road units. *M.D. McCarter, collection of Don Heimburger*

A Nickel Plate Road ex-Wheeling & Lake Erie offset-cupola caboose brings up the rear of a westbound oil train between Fostoria and Arcadia, Ohio in 1943. Railroads shipped wartime oil to protect it better than ships, which were vulnerable to torpedo attacks. *William Rittase, Jay Williams collection*

Long New York Central oil freight clips along with H-10a 2-8-2 #2240 at a good pace on well maintained and ballasted main line trackage on the Belt Line at Brooklyn, Ohio in June of 1945. The war was fast coming to an end. *Jay Williams collection*

Oil Transportation Breaking All Records

The flow of oil from the Southwestern fields to the Eastern seaboard in solid trainlots of from 50 to 60 cars per train increased during the week of August 21 to include more than 75 percent of the 4,000 tank cars loaded daily for Eastern consumption, the Office of Defense Transportation announced recently. A week previous, ODT officials estimated that two-thirds of the eastbound oil had been gathered into the train-lot movement.

This increase was considered an important factor by ODT in the record-breaking delivery to the Eastern seaboard of 830,820 barrels of oil daily during the week ending August 15.

Reports from ODT field representatives in District No. 3 (the oil field area) say that in the week of August 21 eight additional trains daily were launched from the producing fields. *Railway Purchases and Stores, September, 1942*

World's Greatest ASSEMBLY LINE

Railroads provide a 236,000-mile assembly line which runs day and night . . . never stops.

It conveys a million barrels of oil a day. It picks up coal and ore from the mine, food and fibre from the farm, wood from the forest. It carries all these raw stuffs through countless stages of processing, parts-making and assembly, until finished war goods are delivered to the millions of men in our camps, and to ships waiting to carry the vital weapons of victory to our fighting forces around the world.

AMERICAN RAILROADS ★ All United for Victory

Oil Loadings Hit Another New High

Carriers transport 525,697 barrels
to the Atlantic seaboard area

Daily tank car movements of petroleum and petroleum products to the East Coast reached another new high of 525,697 barrels during the week ended April 4, according to an announcement from Petroleum Coordinator Harold L. Ickes. This is the fifth consecutive week that a new high has been established. The previous record of 506,025 barrels per day was established in the week ended March 28.

At the same time the Coordinator made public a report showing that rail shipments of oil and its products from California into Oregon and Washington increased 20% during the week of April 4. The seven oil companies participating in the northwest movement, which is being developed as a substitute for tanker transportation, reported loading a total of 504 cars during the week, compared with 422 cars in the week ended March 28. In terms of oil, declared Ickes, this represents an average daily movement of 16,200 barrels for the week of April 4.

Figuring the time required for cars to return to California after unloading, it is estimated that 1,150 tank cars are now engaged in the Pacific Northwest service.

In moving 525,697 barrels each day into the East, 19 oil companies reporting loading a total of 16,355 cars. Including cars which were on the way back west for reloading, this means that approximately 39,000 tank cars are now engaged in the East Coast service.

At the same time Ickes announced the additional curtailment of East Coast and Pacific Northwest gasoline deliveries, effective April 16, as a step toward meeting the supply deficiency foreseen for the balance of the year. The order will bring the total curtailment to $33\frac{1}{3}$% of the calculated normal consumption. The terms are embodied in an amendment to the War Production Board's previous order, which cut deliveries by 20%. *Railway Age, April 18, 1942*

New York Central 2-8-2 #2124 makes time with an oil consist at Bond, Illinois in April of 1943. Oil companies participated in striving to increase capacity of output and loadings of oil tank trains. *Jay Williams collection*

This United States Army 10,000-gallon petroleum 56½"-gage tank car USAX was used in domestic service. *Don Heimburger collection*

At the New York Central's Paris, Illinois rip track in 1942, Ed Novak shot this photograph of carmen repairing oil tankers so they could be placed back into wartime service quickly—every car was needed for the important, essential task at hand. *Jay Williams collection*

"Come down, Daniel Webster, and tell about the Railroads!"

"Here's an eloquent victory, Dan'l, that deserves your golden words:

"Tell them how the railroads move raw-stuffs by hundred-ton loads to war-plants . . . how our war-weapons reach destinations *on time,* meeting the men who will be using them, men who are carried by the trains—full—first-class, complete with hot shaving-water and smiling porters.

"Tell them, Daniel Webster, how railroads transport food for our nation and a large part of the world . . . how they kept oil flowing to the East Coast after U-Boats stopped our tankers.

"Tell them how—whatever the weather—the trains come through."

As a working teammate of the railroads, General American Transportation is helping maintain their amazing efficiency. Tank, refrigerator, milk and stock cars are all part of the General American fleet, speeding materiel for war and essentials for "home-folks."

GATX GENERAL AMERICAN

A SYMBOL OF INTEGRITY FOR OVER 40 YEARS

GENERAL AMERICAN TRANSPORTATION
CORPORATION
Chicago
BUILDERS AND SUPPLIERS OF RAILROAD FREIGHT CARS

Chris Burritt

This view shows the New York Central's Mt. Carmel, Illinois yard with a loaded oil train heading north en route east while a train of empties waits to pull out for Norris City behind an H-7E 2-8-2 type. The engine in the foreground is an 0-8-0 type Class U-7E. *Courtesy New York Central Railroad*

"Out of your range, Nazi!"

When Hitler's packs of undersea wolves struck at domestic shipping along our shores, he forgot about the American railroads—and thereby started driving more spikes into his coffin.

When Axis submarines struck, the Nation's railroads were called upon to move the major part of the oil supply for the East from Southwestern producing centers; to bring Pacific Coast lumber and the bulk of Pacific Coast canned goods to the East; to more than double the all-rail movement of bituminous coal from Southern Appalachian fields into New England; and to transport many other unexpected and unaccustomed loads. Result: today, the greater part of coastwise and intercoastal traffic is being moved safely and efficiently by the all-rail route, and hundreds of vitally needed tankers and other ships have been diverted direct to war purposes.

The Norfolk and Western Railway is carrying its full share of that essential traffic which formerly moved by water. Here's just one example: during the first ten months of 1942, this railroad moved over its Shenandoah Valley line—Roanoke, Va., to Hagerstown, Md.—approximately 2,700,000 tons of bituminous coal consigned to Northern and New England States—2,700,000 tons of coal diverted from the Port of Norfolk and the water route to N. & W. rails—rails that are "out of your range—Nazi!"

FOR VICTORY
BUY UNITED STATES WAR BONDS AND STAMPS

Norfolk and Western Railway

Norfolk & Western timetable, December 6, 1942

Joe figures he's *still* in the fight

Joe was an Illinois Central fireman before he put on a G. I. helmet and waded ashore on a foreign beach. That's where he picked up the reason for the medical discharge that brought him back to us.

Joe didn't want to be shipped home. He wanted to stay with his outfit. But now that he's back on the job as a fireman again, he feels better about it. Particularly when he looks back over a long string of oil cars. Because Joe has seen oil in action. He knows what it—and other war freight—means to men at the front.

That's why Joe figures he's still in the fight. Next

to shooting a gun, he can't think of any job more important than the one he's doing.

Joe has figured out something else, too. He understands that railroad work will be equally important when peace comes again . . . that railroad progress will make many opportunities for thousands of fine young men and women now serving Uncle Sam.

With the help of our people in the armed forces and our 43,000 other Illinois Central folks at home, one of these days the war will be won. Until then, our main concern is victory. After that, all we have learned during the war years will be turned to account in improving Illinois Central service. We want to *keep on* earning your good will.

J. L. Beven
PRESIDENT

Railroad jobs are war jobs. Men and women are needed in all branches of the service. Consult any Illinois Central representative or the Railroad Retirement Board.

Illinois Central magazine, October 1944

The War YOU are going to Win!

Faster "Turn Around" Will Turn The Tide!

Freight cars . . . particularly tank cars . . . are vital to Victory. They must be loaded, unloaded, kept moving with all possible speed. Delays may cost lives. Keep 'em rolling!

Take pride in those trains of tank cars thundering along the rails to the Nation's warworking factories. Your investment in War Savings Bonds, together with your patriotic "doing without," help fill those tank cars with the essentials needed by our armed forces.

Vitally-needed liquid commodities are rushed in tank cars to the Production Front—thence to the farflung Battle Front. The cargoes of these tank cars are an expression of your determination to "see the thing through."

The GATX Fleet of more than 55,000 specialized freight cars cooperates wholeheartedly with the railroads to make our National cooperation win through—to Victory.

GENERAL AMERICAN TRANSPORTATION
CORPORATION
Chicago
Builders and Suppliers of Railroad Freight Cars

Railroad Purchases and Stores

Santa Fe 4-8-2s #3726 and #3731 nearing Chicago pour on the coal as they double-head a manifest freight bringing war materiels to factories in the Windy City in 1945. *Gordon Glattenberg, Don Heimburger collection*

The North Platte Canteen

U.S. soldiers from all across America rolled through North Platte, Nebraska on troop or passenger trains during the war, enroute to stateside military bases or embarkation points for overseas duty in Europe or the Pacific.

As they traveled by train, some for long distances across the country, they were generally kept on the trains or required not to wander far when they did receive permission to leave the train. Canteens, or "food depots," organized mostly by local women volunteers, sprang up all over the country to offer food, conversation and a smile to soldiers as they made their journeys. Some of the women staffers had lost sons in the war, and they came to talk to the soldiers.

The most famous canteen, established on Christmas Day in 1941 at the Front Street Union Pacific depot, was in North Platte, Nebraska, a dusty 12,000-population town on the windswept plains of the Midwest. The canteen opened at 5 a.m. and closed after the last troop train left after midnight. By the end of the war, more than six million soldiers had passed through the North Platte canteen.

When the troop trains stopped, usually for only 10 minutes, "the people of North Platte made those ten minutes count," says Bob Greene, author of *Once Upon A Town*.

JACK DELANO'S
WAR CONTRIBUTION

Jack Delano worked for the Farm Security Administration (FSA), having graduated from the Pennsylvania Academy of Fine Arts where he studied between 1928 and 1932. At the Academy he won the Kesson Traveling Fellowship and then went to Europe, where he purchased a camera and became interested in photography. Delano applied for and received a $2,300-a-year job at the FSA, and during WWII was assigned to take photographs of the railroads in the U.S. His work has become very popular because of the clarity of his pictures, as well as his keen sense of picture arrangement. Delano, who was born in Russia in 1914, died in 1995. *Photos courtesy Chicago & North-Western Railway Historical Society and Joe Piersen*

Behind the Scenes
OF A
RAILROAD
AT WAR

New York Central

NEW YORK CENTRAL SYSTEM

AT WAR

During WWII, the New York Central issued this booklet, partially re-printed here, to show how it was fulfilling its duty by helping the nation move large quantities of goods and people.

Modern "MOHAWKS" on the Warpath

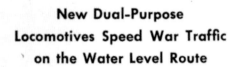

New Dual-Purpose Locomotives Speed War Traffic on the Water Level Route

THERE'S a full-throated roar from her stubby stack as "Mohawk 3112" swings into the straightaway with a string of troop-filled Pullmans in tow. There's an answering roar from her twin locomotive, eastbound with a mile-long train of war freight.

Two engines of a kind. Two of New York Central's versatile "Mohawks" . . . with their big, six-foot drivers . . . able to haul heavy freight on the Water Level Route or speed the 20th Century Limited through on schedule.

Made possible by this almost gradeless route, "Mohawks" are newest among Central's fleet of steam, electric and Diesel locomotives. And their adaptability to freight or passenger use means much to wartime efficiency on this vital east-west link in America's railroad supply line.

Thundering through valleys where Mohawk braves once fought, these "Mohawks" too are on the warpath. And even as they speed the Victory traffic . . . their efficient performance guides Central designers in planning the finer locomotives of tomorrow.

MODERN MOTIVE POWER
Latest New York Central locomotive weighs only 198½ tons. Yet develops 5,400 h.p. . . . ample for heavy freight on Water Level Route.

STOKER CONTROLS

LEVER OPENS FIREBOX DOORS

WHISTLE VALVE

TRACK PAN SUPPLIES WATER

AIR BRAKES

SIX-FOOT DRIVERS

POWER-OPERATED REVERSE GEAR

15,500-GALLON WATER TANK

NEW YORK CENTRAL

"GREEN OVER GREEN." The fireman shouts his readings of signals to the engineer as a double check. It's also part of his training as a future engineer.

EXPERT HAND ON THE THROTTLE. Though New York Central engineers average 20 years' experience, each must pass frequent tests for physical fitness and knowledge of train operating rules.

NO MORE SHOVELING. This automatic stoker feeds the fire at a twist of the fireman's wrist.

600 MILES ON A TENDERFUL. The "Mohawk" of today pulls a passenger train 600 miles on one tender of coal. It gets ⅓ more power per ton than engines of World War I.

AUTOMATIC TRAIN CONTROL. Electric control on right of tender would automatically stop the train if a caution or red signal were passed . . . one of many modern safety devices on every "Mohawk."

New York Central
One of America's Railroads All United for Victory

NEW YORK CENTRAL SYSTEM

LET YOUR DOLLARS FIGHT INFANTILE PARALYSIS

What life is like on a troop train...

speeding over the Water Level Route

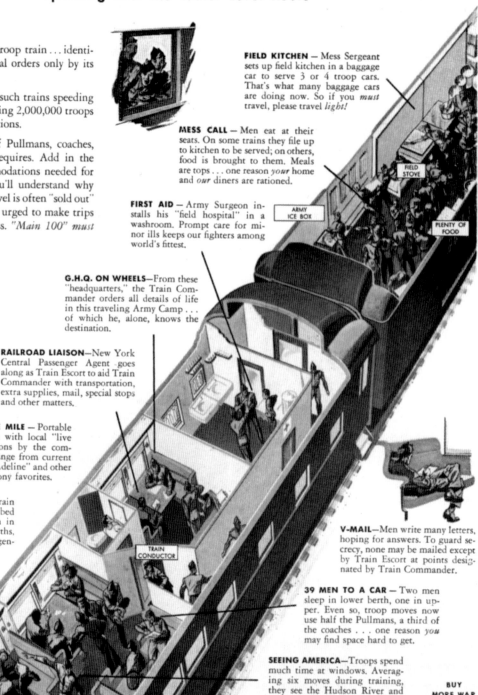

This is "Main 100"...a troop train...identified on New York Central orders only by its code number.

It's one of a vast fleet of such trains speeding over American rails, moving 2,000,000 troops a month to secret destinations.

Picture the thousands of Pullmans, coaches, baggage cars this task requires. Add in the large number of accommodations needed for fighters on furlough. You'll understand why train space for civilian travel is often "sold out" ... and why civilians are urged to make trips *only* on essential business. *"Main 100" must have the right of way.*

FIELD KITCHEN — Mess Sergeant sets up field kitchen in a baggage car to serve 3 or 4 troop cars. That's what many baggage cars are doing now. So if you *must* travel, please travel *light!*

MESS CALL — Men eat at their seats. On some trains they file up to kitchen to be served; on others, food is brought to them. Meals are tops...one reason *your* home and *our* diners are rationed.

FIRST AID — Army Surgeon installs his "field hospital" in a washroom. Prompt care for minor ills keeps our fighters among world's fittest.

G.H.Q. ON WHEELS—From these "headquarters," the Train Commander orders all details of life in this traveling Army Camp... of which he, alone, knows the destination.

RAILROAD LIAISON—New York Central Passenger Agent goes along as Train Escort to aid Train Commander with transportation, extra supplies, mail, special stops and other matters.

MUSIC BY THE MILE — Portable radios compete with local "live talent." Selections by the company quartet range from current hits to "Sweet Adeline" and other old close harmony favorites.

PREPARING FOR TAPS — Train Commander sets hour for bed (usually later en route than in camp). Porter makes up berths, as carefully as for the most generous Pullman passenger.

FIELD STOVE

ARMY ICE BOX

PLENTY OF FOOD

TRAIN CONDUCTOR

V-MAIL—Men write many letters, hoping for answers. To guard secrecy, none may be mailed except by Train Escort at points designated by Train Commander.

39 MEN TO A CAR — Two men sleep in lower berth, one in upper. Even so, troop moves now use half the Pullmans, a third of the coaches ... one reason *you* may find space hard to get.

SEEING AMERICA—Troops spend much time at windows. Averaging six moves during training, they see the Hudson River and Great Lakes this trip ... perhaps California next.

BUY MORE WAR BONDS

New York Central
ONE OF AMERICA'S RAILROADS—ALL UNITED FOR VICTORY

NEW YORK CENTRAL SYSTEM

Wartime Guide to Grand Central Terminal

STEP FROM the heart of New York into the cathedral-like beauty of Grand Central Terminal.

Here beneath this high, blue-vaulted ceiling now pass some 54,000,000 travelers a year. Boys on their way to war, watched to the train gates by bravely smiling parents. Workers journeying to war jobs in faraway cities. Business leaders speeding to win production battles.

Together they form part of the greatest traffic America's railroads have ever carried. A tremendous task, vital to Victory, and rich in promise for the future.

Out of this experience will be born the finer rail transport of tomorrow... when Grand Central Terminal will echo to the footsteps of a free, victorious people bound on swift errands of peace.

❶ 14,800 QUESTIONS AN HOUR
Terminal information men now answer as many as 14,800 questions an hour. To save holding up ticket lines, get information *in advance* at this booth or by telephone.

❷ GRAND CENTRAL SERVICE FLAG
Honors 21,314 New York Central employees. Thousands of other Central workers have sons and daughters in uniform... an added drive behind this railroad's war effort.

❸ TICKET OFFICE 90% BUSIER
Though we've added extra windows and personnel to meet the rush, war-wise travelers prefer to buy tickets at quieter mid-morning and early evening hours.

❹ SERVICE MEN'S LOUNGE
This lounge is busiest on weekends when thousands travel on furlough. To give them room on weekend trains, plan trips you *must* make for *mid-week*.

❺ 54,000,000 PASSENGERS A YEAR
Through these train gates pass a record number of essential passengers...including many thousands of former auto travelers who must now be carried by train.

❻ BAGGAGE CHECKING COUNTER
Some 150,000 pieces of baggage a month are now checked through Grand Central. People have learned to travel light, checking larger luggage, carrying only *one small grip* on crowded trains.

❼ MAIN WAITING ROOM
Here some traveler may have to wait for a later train if *you* fail to cancel an unwanted reservation promptly. These days, cancel reservations the *minute* your plans change.

❽ TROOPS ON THE MOVE
Half the nation's Pullmans and 30% of its coaches are busy moving 2,000,000 troops a month. One more reason railroads can't always provide the accommodations you want.

FREE WARTIME GUIDE TO GRAND CENTRAL
A fascinating booklet that takes you behind the scenes of the Terminal. Write Passenger Dept., Room 1261A, 466 Lexington Ave., New York, N. Y.

New York Central

ONE OF AMERICA'S RAILROADS—ALL UNITED FOR VICTORY
BUY MORE WAR BONDS AND STAMPS

161

Wartime Housekeeping on Wheels

How we serve 3,000,000 EXTRA meals a year on the Water Level Route

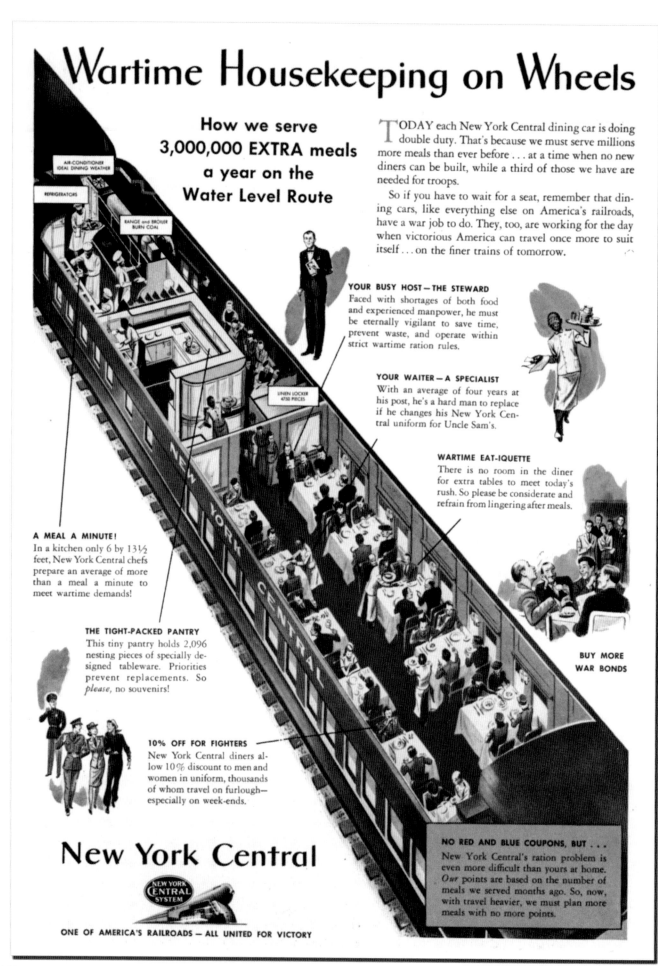

AIR-CONDITIONER IDEAL DINING WEATHER

REFRIGERATORS

RANGE and BROILER BURN COAL

LINEN LOCKER 4750 PIECES

TODAY each New York Central dining car is doing double duty. That's because we must serve millions more meals than ever before . . . at a time when no new diners can be built, while a third of those we have are needed for troops.

So if you have to wait for a seat, remember that dining cars, like everything else on America's railroads, have a war job to do. They, too, are working for the day when victorious America can travel once more to suit itself . . . on the finer trains of tomorrow.

YOUR BUSY HOST—THE STEWARD
Faced with shortages of both food and experienced manpower, he must be eternally vigilant to save time, prevent waste, and operate within strict wartime ration rules.

YOUR WAITER—A SPECIALIST
With an average of four years at his post, he's a hard man to replace if he changes his New York Central uniform for Uncle Sam's.

WARTIME EAT-IQUETTE
There is no room in the diner for extra tables to meet today's rush. So please be considerate and refrain from lingering after meals.

A MEAL A MINUTE!
In a kitchen only 6 by 13½ feet, New York Central chefs prepare an average of more than a meal a minute to meet wartime demands!

THE TIGHT-PACKED PANTRY
This tiny pantry holds 2,096 nesting pieces of specially designed tableware. Priorities prevent replacements. So *please*, no souvenirs!

BUY MORE WAR BONDS

10% OFF FOR FIGHTERS
New York Central diners allow 10% discount to men and women in uniform, thousands of whom travel on furlough—especially on week-ends.

New York Central

NEW YORK CENTRAL SYSTEM

ONE OF AMERICA'S RAILROADS — ALL UNITED FOR VICTORY

NO RED AND BLUE COUPONS, BUT . . .
New York Central's ration problem is even more difficult than yours at home. *Our* points are based on the number of meals we served months ago. So, now, with travel heavier, we must plan more meals with no more points.

The "SIGNAL CORPS" in action!

How the Men of Tower X Speed Wartime Trains on the Water Level Route

THIS IS Signal Tower X. You may have glimpsed it from your train window. Just a little, two-story building beside the tracks. Yet, from here are set the signals and switches that control the steel giants of the rails. And here, day and night, men of New York Central's "signal corps" play their vital part in today's critical battle of transportation.

Once, Tower X bristled with tall levers, labori-ously worked by hand. Today, its electric controls set the heaviest and most distant switch at the twist of a towerman's wrist.

And tomorrow? Well, in New York Central's newest towers, even more automatic controls are already installed. And when Victory again frees production, Tower X and others on the Water Level Route will get still finer equipment to serve the faster rail transportation of the future.

50 MILES AT A GLANCE
This chart maps the part of the Water Level Route controlled by Tower X . . . a 50-mile network of tracks. Electric lights and indicators show instantly the movement of every train and the setting of every switch.

CIRCUIT SLEUTH
A Signal Maintainer is on duty in every large New York Central Tower, checking the hundreds of electric circuits and keeping equipment in perfect order. Other Maintainers work in the yards and on the line.

MISTAKE-PROOF MACHINE
This electric signal machine is typical New York Central tower equipment. Controls are so "interlocked" that Levermen cannot possibly set up conflicting routes.

MASTER STRATEGIST
On the Tower Director's quick thinking depends the smooth flow of wartime traffic over this portion of New York Central. He "calls the routes" to Levermen who set switches and signals according to his orders.

ALL EYES AND EARS
The Operator notes on his Train Sheet (and reports to the Dispatcher) the time each train passes, its engine number, how many and what type cars it carries. He also watches and listens to make sure all cars are running smoothly, and signals the rear brakeman.

LEVERMAN "SETS UP" ROUTES

REMOVABLE PANELS FOR MAINTENANCE

SWITCH LEVERS ARE BLACK

SIGNAL LEVERS ARE RED

"POST-WAR" TOWER TODAY!

This "electric brain" is already at work in New York Central's latest signal tower. It automatically selects routes, sets switches and signals at the touch of a button!

New York Central

ONE OF AMERICA'S RAILROADS

ALL UNITED FOR VICTORY

BUY MORE WAR BONDS

"**N**either snow, nor rain, nor heat, nor gloom of night stays these couriers from the swift completion of their appointed rounds."

Herodotus

Traveling on a
POSTAGE STAMP

How 3 billion pieces of wartime mail a year speed over the Water Level Route

NOT ONE of the passengers aboard the 20th Century Limited ever sets foot here. This car is reserved for wartime travelers of a different kind ...tiny V-mail...important business letters...registered envelopes packed with war contracts and blueprints... all part of the three billion pieces of mail that now speed each year over the New York Central.

Hour after hour, as the Century bores through the night, deft-fingered postal clerks sort this cargo of "preferential mail." And tomorrow, on arrival, the pouches and sacks will be ready for immediate forwarding or delivery.

Winter or summer, through storm or fair weather, these "post offices on wheels" provide lowest cost transportation for 96% of the nation's vast mail tonnage. A vital war service of American railroads today. A service that will be even swifter and more efficient on the finer, faster trains of tomorrow.

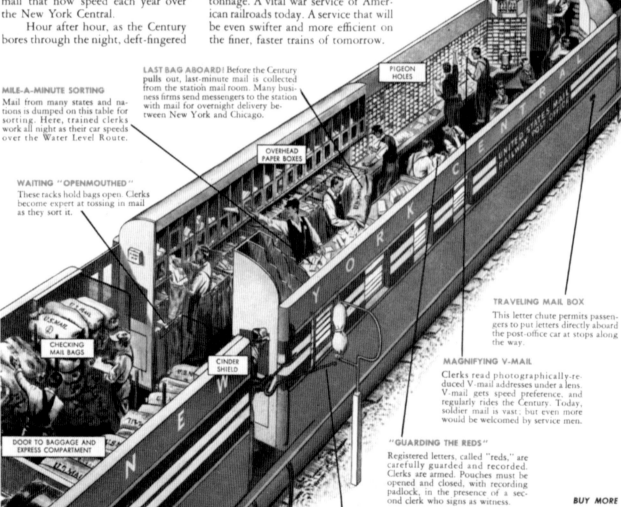

WASH ROOM AND LOCKERS

PIGEON HOLES

LAST BAG ABOARD! Before the Century pulls out, last-minute mail is collected from the station mail room. Many business firms send messengers to the station with mail for overnight delivery between New York and Chicago.

MILE-A-MINUTE SORTING
Mail from many states and nations is dumped on this table for sorting. Here, trained clerks work all night as their car speeds over the Water Level Route.

OVERHEAD PAPER BOXES

WAITING "OPENMOUTHED"
These racks hold bags open. Clerks become expert at tossing in mail as they sort it.

CHECKING MAIL BAGS

CINDER SHIELD

DOOR TO BAGGAGE AND EXPRESS COMPARTMENT

TRAVELING MAIL BOX
This letter chute permits passengers to put letters directly aboard the post-office car at stops along the way.

MAGNIFYING V-MAIL
Clerks read photographically-reduced V-mail addresses under a lens. V-mail gets speed preference, and regularly rides the Century. Today, soldier mail is vast; but even more would be welcomed by service men.

"GUARDING THE REDS"
Registered letters, called "reds," are carefully guarded and recorded. Clerks are armed. Pouches must be opened and closed, with recording padlock, in the presence of a second clerk who signs as witness.

"PICKER-UPPER"
On most trains, this Catcher Arm is swung out to snatch mail bags at way stations, providing fast mail service for even small towns.

BUY MORE WAR BONDS

NEW YORK CENTRAL SYSTEM

New York Central
ONE OF AMERICA'S RAILROADS—ALL UNITED FOR VICTORY

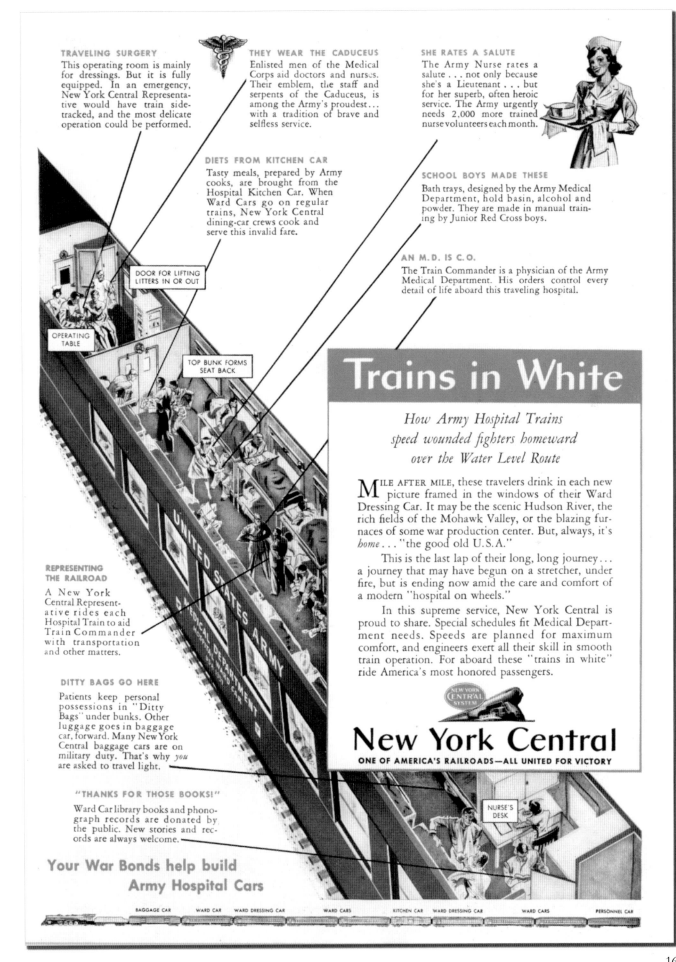

TRAVELING SURGERY

This operating room is mainly for dressings. But it is fully equipped. In an emergency, New York Central Representative would have train side-tracked, and the most delicate operation could be performed.

THEY WEAR THE CADUCEUS

Enlisted men of the Medical Corps aid doctors and nurses. Their emblem, the staff and serpents of the Caduceus, is among the Army's proudest... with a tradition of brave and selfless service.

SHE RATES A SALUTE

The Army Nurse rates a salute... not only because she's a Lieutenant... but for her superb, often heroic service. The Army urgently needs 2,000 more trained nurse volunteers each month.

DIETS FROM KITCHEN CAR

Tasty meals, prepared by Army cooks, are brought from the Hospital Kitchen Car. When Ward Cars go on regular trains, New York Central dining-car crews cook and serve this invalid fare.

SCHOOL BOYS MADE THESE

Bath trays, designed by the Army Medical Department, hold basin, alcohol and powder. They are made in manual training by Junior Red Cross boys.

AN M.D. IS C.O.

The Train Commander is a physician of the Army Medical Department. His orders control every detail of life aboard this traveling hospital.

DOOR FOR LIFTING LITTERS IN OR OUT

OPERATING TABLE

TOP BUNK FORMS SEAT BACK

Trains in White

How Army Hospital Trains speed wounded fighters homeward over the Water Level Route

MILE AFTER MILE, these travelers drink in each new picture framed in the windows of their Ward Dressing Car. It may be the scenic Hudson River, the rich fields of the Mohawk Valley, or the blazing furnaces of some war production center. But, always, it's *home*... "the good old U.S.A."

This is the last lap of their long, long journey... a journey that may have begun on a stretcher, under fire, but is ending now amid the care and comfort of a modern "hospital on wheels."

In this supreme service, New York Central is proud to share. Special schedules fit Medical Department needs. Speeds are planned for maximum comfort, and engineers exert all their skill in smooth train operation. For aboard these "trains in white" ride America's most honored passengers.

New York Central
ONE OF AMERICA'S RAILROADS—ALL UNITED FOR VICTORY

REPRESENTING THE RAILROAD

A New York Central Representative rides each Hospital Train to aid Train Commander with transportation and other matters.

DITTY BAGS GO HERE

Patients keep personal possessions in "Ditty Bags" under bunks. Other luggage goes in baggage car, forward. Many New York Central baggage cars are on military duty. That's why *you* are asked to travel light.

"THANKS FOR THOSE BOOKS!"

Ward Car library books and phonograph records are donated by the public. New stories and records are always welcome.

NURSE'S DESK

Your War Bonds help build Army Hospital Cars

BAGGAGE CAR   WARD CAR   WARD DRESSING CAR   WARD CARS   KITCHEN CAR   WARD DRESSING CAR   WARD CARS   PERSONNEL CAR

"RUNNING BOARD" IS TRAIN-TOP WALK

CONDUCTOR IS IN COMMAND of train operation. Here he is making up his "Wheel Report" on the origin, destination, and content of each car.

LOCKERS FOR CLOTHES, SUPPLIES

ICE BOX

Last but not Least...
the CABOOSE

Command Car of a Mile-Long War Freight Train Rolling over the Water Level Route

THIS IS a New York Central caboose. A workaday little car. Yet it's a *field headquarters* in today's critical battle of transportation.

Every hour, 1,000 freight trains start over the rails of America . . . each commanded by a train crew in just such a caboose as this.

Storms may lash the platforms. Fog or snow may dim the windows. But you'll find the men of the caboose at their posts, safeguarding those precious, heavy-laden cars up ahead.

Today, they're helping to move the greatest traffic of all time, over fifty-billion ton-miles a month. And from this Victory task are growing new efficiencies that will mean still finer rail transportation when Victory is won.

New York Central

BUY
MORE
WAR BONDS

ONE OF AMERICA'S RAILROADS—ALL UNITED FOR VICTORY

OBSERVATION POST. From this seat in the caboose cupola, a brakeman keeps watch over the train ahead.

RAILROAD WIGWAG. Railroad men on duty watch each passing train and signal to the train crew if anything needs attention. The rear brakeman acknowledges these signals. A raised arm means, "All okay."

HERE'S WHAT WE HAUL IN ONE WAR YEAR—194,300,000 TONS
Enough to load all these solid trains, totaling more than 43,000 miles in length.

4,454-MILE OIL TRAIN—Carrying 16,312,298 tons of gas and oil.

1,408 MILES OF OTHER FARM PRODUCTS (4,641,145 tons.)

4,664-MILE FOOD TRAIN Wheat and meat lead in its 15,056,335-ton load.

1,256 MILES OF FOREST PRODUCTS Lumber, pulp wood, etc.—4,296,799 tons.

2,507-MILE ORE TRAIN Ore and mining products totaling 18,026,229 tons.

1,573-MILE BUILDING MATERIAL TRAIN Brick, cement, pipe, roofing, etc., totaling 8,353,027 tons.

2,490-MILE IRON AND STEEL TRAIN New and scrap metals totaling 12,357,067 tons.

11,655-MILE TRAIN OF MANUFACTURES This 32,891,493-ton load includes everything from tacks to guns.

12,699-MILE COAL TRAIN Load of coal and coke totals 79,825,290 tons.

MILITARY SECRET! We can't reveal how much strategic war materiel New York Central carries...but it bulks large in today's record freight traffic.

NEW YORK CENTRAL SYSTEM

ON THE HOMEFRONT . . . AT WAR

New Panama Limited Almost Ready

Cars for the Panama Limited of the Illinois Central, which were frozen under limitation orders L97 and L97a issued by the War Production Board on April 4, have now been released and delivered to the railroad. The cars include Pullman sleeping cars and railroad-owned dining cars. Dormitory cars, the completion of which has been delayed awaiting parts, are expected to be completed before the end of the month. The tentative date for inauguration of the train is May 3. *Railway Age, Vol. 112, No. 17, 1942*

Illinois Central: A Wartime Weapon

The Illinois Central, through preparedness, handled the huge wartime traffic presented to it efficiently and well. With 6,347 miles of line operated, the I. C. is fourteenth among the railways in the country in mileage. In 1944, however, it was seventh in freight revenues, with $200,809,714; eighth in total operating revenues, with $259,271,903; fifth in total cars handled, 2,333,543; fifth in revenue tons carried, 80,333,189; and eighth in revenue tons carried one mile, 23,823,779,000. This reflects the importance of the geographical position of the railway which, extending from the Gulf of Mexico to Lake Michigan, and with lines to Louisville, Birmingham, St. Louis and Omaha as well, bisects or connects with all the important east-west traffic routes in the United States. *Railway Age, October 20, 1944*

Baldwin Post War Plan

The Baldwin Locomotives Works has retained a national engineering firm to prepare a program of post war activity looking to improvement of present products and development of new products in the heavy industry field, it is announced by Ralph Kelly, Baldwin president.

This arrangement was decided upon, Kelly said, "So that Baldwin could go forward in postwar planning without interfering in any way with its first and most important task—maximum production of war materiel. It gives the company the benefit of expert outside engineering experience and ability and enables our own executives and engineers to devote full time to the job of producing for victory." *Denver, Colorado Post, October 4, 1943*

Mr. Eastman on Railway Magazines

"The war has given American railroads the biggest job they have ever been called upon to perform. One of the reasons why they have been able to do the job, and do it well, is that their employees have understood the vital importance of transportation in the waging and winning of the war. They have understood that their work is an essential part of the nation's war effort. I believe that the splendid way in which railway employee publications have utilized their opportunity to drive home these facts to their readers is in no small measure responsible for the railroads' fine record of performance. By making railroad workers realize that they are war workers doing a most necessary job on the home front, and by keeping them fully informed of the obstacles to be overcome, and the progress achieved in the battle of transportation, these publications are highly influential in building and protecting morale during a period of unusual strain. The railway employee magazines and newspapers can be depended upon, I feel sure, to continue this valuable work." *Simmons-Boardman Publishing Co.*

Baldwin in the News

Sub-contracts of approximately 65 million dollars of war orders were awarded by The Baldwin Locomotive Works and its wholly-owned subsidiaries during the first six months of 1943, Ralph Kelly, Baldwin president, announced today. This is an increase of approximately 15% over the corresponding 1942 figure. *Washington, D. C. Post, Aug. 5, 1943*

A trainload of Medium M-4 tanks forms a background for British visitors to Baldwin Locomotive's Eddystone plant. From left to right: C. G. Pinney; Colonel F. H. Petty, British Army staff; Ralph Kelly, President of Baldwin; Lord Pentland, British Ministry of Production; and C. A. Campbell.

Freight Car Material Prices

In order to facilitate the freight car building program laid down by the War Production Board, a schedule of maximum prices for surplus freight car materials and parts, which cuts across all previous schedules affecting those materials, has been established. These materials have been placed under one regulation "Maximum Price Regulation No. 174—Freight Car Materials Sold By Car Builders" to expedite the transfer of surplus freight car parts between car builders and railroads. It was emphasized that only surplus car materials sold by one car builder to another car builder, or by a car builder to a railroad, whether or not the railroad is a car builder, fall under the provisions of this regulation which became effective July 2 and terminated December 31, 1942. *Railway Purchases and Stores, August, 1942*

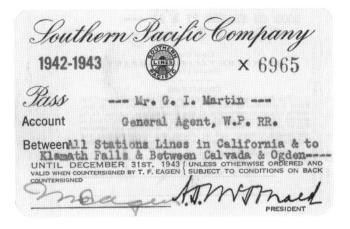

" . . . . they performed miracles"

"During the past twelve months we've had to move about three million troops, plus their equipment and supplies. The railroads have had a tremendous job, and to-date, they've done it well. During the seven critical weeks after Pearl Harbor **they performed miracles.**"

Major General C. P. Gross, Chief
Transportation Corps, Services of Supply

Missouri Pacific timetable, Sept 20, 1942

Pennsylvania Railroad timetable, September 26, 1943

Railroads Handling Heavy Troop Movements

In the nine-month period beginning December 7, 1941, troop movements by rail totaled approximately 6,500,000, compared with 1,916,417 in the first nine months of the last war. In June of 1942, the Transportation Corps moved almost a million soldiers by rail, compared with 308,000 in June 1917. "The rapid development of the 1941 emergency movements," the War Department said, "was achieved with less rolling stock than was available during a like period in 1917." At the time of 1917 mobilization, a nationwide inventory showed 2,596,252 locomotives, coaches, freight, passenger and baggage cars in the service of the railways, whereas at the start of hostilities in 1941, less than 2,000,000 cars and locomotives were at the disposal of the Army.

The present expeditious movement of troops may be accounted for by several factors, perhaps the most important of which was detailed advance planning by the Transportation Corps. Mechanical elements contributing to the success of the operations included more effective motive power, permitting longer trains, a decrease in turn-around time, a better coordination between the Army and the railroads, and increased speed of trains. In 1917, the average speed of special troop trains was 19.6 miles per hour, compared with the average speed today of 30 miles per hour. *Railway Purchases and Stores, October, 1942*

Attending the dedication ceremony of the "Spirit of the Union Pacific" bomber are (left to right) H. O. West, executive vice-president, Boeing Aircraft Company; Walter Wilson, chairman, Union Pacific War Bond Committee; F. W. Madden representing the Brotherhood of Railway Clerks; John D. Beard, Brotherhood of Maintenance-of Way-Employees; L. A. Collins, superintendent of the Oregon Division of the railroad; D. W. Hood, of the Brotherhood of Railroad Trainmen; and Arthur A. Murphy, assistant to the president of the U. P. *Railway Age, September 11, 1943*

Note New Haven rail siding into plant, located on Blachley Avenue.

The A.C. Gilbert Company helps in fight

The A.C. Gilbert Company in New Haven, Connecticut, makers of the famous Erector sets, American Flyer trains, Gilbert scientific and educational toys, Gilbert and Polar Cub motor-driven appliances and electric fans, lent its considerable manufacturing muscle to the war effort. Flares and bombs were two of the war production items that were made, and trains and toys were not produced. An Army-Navy Production Award, accompanied by a large award book measuring 10½" across by 14¼" deep, was presented to Gilbert on at least three occasions, adding a second White Star to its flag. The War Book described the various Gilbert departments and showed photographs of the workers, but it carefully avoided stating what the plant made, for fear of the Axis powers finding out and trying to sabotage the plant. In the book's opening statement by A.C. Gilbert, he writes, "I want the good customers and friends of The A.C. Gilbert Company to know more intimately the members of this great team, the various departments that work together, pull together, plan together, engineer, create and produce the things that strengthen the hands of our fighting men." At the end of the book is a list of the men and women, employees of the company, who were in service to the country at that time. Women in the military were noted with the branch of service after their names.

Dwight Bradley (inset), manager Electrical Department-East Wing

New Equipment

LOCOMOTIVES

The Central of Georgia has ordered from the Electro-Motive Corporation one Diesel-electric switching locomotive of 1,000-h.p.

FREIGHT CARS

Denver & Rio Grande Western Railroad has received approval from the Federal Court on its petition to purchase six heavy steam freight locomotives to haul increasing freight traffic on its line through Colorado and Utah.

The Chicago & NorthWestern, upon receiving authorization from the War Production Board on June 4, is constructing 25 70-ton capacity, 53-ft., 6-in. cast steel underframe flatcars at its Proviso, Ill., yards.

The Denver & Rio Grande Western has ordered 1,000 new gondola cars; 450 50-ton tight-bottom gondolas ordered from the Mount Vernon Car Manufactuing Company; and 500 general service and 50 65-ft. mill-type gondolas from the Pressed Steel Car Company.

The Lehigh Valley has received authorization from the War Production Board for 1,000 hopper cars, 440 of steel construction and 560 of composite wood and steel construction to be built by the Bethlehem Steel Company.

The Missouri Pacific Lines has ordered 650 gondola cars from the Pressed Steel Car Company, upon receiving a release from the War Production Board. *Railway Purchases and Stores, August 1942.*

Baldwin in the News

The 70,000th locomotive built by The Baldwin Locomotive Works, Philadelphia, Pa., has just been turned over to the United States Army. The engine is of the same type as many now being used in military operations abroad. During the 112 years since Mattias Baldwin built the first "Old Ironside," the company has averaged one completed locomotive every fourteen hours for 365 days in the year and twenty-four hours a day. Since on an average, however, the plant has probably operated only, say, ten hours a day for 300 working days a year, it might be said that the plant has completed a locomotive about every five working hours during a period of 112 years. *Machinery, March 1944 (See pages 45, 323)*

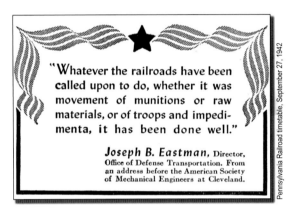

"Whatever the railroads have been called upon to do, whether it was movement of munitions or raw materials, or of troops and impedimenta, it has been done well."

Joseph B. Eastman, Director, Office of Defense Transportation. From an address before the American Society of Mechanical Engineers at Cleveland.

Pennsylvania Railroad timetable, September 27, 1942

Many American railroads and interurban lines displayed wartime patriotism such as the Denver Tramway streetcar shown here at 13th and Arapahoe streets in downtown Denver around 1942. A few male civic leaders and a WAC gather at the doorstep for a photo to show their support of the efforts to "Back the Attack" and win the war. *Denver Public Library*

Scrap campaigns pay in many ways

Information supplied by "Railway Purchases and Stores"

Effective scrap campaigns should mean even more to the railroads than to other industries. They know, if anyone does, what material shortages mean. They are particularly hard pressed for the means to keep operating.

Even if it were only a matter of getting scrap to the furnaces that need it so badly, collection campaigns would be worth while. But experience shows that they help in other ways.

A really effective campaign means a thorough housecleaning of yards, storage yards, shops, and even locker rooms. As a result, a surprising number of items, spare parts, tools, wire and others, come to light that can either be used as they are, or reclaimed for use.

Besides, employees quickly appreciate the importance not only of turning in everything they are not using, but of being careful of the equipment and tools that they are using. This conservation of materials is a help to everyone concerned.

CLIMAX FURNISHES AUTHORITATIVE ENGINEERING DATA ON MOLYBDENUM APPLICATIONS.
MOLYBDIC OXIDE—BRIQUETTED OR CANNED • FERROMOLYBDENUM • "CALCIUM MOLYBDATE"

Climax Mo-lyb-den-um Company
500 Fifth Avenue · New York City

Railway Purchases and Stores, August 1942

Outmoded, and too small to accommodate traffic between Kansas City and Salina, the pioneer *City of Salina* streamliner was junked—so that its precious aluminum could help in the fight. This train was first inspected by President Roosevelt barely nine months after the announcement by W. A. Harriman in May, 1933, that the world's first streamlined train would be built for the Union Pacific by the Pullman-Standard Car Manufacturing Company. The train was delivered on February 12, 1934, and in May of that year completed a nationwide tour during which 1,195,609 persons passed through its cars in 65 cities. *Railway Age, 1942*

In WWII, the Great Northern handled an unprecedented volume of freight, rising from 32.8 million tons in 1939 to 59.7 million in 1942. In this view, a GN magnetic crane piles scrap on a gondola in a rail yard to be melted down to make new steel. *Railway Purchases and Stores, September 1942*

Save Steel for MORE TANKS

By the RECLAMATION

AMERICAN LOCOMOTIVE COMPANY
Railway Steel Spring Division
30 CHURCH STREET, NEW YORK, N. Y.

Railway Purchases and Stores, July 1942

173

Behind the Fighting Front...

BUY U. S.
WAR BONDS
AND STAMPS

Grim and tough, he and his buddies are out there somewhere—fighting. And here at home, millions of more Americans are training intensively . . . toughening up . . . getting ready . . . and moving out . . . to join them.

The tremendous expansion and intensive training of our armed forces demanded the biggest transportation job in history. That meant railroad transportation—the continuous, mass transportation of men, munitions and equipment throughout the vast expanse of this land. These demands are being met—efficiently and safely.

Called on overnight, after the enemy struck at Pearl Harbor, the American railroads carried in organized movements during the first ten months of this war, more than 8,000,000 troops! Nearly four times more than in the same period of World War I. In addition, unknown numbers on furlough have traveled on regular trains.

It takes a lot of railroad equipment to handle the nation's armed forces. For example: To move one triangular infantry division of 15,000 men with their fighting equipment, requires 65 trains with 1,350 cars. Moreover, soldiers in this war are moved from five to six times during the training period, as compared with three times in the last war. They use 40 per cent of the sleeping cars—65 per cent travel in Pullmans—and 15 per cent of the coaches, continuously. And they have first call on all the rest. On top of that, the railroads are carrying millions of persons who formerly traveled by highway.

It all adds up to a tremendous increase—and when war necessities have made it impossible to get additional equipment. The railroads are getting every spark of service out of every unit of equipment they own. So, please remember this: When you can't get what you want on a train today, it is because our fighting men have the right-of-way. That's as it should be, and as every patriotic American wants it to be.

The Norfolk and Western Railway and the Norfolk and Western Family are in this war with everything they have. And they are proud that they can carry their full quota of America's fighting men, who will win complete and uncompromising Victory.

Norfolk and Western Railway

ONE OF AMERICA'S RAILROADS . . . *All* MOBILIZED FOR WAR!

WARTIME DINING CAR SERVICE

More diners . . . but no more dining cars.

More meals to serve . . . but less of many important foods to go around.

That is the wartime dining car situation.

With no additional dining cars being built . . . with some of our present cars busy serving the armed forces . . . the number available for our greatly increased passenger traffic will remain limited for the duration.

At the same time, many of our chefs, stewards and waiters . . . hard men to replace . . . have exchanged their New York Central uniforms for those of Uncle Sam.

That is why most dining cars and crews must now do double wartime duty.

That is why some peacetime niceties are omitted . . . why meals are simplified to speed service . . . and why menus are planned to make the most of rationed foods.

From now till Victory we will go on serving you to the best of our ability. In the meantime, thanks for your aid and understanding in today's difficult situation.

NEW YORK CENTRAL

Our Iron Horses ARE ON THE WARPATH!

The Seaboard's mighty fleet of freight and passenger trains is all-out these days to aid in getting Uncle Sam's fighting men and materials where and when he wants them and in maintaining its high standard of service for civilian needs. The Seaboard and its organization is dedicated to this purpose until victory is accomplished.

SEABOARD
AIR LINE RAILWAY

Baldwin Orders Show Sharp Increase

The dollar value of orders taken in August by The Baldwin Locomotive Works and wholly-owned subsidiaries was $37,650,547, as compared with $6,232,417 for August, 1941, according to a company announcement September 23. The month's bookings brought the total for the eight months of 1942 to $301,881,233, as compared with $64,470,830 for the same period of 1941.

Sales billed by The Baldwin Locomotive Works and wholly-owned subsidiaries in August aggregated $13,981,264, including billings of cost-plus-a-fixed fee contracts, as compared with $5,712,901 in August, 1941. Sales billed for the eight months of 1942 were $101,521,513 as compared with $30,038,298 for the same period of 1941. On August 31, 1942 unfilled orders amounted to $363,259,890. *Railway Purchases and Stores, October, 1942*

Maine Central DELIVERS BOILERS FOR BRITAIN

BIG? It was almost like the hind-sighted home cellar boat builder who forgot to measure the bulkhead door. Each boiler was nearly 18 feet in height and 102,000 pounds in weight. And there were 90 of them.

AWKWARD? It was like trying to make the lawn grass roller "stay put" in the garage. They were round and they wanted to get rolling.

AND, OH THOSE CUTS, CURVES AND BRIDGES! Their peaceful layout was disturbed. One bridge was changed to gantlet tracks, three were elevated, several cuts were widened, tracks shifted as much as 8 feet.

BUT THE QUEER LOOKING CARS CAME THROUGH. Three new types of specially designed cars were made. The route survey showed that 381 miles were necessary for the trip to avoid other obstacles, instead of the usual 283 from where boilers were made, to the Maine coast shipyards.

Not every war-time task is as spectacular as this one, and we look upon it as only one of many war movements which are a part of the job Maine Central is doing to help win the war.

MAINE CENTRAL *Railroad*

ENGINE of WAR

"Our railroads are essential to our nation's capacity to make war. That was proved in World War 1 and has become again overwhelmingly evident in this war. They must be sustained by the American people with full appreciation that they are vital to us and must always be prepared to go into action to make effective the might of the United States."

C. P. GROSS
Major General
Chief of Transportation
United States Army

Association of
AMERICAN
RAILROADS

Troop-Train Operation

On some railroads, all troop trains, whether mixed or not, are operated with cabooses. Other lines operate troop trains at first-class speeds, 75 and 80 miles per hour. Almost all roads are using freight engines on many of these trains, due to the shortage of power. And some troop trains run as high as 18 and 20 cars. *Trains, July 1944*

Box Cars Handle Christmas Presents

Because of so many baggage cars being used in troop service this year, many of the large railroads used box cars for handling the Christmas parcel post. Many of these cars are equipped with steel wheels and steam heat connections and thus could be operated in regular passenger trains. *Trains, February 1945*

BILL, THE PLATFORM MAN

It is 4 minutes to midnight—11:56 P.M.—in a Railway Express terminal. The man is a Railway Express platform man, one of many thousands stationed around the country. The package is a shipment of medical instruments. The destination—a military secret.

The package might have been some other type of war material or a commercial shipment to some factory which must "keep going". It might have been . . . anything.

To Bill, the platform man, and to any other of the thousands of employes who work for Railway Express, their job is to keep things moving so that trains and vehicles may maintain their ceaseless deliveries to the four corners of the nation.

RAILWAY EXPRESS AGENCY

NATION-WIDE RAIL-AIR SERVICE

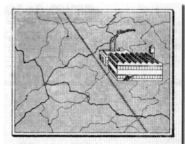
ODT Endeavoring to Increase Locomotive Efficiency

With the heaviest long-haul tonnage demands in history being placed upon the nation's steam freight locomotives, the Office of Defense Transportation is seeking to avert a motive power shortage by taking steps to increase the efficiency of locomotive operation. The number of serviceable freight locomotives now available is about 18,000. Material allocations to locomotive builders by the War Production Board will make it possible to turn out only about 265 new steam locomotives during the remainder of 1942.

NEW RECORD HAUL

Whether this fleet of freight engines will be large enough to meet the motive power requirements of the near future is problematical, according to Joseph B. Eastman, Director of Defense Transportation. During the first four months of 1942, the 121 major rail systems hauled 188-billion revenue ton-miles—188-billion tons of paid freight one mile. The former all-time peak was the first four months of 1929 when 141-billion tons of paid freight moved one mile, a 25 percent increase. In these first four months of 1929 the Class I roads had 24,616 serviceable steam freight locomotives to do the job. In the first third of 1942, 17,893 freight engines took care of the new record haul.

DIFFERENCE IN THE NUMBERS

This difference in the number of locomotives, showing a decrease of more than a third under the 1929 figure, does not mean that the railroads today are working miracles with the engines they have available, Mr. Eastman said. It means that the engines are bigger, that they have a greater tonnage capacity, and that they are handling longer hauls of more heavily-loaded cars. *Railway Purchases and Stores, August, 1942*

Railroads Ready for Autumn Traffic Peak

Facing the heaviest movement of revenue freight traffic in history, America's railroads stand ready to meet autumn peak demands with more than 200,000 miles of trunk lines virtually clear of congestion, Joseph B. Eastman, Director of Defense Transportation, said recently. As of midnight August 31, reports on car and train movements of 108 Class I railroads, compiled by the Traffic Channels Section of ODT's Division of Traffic Movement, showed green lights burning for the mounting flow of war freight.

The traffic channels system, which has now been in operation four months, has been a helping factor in keeping the green lights showing, Mr. Eastman said. Daily studies prepared by the Traffic Channels Section on the basis of operating data submitted by the railroads indicate threatened bottlenecks, particularly over large areas, long before any serious congestion can develop. At the first sign of congestion, cooperative action with the railroads involved making it possible to prevent serious trouble. If necessary, traffic can be diverted around the congested area.

Operation of the traffic channels system has been speeded up in recent weeks by the installation of three commercial telegraph circuits in ODT's Washington headquarters, Mr. Eastman disclosed. Previously, data submitted by the railroads was sent by airmail. The improvement in the transmission system has made possible a savings of 24 hours in the time required for compilation of car and train movements covering a single day. *Railway Purchases and Stores, October, 1942*

The service flag for October, 1944 reveals that 75 Illinois Central men had lost their lives in the war. Of the 8,604 IC employees in the Armed Services, eight were known to be prisoners of war. *Illinois Central magazine, October 1944*

Ed. Note: The following chart, issued by the office of W. G. Carl, assistant to vice president Van Horn, showing (according to job classification) the number of B&O men in military service, will we believe be of special interest to our readers. In studying this compilation, however, several points should be kept in mind, notably the fact that many classifications showing small representation in military service do so because originally they include but few employees. In some cases it may be difficult to determine the classification into which a particular job falls. However, all groups are included and are reported as complete as available information would permit. All figures shown are inclusive of December 31, 1943.

Cumulative Total of B&O Men in Military Service

CLASSIFICATION	NUMBER SERVING
Executives, General Officers and Assistants	3
Professional and Sub-Professional Assistants	33
Chief Clerks and Assistant Chief Clerks and Supervisors and Cashiers	19
Clerks (B&C), including Baggage Checkmen	1067
Mechanical Device Operators (Office)	10
Stenographers, Secretaries and Typists	209
Storekeepers and Assistants, Sales Agents and Buyers	15
Telephone Switchboard Operators and Office Assistants	6
Messengers and Office Boys	103
Elevator Operators and Other Office Attendants	9
Patrolmen and Watchmen	157
City Passenger Agents and Traveling Freight Agents	16
Claim Agents or Investigators	6
Motor Vehicle and Motor Car Operators	30
Janitors and Cleaners	28
Carpenters	70
Painters	17
Extra Gang Foremen	24
Masons, Bricklayers, Plasterers and Plumbers	6
Skilled Trade Helpers and Apprentices (MofW)	212
Extra Gang Laborers	472
Section Men	2243
Assistant Signalmen and Assistant Signal Maintainers	31
Signalmen and Signal Maintainer Helpers	95
General Foremen and Foremen	6
Blacksmiths	12
Boilermakers	20
Carmen	214
Electricians	17
Machinists	74
Molders	1
Sheet Metal Workers	22
Skilled Trades Helper (MofE and Stores)	2039
Regular Apprentices (MofE and Stores)	865
Coach Cleaners	22
Gang Foremen (Stores)	4
Classified Laborers (Shop, Enginehouse and Power Plant)	419
General Laborers (Shop, Enginehouse and Power Plant)	560
General Laborers (Stores)	358
Stationary Engineers, Firemen and Oilers	9
Station Agents, Agent-Operators	9
Telegraphers, Telephoners and Towermen	52
Truckers	604
Common Laborers (Station-Warehouse)	84
Stewards	4
Chefs and Cooks	89
Waiters	148
Bargemen	3
Train Porters	53
Crossing Watchmen and Pumpers	18
Yardmasters and Assistants	6
Switchtenders	3
Hostlers and Hostler Helpers	3
Conductors (Passenger, Freight and Yard)	20
Trainmen (Passenger, Freight and Yard)	1257
Engineers and Motormen (Passenger, Freight and Yard)	5
Firemen and Helpers (Passenger, Freight and Yard)	734
Chief and Trick Dispatchers	2
TOTAL	12,617

Baltimore & Ohio magazine, March 1944

A LITTLE EXTRA SERVICE

Day after day, uniformed men pour into the Union Station at Omaha, Nebraska. They come from New York, Chicago, San Francisco ... from Albert Lea, Minnesota ... Brady, Montana ... and other points from coast to coast.

To them, Omaha is a city of strangers; just a "stop over" on their way to a destination. So, to help them feel at home, the Railroads serving the Omaha Union Station have provided air-conditioned quarters for a recreation room, shower baths, canteen, and first-aid station in

charge of Registered Nurses. Local concerns and townspeople have contributed complete equipment and supply refreshments daily. Volunteer workers give generously of their time. Day and night, a neon sign displays this greeting—"Service Men's Center —Everything Free."

This is a small thing as compared, for example, to the vital job the railroads are doing in transporting huge quantities of war materials and trainloads of troops. But it is one way in which we on the home front can give a *little extra service* to our men who are fighting for their Country.

The Progressive

UNION PACIFIC RAILROAD

ROAD OF THE STREAMLINERS AND THE CHALLENGERS

CHAPTER FIVE

Personal Glimpses of the War

"The path ahead of us will not be easy. But by working together, the job, whatever it develops into, will be done, and done well." —Joseph B. Eastman, Director of Defense Transportation

When Americans learned that Europe was in turmoil in the late 1930s and early 1940s, many already believed that at some point, the United States would become involved.

Despite the fact that many Americans didn't want to enter a war, and despite the fact that elected officials longed for a diplomatic solution to the problems in Europe, many felt that time was marching on, and that the dramatic events taking place would not allow the U.S to sit out the conflict.

Czechoslovakia was invaded by the Germans in 1938. In 1939 Poland and Finland were invaded. In January of 1940 Congress filed its first request for defense appropriations in the Budget Message. Denmark and Norway were invaded in April of 1940. In June of 1940 France capitulated. In September of 1940, Egypt was invaded, and the Selective Service Bill was authorized. In October of that year, Rumania was invaded, followed by Yugoslavia in April of 1941, and a bit later Crete was lost. Americans wondered if they would be next. Then, in December of 1941, Pearl Harbor was attacked.

An advertisement sponsored by Bell Aircraft in the April 12, 1943 edition of *Time* magazine, told the story: "They asked for it. Axis gangsters took the miracle of aviation and made it a weapon of destruction. They bred their birds of prey, unleashed them. Now they hear a tougher breed roaring overhead. Army Aircobras, made at Bell Aircraft, bringing sudden death. In three years—starting from scratch—we Americans created the largest aircraft industry in the world."

The general temperament of the United States had been for peace, plenty and prosperity. But that would change. And when it did, America put its full muscle into the dangerous endeavor.

EVERYONE HELPED

In the meantime, thousands were drafted or asked to help in some way: men, women and families. Everyone needed to contribute to win the war.

America's rail employees, suppliers of industrial goods and services, and troops, all helped the war effort, and each had a specific part to play—and a personal story to tell.

In the first 12 months of WWII, 891,827 troops had been embarked for overseas duty, as well as 10,474,923 measurement tons of Army cargo. People from all walks of life were part of the war now. Soldiers left their loved ones to board troop trains that would take them to a port of embarkation. Engineers and firemen would take the control of their locomotives that pulled long trains of military materiel and guns. Carmen and welders were busy doing their important jobs on the railroad. Many U.S. railroaders and troops still remember the War Years. They're glad they are over, but the memory of certain things that happened during those times remains forever.

Rail Photography during the War Years could be a Problem

by Hal Carstens

Railroad photography was generally a no-no during WWII as railroads were a vital war industry, and film and good cameras were scarce. I managed to shoot these photographs in St. Louis and other places: Memphis on the Rock Island, Abilene on the Texas & Pacific, and later I was able to shoot some railroad photos on the Manila Railroad in Luzon. Despite photographic restrictions, I shot Texas electric interurbans, trolleys in Kansas City, Sacramento and Youngstown, New York, and the battered hulks of the Manila Electric Railway which never ran again. These photos, more than 65 years old, were shot with a low-cost 35mm Argus whose lens left much to be desired. The first thing I did on being mustered out was to buy a new Kodak 620 Medalist camera.

Soldier Hal Carstens on board a troop train in WWII had his Kodak camera at the ready.

Dinner in the Art Deco Diner
by Frank Nolte

In early February of 1944, I was in Chicago's Chicago & NorthWestern Station preparing to board the San Francisco *Challenger* headed back to Sacramento after my furlough in Detroit. I had arrived in Chicago on the New York Central/Michigan Central *Mercury,* a daily limited express train on the Detroit-Chicago run. I arrived around 5 p.m., and the *Challenger* was scheduled to board around 9:30 p.m.

It was met in the station by Father August Preganzer, a Redemptorist priest serving at St. Michael's Parish in Chicago. His identical twin brother, Otto Preganzer, was a parish priest at our home parish in Detroit.

FRIENDLY FATHER PREGANZER

It was not entirely clear to me if Father Preganzer was a train nut, or if he was a quasi-official railroad chaplain. That said, he was clearly familiar with the Chicago railroad complex. As we dined in the station restaurant, and as we walked through the concourse, he was greeted on all sides by station personnel.

Through a series of back doors and stairs unknown to the average passenger, Father Preganzer took me to the platform where the *Challenger* awaited its call to board. He found the conductor, and I was seated in a modern car with upholstered, reclining seats. Normally, GI's like me would have traveled in antiquated cars that had hard wicker seats, gas lights and uneven heat.

ACQUIRED LIEN

The conductor removed a small stub from my ticket and inserted it in a clip at the back of the seat ahead of me. In so doing, I had acquired a lien on my seat. This is important, because such accommodations were usually restricted to commissioned officers, not PFCs like me.

The conductor stated that this was a public train and that having been assigned a seat I was not to surrender it to any officer. He agreed to support me if I was pressed to move—and he was right. The officers wanted me removed, and the conductor said "No." He went so far as to say that trains were so crowded that if I were evicted, there was no other place on the train for me to go. The officer seated next to me supported me in the face of his indignant fellow officers. This was to be my seat for the next 2½ days of transcontinental travel.

ART DECO DINER

This train had a real honest-to-goodness 1935 movie set-style Art Deco diner. Tables were affixed to the wall along

Frank Nolte's furlough ticket on his February, 1944 *Challenger* ride from Chicago to Sacramento on the Southern Pacific.

the left side of the car by the windows, and there were tables with linen tablecloths and napkins, sparkling silverware, tall stemmed-glass, tumblers of water and a menu.

Two people dined seated facing on either side of the table. A waiter, black and appropriately dressed, arranged seating, took orders and served the food.

I will never forget rolling through the winter wonderland of Illinois, Kansas, Nebraska and Colorado. I was seated in warm comfort, dined in elegant style and looked out at expanses of snow-covered open country, seeing cars behind crossing guard gates as we rolled along.

As the saying goes, "Dinner in the diner...nothing could be finer."

350th Engineer Service Regiment
Rides the Rails

by William Sabel

The 350th Engineers left Camp Shelby, Mississippi on January 9, 1943 for overseas duty. Four different trains were required to transport the regiment and its equipment to the port of embarkation at San Francisco, California.

The regiment consisted of 1,222 enlisted men, two warrant officers and 51 officers. We didn't know where we were going, although we had exchanged our woolen GI clothing for summer khaki uniforms. Train #1 consisted of the vehicles of the regiment loaded on flatcars and the organizational equipment loaded into box cars.

There was a guard of one officer and 10 enlisted men who accompanied the train. Their subsistence consisted of "C" rations and coffee money at the rate of 24 cents per day per man. During the movement, three men were hospitalized due to frostbite. There was some difficulty encountered by the officers in charge in keeping the train intact. At various junctions, railroad officials attempted to break the train into smaller sections, but refrained from doing so at the insistence of the officer-in-charge.

SEVEN TRAVEL DAYS

The trip required seven days traveling over the Mississippi Central, the Texas & Pacific and the Southern Pacific, and Train #1 had to leave Camp Shelby two days prior to the departure of the trains carrying troops.

Train #2, a troop train, composed of two baggage cars, one stateroom car for the officers and 10 tourist cars for the enlisted men, pulled out of the station at 5:40 p.m. on the same day. A prepared loading plan made it possible for the personnel, consisting of Companies A and B, to march from the regimental area to the train to the music of the Drum and Bugle Corps and by proper military maneuvers, load into all cars at the same time. It did not take more than five minutes to load all the personnel. The performance of the Drum and Bugle Corps, and the cheers of the on-looking civilians, made the departure a pleasant occasion to remember. A good meal was served as soon as the train was under way.

Train #3 was occupied by Companies C and D and detachments of Headquarters and Service Company. At midnight, the train arrived at Memphis, Tennessee. Many of the men missed seeing this Southern metropolis, as the excitement of the day had completely exhausted them and the majority were fast asleep.

LOOKING INTO THE FUTURE

Frisco, while fulfilling present-day transportation needs, is working and planning ahead for the resumption of operations under peacetime conditions. Constant improvements are being made every day to facilitate service now and to be ready for the new era of rail transportation that inevitably will follow Victory.

Frisco serves one of the nation's most progressive territories... Frisco has and will keep faith with its territory by meriting its reputation as "A Great Railroad."

5,000 MILES IN 9 STATES

FRISCO FASTER FREIGHT

FRISCO LINES ST.LOUIS-SAN FRANCISCO RY.

A GREAT RAILROAD IN WAR AND PEACE

Meals were served at regular hours from the kitchens located in the baggage cars, and the routine was as nearly normal as could be expected of a group in transit. In the kitchen cars, company cooks prepared meals on the company's gasoline stoves which they would be using when we arrived at our overseas base.

FIRE ON BOARD

The menu consisted of easily prepared dehydrated canned foodstuffs. I guess they were preparing us for the food we would be eating for the next 2½ years. On one of the lead trains, the cook was filling the tank on one of the gasoline stoves when it ignited. The fire was quickly extinguished, but he became excited and jumped off the train traveling at 40 piles per hour. Fortunately, he wasn't injured and was picked up by the following troop train.

The floodwaters of the Ohio River between Carbondale and Pickney, Illinois provided a very impressive scene. In several places water covered the rails. Upon arrival at St. Louis, a transfer was made to the Rock Island. The train arrived in Kansas City at midnight the following day.

ONE AIM VICTORY! BUY BONDS

Katy Fireman Captured as a 'Spy'

by Sharon Weldon Hudgins

My late father, Lawrence Munn Weldon (1920-1999), worked for 20 years on the Missouri-Kansas-Texas (M-K-T, or Katy) Railroad—and remained a railroader at heart all his life, long after he went on to pursue a second career in the movie business.

In 1942, shortly after the United States entered World War II, he—like all the other patriotic young men in his hometown of McAlester, Oklahoma—eagerly went down to the recruiting office to enlist in the military. But, to his disappointment, he was rejected because of a slight medical condition that he didn't even know he had—and for the more important reason that he was already employed by an industry vital to the defense of America, the railroad.

As a young newlywed fireman stoking coal on steam engines during those early war years, he sometimes worked on trains that delivered prisoners and supplies to POW camps in Oklahoma. My mother worked at two of those camps herself as an assistant to an Army Major who provided dental care for the foreign prisoners. Four days a week she worked at a camp near McAlester, but on Thursdays she was assigned to accompany the dentist to another, smaller camp somewhere else in the state.

Katy Fireman Lawrence Munn Weldon and his Frisco locomotive, #410.

AVID PHOTOGRAPHER

My father was an avid and talented amateur photographer who often carried his still camera and 8 mm movie camera with him, just in case he came across any good subjects to shoot. One morning, no different from many other mornings, he was the fireman on a train delivering German prisoners to the POW camp where my mother worked. But on that particular day he had also brought his cameras along with him. As the train full of prisoners was nearing the camp and pulling onto the siding to unload, dad leaned out of the cab with his movie camera in hand, filming the approach to the camp. After the train came to a stop and he was climbing down from the engine, he suddenly felt a gun stuck into his back and heard someone shout, "Halt! Put up your hands!"

He raised his hands above his head and slowly turned around to see a military police guard pointing a gun at him and scowling. "You're under arrest!" barked the guard. "What for?" asked my father, who was completely bewildered by the bizarre situation. "For photographing a military installation," replied the guard, who promptly marched dad off to the brig.

'SPY' CAUGHT RED-HANDED

My father's cameras were confiscated by the guards before he was jailed, and later in the day he was interrogated by two of the camp's military officers who accused him of being a spy. Dad kept claiming his innocence and reiterating that his wife was a camp employee in the dentist's office, who could vouch for him. But that happened to be one of the Thursdays when she was away working at the other POW camp in Oklahoma, so there wasn't anyone who could even confirm the identification papers found when the interrogators looked through his wallet. And the camp commander—with a spy caught red-handed—refused to let my father communicate with anyone outside his solitary-confinement cell, not even a phone call to a family member or friend.

SENSE OF HUMOR

It wasn't until much later the next day, several hours after mother had reported for work at the camp and been questioned at length herself, that my father was finally released from jail. The Army returned his cameras to him—minus all the film—and sent him away with a stern warning against ever filming any military sites again.

Dad didn't take it personally. He strongly supported the war against the Axis powers and was as jubilant as every other American on V-E and V-J days in 1945. But he also had a great sense of humor and was an engaging storyteller. The rest of his life he enjoyed recounting how he'd been rejected as a soldier for the U. S. Army, then captured as a "spy" by that same Army while working on the Katy Railroad in Oklahoma.

Ironically, he happened to tell that story to a group of Germans and Americans at a Christmas dinner in a village near Wiesbaden, Germany, 30 years after the end of WWII. And—you guessed it—dad discovered that one of the Germans at that holiday meal had been a prisoner at the same camp where my mother had worked as a dental assistant, and he himself had been captured as "a spy."

After swapping stories about their experiences in Oklahoma during the war, they all raised their glasses in a toast to the past they'd lived through, to the present they were thankful to enjoy, and to a future where they hoped their people would never be enemies again.

I Never Got a Chance to Say Thanks
by Regi Cordic

My U.S. Navy ticket read "Miami, Florida, to Oakland California. For Further Transfer: Seventh Fleet." To an 18-year-old sailor/railfan's sense of justice, it seemed like a pretty fair return for the months of diligent work I had just devoted to mastering the fine art of naval anti-aircraft fire control and gunnery. The time had come to put my knowledge to use aboard a destroyer escort in the Philippines in these final years of World War II.

Bands played as hundreds of white uniforms marched along the platforms of Florida East Coast's Miami passenger depot. Clusters peeled from the ranks to enter various of the vintage Pullman cars that seemed to stretch to the horizon; mine was near the rear. A 4-8-2 type locomotive simmered at the headend. Soon, under a cloud of black smoke and the roar of slipping drivers, the odyssey began that would take me to the coast of Mindinao and the decks of DE 345.

It's hard to explain why, all these years later, I still revere that cross-country journey as one of the most memorable train trips I ever experienced. So many vignettes are almost as alive today as the moment they were burned into my memory.

RED CROSS LADIES

I recall the gentle sincerity in the faces of the Red Cross ladies who met the train in a small Southern crew-change town as they passed out little grooming kits and wished us a safe return.

Who can ever forget his first look at the Rocky Mountains at sunrise? It's the stuff that patriots are made of. Why, you could almost hear the choir singing of "purple mountain majesties" as the low sun rays turned the misty car sides to a bright, shimmering orange and highlighted the flashing rods of the pair of 4-8-4's leaning into a lefthand curve. "God shed His grace on thee."

I remember an old crossing watchman who held a salute until the whole train passed by. Cornball? Maybe, but it was a different time. You had to be there.

You had to be there, too, on the banging vestibule deck with the top half of the Dutch door open to savor the fragrant smells of the land and the pungent blasts of coal smoke from up ahead. On troop trains, conductors were often lenient about the rules. And, oh, the glorious racket! The constant banging of the diaphragms and the deck plates and the hundred variations of the tempo of the wheels on the rails. Whistles high and low,

screaming and moaning. A brakeman tells me there's a hot-shot on our tail. "Hang on, kid!" That was railroading!

AMERICA'S BACKYARDS

Through America's backyards. A fleeting view of a trackside home and a family at dinner. An instant in time with the power to generate an incredible wave of melancholy. What were my folks at home doing now? A little loneliness was part of the bargain in any big adventure. It's what makes kindness loom large.

One event in particular stays with me. Weary from train-watching, I slumped in my seat. It was twilight, and a little drizzle was spreading across the flat Missouri farmland beyond my reflection in the window. A pickup truck paced the train on the parallel two-lane road, slowly falling behind as we picked up speed. The truck's headlights glistened on the wet pavement.

We were rolling again, having made what Navy passengers learned to consider the most important stop of the day: tacking the dining car onto the rear of our lengthy train.

184

This was the ritual as our MAIN (lingo for military or troop train) crossed the continent, passing from one railroad to another. With each line came the best the carrier could provide. Some cars were old and creaky, some sleek and polished, fresh off the streamliner. The food and the service fluctuated as well.

"All right now, chow down! Stay in your seat till I give you your meal ticket." The salty Shore Patrolman, hat forward, billy club on his belt, swaggered down the aisle passing out the small blue sheets that had been counted to equal the available seats. He gestured with his clipboard, "Ya go two cars aft!"

The dining car steward reminded me of my textbook sketch of Ichabod Grantlean and was very tall. The cuffs of his blue jacket exposed a little too much white shirt sleeve when he gestured to a few empty spaces at the kitchen end of the car. His receding hairline lengthened his angular face. Awkward though he seemed, he moved with unexpected grace as the swaying became more pronounced and the silverware tapped Morse Code messages against ice water glasses.

Over the hubub of conversation, his surprisingly strong voice commanded silence. "Gentlemen, could I have your attention, please." "Now what?" someone mumbled. "They forgot to load the damn food!" someone else down the aisle responded. Derisive laughter.

ON THE C&A NOW

If the steward heard it, he paid no attention. "You are now on the Chicago & Alton Railroad," he continued. "Our management knows that troop trains mean extra long hours for dining car crews. So, they have instituted a policy of additional compensation for the men who will be serving you. On this car, tips will not be accepted. Any money left on the table after the meal will be given to the Red Cross."

This was a stunning contrast to some of our earlier experiences when our limited funds for gratuities determined the quality of service we saw. There were no wisecracks now.

He had finished the official greeting and now spoke for himself. "I know it's not much, fellas, but this is our way of expressing our thanks to you. We're proud to have you on the Chicago & Alton."

There came an awkward pause, as if none of us knew exactly what to say. The truth was, we didn't until someone up front yelled, "All right you guys, come on. Let's hear it for the Chicago & Alton." Then the football cheers and applause filled the car and brought a broad, shy smile from our host.

The next morning we were fed and watered in the cavernous Union Station at Kansas City. When we departed, the Alton diner, of course, remained behind. I was sorry that I never got a chance to say thanks. *Reprinted from the June 1994 Trains; used with permission of Kalmbach Publishing Co.*

Baltimore & Ohio magazine, March 1944

Early Military Memories at La Junta

by Delbert Spencer

With the advent of gasoline rationing, public transportation was heavily used in the war years. Most of my early memories at La Junta, Colorado were of the military moving through. Sometimes there were entire trains, commonly called troop trains, and other times just a car or two.

In 1941 when I was 15 years old, I was already 6 foot tall and pretty strong, except for my left leg which was decimated from polio at the age of two. Having been so afflicted from that early age, I had learned how to cope. Other than

a slight limp, I was not visibly handicapped, as long as I had long pants on. I felt my height made me look older than 15, so I applied for a job at Fred Harvey, lied about my age and was hired as a part-time worker since I was still in school, but working full time in the summer and on weekends. My main job was to supply food to the passenger dining cars, and to supply the hotel kitchen, plus whatever else needed to be done.

I was working on Sunday morning, December 7, when the radio announced the Pearl Harbor attack. Every young man was ready to join up, and many did, but my bout with polio made me 4-F, and I was a bit too young. The Army was stricter about age than Fred Harvey! I was there when the first military equipment train came through La Junta. Everyone was frustrated with the sudden increase of traffic, and especially with military requirements and their security demands. The yardmaster put this long military freight train on passenger track #1 for security reasons, thereby blocking any access to the entire passenger yard. The military train had many flat cars loaded with war materiel.

15 MINUTES TO SERVE

Shortly thereafter the streamliners arrived on tracks 2, 3, and 4, and I had a baggage truckload of food to supply the diners, with a maximum of 15 minutes to service them. I could see the diners, but could not reach them, so I did what any thinking person would do. I pulled up to a flat car and started sliding the food across. The next thing I knew, a very large bore machine gun was sticking between my eyes, with a very stern young soldier barking orders at me to "get the hell out of there!" The dining cars did not get serviced, and I was scolded by my boss.

Most military trains had their own dining cars in later years, but in the beginning troop trains and individual military cars moving in regular passenger trains usually were fed in the Fred Harvey Hotel dining room if the timing was right. Many local girls were hired to serve. The men were fed pretty fast, but the girls still worked long hours. Since most banquets were for local dignitaries, the serving equipment was such as found in elegant dining rooms. My wife Dot worked there at times, and remembers coffeepots with straight handles sticking out the side, and after hours of serving, made for aching wrists!

One night, the *California Limited* Train No. 3, had a sleeper car of WAVES (Navy women) on the rear, and the *Fast Mail & Express* Train No. 7 had a sleeper car of soldiers. Mail trains were somewhat like freight trains with no services other than heat, air conditioning and electricity. Someone got the bright idea to combine the two cars on No. 3 in order for both cars to have access to passenger train conveniences. They hooked them together for about 20 minutes, which was a bad move!

A lot of the equipment had been resurrected from the scrap yard to meet wartime needs and was not in the best condition. Air conditioning on some of the sleepers was not mechanical, but was "ice activated" which required blocks of ice from the ice house in the backshop area.

TRAIN LEAVES WITHOUT HIM

Occasionally a passenger would stroll uptown on some errand and find himself stranded when they returned to the depot. One night, a soldier from Train No. 3 came back to find the train departing without him. He still had the brick depot platform to run on, and got to the last third of the train but was unable to find an open door. In desperation he hooked onto the grabirons on the last car and was beating on the door and yelling when I lost sight of him in the darkness.

We had no two-way radios at that time, but if the station at Timpas (17 miles away) was open, the train could have been flagged. The next station would have been Thatcher, 45 miles away, if it was open, and his last chance would have been Trinidad \ rode a few miles in cold desperation!

Several times, passengers who missed their trains would hire a local driver to speed down the road trying to beat the train to the next open depot. Catching a train by car was not easy. The superintendent brought a mail pouch to the depot one evening with instructions to put the package on the Assistant General Manager's business car on Train 13 to Denver without fail! I can't remember the man responsible, but as the train was leaving, he noticed the pouch laying on the counter. Taking his car, he missed the train at Swink (4 miles), Rocky Ford (7 miles), Manzanola (16 miles), but did get to Fowler (24 miles) in time to throw the pouch on the observation platform of the business car as it went by, and called Pueblo by phone telling them where it was. This was a two lane road with a 60 mph speed limit, and three towns. His guardian angel must have been very busy that night!

We had occasional chair cars with tightly-guarded German or Italian prisoners of war, probably going to the prison camp at Trinidad, Colorado. One car was in the passenger yard

for several hours, with armed military guards patrolling. Patriotism was high, and a number of local people came to stare at them. Some vented anger and did some taunting. The guards were usually tolerant with the locals, however, when things would get too bad, they would exercise their authority.

PRISONERS OF WAR

We had soldiers from the La Junta Army Air Corps base who helped on the mail crew in their spare time. One night we had a coffin with a corpse in a "rough box" (shipping container) to move from one train's baggage car to another, however, we had two military trains between the two trains. Most military trains had kitchen cars, with a wide door in the middle of the car on both sides. We took the coffin alongside the troop train until we found a kitchen car, and shoved it through the first train.

On the second train we also found a kitchen car, and we had the coffin in the door when someone said something about it being a coffin with a corpse, and these soldiers would not have anymore to do with it. The military train wanted to leave, but could not until the coffin was removed. We had some tense moments until the situation was finally solved with personnel who were not so superstitious.

How Trains Helped Win a War
by Dr. Richard C. Roberts

The good times of the 1920s came to an end in Ogden, Utah, as in other parts of the United States, during the Great Depression of the 1930s. Business declined, and many companies and industries even went broke. The railroads suffered along with other businesses. Both freight and passenger traffic declined.

Thor Blair, who ran a newsstand at the Ogden Union Station, remembered that during the 1930s the trains were "sporadically" ridden by "gaunt men led by a faint hope of finding some employment" in a city somewhere along the line. Sometimes the passenger cars ran almost empty.

The 1930s were hard times, but the 1940s brought new business to the railroads as trains became a part of the nation's military system during World War II. The railroads did their greatest volume of business carrying materiel and troops for the war effort. By 1944 the total railroad volume in the United States had increased to 783 billion ton-miles of freight. Passenger travel saw similar increases, with 95 billion passenger-miles recorded in 1944. During the war American railways carried 43 million members of the Armed Forces in 114,000 special troop trains.

SIXTY-TWO TRAINS A DAY

The Ogden Union Station on America's main east-west rail line serviced a tremendous amount of this wartime freight and passenger traffic. LeRoy Johnson, a Red Cap at the Ogden Union Station for more than 40 years, recalled those busy days: "At one time, during World War II, 62 passenger trains left the depot every day—streamliners from all over the nation carrying presidents, kings, ambassadors, movie stars, doctors, lawyers, authors, poets—and just people—thousands of them, every day, from all walks of life." During that time 18 Red Caps "worked around the clock to help all these people on and off the trains." Tom Zito, who worked in the Ogden Union Pacific Railroad shops beginning in 1941, also remembered the war years at the station. He said the troop trains "would come in there so fast and so thick that people [would] just run around in circles. There were just too many people. Nobody knew where they were going or where they came from."

Sometimes the soldiers passing through Ogden got off the trains to relax or have some fun. Zito said, "Boy those soldiers just didn't care where they went, how they went or when they came back. They were just out for all the fun they could have. Some of them had no way of cleaning themselves up, they had whiskers and they were actually dirty. But then there were so many of them that they couldn't keep the passenger trains clean because those poor soldiers would be riding for days and nights getting to where they wanted to go. They would sleep in the aisle and anywhere they could curl up and get a little rest...much of the time...

Ogden Union Station, Ogden, Utah around 1944 saw between 100-120 trains a day. Troops on passenger trains were served food at the station from canteens, operated by local women's groups. This view shows the station looking west toward the station entrance and the parking area. Local establishments along 25th Street near the station attracted soldiers who had a layover. *Ogden Union Station collection*

This familiar scene was repeated over and over all across the country during wartime—soldiers of all military branches checking in prior to departing on trains for furlough or their next duty assignment.

there wasn't enough food. It was just the wildest place you were ever in around the depot."

GO OUTSIDE AND DROP

"Some of the soldiers looked for a place to rest away from the crowds and confusion. They would just go outside in the summer time and drop anywhere they could get a little sleep. Of course they moved them out as fast as they could... for a long time during the war a passenger train [came] in and out of the depot every five minutes around the clock."

Angus Hansen, who worked as a carman and welder for the Union Pacific in Ogden, said of the war years, "At the time I worked there it was actually the peak during World War II. They had freight and passenger train service. I don't think you could go down to the depot anytime, night or day, that you didn't find that depot full of people wanting to ride the trains. Of course, during the war there was a restriction put on [civilian] travel to a certain extent, because they didn't have enough passenger trains to handle the service or military personnel."

The freight load was heavy, too, Hansen remembered, and in addition, "Our freight trains had an awful lot of repair work. There wasn't a time when there wasn't four or five tracks that we used for repair work. You would never find anytime that there wasn't three out of those four that were full of bad-order cars that needed repair."

Lamar Belnap, who was a switching engineer for the Union Pacific Railroad, remembered the soldiers:

> I was down there when the war first started. These troop trains would come in, the soldiers had been confined to the trains and were anxious to get out...They'd head up 25th Street and find a bottle or drink. There were a lot of troop trains going through Ogden to the West Coast. When a hos-

pital train came in, they were marked with red crosses on the cars. The soldiers who could walk would get off the train and walk around. It was a sad deal seeing a lot of the fellows...on crutches and bandaged up.

UNUSUAL CARGO ON TRAINS

When trains with unusual cargo arrived at Ogden they got special treatment. Belnap remembered trains loaded with gasoline coming into the depot. When they stopped they were immediately surrounded by armed guards to protect the cargo. Another time, a train carrying gold bullion came to Ogden. The bullion was shipped in special cars that had "U.S. Army" written on them. They were a short car with an extra set of wheels under them to help support the weight. They were a kind of square car...only one-half the size of a regular box car. They had a little platform on the sides so the armed guards could sit on the outside and guard them, especially when they stopped. I don't think they rode on them when they were moving...they were very noticeable with the U.S. Army signs and warning signs all over.

During the war years as many as 120 trains a day moved through the Ogden Union Station. There were 17 tracks for passenger service. An underground passageway led from the station to the platforms so that passengers didn't have to walk across the tracks.

The 1940s were the busiest times for the Ogden Union Station. They were also good economic times for the workers. The war years were not the happiest of times, however, because war brings with it much tragedy, as those at the station witnessed when troop trains and hospital trains arrived. Another kind of tragedy occurred when the Southern Pacific Railroad suffered a major train wreck. The Ogden depot served as the center for receiving the dead and injured.

The Sub that Sank a Train
by Dr. Richard C. Roberts

It was after 4 a.m. and Commander Eugene Fluckey rubbed his eyes as he peered over the map spread before him. It was the twelfth war patrol of the submarine *U.S.S. Barb*, the fifth under Commander Fluckey. What could possibly be left for the Commander to accomplish who, just three months earlier, had been in Washington, D.C. to receive the Medal of Honor?

He smiled to himself as he looked again at the map showing a rail line that ran along the Japanese coast near Karafuto. This final patrol had been promised as the *Barb's* "graduation patrol," and Fluckey and his crew had cooked up an unusual finale. Since June 8 they had harassed the Japanese by destroying enemy supplies and coastal fortifications with the first submarine-launched rocket attacks. Now his crew was buzzing excitedly about bagging a train.

The rail line itself wouldn't be a problem. A patrol could go ashore under cover of darkness to plant the explosives, one of the sub's 55-pound scuttling charges. But on this early morning, Commander Fluckey and his officers were puzzled how they could blow not only the rails, but one of the frequent trains that shuttled supplies to equip the Japanese war machine. Such a daring feat could handicap the enemy's war effort for several days, a week or perhaps even longer.

EXCITING NEW IDEA

Cruising slowly beneath the surface to evade an enemy plane circling overhead, the crew had an exciting new idea. Instead of having crewmen on shore to trigger explosives to blow both rail and a passing train, why not let the train blow itself up by a special mechanism? "To complete the circuit (detonating the 55-pound charge) we could hook in a microswitch between two ties so the train sets it off," said crewman Billy Hatfield. Not only did Hatfield have a plan, he wanted to be part of the volunteer shore party.

The solution found, there was no shortage of volunteers, and all that was needed was the proper weather, a little cloud cover to darken the moon for the mission ashore. Fluckey established his own criteria for the volunteer party: no married men would be included, except for Hatfield; the party would include members from each department; the opportunity would be split between regular Navy and Navy Reserve sailors; and at least half of the men had to have been Boy Scouts, experienced in how to handle themselves in medical emergencies and in the woods.

In the meantime, there would be no more harassment of Japanese shipping or shore operations by the *Barb* until the train mission had been accomplished. The crew would "lay low," prepare their equipment, train for the attack and wait for the weather.

During the next four days the saboteurs anxiously watched the skies for cloud cover over Patience Bay and the inventive crew of the *Barb* built the bomb's microswitch. When the need was posed for a pick and shovel to bury the explosive charge and batteries, the *Barb's* engineers cut up steel plates in the lower flats of an engine room, then bent and welded them to create the needed tools. Time was running out. Only five days remained before the *Barb* had to return to base.

The eight saboteurs were: (L to R) Paul Saunders, William Hatfield, Francis Sever, Lawrence Newland, Edward Klinglesmith, James Richard, John Markuson and William Walker.

Anxiously watching the skies, Commander Fluckey noticed plumes of cirrus clouds, then white stratus clouds capping the mountain peaks ashore. A cloud cover was building to hide the three-quarters moon. This would be the night.

WALK ON JAPANESE MAINLAND

By midnight on July 23, 1945 the *Barb* had crept within 950 yards of shore. No one would suspect an American submarine so close to shore or in such shallow water. Slowly the small shore boats were lowered and the eight men paddled toward the beach. Twenty-five minutes later they pulled the boats ashore and walked on the surface of the Japanese mainland. Having lost their points of navigation, the men landed near the backyard of a house. Fortunately the residents had no dogs, though the sight of human and dog tracks in the sand along the beach alerted the sailors to the potential for unexpected danger.

Stumbling through noisy waist-high grasses, crossing a highway and then stumbling into a 4-foot drainage ditch, the men made their way to the railroad tracks. Three men were posted as guards. The *Barb's* auxiliary man John Markuson climbed the ladder to a water tower, then stopped in horror as he realized it was an enemy lookout tower. Fortunately the Japanese sentry was sleeping peacefully, and Markuson quietly withdrew to warn the raiding party.

The news from Markuson caused the men digging the placement for the explosive charge to continue more slowly and quietly. Suddenly, from less than 80 yards away, an express train was heard bearing down on them. The appearance was a surprise; it hadn't occurred to the crew that there might be a night train. When it passed, the brave but nervous sailors extracated themselves from the brush to continue their task. Twenty minutes later the holes had been dug and the explosives and batteries hidden beneath fresh soil.

Watching from the deck of the *Barb*, Commander Fluckey gave a sigh of relief as he noticed a flashlight signal from the beach announcing departure of the shore party. He had skillfully, and daringly, now guided the *Barb* within 600 yards of the enemy beach. There was less than six feet of water beneath the sub's keel, but Fluckey wanted to be close in case trouble arose and a daring rescue of his men became necessary.

The two boats were only halfway back to the *Barb* when the sub's machine gunner yelled, "Captain! Another train coming up the tracks!" The Commander grabbed a megaphone and yelled through the night, "Paddle like the devil!" knowing full well they wouldn't reach the *Barb* before the train hit the microswitch.

The darkness was shattered by brilliant light and the roar of the explosion. The boiler of the locomotive blew, shattering pieces of the engine 200 feet into the air. Behind it the cars began to accordian into each other, bursting into flame and adding to the magnificent fireworks display.

Five minutes later the men were lifted to the deck by their comrades as the *Barb* turned back to safer waters. Fluckey's voice came over the intercom: "All hands below deck not absolutely needed to maneuver the ship have permission to come topside." He didn't have to repeat the invitation. Hatches sprang open as the proud sailors gathered on the decks to watch the distant fireworks display. The *Barb* had "sunk" a Japanese train!

CHAPTER SIX

Built with Pride for the War Effort

"Never before in history has the freight car meant so much to the nation. Never before has so much depended upon the service it performs. Never before has its proper use been so important." —John J. Pelley, President, Association of American Railroads

During the initial war years, America's railroads hummed successfully, but soon the railroads and American industry thought about the bigger picture. How could the U.S. cope with such a tremendous buildup of military and passenger traffic if the war continued? And what would the railroads—and the American public—expect after the war was won?

Hotshot freights, double and tripleheaded trains, peak-capacity troop and regular passenger trains rode the high iron from east to west, crowding the rails. Railroads needed more capacity, larger locomotives and more modern equipment. More than four-fifths of the nation's wartime increase in

freight traffic was carried by the railroads. More than 93% of all of the Army's freight and express, and more than 80% of armed personnel was transported by the railroads.

In the first 20 months of WWII, the railroads carried 2½ times more troops as in the 19 months of WWI, and that did not include servicemen and women who traveled while on leave or on their own.

TRAINS HIGHLIGHTS WAR EFFORTS

In the December, 1943 issue of *Trains* magazine, the column entitled "Portfolio of Railroad Pictures" shows cab-forward articulateds, bright red and orange 4-8-4 Daylights

LEFT AND ABOVE. In 1941 and 1944, Lima Locomotive Works manufactured a series of 24 beautiful 2-8-4's for the Pere Marquette, a road that merged into the C&O in 1947. During WWII the railroad hauled primarily automobiles and auto parts, while merchandise was also a primary source of revenue. These engines were at the center of much of the lines' Michigan automobile wartime tonnage. *Jay Williams collection*

running between Los Angeles and San Francisco, the Reading's Pacific #105 pulling a fast New York-Philadelphia express, and the Santa Fe's diesel-powered *El Capitan* climbing the 2.2% eastbound grade of Cajon Pass.

At West Philadelphia, the Pennsylvania Railroad shows numerous steam locomotives simmering near the roundhouse—a show of strength in these war years.

Even pictures of the Rio Grande's big, husky 2-8-8-2 compound Mallets are shown pulling the fast freight *Ute* on the Moffat Route near Plainview, Colorado. In another story, *Trains* goes to Southeastern Junction at the city limits of St. Louis, to record the smoky wartime action on the Frisco Lines, where the single operator-leverman is kept "plenty busy. And there is a long, long parade of fast freight trains outbound at night, inbound in the morning, and an astoundingly continuous string of oil trains," reads the article.

PLAN NEEDED FOR FUTURE

Railroads needed a plan for growth and expansion. And they needed it in all areas of their operations including locomotives, freight and passenger cars, signaling and trackwork, computing and management. As railroad traffic grew, more plans were developed to sustain the vital rail link already established and build new equipment to match the future needs of America.

Everyone got involved—railroads, the government and industry. Soon a revolution began that propelled the railroads and the rail industry into the future.

> "We at Baldwin see clearly the need for new and better locomotive types, and we are working diligently toward that goal."—*Ralph Kelly, president of the Baldwin Locomotive Works in 1945.*

BELOW AND ABOVE. Lima turned out Nickel Plate Road locomotive #757 in 1944 in the series #755-762 S-2 Class 2-8-4 in August. This locomotive last operated on June 15, 1958 on a run between East Wayne and Bellevue, Ohio. Later it went to the Railroad Museum of Pennsylvania at Strasburg. *Jay Williams collection*

194

These pictures show a C&O H-8 2-6-6-6 being built at the Lima Locomotive Works in Lima, Ohio in mid-1944. The C&O ordered 10 of these mighty monsters, then another 15 for the war in that year, and they, along with 35 other C&O Alleghenies, were the final refinement of super-power. The locomotives carried the railroad during the WWII years, as well as the years that followed. *Jay Williams collection*

Detroit, Toledo & Ironton 2-8-2 #808 was delivered new and ready for battle by Lima in June of 1944. Lima's large shops were located between the B&O's Cincinnati-Toledo main line and the NKP's main line and shops in Lima, Ohio. *Jay Williams collection*

In 1941 the Milwaukee Road received its first 5,400-hp FT four-unit road diesels in A and B configurations and numbered 40A, B, C and D, setting the stage for other diesels to follow. During the year of 1944, the Milwaukee owned 622 freight locomotives, 56,000 freight cars, 182 passenger locomotives and 950 passenger cars. *Jay Williams collection*

In 1943 the Norfolk & Western Railway Roanoke facilities outshopped C&NW 2-8-2 #2309 for unknown reasons, but it could have been because the C&NW needed the locomotive sooner than its own shops could rebuild it because of the war schedule. *Jay Williams collection*

In 1944 the last cab forward was delivered to the Southern Pacific from Baldwin, with 4-8-8-2 #4294 among the final group numbered 4275-4294. With 63" drivers, this grouping of AC-12s ended an era of railroading for the SP which began in 1910 with the first cab-in-front engine. These locomotives helped SP with wartime movements and gave plenty of power to freights needing that extra push. *Jay Williams collection*

With the war at full throttle, and the Pennsylvania needing more rugged power to cross the Pittsburgh Division mountains as well as hot-shot locomotives elsewhere, management went shopping. But wartime restrictions wouldn't allow the railroad to design a new engine, so the C&O lent a 2-10-4, and soon Pennsy's Altoona Shops were busy constructing the J1 Class. The first was delivered in December of 1942; in all, 125 Texas types, J1's and J1a's, were made. *Jay Williams collection*

In the June, 1942 Baldwin Locomotive Works magazine, this Frisco 4-8-4 was featured pulling wartime tonnage in a tribute to the fine locomotives being built during WWII. *Baldwin magazine, First Quarter 1944*

Other Baldwin locomotives built during WWII . . .

• Frisco • Southern Pacific
• Duluth, Missabe & Iron Range
• Northern Pacific
• Richmond, Fredericksburg & Potomac

ABOVE AND LEFT. Southern Pacific cab forward articulated locomotives #4205 and #4242 were of the AC-10 Class with 63" drivers, 250 pounds of boiler pressure and built by Baldwin in 1942 to help turn the tide of the country's emergency. The class consisted of 39 locomotives, #4205 to #4244. *Baldwin magazine, December 1942*

BALDWIN

Baldwin magazine, First Quarter 1944

Baldwin magazine, First Quarter 1944

Baldwin disc driving wheels are used by the Richmond, Fredericksburg & Potomac on their 4-8-4 type locomotives. *Baldwin magazine, December 1942*

Norman Call, president of the Richmond, Fredericksburg & Potomac Railroad Company, and his wife inspect the *Governor John Letcher* during a visit to the Baldwin plant at Eddystone during the war.

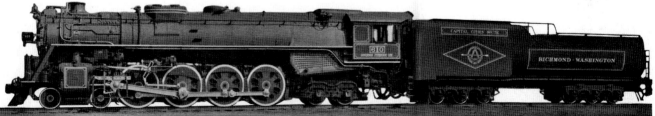

Baldwin magazine, December 1942

Number 1106 was one of the 2-6-6-4 type locomotives built by Baldwin for the Pittsburgh & West Virginia during WWII. Note the new style of lettering and the monogram on the side of the tender. *Baldwin magazine, October 1943*

**Steam Locomotives
built for the war**

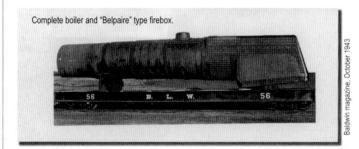

Complete boiler and "Belpaire" type firebox.

Baldwin magazine, October 1943

Interior of cab on engineer's side.

Front view of number 1101 shows the air pumps mounted on the smokebox front.

Baldwin magazine, October 1943

**One of the Baldwin-built 2-6-6-4 type locomotives delivered
to the Pittsburgh & West Virginia Railway in 1943**

Cylinders (4) . . . . 123" x 32"		Fuel . . . . soft coal	
Steam pressure . . . . 225 lb		Heating surface . . . . 5,914 sq ft	

Louisville & Nashville's new 2-8-4 #1954 was built by Baldwin in 1942 with 25" x 32" cylinders and steam pressure of 265 pounds. *Baldwin magazine, December 1942*

Baldwin magazine, December 1942

NEW LOCOMOTIVES
FOR THE WAR DEPARTMENT
United States Government

Baldwin magazine, December 1942

Baldwin magazine, December 1942

Superheating surface	1873 sq ft	Weight, engine and tender .905,640 lb
Grate area	102.3 sq ft	Tractive force (main cylinders). .97,000 lb
Drivers, diameter	63"	Tractive froce (booster. .16,000 lb
Weight on drivers	397,300 bl	Tender water capacity .20,000 U.S. gal
Weight, total engine	.528,040 lb	Tender fuel capacity . 20 tons

Baldwin magazine, October 1943

Victory Power

At this time when everything depends on a free flow of traffic, the American transportation system has the leading role in our struggle against oppression. Even before planes, ships, tanks, and guns are made, the raw materials must be produced and transported thousands of miles to all parts of the nation. Whitcomb locomotives will be found in most of our strategic industrial areas on the roughest, toughest hauling jobs.

This war is world-wide and it is only natural that Whitcomb locomotives should be on the job in other vital areas. Hauling supplies in many theatres of war, bauxite in the jungles of British and Dutch Guiana, local transportation at Trinidad, Pearl Harbor and Nassau— from Vladivostok to Melbourne, if there are rails to run on, you will probably find a Whitcomb. You'll find, too, that they are doing these jobs the way they must be done . . . fast, economically, efficiently, with top performance from start to finish.

THE WHITCOMB LOCOMOTIVE CO.

ROCHELLE, ILL.

Subsidiary of THE BALDWIN LOCOMOTIVE WORKS

Baldwin magazine, December 1942

New United States Army locomotive is inspected by (left to right) Colonel E. F. MacFadden, Major J. W. Marsh and Colonel W. G. Knight, all of the Corps of Engineers, United States Army. *Baldwin magazine, December 1942*

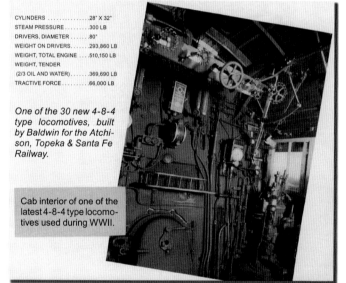

CYLINDERS	.28" X 32"
STEAM PRESSURE	.300 LB
DRIVERS, DIAMETER	.80"
WEIGHT ON DRIVERS	.293,860 LB
WEIGHT, TOTAL ENGINE	.510,150 LB
WEIGHT, TENDER (2/3 OIL AND WATER)	.369,690 LB
TRACTIVE FORCE	.66,000 LB

One of the 30 new 4-8-4 type locomotives, built by Baldwin for the Atchison, Topeka & Santa Fe Railway.

Cab interior of one of the latest 4-8-4 type locomotives used during WWII.

Baldwin magazine, Third Quarter 1944

NEW LOCOMOTIVES
on the Santa Fe

The Santa Fe 4-8-4 2900 Class

Baldwin magazine, Third Quarter 1944

Pennsylvania's streamlined T1 Class

Wartime Loewy-styled Duplex locomotives

Baldwin magazine, December 1942

This is the mammoth boiler of the Pennsylvania T1 #6110 at the Baldwin Locomotive Works plant while still under construction in 1944. *Baldwin magazine, December 1942*

Interior of the cab of a Class T-1 locomotive shows the arrangement of gauges, valves and other fittings on the backhead of the boiler. It is an orderly arrangement insuring maximum convenience and safety for the operators.

Baldwin magazine, December 1942

Baldwin magazine, December 1942

In 1942, the Chicago & NorthWestern placed a Whitcomb 80-ton, 650-hp diesel-electric locomotive in service at Sheboygan, Wisconsin. The C&NW used the centercab unit for switching in the yard, pusher service and transfer of cars at the coal docks on the Sheboygan River. *Baldwin magazine, 1944*

Joseph B. Eastman, Director of the Office of Defense Transportation and an Interstate Commerce Commissioner, right, peers out a locomotive cab window during the war. Eastman was considered the nation's best known and most honored civil servant. He died in March of 1944. *Press Association*

Passenger Service Cut

The O. D. T. has ordered that all passenger trains which handled less than a 35% load last November must be discontinued. And, although passenger schedules have been practically frozen since the beginning of the war, it has ordered discontinuance of all special services to resorts. Rumors persist that diners will be ordered off all runs of less than 350 miles, but as yet nothing has been done along this line.

New Equipment

Class 1 railroads during 1944 put 40,392 new freight cars and 938 new locomotives in service, the A. A. R. announces. This was 11,684 cars and 165 locomotives more than in 1943. In 1942, the railroads put 63,009 new freight cars and 712 new locomotives in service. The new locomotives installed in 1944 include 329 steam, 1 electric, and 608 Diesel. Most new cars were box and hopper. *Trains magazine, March 1945*

Baldwin magazine, October 1943

"One thing the recent war provided is the country's utter dependence on its railroads for the transportation on which military success depends," said *Railway Age* in its August 24, 1946 issue. So after the war, the Gulf, Mobile & Ohio added 55 1,500-hp Alco-GE FA-1s to its roster in 1946-7, each featuring 60,000 pounds of tractive effort. They were built at the Schenectady, New York plant. *Don Heimburger collection*

LEFT. Baldwin-Westinghouse 2,000-hp diesel-electric road locomotive makes a station stop in 1943 during an experimental run on the lines of the Central Railroad of New Jersey. *Baldwin magazine, October 1943*

Wartime Pennsylvania #6131, a Class Q-2 4-4-6-4 constructed in the Pennsylvania Railroad's own Altoona shops in August of 1944, was one of the largest and most powerful 10-drivered locomotives built. In the railroad's own tests at Altoona, the Q-2 showed it was capable of producing a 8,000 horsepower rating. The Q-2 series #6175-6199 was built between 1044 and 1945, with the #6131 an experimental unit among five Q-2s built before the production run. *Don Heimburger collection*

ABOVE AND BELOW. These giant Southern Pacific cab forward articulated engines were used primarily for freight trains, but sometimes were found heading up passenger trains as well. Engine #4262 is at El Paso, Texas in 1945, while #4238 waters up at Lancaster, California. *Jay Williams collection*

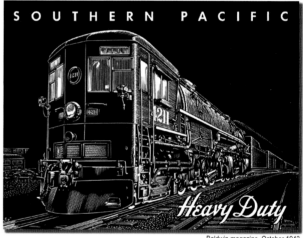

Baldwin magazine, October 1943

"It's hard to realize," says noted veteran railroad historian Joe Collias, "the tremendous impact war had on rail traffic. For all practicable purposes, all military traffic moved via rail." So in 1943, Baldwin Locomotive Works delivered this monster Missouri Pacific 4-8-4 #2208 in Class N-73 (numbers 2201-2215). A tractive force of 67,200 lbs., 73" drivers and 285 lbs. boiler pressure was wrapped up in this machine, which was 17,000 pounds heavier than the Denver & Rio Grande Western's big M-68 4-8-4s. Because of rationed bronze, these engines featured lead bells which produced a "dink" instead of a "clang," says Collias. The 2200 Class was put to work on the MoPac hauling redball freights between St. Louis and Kansas City, as well as heavyweight passenger trains. *Don Heimburger collection*

U.S. railroads needed newer and heftier motive power between 1941 and 1945 and immediately thereafter. Wabash 4-6-4 #703 was rebuilt from a Class K-5 2-8-2 (#2603) at the railroad's sprawling Decatur, Illinois shops, and was one of seven such rebuilds (Nos. 700-706) between 1943 and 1947; all were scrapped by 1956. *Charles Felstead, Don Heimburger collection*

Norfolk & Western's 4-8-2 Mountain Class K-3 #200, shown here built new in 1926 at Roanoke, was used mostly on the Norfolk and Scioto divisions. But during WWII, it was declared surplus power, and was sold to the Richmond, Fredericksburg & Potomac in early 1944. *Glen Kratt, Don Heimburger collection*

Equipment and Supplies

Heavy locomotive buying in March
Large steam power orders placed; car buying declines as deliveries lag

Continued heavy railroad purchases of steam locomotives highlighted the domestic railway equipment market during March. Orders were placed during the month for 102 steam engines, more than placed in any preceding March since the 133 units ordered in March, 1929.

An additional large number of locomotives were comprised in inquiries by railroads that came into the market for steam power during March but had not placed orders at the month's end. These in part included the Bessemer & Lake Erie inquiry for five 2-10-4's and two 0-8-0's; the Duluth, Missabe & Iron Range inquiry for ten 2-8-8-4's;

Westinghouse, June 1942

the Indianapolis Union inquiry for one or two 0-8-0's; and the Western Pacific inquiry for six 4-8-4's. Directors of the Illinois Central approved a large locomotive-buying program.

Also reported unfilled at the end of March was an earlier inquiry by the Argentine State Railways for ten, twelve, or fifteen 4-6-2's and three 2-10-2's for which, it was understood, the Argentine government would request a high priority rating.

Together with 85 steam locomotives ordered in February, and the above-mentioned unfilled inquires, the 102 steam engines purchased in March will probably rank the current months as one of the most concentrated buying

periods in recent steam locomotive history. These orders and inquires, made despite large backlogs of orders already on builders' books from the carrier—and at a time when the country's steam locomotive building capacity is largely devoted to the completion of recent large government orders—evidences the scope of managerial foresight and preparation for late 1942 and 1943 traffic requirements.

A total of 42 diesel-electric locomotives were also ordered by the railroads during March, including nine freight engines of 5,400 hp. each and 33 switching engines of 1,000 hp. each. This compares with 79 Diesel-electric units ordered in the proceeding month of February and with 95 ordered in March, 1941. *Railway Age, April 4, 1942*

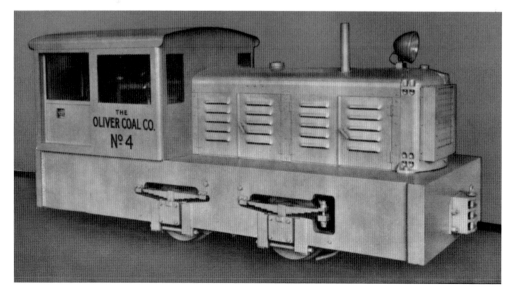

In the nation's coal industry during the war, new motive power was introduced, such as this low-height Oliver Coal Company Hercules Model DOOD engine rated at 56 hp for a mine at an altitude of 6,100 feet. *Baldwin magazine, First Quarter 1945*

The New York Central went shopping for new power and ordered 4-8-2 Mohawks from Lima in 1943. Both the L-4a's (shown here as #3103) and the L-4b's were fitted with the largest tender yet used on the NYC system, featuring a coal capacity of 43 tons of the black gold. Noted NYC steam buff Alvin Staufer said, "...the wartime service they performed was almost beyond belief. It was nothing for them to come in on a heavy freight drag, be serviced, and leave a few hours later at the head of one of the Great Steel Fleet." Here the 72"-drivered #3103 steams at Englewood (Chicago) in April of 1943 with a passenger train in tow. *Don Heimburger collection*

Pennsylvania's Altoona-built Q1 Class duplex 4-6-4-4 was ultra modern and shrouded, but too costly to operate with diesels arriving. And U.S. railroads were already trimming their expenses during the latter part of the war. The #6130 had 77" drivers and different sizes of front and rear cylinders, an oddity. The impressive-looking Q's didn't last long, and by 1949 most were inactive. *Don Heimburger collection*

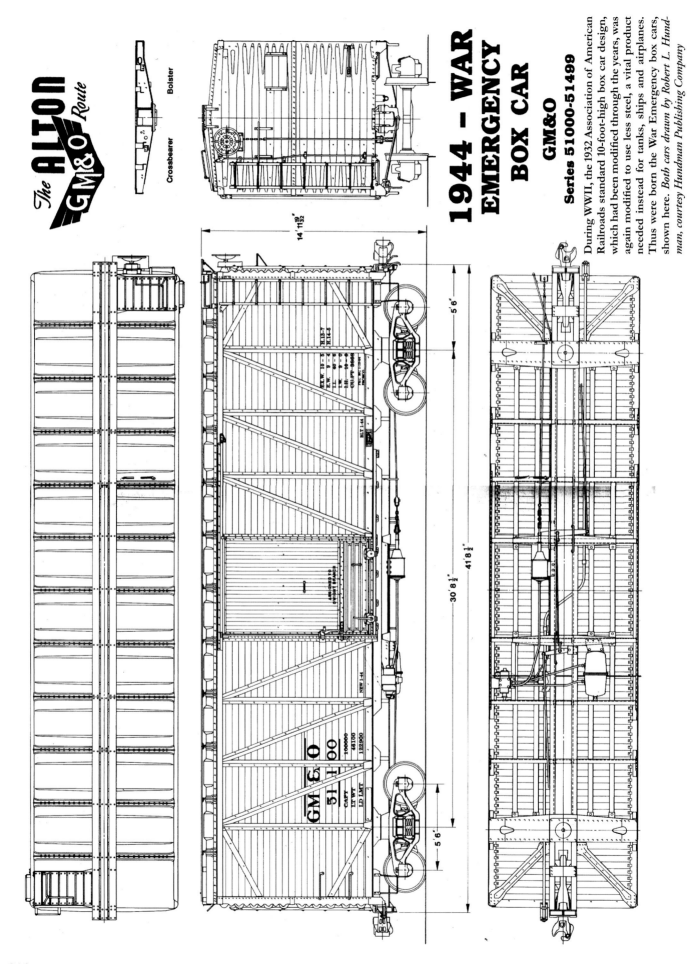

1944 – WAR EMERGENCY BOX CAR

GM&O

Series 51000-51499

During WWII, the 1932 Association of American Railroads standard 10-foot-high box car design, which had been modified through the years, was again modified to use less steel, a vital product needed instead for tanks, ships and airplanes. Thus were born the War Emergency box cars, shown here. Both cars drawn by Robert L. Hundman, courtesy Hundman Publishing Company

Bolster

Crossbearer

14' 11 9/32"

5' 6"

41' 8 1/2"

30' 8 1/2"

5' 6"

War Emergency Box Car

AT&SF
Class Bx-38

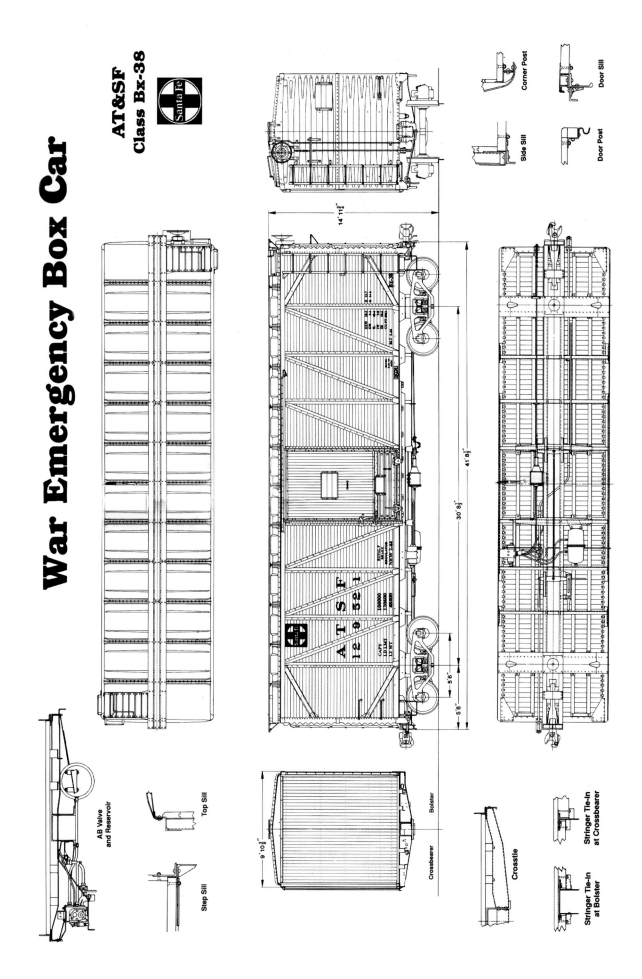

Corner Post

Door Sill

Side Sill

Door Post

AB Valve
and Reservoir

Top Sill

Step Sill

Bolster

Crossbearer

Crosstie

Stringer Tie-In
at Crossbearer

Stringer Tie-In
at Bolster

ATSF
12 9 52 1

14' 11⅜"

41' 8½"

30' 8½"

5'6"

5'6"

9' 10⅜"

One of five 1000-horsepower diesel-electrics delivered to St. Louis-San Francisco Railway last year. Baldwin now has an order for eight more 1000-horsepower and two 660-horsepower locomotives.

Atlantic Coast Line Railroad is operating two of these Baldwin 1000-horsepower locomotives delivered in 1941. Four duplicate locomotives are now on order.

A Baldwin 660-horsepower locomotive built early in 1942 for the Akron and Barberton Belt Railroad.

The Upper Merion and Plymouth Railroad now has two of these Baldwin 660-horsepower locomotives.

More new diesel switcher locomotives produced in 1942 by Baldwin for wartime work in the U.S. were distributed to both large roads like Frisco and smaller, obscure roads such as the Upper Merion & Plymouth. *Baldwin magazine, June 1942*

WWII Tank Cars

United States Army 10,000-gallon tank car #11278 was built in October of 1942 to a particular specification, USG-A, which was a unique plan used during national wartime periods. This car was riveted and did not feature heating coils. The car had a steel frame, and rivets were used to attach handrails, domes and other appliances to the car. The car was made of six sheets of metal, and the tank rested on four hardwood pads, one on each corner. The wheels had friction bearings. *Thornton Waite; photos by the author*

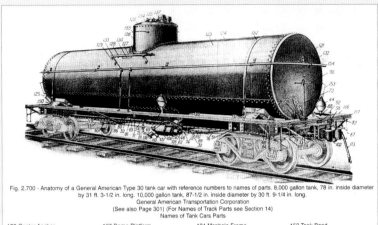

Fig. 2.700 - Anatomy of a General American Type 30 tank car with reference numbers to names of parts. 8,000 gallon tank, 78 in. inside diameter by 31 ft. 3-1/2 in. long. 10,000 gallon tank, 87-1/2 in. inside diameter by 30 ft. 9-1/4 in. long.
General American Transportation Corporation
(See also Page 301) (For Names of Track Parts see Section 14)
Names of Tank Cars Parts

120 Center Anchor	127 Dome Platform	134 Manhole Frame	152 Tank Band
121 Tank Head	128 Dome Platform Angle	135 Manhole Cover	153 Tank Head Grab
122 Dome Head	129 Dome Platform Bracket	136 Manhole Cover Safety Guard	154 Hand Rail Pipe and Fitting
123 Outer Shell Sheet	130 Dome Platform Grab	(not shown)	155 Dome Grab
124 Inner Shell Sheet	131 Inside Tank Ladder (not shown)	137 5 in. Safety Valve	
125 Bottom Sheet	132 Hand Rail Bracket	150 Tank Band Turnbuckle	
126 Dome Sheet	133 Dome Ladder	151 Tank Band Bolt	

Simmons-Boardman Publishing Company

213

Troop Sleepers and Kitchen Cars
America's Railroads Serve the Nation
During its Wartime Emergency

The advent of World War II placed extreme demands upon America's railroads regarding the amount of freight ton-miles required for the handling of the raw materials and finished weapons of war that would be needed until final victory was achieved.

Railroad revenue ton-miles increased from 373.3 billion in 1940 to 740 billion in 1944, a doubling of traffic in just four years. During the war years, America's railroads were also required to provide for the transportation of millions of soldiers, sailors and Marines from their training bases and camps throughout the country to the ports of embarkation and naval bases on the East, West and Gulf coasts.

At the same time, they accommodated the needs of untold numbers of civilian passengers traveling between America's far-flung cities and towns. Consequently, revenue passenger-miles increased from 23.8 billion in 1940 to 96 billion in 1944, a fourfold increase in only four years. As a further complication, the War Production Board severely restricted the number of conventional passenger cars that were built during this period. Only 242 passenger train cars were built for domestic railroads in 1942 and none in 1943 and 1944. Asking civilians, "Is your trip essential?" and to limit their travel if the answer was "no," only provided partial relief for American railroads' overtaxed passenger handling capacity.

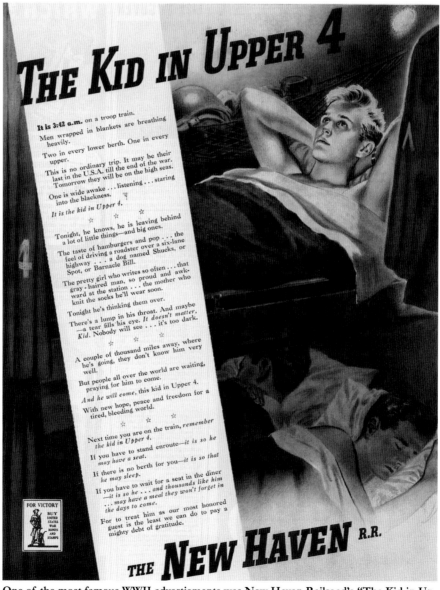

One of the most famous WWII advertisments was New Haven Railroad's "The Kid in Upper 4," which describes a young soldier's sleepless nights and emotional thoughts about going to war. The ad first appeared in the December 21, 1942 issue of *Life* magazine. *John Kelly collection*

Northern Pacific 4-6-6-4 #5123 with a long string of troop cars trailing, stops at Missoula, Montana a few months after the war ended to give soldiers a break and stretch their legs, although it appears officers told them not to venture far from the train. Locomotive #5123, particularly clean over its massive length, featured 70" drivers and was of the Class Z-7, of which six were built by Alco, all in 1941. This engine was dismantled in 1956. *R.V. Nixon, collection of J. Michael Gruber*

As a stopgap solution, hundreds of surplus Pullman tourist heavyweight sleeping cars, primarily having 12 open sections and one drawing room (usually Plan 2410 cars), were pressed into troop train service. Each car could handle as many as 39 passengers: one soldier slept in an upper berth while two soldiers were assigned to a lower berth. In contrast, the Navy assigned only one sailor to a lower berth.

To provide food for the troops, baggage cars were temporarily converted into kitchen cars by the inclusion of field stoves and iceboxes. These cars were placed in the charge of a mess sergeant who was assisted by mess stewards and the "kitchen police" (soldiers assigned to KP duty).

Each mess unit stocked these cars at departure points and removed its equipment at the final destination. In most instances, the men remained in their seats, and the "chow" was brought to them by the mess stewards. As another stopgap measure, 40 PRR X32 50-foot round-roof automobile cars were converted into troop sleeping cars (#8200 to 8239), and five additional X32 automobile cars were converted into kitchen cars (#6201 and K-500 to K-503) in 1943.

Even though these makeshift procedures were a much needed help to America's wartime transportation needs, there were still not enough spare Pullman tourist sleepers and available baggage cars to outfit all of the troop trains needed as America's participation in the war increased. As a consequence, the Defense Plant Corporation contracted for the new construction of 2,400 troop sleeping cars, 800 troop kitchen cars, and 40 hospital kitchen cars beginning in 1943 and ending in 1946. The troop sleeping and kitchen cars were government-owned but operated and maintained by the Pullman Company as part of its normal "pool." The

food service provided to the troops was normal Army rations handled by regular Army mess crews.

In order to save money and time, designs for the troop sleeping and kitchen cars were based on the A.A.R. standard 50' 6" box car. While the cost of building the cars was a small fraction of the cost of a standard Pullman sleeping car, the Pullman Company made it clear to their employees that, "Our service in these cars is to conform in every respect to the customer service you are accustomed to deliver in connection with the regular Pullmans. These cars will bear the name Pullman."

PULLMAN-STANDARD TROOP SLEEPERS

The 2,400 production triple-deck troop sleepers were built by the Pullman-Standard Car Manufacturing Company in their Michigan City plant in two lots: car numbers 7000 to 8199 from October 1943 through March 1944 (Lot 6704) and car numbers 8300 to 8499 and 9000 to 9999 from October 1945 through May 1946 (Lot 6753).

A single unnumbered test car was also built by Pullman-Standard in 1945 (Lot 6753-A). The troop sleepers were of riveted carbon-steel construction with heavily reinforced ends. The first series weighed 76,300 lbs. The length over buffers was 54' 2½". The width was 9' 9⅝" over side sills. Truck centers were spaced 40' 8½". The flooring was 1¾" by ⁵⁄₁₆" tongue-and-groove material which was applied across the car the same as in a freight car and was bolted directly to the side sills and floor stringers.

The top flooring was brown asphalt tile cemented directly to the wood flooring. Sloping ramps covered with non-slip metal treads brought the floor height up to the standard passenger car floor height at the car ends. The cars were

At Philadelphia soon after the war ended, troops and equipment were still moving throughout the U.S. In this picture, a loaded troop train sits on the near track, a clerestory-roofed heavyweight troop train is on the middle track and additional heavyweights and military loads on flatcars are on the farthest tracks of this rail yard. The average troop train carried from 250 to 500 men, and some troop trains were as long as 35 cars in length. *Collection of J. Michael Gruber*

equipped with two AB-1-B type control valves, two air reservoirs, two type "C" slack adjusters and two UAH 10" by 12" brake cylinders, operating each truck brake independently.

The Westinghouse AB-1-B brake equipment was a modification of the standard AB freight car brake system. It was designed for use on freight cars that operated in both freight and fast passenger service. The AB-1-B control valve incorporated an additional connection to the passenger signal pipe. When the signal line was charged with air, the brake valve automatically adjusted the equipment for passenger train service. This eliminated operation of the "controlled emergency" necessary for long freight train service and enabled the emergency rate of the brake cylinder application appropriate to passenger train operation.

Also, the UAH brake cylinders accommodated additional air lines to power the automatic slack adjusters. Rods were provided on each side of the car for releasing the brakes. A single hand brake operated on only one truck, and train crews were cautioned to inspect both trucks to ensure that the hand brake was released before moving the car.

High-speed Allied Full Cushion trucks, along with steam and signal lines, allowed the cars to be operated in all passenger trains. The water supply consisted of 150 gallons per car stored in overhead gravity-flow tanks. The tanks were filled through nozzles at the side sill level at each corner of the car just inside the trucks.

The end doors were similar to those on standard railway passenger cars. There were no vestibules, but each car was fitted with passenger car diaphragms and face plates. Sliding doors on each side at about the center of the car facilitated loading and unloading. The side doors on the first lot of cars were provided with trap doors and step walls closed with pressed pans. Those on the second lot lacked the wells and had simple flat section steel steps.

On each side of the car were 10 sliding windows about 2½' by 3' high. Each window was equipped with roll shades and mesh screens. In addition to the main windows, there were smaller windows at each end of the car opposite the wash basins and for each toilet room.

Eight exhaust ventilators in the roof and inlet ventilators in the side near the eaves provided ventilation. A low-pressure steam vapor heating system with fin radiators was installed in the cars and perforated grills covered all heating pipes. The heat was manually controlled by four hand valves, two placed on each side of the car, with stencil markings showing their location. The cars were insulated, and the ceilings and interior sides were lined with a composition material painted in three-tone tans.

BERTHS ACCOMMODATE 30 PASSENGERS

When made up for night occupancy, the cars had sleeping accommodations for 29 passengers and one porter with each having an individual bed. The berths were arranged in tiers of three running crosswise with the aisle along one side instead of in the center as in a conventional sleeping car. One of the end upper berths was enclosed and reserved for the porter. It was accessible only from the transverse corridor that was opposite the end door. For daytime use,

The Wabash Railroad used a number of old troop cars after the war for maintenance-of-way trains. These cars, with lights burning and crews inside, could often be seen on sidings along the main line in the evenings in the 1950s. *Don Heimburger*

the top berths remained fixed, forming a ceiling for the sleeping section and space for the storage of bedding and linen. The middle berth dropped down to form a back for the seat converted from the lower berth. Each tier of berths had curtains for use when the cars were operated in regular trains or when the cars were occupied by WACs or WAVES, or other women members of the military.

Standard Pullman bedding, consisting of sheets, pillows, pillowcases and blankets was furnished for each berth, and the linen was changed every night while the cars were in service. Two wooden coat hangers were permanently attached to each berth. Each berth was also furnished with a rack for the soldier's rifle.

There were four wash basins, two at each end of the car, with cold and hot water faucets, and two enclosed toilets, one at each end of the car. Above the wash basins were wide mirrors, and nearby was located a paper towel dispenser and waste rack for used towels. A drinking water cooler with a dispenser for sanitary drinking cups was provided at one end of the car.

An emergency tool rack, enclosed in glass, was located above one of the side doors for easy accessibility. Two chemical fire extinguishers, also enclosed in glass cases, were installed in each car. Additionally, a first-aid package was located in a locked container on one of the side walls.

The current for the electrical lighting system was furnished by replaceable dry cell-type batteries. The batteries were housed in large steel boxes mounted on the interior side wall, approximately 7' above the aisle floor. There were 12 low-voltage light fixtures throughout the car. Two fixtures were mounted over the wash basins, one at each end of the car, two on each car between the side doors, and eight arranged in pairs on the side wall in each section. The illumination provided by these lights permitted soldiers to read, write letters and play cards. For night lights, there was one ceiling fixture in each toilet, one in front of each end door, and two in the ceiling of each passageway.

AMERICAN CAR & FOUNDRY CARS

The 800 troop kitchen cars were built by the American Car & Foundry Company in its Chicago plant from October

1943 through March 1944 (Lot 2635, car numbers K-100 through K-499) and in their Berwick, Pennsylvania plant from October 1945 through January 1946 (Lot 2852, car numbers K-600 through K-999).

The steel framing for the underframe, sides and roof closely followed the corresponding A.A.R. standard box car design. The end framing with end-door opening was designed to meet A.A.R. requirements for passenger train equipment. The light weight of these cars was 77,500 lbs. The length over buffers, coupled, was 54' 2 1/8". Truck center spacing was the same as that for the troop sleepers, 40' 8 1/2".

A double wood floor was provided of tongue-and-groove yellow pine, the bottom course being 1 3/4" laid crosswise and the top course 1 5/8" laid longitudinally. A ramp of non-skid steel floor plate was provided at each side door to account for the difference in elevation between the platform floor level and the car body floor. Eight floor drains with hinged flush covers permitted washing out the kitchen with a hose.

Like the troop sleepers, each car had air signal lines along with twin Westinghouse AB-1-B air brake equipment having two brake cylinders, two air reservoirs, two C-26-DX-90 automatic slack adjusters and two control valves. The kitchen cars lacked A-2-A quick service valves that were

THROUGH THE DARKEST HOUR

The railroads are part and parcel of the vital service of supply on which fighting men depend. They know first-hand the darkness of the hour before the dawn. ● They follow the progress of the war by the nature and urgency of the burdens they carry—burdens that never lighten through the whole 24 hours of the day. ● So through sunshine and shadow, railroad men serve the needs of war. Short on help, short on time, they know the value of every hour and every car. They know that a fighting nation counts on them to deliver the goods that Victory is made of—and doggedly, devotedly, they are sticking to that job. ● Some day the dark hour will be behind us. Then our nation will look back on the courage and the will with which we faced it and judge our fiber as a people. ● The railroads are working now so that when that day dawns they can, in clear knowledge of a job faithfully discharged, look forward with confidence to finer things to come.

ASSOCIATION OF
AMERICAN RAILROADS
ALL UNITED FOR VICTORY

National Geographic, August 1944

usually a component of the AB-1-B air-brake system. A hand brake was installed at one end of the car located inside the main body end post. The brakes on only one truck were operated by the hand brake. As on the troop sleepers, high-speed Allied Full Cushion trucks and steam lines allowed the kitchen cars to be operated in all passenger trains.

The water supply was furnished from an air pressure water system with air supplied from one of the emergency reservoirs of the air brake equipment, a reducing valve and a low-pressure 14" by 30" air reservoir. A hand-operated pump was located under the sink for emergency use when the cars were standing without an air connection. Separate water supplies were provided for the sink and crew shower. Two 200-gallon cold water tanks and one 40-gallon hot water tank furnished the sink supply, and one 82-gallon cold water tank and one 30-gallon hot water tank were connected to the shower. Water for the shower was heated by a Vapor water heater and for the sink by a similar heater and the water backs of the ranges.

The end door openings were 2' 3" wide, and the side door openings were 4' wide by 6' high. A safety bar was provided across each end door opening which was pivoted to a bracket on the main body endpost. The side door openings were protected by door guards of standard pipe with a pivoted bottom section of expanded metal. There were 14 windows (six on one side and eight on the opposite side) having a sliding sash and inside screens, both of which could be raised by the kitchen crew. Each window also had a roller curtain which overlapped the window opening at all edges. Similar curtains were also provided at the end door and side door windows.

VENTILATED OPENINGS

Nine pivoted ventilating openings with flush outside screens were installed in the sides of the cars close to the side plate, and 11 galvanized steel exhaust ventilators were installed on the roof with screened openings outside and adjustable shutters inside. The cars were heated by the Vapor Car Heating Company's system of steam heat having four plain pipe coils, one located in each corner of the car. Four manual steam supply valves allowed control of heat provided to the car.

The kitchen car interior equipment consisted of two U.S. Army coal ranges connected in tandem. Each range was equipped with a back filled with water and was connected to a shared positive exhaust smokejack. A canopy was installed over the ranges with connections to two roof exhaust ventilators. The ranges were located on one side of the car adjacent to the side door opening.

A coal box of half-ton capacity was located opposite the range and had a roof hatch for loading the coal. An expanded metal bin was installed next to the range for wood. Adjacent to the range was a deep sink of heavy galvanized steel having a center partition with wooden drain boards and a splash back. A single swing faucet was provided for the hot and cold water supply. Across from the sinks was a cook's work table.

Across the car from the range was a utensil cupboard with sliding doors, and on the other side of the door opening

This is the same troop kitchen car as in the photo below, but apparently this photo was taken with representatives of the U.S. military and plant supervisors when the car was just completed.

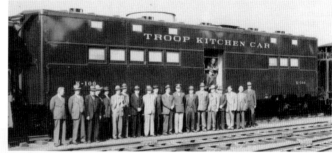

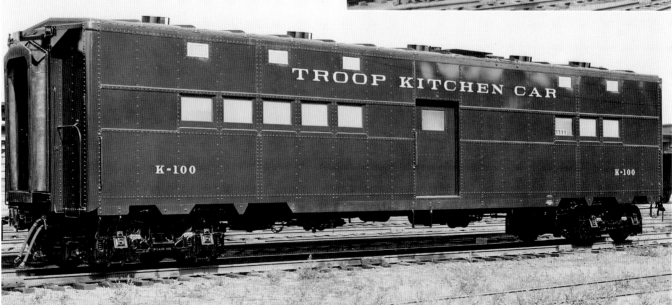

ABOVE AND OPPOSITE PAGE. Troop cars K-100 and #7000 are shown when new. *Courtesy Kalmbach Publishing Company*

Triple-Deck Troop Sleeping Cars

*The first passenger cars authorized since the beginning of the
war and the first ever built exclusively for carrying troops*

On the principle that nothing's too good for American fighting men, a new type of Pullman sleeping car, built by the Pullman-Standard Car Manufacturing Company and designed for transporting service men with emphasis on comfort and efficiency, will be placed in service in October. Previewed at Washington, D. C., on September 4 by officers of the Transportation Corps, Army Service Forces, who originally approved the design, it was the first of 1,200 cars incorporating a special triple-deck berth arrangement. Production schedules call for completion of the order by the first of the year.

CAR'S PRINCIPAL FEATURES

The new Pullman triple-deck sleeper embodies primarily riveted carbon-steel construction with heavily reinforced ends and weighs 76,300 lbs. It is designed for full interchangeability with all other cars, is equipped with high-speed passenger-train car trucks and springs, and therefore can be operated in any type of passenger railway train. There are no vestibules. Sliding doors on each side at about the center of the car, with trap doors and steps, facilitate loading and unloading. On each side of the main body of the car there are 10 sliding windows about 2½ ft. wide and 3 ft. high. Each window is equipped with roll shades and steel mesh screens.

These large windows give ample light in the daytime, and, with the seats arranged for daytime occupancy, clear and unobstructed vision to the outside. Each window is easily raised or lowered so that fresh air may circulate freely throughout the car, as required. In addition to these main car windows, there is a window at each end of the car beside the wash basins and a window in each toilet room.

The car is thoroughly insulated. Eight exhaust ventilators in the roof and inlet ventilators in the sides near the eaves insure adequate ventilation under all conditions. A low-pressure, Vapor heating system, with fin-type radiation, is installed. The heating is controlled by four hand valves, two placed on each side of the car, with stencil markings showing their location. The ceilings and sides of the car are lined with a composition material which makes a smooth interior, painted in three-tone tans.

When made up for night occupancy, with sleeping accommodations for 30 passengers, each in an individual bed, the car has berths arranged in tiers of three running crosswise, with the aisle along the side instead of in the center as in the conventional sleeping car. The floor is covered with brown asphaltum, designed to be durable and long wearing but soft and springy to the touch. *Railway Age, 1943*

was a refrigerator of counter height. It had two ice wells of about 7.5 cubic-foot capacity apiece with a food compartment in between of about 15.5 cubic-foot capacity. Next to the refrigerator was the cook's meat-cutting table. On the opposite side of the car, adjacent to the door opening, was a bread locker. Drawers were provided above the refrigerator and cook's work table as well as below the meat-cutting table, cook's work table and bread locker. All shelves were furnished with a railing of 3/8" pipe. Next to the bread locker toward the end of the car was a service table that could be folded against the side of the car. In one corner of the car was a crew shower with a pre-cast reinforced concrete base. Connections were provided for hot and cold water. The front opening of the shower was covered by a white cloth curtain.

BATTERY SYSTEM

The cars were lighted by a battery system using National Carbon Company's replaceable "Eveready" dry cell batteries which provided six volts for the light fixtures. These bat-

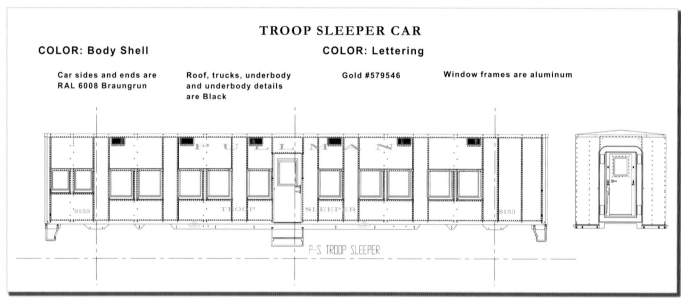

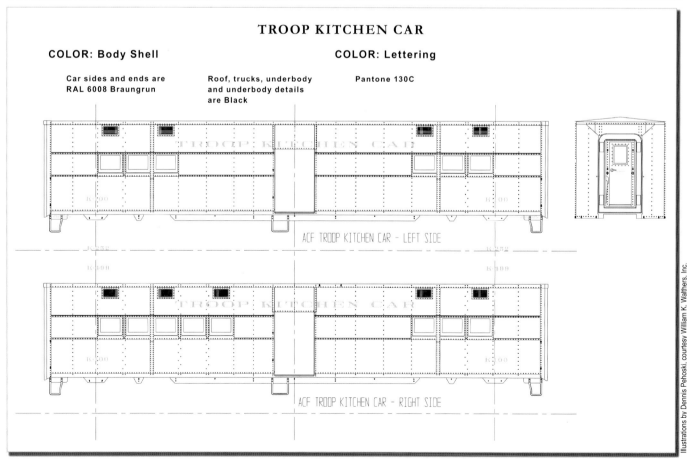

teries lasted approximately six months under normal lighting requirements. Twelve lighting fixtures were arranged on two circuits with snap switches, and one night light fixture at each end of the car was operated by pull-chain switches.

The troop kitchen cars were usually located near the center of the train to permit dispensing food from each end. Each kitchen car was capable of furnishing meals for 250 soldiers. The cars were stocked with food and kitchen uten-sils by unit mess sergeants. Each military unit employing the car provided its own cook and mess crew. Aside from the cooking utensils, all equipment was stationary. At mealtimes the men were issued paper cups and plates. Bread and cubes of butter were served from paper cartons. The entrée was carried in stock pots by two men, with a third following to serve it as the trio proceeded through the train aisles. Coffee and dessert were served in a similar fashion. Af-

Troop sleeper #7271 is on display today at the Illinois Railroad Museum, in Union, Illinois. *M.D. McCarter*

This Wabash troop sleeper, #7021, was spurred at Moberly, Missouri on October 12, 1947. *M.D. McCarter*

ter the meal was consumed by the troops, a kitchen police crew gathered up any remaining leftovers and trash which was burned at the first opportunity.

AC&F HOSPITAL KITCHEN CARS

The 40 hospital kitchen cars were built by AC&F in its Chicago plant from February 1944 through March 1944 (Lot 2654, car numbers 8731 to 8770). These cars were used in conjunction with the hospital ward cars that were converted at the same time in AC&F's St. Charles, Missouri plant. The hospital kitchen cars were essentially identical to the troop kitchen cars except that 32-volt axle-generator equipment with storage batteries and suitable fixtures were used for car lighting.

PAINTING AND LETTERING

According to the AC&F bill of materials, the sides and ends of the first 400 troop kitchen cars were painted with Pullman-Standard green enamel paint. The roof, brake parts and trucks were painted black. Lettering was medium yellow paint mixed with gold stencil paste. The side and ends of the second 400 troop kitchen cars were painted with Pittsburgh Pullman-Standard synthetic green enamel. The roof, brake parts and trucks were black. Lettering was Pittsburgh gold enamel paint. The U.S. Army hospital kitchen cars were painted dark olive drab with a black roof, white lettering and red crosses. The Pullman-Standard troop sleeping car were painted in the same manner as the troop kitchen cars.

In 1947 the U.S. War Assets Administration Office of General Disposal offered 2,290 troop sleepers and troop kitchen cars for sale to the railroads at a fraction of their original cost. The cars were considered to be very suitable for conversion to headend baggage and express cars for passenger train service, especially the last group of troop

sleepers from Lot 6753. The side door step wells in the earlier Lot 6704 cars weakened the side structure of the cars which made them less desirable for postwar conversions.

TYPICAL TROOP TRAIN CONSIST

The typical troop train in 1944 or 1945 would most likely have consisted of a single 4-6-2, 4-8-2, 4-6-4 or 4-8-4 steam locomotive followed by one or more baggage cars, perhaps an express refrigerator car, three or more troop sleepers, two or more troop kitchen cars and six or more Pullman tourist sleeping cars, usually having a 12-section, 1-drawing room configuration. The latter would most likely be Plan 2410 type cars without air-conditioning that were unnamed but were numbered 1100 through 2511. The cars would be found in almost any order, however, the kitchen cars tended to be near the center of the train or spread evenly throughout the consist in order to expedite the feeding of troops riding in sleeping cars. *Pat Wilder, Railway Prototype Encyclopedia, Volume 5*

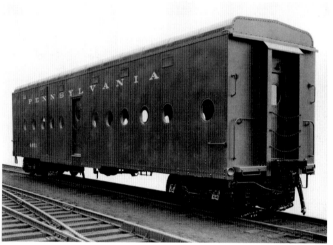

This tall Pennsylvania Railroad troop sleeper with 11 circular windows each side, plus one in the door, is an oddity. *Jay Williams collection*

Troop kitchen car #K341 was photographed after the war at Jersey City, New Jersey on September 14, 1946. The lettering was centered over the middle of the car. *Collection of J. Michael Gruber*

PULLMAN TROOP SLEEPER INTERIOR LAYOUT

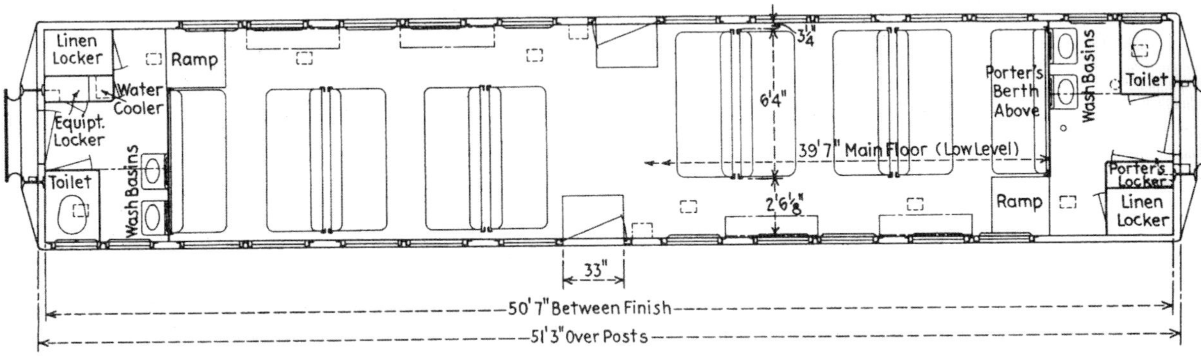
Linen Locker
Ramp
Water Cooler
Equipt. Locker
Toilet
Wash Basins
6'4"
39'7" Main Floor (Low Level)
Porter's Berth Above
Porter's Locker
Linen Locker
Toilet
Wash Basins
Ramp
33"
50'7" Between Finish
51'3" Over Posts

Railway Prototype Cyclopedia, Vol. 5

PULLMAN TROOP KITCHEN CAR INTERIOR LAYOUT

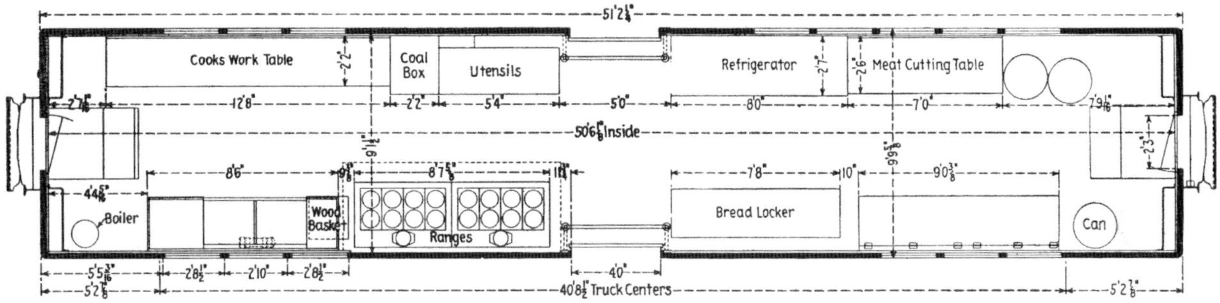
Cooks Work Table
Coal Box
Utensils
Refrigerator
Meat Cutting Table
Inside
Bread Locker
Boiler
Wood Basket
Ranges
Can
Truck Centers

Railway Prototype Cyclopedia, Vol. 5

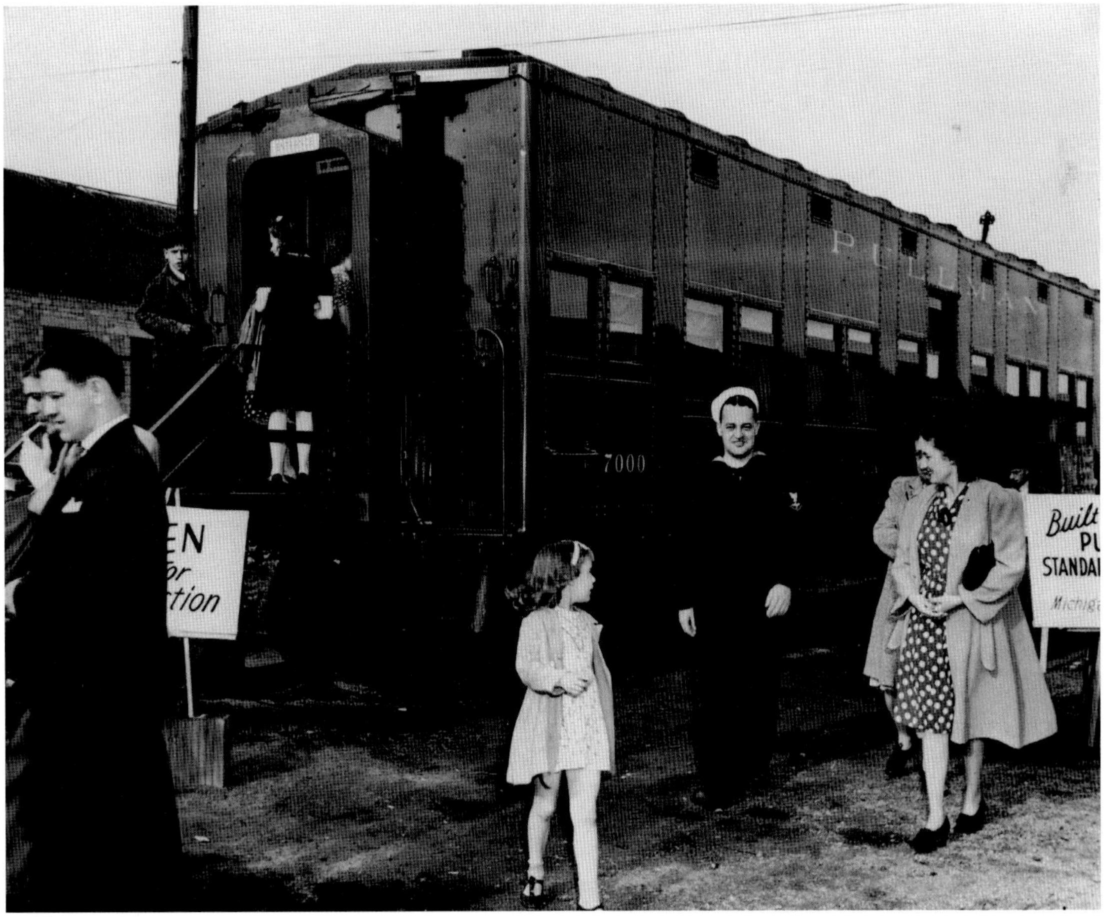
PULLMAN
7000

Seaman Louis Myers, a gunner in training at the Great Lakes Naval Training Center in Wisconsin, visits the new Pullman-Standard built troop cars on display in Chicago in 1944. *Photo courtesy David Myers*

A Southern Pacific cab forward lifts a long troop train over snow-covered Western mountains during the war years. *David Myers*

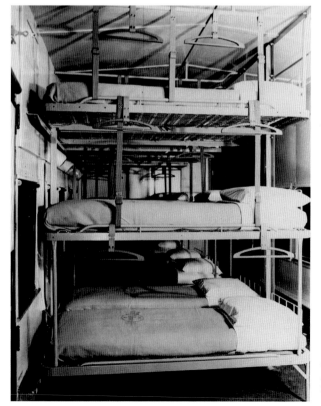

Troop sleeper #8099 is newly-built and ready for action. *David Myers*

The interior of a troop sleeper was pretty sparse, with a triple layer of bunk beds. *David Myers*

Railway Express Agency box car #6685 began life as a troop sleeper; note the side windows have been riveted over with metal panels. Photograph taken February 25, 1968 at Phoenix, Arizona Union Station. *M. D. McCarter*

Wabash maintenance-of-way crew car #5667 was once a troop sleeper. It was photographed at Lafayette, Indiana in September of 1951. *L. G. Issac photo, collection of Don Heimburger*

Wabash #5600, used as part of the railroad's maintenance-of-way equipment after the war, was photographed at Decatur in central Illinois, location of one of the railroad's division points. *M.D. McCarter*

225

TROOP TRAIN EQUIPMENT

A 12-1 Pullman can sleep 36 in the sections (one in the upper, two in the lower) plus three in the drawing room, enough room for a typical Army platoon and its three leading sergeants. The less common 16-section cars are prized for their higher capacity of 48. Being Pullmans, the 16-section cars came complete with a porter and all the usual amenities one expects on a Pullman sleeper.

The Great Depression had sidelined almost all of the early first generation "Gothic" heavyweight cars, which sat on storage sidings for years. In the late 1930's, a number of the 12-1 and 16-section sleepers were rebuilt into some of the all-room versions that were popular at the time. Still, when a State of Emergency was declared in 1940, most of them were still in storage. Pullman had not scrapped them (even though they were obsolete and surplus at the time) because the equipment trusts were still in effect: they had not yet been paid for.

'GOTHIC' CARS RETURNED

WWII returned nearly 1,500 "Gothic" cars to service, where they lived up to their builder's reputation for quality and durability through four long years of nonstop service with no more than essential maintenance. Once the war ended, most of these cars—now worn out—were scrapped.

The shortage of diners was even more critical as there were fewer of them, and most were owned by individual railroads and were needed for the packed civilian trains. So, at War Department insistence, various railroads converted older headend cars into field-expedient kitchen cars such as the old trussrod wood baggage cars.

Facilities of these cars was minimal: at either end of the car were iced coolers. In the center was any of a variety of ad-hoc cookstoves, many welded of plate and angle iron in the car shops, together with a coal bin. There was also a sink and a pair of garbage cans.

Even with 40% of Pullman's inventory committed to troop train service, there was still a critical shortage of rolling stock. It was quickly realized that the campaigns ahead would require massive troop movements and that more equipment had to be built. However, both Pullman and the

16-section Pullman tourist sleeper

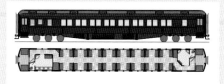

Plan 2412F - built 1916 - 16 open sections
capacity 32 - 155 cars total

War Department were not happy with the time and materials needed to build that many conventional passenger carbodies. So Pullman, at War Department insistence, developed a fast and inexpensive troop sleeper based on the ubiquitous PS-1 box car.

What these cars lacked in style, they did not make up in comfort. During the day, the upper two bunks were folded away and the lower used for three-across seating. At either end was a washroom and toilet. Nominal capacity was 29 plus the porter. As the war progressed, the practice of assigning porters to these cars gradually diminished.

ALLIED TRUCKS

The cars were not air conditioned and ventilation was a haphazard process of opening the windows or doors. What made it worse was that these cars rolled on an experimental four-wheel high speed truck known as the "Allied" truck. These trucks were rough riding, maintenance intensive and prone to derailment. They have since been outlawed in interchange service.

American Car & Foundry also built 800 kitchen cars after the PS-1 box car pattern. The kitchen facilities followed the same basic pattern as the ad hoc baggage car conversions, but were better laid out. Notable additions were more table space, a sink for washing utensils and next to the coffee urns, a milk machine. Unlike their predecessors, these cars also featured a large overhead water tank. Most were disposed of after the war and were used for M-o-W service. However, unlike the sleepers, several dozen of these cars remained in War Department inventory through the Korean War.

60-foot express car converted to kitchen car

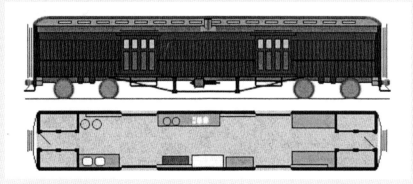

The invasion of Japan was expected to produce as many as a million Allied casualties. In anticipation of the deluge of wounded, the War Department contracted early in 1945 for several lots of hospital cars, including an order built by American Car & Foundry.

MODERN CARS

These are a peculiar design: a lightweight carbody sitting on six-wheel drop-equalized heavyweight Pullman trucks for a smooth ride. Other than that, they were modern, lightweight passenger cars in every sense: thermopane windows and welded truss carbodies.

The cars featured a loading door for stretcher cases (ambulatory patients entered through the vestibule door). Inside was a triage area where patients were examined, given rudimentary treatment such as changing bandages, then moved down the corridor to the berths. At the end of the car was a toilet and an ice locker for perishable medical supplies.

Leaving the triage area, there were a pair of sections for ambulatory patients who could sit up. The hospital staff made the berths up at night. Next to that were some of the several lockers for medical supplies. The center of the car had two rows of double stacked permanent berths for stretcher cases.

At the other end of the car was a medical station where routine treatment such as changing bandages took place. Normally, no operations were performed on board these cars, although emergency surgery could be performed in urgent cases. Around the medical station were lockers for surgical supplies, wash sinks and a desk for the duty medic.

The war ended without these cars having to go into service. In the postwar selldown, the cars were snapped up by the Monon, which rebuilt them into luxury lightweight chair cars. *North East Rails, Clint Chamberlin, Those Classic Trains, Kalmbach Publishing Co.*

Norfolk & Western timetable, October 15, 1942

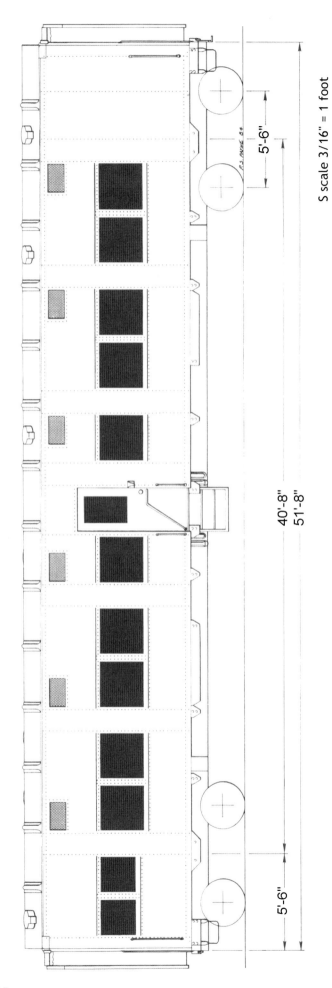

S scale 3/16" = 1 foot

5'-6"

40'-8"
51'-8"

5'-6"

Troop Cars
Illustrated by P. S. Payne

Between 1945 and 1946, wartime troop movements on U.S. railroads declined 77%. During July of 1946, 248,421 service personnel and prisoners of war were carried by rail in organized movements, as compared with 1,087,300 in December of 1945.

Near the end of WWII, 2,400 troop sleepers and more than 500 kitchen troop cars were returned to the Reconstruction Finance Corp. The cars were constructed by Pullman-Standard. The all-steel sleepers held 30 men each and were the only passenger cars built during WWII. The unused cars were stored at an unused Army ordnance plant at Illiopolis, Illinois.

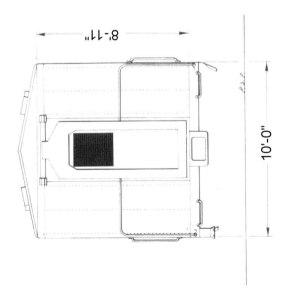

8'-11"

10'-0"

To ease the strain of the railroads' overtaxed passenger capacity, hundreds of heavyweight Pullmans were converted to troop sleepers, as shown here. *Bob's Photos*

United States Navy 0-4-0T locomotive is shown at the Navy Supply Depot at Pasco, Washington, a town which provided excellent transportation facilities by rail, land and water for military movements. Pasco received its name from Virgil G. Bogue, a construction engineer for the Northern Pacific Railroad. In 1889, the Northern Pacific moved their facilities from Wallula Junction to Pasco. *Mallory Hope Ferrell collection*

Military Camp Railroads

"This war is, above all, a war of movement—movement of ground forces, air forces, and their supplies between induction stations, training centers, mobilization points, ports of embarkation, and 'fronts'—wherever flies the flag of the Army of the United States." —Brigadier General C. P. Gross, Chief of Transportation, United States Army

In order to win the war, the U.S. needed help from many sources. It needed good transportation services between its many military camps and military installations scattered throughout the U.S., as well as its more secretive camps and ordnance supply depots. It required rail connections for movement of men, materiel and machinery between military camps, factories and plants, and ports of embarkation.

There is no doubt that the railroads played an extremely important and vital role in the transportation of everything military during the war. From Ft. Leonard Wood, Missouri, Bremerton Navy Yard in Washington, to Ft.

Meade, South Dakota and Ft. Sill in Oklahoma, to Camp Lee, Virginia to Ft. Bragg, North Carolina, the military establishment and railroads were connected by ribbons of steel. Looking at a map of the camps, forts and posts, airfields, airdromes and bases, you can see the tremendous coordination that was needed to move men and materiel between one point and another.

Fortunately, most of this steel rail network was already in place as the U.S. entered the war. In this chapter, we will take a brief look at the equipment used at some of these camps and bases, and offer a more extensive look at Ft. Eustis, Virginia.

The United States Navy 0-4-0 locomotive #6992 at Pasco, Washington featured a front boiler headlight slightly lower than normal and an overhanging metal awning to keep rain off the fireman and engineer. *Mallory Hope Ferrell collection*

Anniston Ordnance Depot (AOD) locomotive #1, built by the Davenport-Besler Corporation, served this 15,000-acre depot which was located in northeast Alabama. It consisted of 500 ammunition storage igloos, six standard magazines, 20 warehouses and several administrative buildings, authorized by War Department General Order No. 11, dated October 14, 1941. *Don Heimburger collection*

Utility railroad layout of a typical Army installation. *Louis Marre*

BELOW. U.S. Army #22, a product of Alco-Richmond (construction number #47981 June, 1910), formerly Washington, Idaho & Montana #22, is at Camp Claiborne, Louisiana (Alexandria) in 1942. The U.S. Army paid $8,500 to purchase this locomotive from the WI&M Railway in April of 1939. Apparently #22 remained in Army service until sometime after completion of the Ft. Peck Dam in Montana. *Thomas Burg*

Camp Pike at Little Rock, Arkansas shows rail lines with numerous troop coaches, flat and box cars with military loads. Note also the horses and wagons, and especially the flat car at lower right with wagons. The camp was established in 1917 for training of the 87th Army Division, and before WWII its name was changed to Camp Joseph T. Robinson. It was used for the training of troops and training in the use of rifles, revolvers, machine guns, grenades, mortars and field artillery. *Don Heimburger collection*

This center-cab Whitcomb switcher, with prominent headlights, bell and classification lamps on the hood, was operated as #2 at the Oakland, California Naval Supply Depot. The depot opened in December of 1941 and was a major source of supplies and war materiel for ships operating in the Pacific. Known for its large warehouses, the depot continued a decades-long expansion after it opened; the depot closed in 1998. *Bob's Photos*

The Quartermaster Corps used this small Plymouth #2051 for switching cars. The Quartermaster Corps is the U.S. Army's oldest logistics branch, established in June of 1775. Quartermaster units and soldiers have served in every U.S. military campaign from the Revolutionary War to current-day operations. *Bob's Photos*

The U.S. Naval Ammunition Depot at Oahu, Hawaii ran this small 36" gauge 35-ton diesel produced by the Atlas Car & Mfg. Co. located in Cleveland, Ohio. This locomotive (construction #1904) was built in October of 1933. It was rated at 265 horsepower. *Bob's Photos*

This H.K. Porter center-cab diesel switches tank cars of precious oil needed for the U. S. war effort at Norfolk, Virginia. A sign on the building at the left and behind the engine reads "Restricted Area." *Bob's Photos*

This Whitcomb diesel appears brand new as it waits its next assignment at the Navy Yard in Brooklyn, New York. On the eve of World War II, the yard contained more than five miles of paved streets, four dry docks ranging in length from 326 to 700 feet, two steel shipways, six pontoons and cylindrical floats for salvage work, barracks for Marines, a power plant, radio station, railroad spur and foundries, machine shops and warehouses. At its peak during World War II, the yard employed 70,000 people, 24 hours a day. *Bob's Photos*

At Mare Island Navy Yard at Napa Junction, California (Vallejo), the #4, an American Locomotive Co. (Alco) switcher, performed its military chores for the cause. *Bob's Photos*

This tiny diesel—shown here in 1945—was operated by the U.S. Naval Ammunition Depot at Iona Island, New York during WWII. The island was composed of 556 acres on bedrock and was purchased by the U.S. Navy in 1900 for ammunition storage. It was closed in 1947. The stubby 0-4-0 locomotive eventually was purchased by Fruit Growers Express. *Mallory Hope Ferrell*

Captain C. J. Streiff, who had recently returned from service in North Africa with a railroad battalion, uses toy trains at Jefferson Barracks, Missouri, to demonstrate practical railroad problems. *Private Lee Marks, battalion photographer*

LEFT. A diesel switcher from McAlester, Oklahoma Ammunitions Plant runs over that facility's 200 miles of track. Between 1943 and 1977, the plant was called the Naval Ammunition Depot. In 1943, the first diesel locomotive was assigned to the plant, and by 1945 there were 13 diesels being operated at the site. *U.S. Army Transportation Museum*

Troops board coaches of the Ft. Benning, Georgia Light Railway during maneuvers. This military railroad was of 60 centimeter gauge. *Mallory Hope Ferrell collection*

Quartermasters Corps #5230 2-6-2T, a Davenport locomotive, highballs with a load of troops in training at Ft. Benning, Georgia. *Mallory Hope Ferrell collection*

A soldier at Camp Bowie, Texas engineers new 35-ton gas-mechanical Davenport locomotive #7571 (Construction #2466) delivered on December 22, 1942. The soldier, Technical Sergeant Carl Smelser, wears a tie while working at the controls. *U.S. Army Signal Corps, Bob Hall collection*

Fort Meade, served by the Baltimore & Ohio Railroad during WWII, was established in 1917 when the United States Department of War acquired 19,000 acres of land west of Odenton, Maryland to develop a training camp. First known as Camp Annapolis Junction, the fort was named Camp Admiral at its opening in 1917. Other name changes occurred after construction of 1,460 buildings on the site: it became Camp George Gordon Meade, then in the 1920s it became Fort Leonard Wood, but by the 1930s it reverted back to Fort George G. Meade. The fort was used as a basic training post and a prisoner of war camp during WWII.

TABLE 2 — FORT MEADE SERVICE

Coordinated Service via BALTIMORE & OHIO R. R.—BALTIMORE & ANNAPOLIS R. R. and WEST VIRGINIA TRANSPORTATION COMPANY

All tickets issued by above lines will be honored via any of the following routes to or from Baltimore

FORT MEADE TO BALTIMORE

Note—Buses via Laurel leave from Old Annapolis Road at 26th Street.
Buses via Jessup leave from Post Bus Terminal.

Service.	Leave Fort Meade.	Arrive Camden Station.	Company.	Route.
Daily	5.45 AM	6.45 AM	W. Va.	Bus Direct
Ex. Sunday	6.00	7.30	W. Va.	Bus-Train via Laurel
Ex. Sunday	7.05	8.05	W. Va.	Bus-Train via Jessup
Daily	8.00	9.00	B. & A.	Bus Direct
Daily	9.15	10.15	W. Va.	Bus Direct
Daily	10.05	11.18	W. Va.	Bus-Train via Laurel
Daily	11.00	12.00	W. Va.	Bus Direct
Daily	12.30 PM	1.30 PM	W. Va.	Bus Direct
Daily	2.00	3.00	B. & A.	Bus Direct
Daily	2.50	3.53	W. Va.	Bus-Train via Jessup
Daily	4.00	5.00	W. Va.	Bus Direct
Ex. Sat., Sun. & Hol.	4.30	5.28	W. Va.	Bus-Train via Laurel
Daily	4.45	5.45	W. Va.	Bus Direct
Ex. Sunday	5.00	6.00	B. & A.	Bus Direct
Daily	5.40	6.55	W. Va.	Bus-Train via Laurel
Ex. Sat., Sun. & Hol.	6.30	7.30	W. Va.	Bus-Train via Laurel
Daily	7.05	8.15	W. Va.	Bus-Train via Laurel
Daily	7.45	8.45	B. & A.	Bus Direct
Daily	9.00	10.00	W. Va.	Bus Direct
Daily	10.30	11.50	W. Va.	Bus-Train via Laurel
Daily	10.45	11.45	B. & A.	Bus Direct
Daily	12.00	1.00 AM	W. Va.	Bus Direct

BALTIMORE TO FORT MEADE

Service.	Leave Camden Station.	Arrive Fort Meade.	Company.	Route.
Daily	2.00 AM	3.00 AM	W. Va.	Bus Direct
Daily	4.45	5.45	W. Va.	Bus Direct
Daily	6.00	7.00	B. & A.	Bus Direct
Ex. Sunday	6.20	7.25	W. Va.	Train-Bus via Laurel
Daily	6.45	7.45	W. Va.	Train-Bus via Laurel
Daily	7.00	8.00	W. Va.	Bus Direct
Ex. Sat., Sun. & Hol.	7.15	8.00	W. Va.	Train-Bus via Jessup
Daily	9.15	10.15	B. & A.	Bus Direct
Daily	10.30	11.30	W. Va.	Bus Direct
Daily	12.00	1.00 PM	W. Va.	Train-Bus via Laurel
Daily	12.15 PM	1.15	B. & A.	Bus Direct
Daily	1.45	2.45	W. Va.	Bus Direct
Ex. Sunday	2.40	3.35	W. Va.	Train-Bus via Laurel
Daily	3.30	4.30	B. & A.	Bus Direct
Daily	5.05	6.25	W. Va.	Train-Bus via Laurel
Daily	5.30	6.30	W. Va.	Bus Direct
Daily	6.00	7.00	W. Va.	Bus Direct
Daily	6.15	7.15	B. & A.	Bus Direct
Daily	7.40	8.40	W. Va.	Bus Direct
Daily	9.00	10.10	W. Va.	Train-Bus via Laurel
Daily	9.30	10.30	B. & A.	Bus Direct
Daily	11.00	12.00	W. Va.	Bus Direct
Daily	11.59	12.59 AM	B. & A.	Bus Direct

New Year's, Washington's Birthday, Memorial Day, Fourth of July, Labor Day, Thanksgiving Day, and Christmas are considered holidays.

TABLE 3 — FORT MEADE SERVICE

Coordinated Service via BALTIMORE & OHIO R. R. and WEST VIRGINIA TRANSPORTATION COMPANY

All tickets issued by above lines will be honored via any of the following routes to or from Washington

FORT MEADE TO WASHINGTON

Note—Buses via Laurel leave from Old Annapolis Road at 26th Street.
Buses via Jessup leave from Post Bus Terminal

Service.	Leave Fort Meade.	Arrive Washington Union Sta.	Bus Train Route.
Except Sunday	6.00 AM	7.15 AM	Via Laurel
Daily	6.30	7.35	Via Laurel
Except Sat., Sun. and Hol.	7.05	8.10	Via Jessup
Daily	11.35	12.50 PM	Via Laurel
Except Sunday	2.15 PM	3.35	Via Laurel
Daily	4.50	6.05	Via Laurel
Daily	8.55	10.05	Via Laurel

WASHINGTON TO FORT MEADE

Service.	Leave Washington Union Sta.	Arrive Fort Meade.	Train Bus Route.
Except Sunday	6.00 AM	7.25 AM	Via Laurel
Except Sunday	7.05	8.00	Via Jessup
Daily	10.30	11.25	Via Laurel
Saturday only	1.45 PM	3.35 PM	Via Laurel
Daily	3.00	3.55	Via Jessup
Except Sat., Sun. and Hol.	4.45	5.35	Via Laurel
Except Sunday	5.32	6.25	Via Laurel
Except Sat., Sun. and Hol.	6.00	6.55	Via Laurel
Daily	7.30	8.25	Via Laurel
Daily	11.00	11.55	Via Laurel

TABLE 4 — B&O TRAIN SCHEDULES BETWEEN WASHINGTON, BALTIMORE, PHILADELPHIA AND NEW YORK

EASTWARD	528	510	2	6	44	4	504	28	8	36
All trains are daily.	AM	AM	AM	AM	AM	AM	PM	PM	PM	PM
Lv Washington	1.00	7.00	8.00	9.15	10.30	11.40	1.25	3.45	5.00	6.30
Baltimore (Cam'n)	1.48	7.40	8.40	9.55	11.20	12.20	2.03	4.23	5.40	7.12
Baltimore (Mt. R.)	2.03	7.46	8.46	10.01	11.26	12.26	2.09	4.29	5.46	7.18
Wilmington	3.28	9.00	9.52	11.06	12.40	1.38	3.10	5.30	6.53	8.33
Ar Philadelphia	4.03	9.28	10.23	11.37	1.15	2.07	3.38	5.59	7.21	9.10
Ar New York—										
Liberty St. (CNJ)	6.50	11.24	12.20	1.34	------	4.04	5.33	7.54	9.20	------
42nd St. Sta.	7.10	11.50	12.50	2.00	------	4.30	6.00	8.15	9.40	------
(Note 1)	AM	AM	PM	PM	PM	PM	PM	PM	PM	PM

WESTWARD	511	35	509	27	45	5	1	3	523	7
(Note 1)	AM	AM	AM	AM	PM	PM	PM	PM	PM	PM
Lv New York—										
42nd St. Sta.	12.20	------	7.05	8.45	------	12.15	1.15	2.55	4.10	6.20
Liberty St. (CNJ)	12.45	------	7.30	9.15	------	12.45	1.45	3.30	4.45	6.50
Philadelphia	3.30	8.01	9.25	11.10	2.15	2.41	3.42	5.26	6.41	8.47
Wilmington	4.00	8.30	9.50	11.35	2.40	3.09	4.07	5.51	7.06	9.12
Ar Baltimore (Mt. R.)	5.50	9.47	10.58	12.38	3.54	4.18	5.16	7.07	8.11	10.22
Baltimore (Cam'n)	5.58	9.52	11.03	12.43	3.59	4.23	5.21	7.12	8.16	10.27
Ar Washington	7.00	10.35	11.50	1.30	4.40	5.10	6.10	8.00	8.55	11.15
	AM	AM	AM	PM	PM	PM	PM	PM	PM	PM

REFERENCE NOTES.

Light-face figures A. M. time.   Dark-face figures P. M. time.

NOTE 1—B&O motor coaches quickly convey you directly between trainside at Jersey City (C. of N. J.) and the Heart of Greater New York, at no extra cost. Four conveniently located motor coach stations— 15 Rockefeller Plaza at 49th St.; 15 Columbus Circle; 122 East 42nd St.; and Washington and Johnson Sts.; Brooklyn, N. Y. Also nine other stops at leading hotels. Ask agent for folder of details.

"One reason why the Nazis are folding up so fast," reads the caption with this 1944 cartoon in *Railway Age*.

This General Electric 44-ton SN-1 U.S. Army spreader was photographed at Holabird Depot in Baltimore, Maryland on August 27, 1949; note the crisp Transportation Corps insignia on the upper righthand portion of the cab. *Bob's Photos*

U.S. Army 3-foot-gauge gas-powered locomotive is at Schofield Barracks, Oahu, Hawaii during WWII. The flatcar is an ex-Oahu Railway & Land piece of rolling stock. *Mallory Hope Ferrell collection*

U.S.A. Davenport 2-6-2T Mid-Pacific RR locomotive and crew is at Schofield Barracks, Oahu, Hawaii. *Mallory Hope Ferrell collection*

238

Ft. Knox, Kentucky, former home of the U.S. Army Armor Center, operated this 1,000-hp Fairbanks-Morse H-12-44 #1846 and a sister H-12-44 which were built after the war in the 1950's. The #1846 is now owned by the Kentucky Railway Museum, New Haven, Kentucky. Ft. Knox is the home of the bulk of the U.S. gold reserve. In World War II, the gold vault at Ft. Knox was used to keep the original copies of the Constitution, the Declaration of Independence, the Magna Carta, and the original draft of the Gettysburg address safe. *Don Heimburger collection*

Sixty-centimeter-gauge #6 Davenport 2-6-2T "Trench Locomotive," operated by the Quartermasters Corps, steams up in the yard area at Ft. Benning, Georgia. *U.S. Army Signals Corps, Bob Hall collection*

During the May, 1969 re-enactment of the joining of the transcontinental railways at Promontory Point, Utah, Lt. Michael Connor from the 714th Railway Operating Battalion, right, joined other dignitaries during the festivities. The 2-8-0 #612 from Ft. Eustis, Virginia made a perfect backdrop for the military photo. *Don Heimburger collection*

History of Fort Eustis

For more than 70 years, first as a camp and later as a post, Fort Eustis has had a heritage of supporting U. S. combat forces. Ft. Eustis was known in colonial times as Mulberry Island and was the residence of John Rolfe, husband of Indian Princess Pocahontas. It became Ft. Eustis and a permanent military installation in 1923 and was garrisoned by artillery and infantry units until 1931, when it became a federal prison, primarily for bootleggers. Prohibition's repeal forced a prisoner decline, and the post was taken over by various other military and non-military activities. The fort was reopened as a military installation in August 1940 as the Coast Artillery Replacement Training Center. In May, 1946 the TC took over operation of Ft.

Eustis as its new headquarters. Military railway schools at Camp Claiborne, Camp Plauche and Ft. Francis E. Warren were closed and consolidated at Ft. Eustis. Training in rail, marine, amphibious operations and other modes of transportation was consolidated at Ft. Eustis.

TRANSPORTATION CORPS HISTORY

The Transportation Corps was established on July 31, 1942 by Executive Order 9082. Transporters have a long history of answering the nation's call. As far back as the Revolutionary War when General George Washington appointed the first Wagon Master, Transporters have been there to move and sustain American fighting forces. With the attack

The engineer gets a signal from the brakeman on the ground to slow his locomotive as it nears a Pennsylvania wooden box car during a switching maneuver at Ft. Eustis in 1947. *Photo by H. Reid, Mallory Hope Ferrell collection*

on Pearl Harbor in 1941, the U. S. began the largest mobilization in its history, and there was no hesitation concerning the control of transportation.

In March 1942, transportation functions were consolidated into the Transportation Division of the newly-created Services of Supply. That same year, on July 31, President Roosevelt established the Transportation Corps. By the end of the war, the Transportation Corps had moved more than 30 million soldiers within the continental United States, and seven million soldiers, plus 126 million tons of supplies, overseas.

Locomotive #1600 in 1947 at Ft. Eustis, Virginia. *Mallory Hope Ferrell collection*

Doubleheading steam locomotives #606 and #611 blast through the Ft. Eustis pine trees in a 1966 H. Reid photo. *Mallory Hope Ferrell collection*

The second engine, a 2-8-0 with 57" drivers, of the 600 Class, built by Baldwin in 1943 and later re-built by Baldwin, doubleheads with #611 at Ft. Eustis. *Mallory Hope Ferrell collection*

Lima-built locomotive #606, a 2-8-0 constructed in 1945, switches in Ft. Eustis' Hanks Yard in December of 1962. *Mallory Hope Ferrell collection*

Three engines—#611, #612 and #606—all 2-8-0's, pour it on at Ft. Eustis on September 3, 1966 on a National Railway Historical Society special excursion. *Mallory Hope Ferrell collection*

U.S. Army locomotive 2-8-0 #612 percolates quietly at Ft. Eustis. *Mallory Hope Ferrell collection*

Locomotive #606, running light with just a cupola caboose, blows off steam at Ft. Eustis. *Mallory Hope Ferrell collection*

Steam was still around in the U.S. military in the early 1960s, but it was just about finished. Engine #606 steams contently in Hanks Yard at Ft. Eustis on December 12, 1962 as it's being looked over by non-commissioned officers. *Mallory Hope Ferrell collection*

Locomotive #607 at Ft. Eustis. *H. Reid, Mallory Hope Ferrell collection*

ABOVE. Locomotive #620, another 2-8-0, crosses a low trestle at Ft. Eustis. *William Gwaltney, Mallory Hope Ferrell collection*

An Army fireman looks out contently at the camera from locomotive #644, a 2-8-0, at the Ft. Eustis military railroad. Note serif lettering on tender; other Ft. Eustis locomotives sported sans serif lettering on tender. *Mallory Hope Ferrell collection*

ABOVE AND RIGHT. Neat, sporty 0-4-0T #714 with safety stripes on its front pilot beam in one photo and no stripes in the other, shows distinct painting/lettering differences between photos. *H. Reid, Mallory Hope Ferrell collection*

Soldiers do a "wash down" on #611's exterior at Ft. Eustis as a railfan records the event at left. *Mallory Hope Ferrell collection*

A small 2-6-2 #7 from the Quartermasters Corps is checked out before the next run. *U.S. Army Transportation Museum*

Center-cab #8501 diesel sits in line-up with other Ft. Eustis locomotives in 1947. *Mallory Hope Ferrell collection*

Shown testing the air mechanism of a dump car on the Rock Island Railway at Little Rock, Arkansas, are left to right: Corporal James E. Harper, an air brake inspector on the Illinois Central at Memphis, Tennesee, for two years before entering the Army; Sgt. Barney E. Glass (under car), of Little Rock, Arkansas, former carman with the Missouri Pacific and Cotton Belt railroads; and Technician Third Class J. M. Gutkoska, former steel worker at Baltimore, Maryland. All are members of the 743rd Railway Operating Battalion, the second battalion to be sponsored by the Illinois Central. *Army Signal Corps photograph; Illinois Central magazine, Octtober, 1944*

U.S. Army locomotive #6997 in 1947 sits at Ft. Eustis. *Mallory Hope Ferrell collection*

The various parts of Ft. Eustis Railway's #644, including the boiler front, are placed back into position. *U.S. Army Transportation Museum*

This three-pronged machine is a military weed burner at Ft. Eustis. Note crawler/dozer in the field across the road. *Mallory Hope Ferrell collection*

U.S. Army box car USAX #2500 with "Transportation Corps" logo on right side, at Ft. Eustis. *Mallory Hope Ferrell collection*

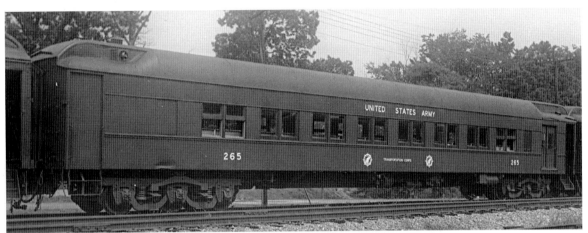

A former clerestory-roofed U.S. Army diner car, #265 and baggage-passenger car #540 are shown at Ft. Eustis, Virginia in 1966. Kitchen car #89620 is at Beecher Falls, Virginia in June of 1977. *Three photos, J. Michael Gruber collection*

The bumper reads "FE 714T ROB 1," and the car on steel wheels sports a siren and white flags. Photo taken at Ft. Eustis in 1947. *Mallory Hope Ferrell collection*

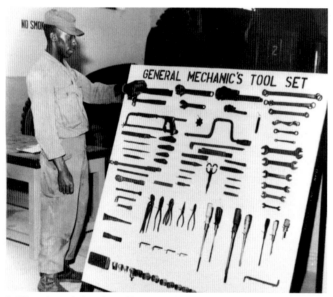

Master Sgt. Malcom R. Darlington is with a railway operating battalion in France, where as assistant chief train dispatcher he had the distinction of dispatching the first train operated in Normandy after the invasion. He is the son of D. B. Darlington, agent at Alburnett, Iowa, and was himself a telegraph operator on the Iowa Division of the Chicago & North Western Railway before he entered the Army in March, 1942. He went overseas to England in July, 1943. *John B. Corson, Iowa Division Editor, Waterloo, Iowa; from Illinois Central magazine, October 1944*

Soldiers in training for railway service at Ft. Eustis needed to have a knowledge of tools used on heavy machinery and steam locomotives. *U.S. Army Transportation Museum*

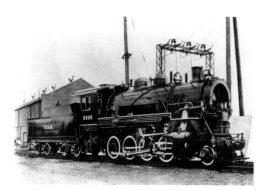

USA steam locomotive #6998, a Lima 2-8-0, with white wall tires, is brand-spanking new in this portrait. *U.S. Army Transportation Museum*

Odd-looking USA #7503 diesel is coupled to a sloped-backed steam engine at Ft. Eustis. *Mallory Hope Ferrell collection*

Locomotive #610 2-8-0, with white-trimmed tires and running boards, sits pretty with white flags at Ft. Eustis.

Transportation Corps #6802 gets serviced at an unknown location. During WWII, U.S. soldiers were trained to operate steam locomotives for use in the States as well as abroad. Note the large "PW" letters on some of the uniforms, likely an indication of "Prisoner of War." With the attack on Pearl Harbor, the United States began the largest mobilization in its history. In March 1942, the transportation functions were consolidated into the Transportation Division of the newly-created Services of Supply. That same year on July 31, President Franklin D. Roosevelt established the Transportation Corps. By the end of the war the Transportation Corps had moved more than 30 million soldiers within the continental United States, and 7 million soldiers plus 126 million tons of supplies overseas. The Transportation Corps is the third smallest branch of the U.S. Army.

Engine #620, a Lima-built 2-8-0, passes a grade crossing at Ft. Eustis; note fireman with helmet on. The well-proportioned #620 with white-wall tires, built in 1941, featured 50" drivers and 21 x 26" cylinders. *Mallory Hope Ferrell collection*

Oil-fired 0-6-0T Vulcan V-1923 (built 1943) with 36" whitewall drivers was meter gauge. *Mallory Hope Ferrell collection*

Docksider 0-4-0T #714 with the U. S. Transportation Corps logo on the boiler jacket, pokes its nose out of the Ft. Eustis shops. *Mallory Hope Ferrell collection*

Transportation Corps Supply

Transportation Corps Supply, like many of its other activities, suffered severely from the fact that the Corps was not established and its procurement responsibilities determined until well after the country had been plunged into World War II.

The lack of experienced personnel, settled organization, and tested methods were basic handicaps which had to be overcome. There were no technical manuals, supply catalogs, spare parts lists or standard nomenclature. Estimates of requirements, approved programs, and production schedules were unrealistic in some respects. There were no depots for Transportation Corps material. Procurement functions were scattered among several headquarters divisions and field installations, with resulting lack of standardization and coordination. The heavy burden which the war imposed upon the well-established services was multiplied in the case of the Transportation Corps because of its newness.

When, in the Army reorganization of March 1942, the first step toward an integrated transportation service was taken, the procurement responsibility of the new Chief of Transportation included only ships, harbor boats and other floating equipment. This responsibility was assigned to the Water Division in the Office of the Chief of Transportation. It was soon agreed that vessels over 1,000 gross tons, and all used vessels of lesser tonnage, would be procured for the Army by the War Shipping Administration. However, the demand for the construction of many types of small boats grew so rapidly that a considerable expansion of the procurement staff was necessary. In July 1942, a Requirements and Procurement Division was established, and in October of the same year an Assistant Chief of Transportation for Supply was designated.

In November 1942, responsibility for the procurement of military railway equipment was transferred to the Transportation Corps from the Corps of Engineers. The procurement function of the Chief of Transportation was stabilized—one year after the U. S. entry into the war—with this large accretion. The procurement of railway equipment covered various types of steam, diesel and electric locomotives, many types and sizes of railway cars, locomotive cranes and other rolling stock, all adapted to the requirements of the foreign and domestic railroads upon which they were to be used.

Altogether there were 158 different types and sizes of floating equipment, 224 different types and sizes of railway equipment, and more than 50,000 different items of replacement parts and expendable supplies.

THE SUPPLY PROGRAM

The annual budget estimates for Transportation Corps supply reflected anticipated requirements. In a world war of such proportions, and with strategical plans repeatedly taking on new aspects, long-range forecasts of overseas requirements were subject to revision, and sometimes wide

Wood-sided Ft. Eustis Railway cupola caboose was a 40-ton piece of rolling stock used in domestic service. *Don Heimburger collection*

revision. The program was designed to provide adequate equipment for the invasion of Continental Europe and the limited war in the Pacific, and after V-E Day to provide additional equipment as the final drive against Japan required. The peak budget estimate was $1,196,161,000 for the fiscal year 1944, which was more than four times as large as the estimate for 1942.

V-E Day brought a reduction in dollar value of less than 1% in the procurement schedule for the calendar year 1945, and an increase of more than 25% in the schedule for 1946. The increase for 1946 was due only in part to Army requirements, since the end of the war in Europe brought a substantial increase in the requirements of equipment (principally railway items) for shipment to foreign countries under the auspices of the Foreign Economic Administration. The greater requirements of FEA, as agent for various foreign governments, more than offset the reduced requirements under Lend-Lease. Following V-J Day, procurement for the Army was virtually cut off, except that pertaining to replacement parts and supplies to keep existing equipment in operation, FEA requirements remained substantial.

REQUIREMENTS FOR EQUIPMENT

Requirements for equipment procured by the Transportation Corps were estimated by overseas commanders, Transportation Corps installations in the zone of interior, and other services and commands using such equipment. Then they were reviewed by the operating divisions in the Office of the Chief of Transportation, which were familiar with the respective items, before being acted upon by the Requirements Division. Estimates of future requirements were obtained bi-annually from all prospective users, and these formed the basis of the Transportation Corps' supply program, which after approval by the Requirements Division, Army Service Forces, became a part of the Army Supply Program. Naturally, it was necessary to process many new requests in the course of the year, and cutbacks in approved programs frequently were necessary to bring them in line with changing conditions.

Year	Estimate
1942	$147,436,682
1943	$224,469,643
1944	$345,869,077
1945	$230,669,235
1946	$49,385,000
Total	$997,829,637

Budget estimates for Transportation Corps railway equipment and supplies for the fiscal years 1942 through 1946, as originally submitted to the U.S. Congress.

In the beginning, great difficulty was experienced with theater requirements for operational supplies, that is, equipment and other material in excess of authorized allowances, needed for assault or other military operations. The Transportation Corps was especially affected, since it was new and did not have time to build up its stockpiles. Theater commanders also were less experienced in estimating their needs for transportation equipment. The operational project system, introduced in the summer of 1943, was of great importance to the Chief of Transportation and his assistant for supply.

OPERATIONAL PROJECTS

Operational projects were of two types. War Department projects included long-range estimates for forthcoming operations directed by the War Department. Theater projects covered equipment and supplies required for operations planned in the theaters. Estimates of requirements made when the operations were projected formed a solid basis for the procurement program than sporadic requests received from time to time. More than 75 projects were submitted, which included transportation equipment. The first major project of this nature, submitted by the European Theater of Operations in August 1943, included the estimated requirements of floating equipment for the operation of four major and eight medium ports, with a daily discharge capacity of 40,000 long tons, which were part of the plan for the invasion of France. The project was augmented later, but the original request, when approved by the War Department, greatly aided the Chief of Transportation in contracting for and scheduling production of equipment needed almost a year later.

The Transportation Corps, in addition to procurement for the U.S. Army, had responsibility for supplying marine and railway equipment to other nations under the Lend-Lease Act and under other authority vested in the Foreign Economic Administration. Foreign requisitions, approved by the appropriate authorities, were processed by the International Division in the Office of the Chief of Transportation, which also coordinated the shipment of such supplies up to the time they were loaded on ships. During the fiscal year 1944, Transportation Corps equipment valued at $131,155,747 was transferred to other countries. The corresponding figure for the fiscal year 1945 was $258,724,355. Of the latter figure, $195,084,121 represented equipment destined to Russia, and $57,843,803 equipment destined to the United Kingdom. The breakdown by type was:

Rail equipment and supplies	$229,752,652
Marine equipment	$20,446,755
Other equipment	$8,524,948
Total	$258,724,355

"We are fighting a war which is at bottom a contest between the natural resources and productive capacities of nations, and we are engaged in a war production program so vast that it staggers the imagination," said Joseph B. Eastman, federal coordinator of transportation, in the August 1942 issue of *Railway Age*. A result of that production are these heavy Army tanks, which the U.S. Third Army is getting ready as maneuvers get under way at Camp Polk, Louisiana in late August of 1942. The medium tanks are being checked on arrival at Boyce, Louisiana. *U.S. Army Signal Corps, Bob Hall collection*

Men of the 16th Armored Division at Camp Chaffee, Arkansas use brute force to help unleash tanks on flatcars on June 3, 1943. *U.S. Army Signal Corps, Bob Hall collection*

ABOVE. Fifteen-ton Christie Convertible tanks, designed by J. Walter Christie, are loaded on a Pennsylvania RR gondola for scrap from the 10th Armored Division at Ft. Benning, Georgia in September of 1942. The rear set of road wheels on a Christie tank were powered from the drive sprocket using a simple chain drive so that the track could be removed and the vehicle run on its wheels for higher speeds. *U.S. Army Signal Corps, Bob Hall collection*

Military tanks on flatcars sit on the post ordnance rail siding at Camp Polk on July 8, 1943, awaiting shipment back to the manufacturer for repairs since Camp Polk did not have facilities to repair them. Construction of Camp Polk began January 28, 1941 on the broad, rolling plains that contained little but cutover pine forests, a few shacks and some rangewire fencing. Thousands of wooden barracks sprang up virtually overnight to support an Army preparing to battle Axis forces on the North African, European and Pacific fronts. The camp, named for Confederate Lieutenant General and Episcopal Bishop Leonides Polk, was completed August 1, 1941. *U.S. Army Signal Corps, Bob Hall collection*

A sergeant from the 502nd Parachute Battalion sits at the controls of a steam locomotive during an operating training course given to parachute soldiers at Ft. Benning in December of 1941. *U.S. Army Signal Corps, Bob Hall collection*

OPPOSITE PAGE, LEFT. Two members of the 502nd Parachute Battalion, as a means of being prepared for "come what may," receive instructions in operating a Pershing steam locomotive in December of 1941 at Ft. Benning. *U.S. Army Signals Corps, Bob Hall collection*

Captain Reuben Whellis of the U.S. Army Transportation Crops tests a small 20-ton Whitcomb warehouse diesel (Construction #40264) at Camp Fannin, Texas in February 1942. Camp Fannin was named in honor of the hero of the 1836 Mexican/Texas Goliad military campaign, Colonel James Walker Fannin. The base was located northeast of Tyler, Texas; in March of 1943 the camp was officially dedicated as an U.S. Army Infantry Replacement Training Center, where more than 200,000 American men became Army infantry replacements between May 1943 and December 1945. *U.S. Army Signal Corps, Bob Hall collection*

Alaska's Railroads Weigh In

"The Alaska Railroad carried almost three and one-half times as much freight at war's end than it had during 1939." —William H. Wilson, *Railroad in the Clouds: The Alaska Railroad in the Age of Steam, 1914-1945*

The U.S. used all its leverage in WWII to bring about a victory for the Allies, including beefing up both the Alaska and the White Pass & Yukon railroads. The military had already established military bases in Anchorage and Fairbanks in 1941 and 1942, and from that time, the railroads of Alaska felt the strain of increased wartime tonnage.

Some of the achievements undertaken on the Alaska Railroad (which ran from Seward in the south to a little past Fairbanks to Eielson in the north) were a $5.3 million rail line on the Kenai Peninsula to ease congestion in 1941; this trackage was called the Whittier Cutoff. A new, expansive three-story depot at Whittier was also built, as was a general

Soldiers of the 770th Railway Operating Battalion, Company B, pose with locomotive #196, a 2-8-2 Mikado, on the Skagway turntable in March of 1944. Troops were called in to run the Alaska Railroad between 1942 and 1946. *Dedman's Photo Shop*

office building in Anchorage. The war also caused railroad employees to leave their jobs for higher-paying positions elsewhere, and there was a desperate shortage of equipment to run the railroad, of which the Army was maintaining 400 miles. In a move to alleviate the labor problem, the Alaska Defense Command ordered soldiers to operate the trains, and extra equipment was sent from a nearby railroad.

The 714th Railway Operating Battalion of Camp Claiborne, Louisiana was finally sent with 25 officers and more than 1,000 enlisted men to operate the railroad, arriving in Seward in April of 1943. Also in 1943, six Baldwin locomotives (later numbered 551-556) were sent to the railroad, as were U.S. Army soldiers to keep the Eska coal mine open from 1942 to 1945.

WHITE PASS & YUKON

On the White Pass & Yukon, which ran from Skagway in the south to Whitehorse, a distance of 110 miles, it was about the same story. Various needed wartime U.S. projects, such as the Alaska Highway, other roads and an oil pipeline, kept the railroad busy and overwhelmed. The 770th Railway Operating Battalion assumed control of the line on October 1, 1942, running the line until May 1, 1946. Construction on railway shops and facilities, as well as accommodations for the troops, began in earnest. New rolling stock was built at Skagway, and more equipment arrived to help. Locomotives #10 and #11 from the East Tennessee & Western North Carolina Railroad; engines #20 and #21 from the Colorado & Southern; and #22, #23 and #24 from the Silverton Northern were shipped to the railroad between 1942-1943. Another eleven 2-8-2 steam locomotives (#190-200), consigned to Iran, were shipped to Skagway after they were converted from meter gauge to standard gauge in 1945. From 1942 through 1945, another 10 steam engines from the Denver & Rio Grande Western Railroad, built by Alco in 1923, operated on the

White Pass as well. As many as 34 trains a day operated over this narrow gauge rail line during the war. In all, as many as 36 locomotives were assigned to the railroad and nearly 300 pieces of rolling stock.

These two Alaskan rail lines served the war effort in an extremely critical capacity, keeping goods, men and materiel out of harm's way from Japanese aircraft, and building up the U.S. defense network in Alaska's rugged territory.

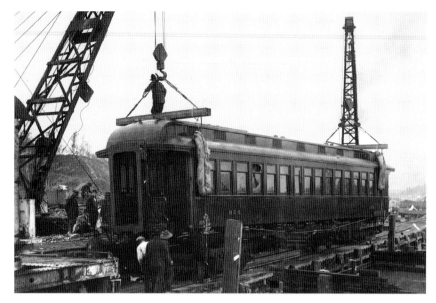

Two heavy cranes lift a heavyweight clerestory-roof passenger coach #864 onto its trucks in Alaska. *National Archives*

NEXT PAGE, ABOVE RIGHT. Goods are taken off box cars on the Alaska Railroad and placed on horse-pulled sleds which negotiated the snow and ice better. *National Archives*

NEXT PAGE, LOWER RIGHT. Some of the United States Railway Service equipment on the Alaska Railroad. *National Archives*

Locomotive #471, on the turntable at Salida, Colorado about 1940, was one of the 10 narrow gauge Denver & Rio Grande Railroad engines that went to the White Pass & Yukon Railroad during WWII for service. *John B. Norwood Jr. collection*

Ambulances, tank trucks, jeeps, Caterpillar dozers and other equipment was ferried to Alaska by rail during WWII, such as these vehicles entering Skagway. *Courtesy Pictorial Histories Publishing*

LEFT. With the Army's Alaska Railroad operations spanning 400 miles, this roving two-car mobile PX was used over the line, offering toiletry items, cigarettes, candy and periodicals. *Courtesy Pictorial Histories Publishing*

Army MT boat #279, a shallow draft tug used in rafting operations on the Tanana River, was brought to Alaska by rail in 1944. *Courtesy Pictorial Histories Publishing*

Color Railroad Promotions Spur War Effort

"Our product is transportation—and, twenty-four hours every day, our plant and personnel are producing more and more of it—in the name of Freedom!" —Pere Marquette Railway, May 23, 1942

I f ever color promotional pieces and advertisements could help the cause, whatever that cause may be, American industry used it during World War II.

America's fighting forces were giving their lives overseas for American independence and freedom, and nothing was too good for "the cause" here at home. Railroads, manufacturers who supplied railroads, and larger businesses that needed to get their point across, considered punching up their advertisements with color in railroad, trade and consumer magazines.

Advertisements helped to let Americans know that their help was vital in ending—and winning—the war. Ads for reducing inflation, rationing of food and goods, conservation of clothing and other essentials, all helped to increase materials for the war effort.

The War Advertising Council and the War Finance Committee both sought to promote the sale of war bonds and wartime rationing, all with the underly-ing theme of boosting American morale on the homefront. The work of these organizations is said to have produced the greatest volume of advertising and publicity ever given to any product or agency in the history of America. Even as the country emerged from war, new diesel locomotives were illustrated in color promotional material to heighten their acceptance and show that railroads were modernizing.

Color ads, especially, stirred patriotic attitudes, the spirit of sacrifice, and the collective conscience of Americans. Railroads and their suppliers were at the forefront of this gigantic effort.

Baltimore & Ohio magazine, July 1943

Newsweek, September 1941

POWER

TO PACE THE FUTURE

Here's the drama that comes off a drawing board . . . first of a series of new engines now in service on the East-West route of the Pennsylvania Railroad! Capable of speeds up to 120 miles an hour . . . different in design . . . this long streamlined giant not only marks another forward stride in the science of railroading — it is indicative of the spirit of progress in an industry vital to the welfare of America, now and in the future.

Pennsylvania Railroad
moves ahead

BUY UNITED STATES WAR BONDS AND STAMPS   ★ *50,265 entered the Armed Forces*   ☆ *492 have given their lives for their Country*

FIRST CHOICE *OF THE RAILROADS TODAY !*

THE streamliner pictured here is more than "the locomotive of tomorrow." It is the No. 1 locomotive of *today*.

Authority for this statement is the fact that American railroads, for the past four years, have bought more GM locomotives than locomotives of any other kind.

And in this achievement you see a typical example of the progressive benefits that General Motors enterprise makes possible.

The Diesel engine that drives these swift and thrifty locomotives was born of General Motors research in internal combustion engines. And from our practical experience in manufacturing motors, generators, frames,

bodies and hundreds of other parts—came the processes by which all such units are now made and assembled into complete locomotives in the largest self-contained locomotive factory in the world.

But equally important as the job of developing these locomotives, is the job they themselves have done in actual operation on the railroads. Many people know their record in passenger service. But railroad men can tell

you also how more than 600 General Motors switchers have accelerated freight handling and pared down costs in railroad yards—that a new high-powered freight locomotive is beginning to extend these advantages to mainline freight operation.

And you can thank the alertness of railroad management for putting this new equipment to work at a record rate—to better still further the service of the finest railroads in the world.

ELECTRO-MOTIVE CORPORATION • Subsidiary of General Motors, La Grange, Illinois

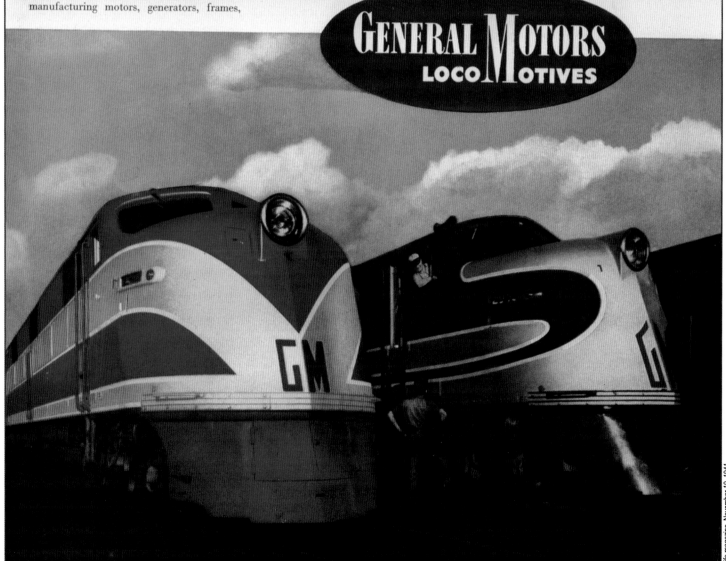

GENERAL MOTORS LOCOMOTIVES

Life magazine, November 10, 1941

Baldwin Locomotive Works showcased the Pennsylvania Class T-1 Nos. 6110 and 6111 in their employee magazine in the December, 1942 issue and again in the Second Quarter 1945 issue. The locomotives were designed for high-speed heavy passenger service.

"Dis pella someting belong wuh-name?"

"What's this?" Joe's asking.

"Paw-paw!" says the native, naming the fruit of the tropical tree.

It's Melanesian Pidgin-English that they're speaking, a "language" described in the War Department's Pocket Guide to New Guinea as:

"*. . . a mixture of words from English, native tongues, Chinese, Malay, German and other languages put together with a minimum of grammar and liberally sprinkled with the salty oaths of early sailormen.*"

Joe's pretty good at pidgin, thanks to the 19 pages of common words and phrases in the Pocket Guides issued to his outfit. And it's lucky that he is for, as those Guides say, it's the *custom of the country* to use Pidgin-English:

"*. . . not only between whites and natives, but also between natives who speak . . . many different little local languages and dialects.*"

That's something new—one of many foreign customs our boys learn as they keep on the move.

There's an *American* custom that's just as new to many boys

whom war keeps on the move *before* they go abroad. It's our custom of *traveling in comfort*—which troops in training do at the rate of 30,000 every night.

The thrill of *going* Pullman is new to lots of those boys now. But no newer to *them* than it will be to *you* when you step aboard two *new-type cars* that Pullman plans to operate when the war is over.

The duplex-roomette is one—a car in which you'll have a completely equipped *private room* for little, if any, more than a lower berth costs now.

The coach-sleeper is the other—a car in which Pullman comfort and convenience will be yours for *less* than the present rate for a berth in either standard or tourist sleeping cars.

When Pullman introduces these new cars, you'll get a new conception of the comfort that has made *going* Pullman *the custom of the country.*

* * *

NOW'S THE TIME TO BUY ANOTHER WAR BOND!

PULLMAN

For more than 80 years, the greatest name in passenger transportation

Copyright 1944, The Pullman Company

National Geographic, August 1944

ON THE JOB FOR UNCLE SAM

This husky fellow was designed to furnish the motive power for one of the Union Pacific fleet of Limited trains providing comfortable passenger transportation between Chicago and the West Coast. Today, he and many like him are performing an important war-time task. Uncle Sam has called on the railroads, not only to move vast quantities of war materials, but also to transport thousands of men in service. Thus, we are not always able to provide preferred accommodations for civilians who find it necessary to travel. To these patrons, Union Pacific wishes to express its appreciation for their patience and cooperation.

The Progressive
UNION PACIFIC RAILROAD
ROAD OF THE STREAMLINERS AND THE CHALLENGERS

National Geographic, January 1943

Santa Fe *Serving America* **in war and peace**
CHICAGO * THE SOUTHWEST * CALIFORNIA

buy more war bonds

Let's all pull together

Military movements come first with American railroads during this all-out war, but you can help maintain adequate passenger service for civilians these days, by cooperating in the following ways:

★ Cancel unwanted reservations promptly ★ Carry least possible luggage, checking all extra pieces to

avoid crowding ★ Label your luggage, ask ticket agent for free sticker or tag ★ Vacate dining cars quickly after meals ★ Travel mid-week, avoid week-end and holiday rush periods ★ Remember, 30 days prior to departure is earliest date advance reservations can be made.

Please turn freely to any Santa Fe agent for help on your travel problems.

Season's Greetings

This Christmas Season
The goods of war roll on
. . . . That Christmas
in the years to come
May once again
mean Peace on Earth
Good Will toward Men

New York Central System

October 10, 1852, the famous Rock Island steam train, the "Rocket," made its initial trip between Chicago and Joliet, Ill. Several years later the Rock Island Lines opened the first bridge across the Mississippi. With true poetic license, the artist has brought these two events together.

The Rock Island Lines operate a fleet of fast and powerful General Motors Diesel freight locomotives known as the "Hercules." They are fitting railmates indeed to the General Motors Diesels which power the new and modern Rock Island "Rockets" of today.

GREAT THINGS ARE HAPPENING IN TRANSPORTATION

When people discuss travel you'll often hear mention of the big, powerful Diesel locomotives that are hauling so many of America's crack trains.

You may, or may not, know that by far the greater number of these new and modern locomotives are built by General Motors. Railroad men know it. And they will tell you, too, how these amazing GM Diesels have changed all previous ideas of speed with comfort and safety for passengers; how they have effected economies and efficiencies beyond all previous railroad experience.

It may be your good fortune to ride behind one of these passenger Diesels on your next railroad trip. Or, perhaps you have seen one of these powerful freight locomotives pulling a mile-long loaded train. If so, you'll know why it's a great new day for railroading—with even greater days to come.

ON TO FINAL VICTORY
BUY MORE WAR BONDS

GM GENERAL MOTORS DIESEL POWER

LOCOMOTIVES . . . . . . ELECTRO-MOTIVE DIVISION, La Grange,

ENGINES . . 150 to 2000 H.P. . . CLEVELAND DIESEL ENGINE DIVISION, Cleveland 11, Oh

ENGINES . . 15 to 250 H.P. . . . . DETROIT DIESEL ENGINE DIVISION, Detroit 23, Mi

What's the Olympian "in the hole" for, Bill?

CONDUCTOR BILL can't talk about his railroad orders in wartime—even to such an old friend of the line as Monty Miller, foreman of the Angle D ranch.

It may be the famous, electrified Olympian has gone "in the hole"—which is railroadese for waiting on a side track—because it's more important for a military train to have right of way.

Station agents, conductors, brakemen, and other railroad men don't like to appear unobliging—but they've pledged themselves for the duration to give no information to anyone about unusual train movements.

That's in the interest of national security. An idle word dropped about a troop train—or a supply train's schedule and destination—might reach enemy ears and lead to an attack on a convoy days and even weeks afterward.

For the most part, passengers realize this situation. They too, keep mum about war traffic they see on the railroad.

If the Olympian, the Hiawathas, the Pioneer Limited or other heavily traveled trains happen to be delayed, there is little complaining among passengers. For this understanding attitude, we of The Milwaukee Road are deeply grateful.

ELECTRIFIED OVER THE ROCKIES TO THE SEA

CHICAGO MILWAUKEE ST. PAUL and PACIFIC

THE MILWAUKEE ROAD

VICTORY IS OUR BUSINESS

FREIGHT PROGRESS IN 1943

GENERAL MOTORS LOCOMOTIVES

ELECTRO-MOTIVE DIVISION
GENERAL MOTORS CORPORATION   LA GRANGE, ILLINOIS, U.S.A.

The Man with the "Thousand Track" mind

● Along the Union Pacific are many types of locomotives—tons of pulsating power—designed for particular tasks.

It's the job of the train dispatcher to know, at all times, what locomotives are available and to assign their "runs."

Heavy wartime traffic—the movement of troops and war materials—has greatly added to the dispatcher's responsibilities. More than ever before, he must be exacting, alert and resourceful—a man with a "thousand track" mind.

Dispatchers, like hundreds of other Union Pacific employes in key positions, are especially trained to handle the heavy traffic which flows over "the strategic middle route." They have the experience and ability. They know that hard work and initiative are recognized and rewarded.

Today, 60,000 Union Pacific workers are carrying on the tremendously important wartime transportation job. An additional 12,000 employes are in the armed forces. Their common objective is victory—to maintain the spirit of freedom, individual enterprise and equal opportunity for all.

★ *Help the war effort by not dealing with black markets nor paying over-ceiling prices.*

THE *Strategic* MIDDLE ROUTE

THE PROGRESSIVE
UNION PACIFIC
RAILROAD

BUY ANOTHER WAR STAMP OR BOND TODAY

Home is the sailor, home from sea . . .

This is our wish for you, for Christmas — that your loved ones may be safe and secure in your arms. But if that is not to be, remember there are other Christmases to come; and the job your fighter is doing now will make them happier Christmases for the whole world.

Help him to do this job, by faithfully performing your important duties here at home. It is necessary to conserve clothing, because the making of clothing uses up precious materials and manpower. The way is simple: buy only what you need, buy it wisely and care for it properly.

Garments made of Pacific Factag Fabrics carry the famous Pacific Factag informative label, which tells you what you need to know about the fabric and how to care for it to get maximum service and satisfaction.

Depend on the Pacific Factag for wise wartime buying; ask for it when you shop. For free booklet, address Pacific Mills, Cotton and Rayon Division, 214 Church Street, New York.

PACIFIC *Factag* FABRICS

———— IDENTIFIED BY AMERICA'S LEADING INFORMATIVE LABEL ————

LOOK FOR THIS TAG on House dresses · Street dresses · House coats · Brunch coats · Pinafores · Aprons · Uniforms · Skirts · Blouses · Slacks Hooverettes · Smocks · Work clothes · Play suits · Sun suits · Nightgowns · Negligees · Slips · Pajamas · Children's wear · Men's shirts, shorts, pajamas; sports shirts, slacks, ensembles · Also ask for your Factag slip with purchases of Pacific Yard Goods, and for your Facbook with Pacific Sheets and Pillowcases

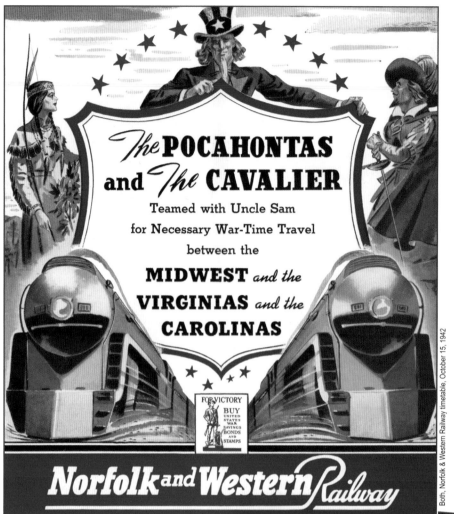

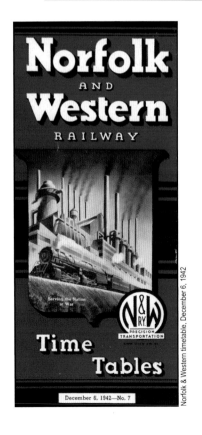

In the world of transportation...

NOTHING SERVES LIKE COPPER

IT WASN'T always "a small world". Modern transportation has made it so...and today is doing a tremendous wartime job...moving more people and more goods in less time than ever before.

And transportation in all its phases makes full use of the combinations of properties found only in copper or its alloys...superior ability to carry electric current and to transfer heat, freedom from rust and resistance to corrosion, ready workability, bearing and spring qualities, strength and durability. No other metals have rendered such dependable service for so many uses, for so long a time.

When the time comes, The American Brass Company, foremost fabricator of copper, brass, bronze, nickel silver and special copper alloys, will be prepared to meet its peacetime responsibilities to transportation and industry at large.

THE AMERICAN BRASS COMPANY
Subsidiary of Anaconda Copper Mining Company
General Offices: Waterbury 88, Connecticut
In Canada: ANACONDA AMERICAN BRASS, LTD.,
New Toronto, Ont.

Special Alloys developed by The American Brass Company, such as Avialite*, Beryllium Copper, Everdur*, Tobin Bronze*, are performing hundreds of important tasks...in engine and operating equipment...in trains, ships, planes, trucks, buses and automobiles. Each of these metals has special properties which contribute to economical and dependable performance.   4508A

*Reg. U. S. Pat. Off.

ANACONDA *Anaconda Copper & Brass*

Keep Faith With Your Fighters and Yourself!
...Buy War Bonds for Keeps

"TO THEIR HEALTH"

Oranges and other citrus fruits are in greater demand today than ever before. As an abundant source of Vitamin C, they are invaluable in maintaining the health of America's fighters in the field and on the industrial home-front.

Union Pacific serves a large part of the Western territory which produces great quantities of citrus fruits. Modern refrigerator cars provide the protective

transportation that keeps these fruits in orchard-fresh condition.

Thus, a transportation service of commercial value in peace-time has become even more essential in war-time. To guard America's health through supplying proper foods might be considered almost as important as the transportation of armament and troops; another job that the railroads are doing efficiently and whole-heartedly.

The Progressive

UNION PACIFIC RAILROAD

ROAD OF THE STREAMLINERS AND THE CHALLENGERS

BUY MORE WAR BONDS

National Geographic, November 1943

Concourse, Union Station, Chicago

Crossroads of War... *America 1943*

HOUR after hour, day after day, you see them—crowding the concourses of the nation's great railroad terminals—file after file of men in olive drab and navy blue and forest green.

Over four million a month—entraining for camps—heading toward secret embarkation ports—coming home on leave. And more and more civilian travelers, on essential missions, swell the ever-growing throngs.

It's America at war—1943, and riding the rails is never before! What the railroads are doing "adds up to the greatest transportation job in history," according to Chairman Clarence F. Lea of the House Committee on Interstate and Foreign Commerce.

New passenger cars are not now available, due to wartime conditions. Yet, by dint of teamwork and resourcefulness and through sparing neither time nor expense, heavier and heavier demands are being met.

On The Milwaukee Road, for example, travel is running three, often four times higher than in recent pre-war years. Freight traffic is at new peaks.

Nevertheless, The Milwaukee Road's 35,000 loyal employees are not complacent simply because they are handling their wartime assignments with admirable efficiency. They know they must keep on fighting America's transportation battle unremittingly every hour and every day of this war.

THE MILWAUKEE ROAD

★ Buy More War Bonds ★

SERVING THE SERVICES AND YOU

Greetings from CAMP CLAIBORNE LOUISIANA

From 1941 to 1946 more than half a million men were stationed at Camp Claiborne, a U.S. Army military camp located in Rapides Parish in central Louisiana. The camp was under the jurisdiction of the U.S. 8th Service Command and included 23,000 acres. It was mainly used for basic training and artillery practice, which included the nearby Winn District-Kisatchie Precision Bombing Range. Engineering unit and special service forces training was also conducted there, including railroad battalion training. *Don Heimburger collection*

PATHFINDERS OF THE DIESEL ERA

The original Burlington Zephyr which inaugurated a new era in American transportation history in 1934. After more than 1,850,000 miles it is still assigned to its daily round trip of 465 miles between Lincoln and McCook, Nebraska.

Latest of the illustrious descendants of the original Zephyr—one of the sixteen 5400-horsepower General Motors Freight Locomotives being put into wartime service by the Burlington Lines.

IT is just ten years since the famous Burlington Zephyr introduced new ideas in railroad travel. It was the world's first Diesel-powered streamlined train. Its power plant was General Motors Diesel. Today hundreds of General Motors Diesel Locomotives are hauling passengers and freight on 75 American railroads. They operate many millions of miles annually with astounding dependability and economy. Day by day additional GM Locomotives are entering that honored field of more than one million miles of operation. Every day brings new records of performance.

And this performance, highlighted by its invaluable contribution to the astonishing war record of the railroads, is providing a glimpse of the greater day of railroading which lies ahead.

Keep America Strong BUY WAR BONDS

GM GENERAL MOTORS DIESEL POWER

LOCOMOTIVES......... ELECTRO-MOTIVE DIVISION, La Grange, Ill.

ENGINES....150 to 2000 H.P....CLEVELAND DIESEL ENGINE DIVISION, Cleveland, Ohio

ENGINES.....15 to 250 H.P........DETROIT DIESEL ENGINE DIVISION, Detroit, Mich.

General Motors, March 1944

... the **biggest** job in railroad history

At a time when congestion or a car shortage on American railroads might have meant disaster for mankind half way around the earth, the American railroads have done the biggest transportation job in the history of the world.

One reason they have been able to handle more traffic than in the busiest year of the first World War with 32% fewer locomotives is because the power of the average locomotive has been increased more than 50% and the speed of freight trains more than 30% in that period.

Many of these locomotives have been Baldwins, with 111 years of knowing-how behind them. Many Baldwin ideas have gone into the spectacular increases in power and speed.

However, Baldwin does more than build locomotives. Its products include hydraulic presses for forming the metal for ships and planes—machines and instruments for testing airplane parts—turbines for power dams— propellers and forgings for ships.

Today, the engineering and manufacturing skill Baldwin has gained in building these products and many more for a vast cross-section of American industry, is devoted to the rapid production of the things needed by America at War, whether they be machines for other vital industries, or tanks, guns, gun mounts and other materiel for our rapidly expanding Army and Navy.

The Baldwin Locomotive Works, Philadelphia, Pennsylvania: Locomotive & Ordnance Division; Baldwin Southwark Division; Cramp Brass & Iron Foundries Division; Standard Steel Works Division; Baldwin De La Vergne Sales Corp.; The Whitcomb Locomotive Co.; The Pelton Water Wheel Co.; The Midvale Co.

Baldwin serves the Nation which the Railroads helped to build

Baldwin magazine, June 1942

The Milwaukee Road Victory Clock

★ 24 hours a day for U.S.A. ★

There's never any stopping the clock on a railroad—but it's when a war is on that railroads must really wheel 'em.

Troop trains must reach embarkation and transfer points with speed, secrecy and precision.

Precious freight must be delivered to its destination exactly when it's needed, or vital hours of production may be lost.

Tracks must be always clear for war cargoes—and often shipments must be rerouted with scarcely any notice in advance. Weather conditions must be anticipated and mastered.

Today the clock on The Milwaukee Road is a Victory Clock in scope as well as in spirit. 35,000 loyal, alert employees in more than 100 different classifications—track men, car men, shop mechanics, roundhouse men, trainmen, dispatchers and division superintendents, to name a few—all fully realize the solemn responsibility of their jobs.

24 hours a day for U.S.A. is the war schedule on The Milwaukee Road. And we're putting all the accumulated experience of 92 years of railroading into every hour of achievement our Victory Clock ticks off.

CHICAGO MILWAUKEE ST PAUL AND PACIFIC

THE MILWAUKEE ROAD

11,000-MILE SUPPLY LINE FOR WAR AND HOME FRONTS

New York Central

SYSTEM TIME TABLES

ONE OF AMERICA'S RAILROADS—ALL UNITED FOR VICTORY—BUY UNITED STATES WAR BONDS AND STAMPS

Effective February 20, 1944—Form 1001

SO WE'LL MEET AGAIN

BUY MORE WAR BONDS

Mr. Sedgwick's Receipt
is now a *Museum Piece*

The practice of giving a receipt for Express shipments began with the first transaction more than a hundred years ago. It is, in effect, a contract setting forth the terms of responsibility of the Express Agency. The receipt taken at delivery is a record of fulfillment of service.

In 1839, Express receipts covered shipments only from Boston to New York and return. Today, Express receipts are written for every conceivable variety of goods — war items, commercial, personal — for delivery throughout the nation. Every foot of the way from shipper to receiver, direct responsibility for safe transportation, by rail and air, remains with Railway Express.

BUY BIGGER BONDS FOR THE BIG 7th

RAILWAY EXPRESS AGENCY

NATION-WIDE   RAIL-AIR SERVICE

Bringing in the HARVEST

...SO VITAL TO VICTORY!

NEVER before in history has food figured so much in American calculations.

Today we are a rationed nation, sharing our food with our boys abroad and their comrades-in-arms.

In order that there may be food for all, the railroads not only are moving great quantities from canneries, packing plants, fruit and vegetable areas but are sending thousands of cars into the harvest fields to haul millions of bushels of grain—your daily bread.

You may wonder how the railroads can take on so big a job as the harvest these days and still keep the war effort rolling. Here is the answer in one word—*cooperation*.

The railroads work together. While crops are still ripening in the fields, their plans are already laid. When harvesting starts, Pennsylvania Railroad contributes a share of its freight cars, along with other railroads, to the great American car "pool"...and there's a reserve army of cars all mobilized to move the crops to elevators and ship sidings.

Result: Plenty of cars for agriculture, the load evenly distributed among many railroads.

It is this sort of teamwork, going on every day, that is enabling the railroads to do for their country what United States Senator Clyde M. Reed of Kansas described as "the most phenomenal job in their history."

PENNSYLVANIA RAILROAD
Serving the Nation

★ 29,842 *in the Armed Forces* ☆ 26 *have given their lives for their country*

Now in full swing on the Great Lakes...

ANOTHER RECORD MOVEMENT OF

Iron Ore for War

Iron ore is vital to the war effort—you can't make steel without it.

So the number of tanks, guns, ships, and munitions we turn out depends upon the amount of ore mined and moved to steel mills.

But iron ore can be moved down the Great Lakes only 8 months of the year, because navigation is closed during the winter months due to ice conditions.

In 1942—under the spur of war

—ore mines, boats and railroads, teaming up, moved from mines to furnaces a total of 92,076,781 gross tons of iron ore via the Great Lakes . . . surpassing the approximately 65,000,000 tons moved in one season during World War I and again in 1929.

But this is 1943. Now navigation is under way. Giant ore boats are steaming full speed ahead. The whole ore movement is in full swing. For Uncle Sam is calling for more ore than ever before.

In fact, the War Production Board's 1943 quota is 95,000,000 tons. So "the great ore ferry" must top last year's all-time record by at least 3,000,000 tons !

Pennsylvania Railroad, as one of those doing the job, knows what mining men . . . boatmen . . . . . . dockmen . . . steel men . . . railroad men . . . can do! And it salutes them as they point for a new all-time record ! Now, pictured here is the job—and how it is done.

Pennsylvania Railroad

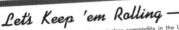

Let's Keep 'em Rolling —

Safe, dependable rail service is a priceless commodity in the United States, particularly in times such as the present. Strategically located as it is, the C&EI has always been actively engaged in moving people of many trades, and goods of various industries.

However, for the past several months, the C&EI has been a combat unit of the transportation industry of America. Our first concern is the fulfilling of Government requirements and our entire resources are pledged to the accomplishment of this task.

But, busy as we may be, we are sincerely endeavoring to keep the needs of our regular travelers and shippers before us—our freight and passenger equipment is dedicated to keep the public adequately provided with the best possible accommodations, and you may be sure we appreciate your patronage just as much now as we did in peace time.

There is also a more personal angle involved—practically every department on our railroad is now represented in Uncle Sam's armed forces —a distinction of which we are proud.

We know you will agree with us that our first job is to serve Uncle Sam with all the means at our disposal. Therefore, we beg your indulgence while we are fulfilling our first responsibility of "keeping 'em rolling" for Uncle Sam.

O'neal

President

Chicago & Eastern Illinois Railroad timetable, December 17, 1942

"NEW GUESTS" ARRIVING AT SAN ANTONIO AVIATION CADET CENTER

ON THEIR WAY

Shades are drawn down. Lights dim low. The landscape is blotted out ...there's just the hum of the speeding train.

These boys know what it means— the troop train is approaching the troop ships.

Some draw a deep breath. A soldier fumbles for a letter. Another wonders if he can make a last telephone call. Another draws out a crumpled photograph.

No, travelers don't see this—but the trainmen of the Pennsylvania Railroad do, daily. And more so than ever now. As the swelling tide of American youth—fine and fit— streams overseas...

Of course, it takes a lot of equipment for these troop movements— but with what remains we are doing our best to serve all essential travelers... efficiently, courteously.

BUY UNITED STATES WAR BONDS AND STAMPS

Pennsylvania Railroad
Serving the Nation

★ *44,823 in the Armed Forces*   ★ *134 have given their lives for their country*

What it takes to move a division

IF, like the eagle, you could look down on the amount of railroad equipment it takes to move a single armored division, here is what you would see...75 trains!

Many passenger trains, many freight trains —all required to move just *one* division. For a division takes all its equipment with it—tanks, jeeps, armored cars, supply trucks, tractors, anti-aircraft guns, many things. And its men, numbering about 12,000, need berths in which to sleep!

What's more, when this division moves by rail, it moves as a unit—that is, trains following one another a few minutes apart.

Now, in terms of trains, those 75 *taken out* of civilian service and *put into military service,* are *about equal to* the number of passenger trains running daily over the Pennsylvania Railroad between *two of the busiest places on the face of the globe*—New York and Washington.

Multiply this one division by the many moving in this country and you can understand why...you may have difficulty

getting a berth...or be obliged to stand in a coach...or arrive at your destination late. In fact, demand for equipment is now so great that on arriving at terminals cars must be put right back into service, so you may find them not quite so spic and span as we would like. Housekeeping facilities are adequate but there's not always time.

But Americans are taking all this like good soldiers. For they know this is a war of movement, and that movement begins right here—*in America, on the rails.*

★ 26,611 in the Armed Forces
★ 21 have given their lives for their country

BUY UNITED STATES WAR BONDS AND STAMPS

 **PENNSYLVANIA RAILROAD**

Serving the Nation

Copyright 1943, The Pullman Company

"Bet I come back hitched !"

Mother will bring him breakfast in bed. Dad will talk of Belleau Woods and how they did it in '18. Mary—well, she's half-way promised—there'll be a moon—and leave it to a Marine with two weeks' leave to get "the situation well in hand"!

So Pullman has *another* passenger tonight—this lieutenant heading home—*another* reason wartime travel is at an all-time high.

And besides the huge load on *regular* trains, an average of almost 30,000 troops a night ride *special* trains of sleeping cars.

So sometimes, it's a pretty tight squeeze to take care of *everyone*, especially in the customary Pullman manner. But most passengers realize the difficulties and are tolerant of short-comings.

And it's not only that they say, "Troops come first with us, as they do with Pullman." It's also that *wartime* travelers don't seem so concerned about the free choice of accommodations and the

lavish services that made peacetime Pullman trips such memorable occasions.

That's probably because what people want from Pullman *now* are the *fundamental features* rather than the frills.

The privacy and comfort that permit a few golden hours of utter relaxation. That present an opportunity to do some quiet thinking beyond the jangle of a telephone. That invite—gently but insistently—the deep, untroubled sleep that "knits up the ravell'd sleeve of care."

These things may seem little in themselves, but

they are of vast importance to those whom war drives hard because a good day's work depends a lot upon a good night's sleep. So ask yourself, "Is my trip *necessary?*" If it is, please:

Cancel promptly, when plans change, and make the Pullman bed reserved for you available to someone else.

Travel light and give yourself and fellow passengers the room that excess luggage would take up.

Ask your Ticket Agent on which days trains may be least crowded on the route you want to take. Try to go on one of those days if you can.

PULLMAN
America's Most Comfortable Way To Travel
—THE SURE WAY TO GET WHERE YOU WANT TO GO

The Pullman Company

FORWARD

...all along the line!

AMERICA is on the offensive wherever the flag flies . . . for one purpose, and one purpose only — to bring this war to a victorious close as quickly as possible.

If this is to be the year, as everybody hopes, then the call is not only for *united* effort — but for that extra "something" from every American on the home front. Count on the 161,922 workers of the Pennsylvania Railroad to do their share!

Count on them to help keep rolling the greatest volume of freight and passenger traffic in the history of railroading...to push war shipments through with speed and efficiency...and to serve the traveling public in the spirit of courtesy and friendliness characteristic of the Pennsylvania Railroad at *all* times — in war or peace.

★ *38,122 in the Armed Forces* ★ *84 have given their lives for their country*

Pennsylvania Railroad

Serving the Nation

283

RAILROADING IS *People*

Nothing in this world is as interesting as—people!
Nothing is as important as people . . . people
who live and grow, love and get married . . . people
with their habits and manners, their likes and
dislikes. Nothing really matters but—people.

The city? We think of it as people. The countryside
is people. And so is the railroad . . .
just folks—all of them!

SOLDIER, SAILOR, MARINE: we wish to serve you well on-your furlough.

Locomotives, cars, equipment . . . all these have
been thought out, designed, engineered, developed and
built by people for people. They are of value
only as they serve people.

We of the Pennsylvania Railroad try to keep in mind
always: everything we do is measured by how we help
people, how we get along with people, how we
treat people. Our greatest reward is in having people
think well of us . . . because we have served them well!

PENNSYLVANIA RAILROAD
Serving the Nation

Buy United States Victory Bonds and Stamps

Life magazine, November 19, 1945

WAR TRAINS *"go to sea by rail"*

on Southern Pacific's Overland Route (DESTINATION TOKYO)

Just west of Ogden, Utah, Southern Pacific's OVERLAND ROUTE leaves the land and heads boldly out to sea toward a distant shore—thirty miles away!

This is the spectacular Lucin Cut-off—a causeway across Great Salt Lake. Southern Pacific built it to save 44 miles. It was, and is, an engineering wonder of the world.

Great Salt Lake fought its conquerors with savage fury. Sudden storms tore away the pilings as fast as they were driven. In one place the builders had to dump *75,000 carloads of rock* before they found firm bottom for the roadbed. But the job was done. It cost $8,000,000.

Eight million dollars to save 44 miles!

America can be thankful now for the courage and vision of the men who built the Lucin Causeway. It is one reason why America's railroads were able, when war came, to do a transportation job which would have seemed impossible before Pearl Harbor.

* * * *

After the war is over, we hope you'll come West

on Southern Pacific's historic OVERLAND ROUTE. You'll ride the swift streamliner *City of San Francisco*, the famous *Overland Limited*, the *San Francisco Challenger* or the *Pacific Limited*. You'll "go to sea by rail" across Great Salt Lake, climb the High Sierra near mile-high Lake Tahoe, and glide down through the mining towns the Forty-Niners built, to San Francisco.

But that must wait. Southern Pacific trains are war trains now.

Our 100,000 men and women know that Southern Pacific serves the main West Coast ports of embarkation from San Diego to Portland, and more military and naval establishments than any other railroad. Night and day they are pushing the war trains through . . .

On our SUNSET ROUTE from New Orleans through the Old South and Texas; on our GOLDEN STATE ROUTE through El Paso and Southern Arizona; on our SHASTA ROUTE down through the evergreen Pacific Northwest, past mighty Mt. Shasta and Shasta Dam; and on our OVERLAND ROUTE, as we have told you here . . .

Night and day we will roll the war trains through until the enemy is defeated.

S·P
The friendly Southern Pacific
Headquarters: 65 Market Street, San Francisco 5, California

STEEL—*and what it takes to haul it!*

THE American steel industry, under the stimulus of war, turned out last year a tonnage never before attained—almost 90,000,000 tons.

For the production of 90,000,000 tons of steel, the railroads moved altogether to steel plants about six and a quarter million carloads of raw materials, such as iron ore, coal, limestone, "scrap," manganese, chromite and other special ores.

Two million cars were provided to haul the finished steel away.

Altogether, the railroads moved more than 8,000,000 carloads of material to and from the steel mills!

Yet that is only one of the major wartime jobs being done by the railroads. Any wonder then that traffic on the rails, at times, has been so heavy as to cause delay and inconvenience to passengers? The Pennsylvania Railroad, however, has found traveling Americans very cooperative—they realize the magnitude of the job railroads are doing.

Pennsylvania Railroad timetable November 26, 1944

ANOTHER GREAT CHAPTER IN RAILROAD HISTORY

Here Currier and Ives, the famous portrayers of American life in the past century, picture their idea of the ultimate in convenient travel —a train of the 70's rolling through the cut outside Jersey City.

Today GM Diesel Locomotives *speed passengers from Chicago to Los Angeles, 2227 miles, in 41¾ hours, a business-day faster than in the middle nineteen thirties. In recent war emergencies GM freight locomotives on the Santa Fe have been an important factor in the rapid movement of precious war material between Chicago and the Pacific Coast.*

THE history of America is a history of progress in transportation. ★ This history is not completed. ★ General Motors locomotives have turned a new page in this record of progress. ★ The flowering of this new era when peace again returns is foretold in the tremendous strides already taken in meeting the challenges of war today.

Pages will be turned too in farm and industrial history. For GM Diesels will be ready to serve wherever America needs power.

GM
GENERAL MOTORS
DIESEL POWER

LOCOMOTIVES.....................ELECTRO-MOTIVE DIVISION, La Grange, Ill.

ENGINES..300 to 2000 H.P....CLEVELAND DIESEL ENGINE DIVISION, Cleveland, Ohio

ENGINES.....15 to 250 H.P......DETROIT DIESEL ENGINE DIVISION, Detroit, Mich.

General Motors

PENNSYLVANIA RAILROAD

Serving the Nation

Sept. 27, 1942

BUY U. S. WAR SAVINGS BONDS AND STAMPS FOR VICTORY!

Pennsylvania Railroad timetable, 1942

Good Soldiers ...All!

Railway Purchases and Stores, November 1942

Eternally Vigilant—

FOR A FREE AND FIGHTING AMERICA

Today, while vigilantly conserving priceless materials, railroad men and equipment are delivering history's most efficient transportation to a free and fighting America.

And as one who serves the great American railroads, we of Dayton are gladly doing our best to help maintain the uninterrupted flow of troops and fighting weapons to the combat zones of both hemispheres.

At your disposal, without cost or obligation, are the services of Dayton's Maintenance and Inspection Engineers to help train maintenance crews, analyze your maintenance procedure, or ferret out any unusual problems concerning V-Belts.

The proper application, alignment of pulleys, and the regular checking of pulley groove wear contributes greatly to the life of V-Belts and Connectors, and so conserves vital materials. Therefore we urge you to read carefully our Catalog No. 65 now in your files for complete instructions regarding the installation, inspection and maintenance of Dayton V-Belt equipment.

THE DAYTON RUBBER MFG. CO.
DAYTON, OHIO

Pioneers of Railway V-Belts and Connectors

THROW YOUR SCRAP INTO THE FIGHT!

Dayton 2" V-Belt Axle Drive

Dayton V Belts

FOR CAR LIGHTING AND AIR-CONDITIONING EQUIPMENT
MADE BY THE WORLD'S LARGEST MANUFACTURER OF V-BELTS

Copyright 1942, The Dayton Rubber Manufacturing Company

service unrationed
on your **2** favorite Trains
to & from **TEXAS**

M·K·T
Katy Lines

Fine . . . Fast . . . Daily

1			2	
7 **THE BLUEBONNET**	**CONDENSED SCHEDULES**		**8** **THE BLUEBONNET**
TEXAS SPECIAL			**TEXAS SPECIAL**	

TEXAS SPECIAL	THE BLUEBONNET	CONDENSED SCHEDULES	TEXAS SPECIAL	THE BLUEBONNET
6:00PM	2:15PM	Lv...ST. LOUIS...Ar	8:30AM	11:40AM
6:10PM	2:25PM	Lv. Tower Grove (StL-SF)..Ar	8:10AM	11:22AM
f10:35PM	7:25PM	Lv...Lebanon......Ar	f3:51AM	6:32AM
12:15AM	9:20PM	Lv...Springfield....Ar	2:15AM	4:15AM
1:35AM	10:35PM	Lv...Monett....Ar	12:58AM	2:55AM
......	6:31PM	Lv....KANSAS CITY....Ar	......	7:15AM
5:05AM	2:45AM	Lv....Muskogee...Ar	9:25PM	10:55PM
	4:15AM	Lv....McAlester...Lv	8:02PM	9:30PM
8:45AM	6:45AM	Ar....Denison.....Lv	5:50PM	7:10PM
11:33AM	9:55AM	Ar....Highland Park...Lv	3:05PM	4:00PM
11:45AM	10:05AM	Ar....DALLAS....Lv	2:55PM	3:50PM
2:25PM		Ar....Waco....Lv	12:20PM	
11:40AM	10:00AM	Ar....FORT WORTH....Lv	2:55PM	3:50PM
1:15PM		Ar...Wichita Falls....Lv		2:30PM
3:24PM		Ar....Temple....Lv	11:22AM	
5:20PM		Ar....Austin....Lv	9:25AM	
7:40PM		Ar...SAN ANTONIO...Lv	7:25AM	
9:50PM		Ar...HOUSTON....Lv		

BEDROOM CARS
on Texas Special
Between
ST. LOUIS and DALLAS—SAN ANTONIO

PARLOR CARS
on Texas Special
Between
DENISON and DALLAS—SAN ANTONIO
and on
The Katy Flyer
Between
PARSONS and DALLAS

Serving the Southwest... and the Nation ...Well

. . . it is this spirit-

Newspapers, magazines and military and government authorities have paid the railroads some mighty fine compliments for the smooth, efficient job they are doing in the transportation of our fighting men. These pats on the back are genuinely appreciated, and spur railroaders on to doing a better and better job.

And now, the Norfolk and Western wants to pay a compliment and express sincere appreciation to the folks in civilian life—who know and accept the fact that Uncle Sam's fighters come first with the railroads; who give the right-of-way to the men in uniform; who do not fuss or criticize when they have to take the best they can get in train travel.

It is this teamwork, this spirit of cooperation between civilian travelers, the railroads, and military authorities, that makes America invincible . . . that gives our fighting men the confidence and courage—to go places and do things!

FOR VICTORY
BUY UNITED STATES WAR BONDS AND STAMPS

NORFOLK and **WESTERN**
Railway

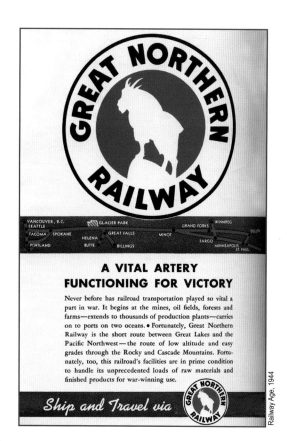

GREAT NORTHERN RAILWAY

VANCOUVER, B.C. GLACIER PARK
SEATTLE
TACOMA SPOKANE GREAT FALLS GRAND FORKS WINNIPEG
HELENA MINOT DULUTH
PORTLAND BUTTE BILLINGS FARGO
MINNEAPOLIS ST. PAUL

A VITAL ARTERY FUNCTIONING FOR VICTORY

Never before has railroad transportation played so vital a part in war. It begins at the mines, oil fields, forests and farms—extends to thousands of production plants—carries on to ports on two oceans. ● Fortunately, Great Northern Railway is the short route between Great Lakes and the Pacific Northwest—the route of low altitude and easy grades through the Rocky and Cascade Mountains. Fortunately, too, this railroad's facilities are in prime condition to handle its unprecedented loads of raw materials and finished products for war-winning use.

Ship and Travel via
GREAT NORTHERN RAILWAY

Fixing 'em on the Fly for Victory

How Santa Fe Is Speeding Up the Servicing Time of War-Vital Freight Cars

Another chapter in the story "Working for Victory on the Santa Fe"

War can't wait. The load on a freight car might win a battle . . . and save the lives of thousands of our fighting men.

There's a battle-winning spirit in the way Santa Fe crews are keeping freight cars rolling these days. They are actually repairing loaded cars without unloading them!

When an inspector reports a flat wheel, a splintered side, or a shifted load on a Santa Fe freight, the car is cut out of the train . . . fixed "on the fly" on a repair track . . . and switched back on the same train, or the one immediately following.

Ready to Roll Again

A Santa Fe gondola has pulled up with a flat wheel. The car and its war load are lifted by pneumatic jacks. Within a few minutes a complete new truck of four wheels is in place, and the car is again ready to roll.

ATSF 169614

Santa Fe

SANTA FE SYSTEM LINES
Serving the Southwest and California
ONE OF AMERICA'S RAILROADS—ALL UNITED FOR VICTORY

Freight Progress In War Number

May 23, 1942

PRICE—ONE DOLLAR

Railway Age

THREE FOR V

UNITED FOR VICTORY

WHAT does it take to move a million tons of freight a mile every minute—as the American railroads are doing?

What does it take to have cars, when and where they're needed—so that every minute a dozen different freight trains start out on their runs?

It takes good equipment, skilled man power and efficient management.

It takes the full, three-way cooperation of those who ship goods, of the railroads which haul them, and of those who receive them.

It's up to the shipper to load his cars to capacity as soon as he gets them. It's up to the railroads to speed them to their destination. And it's up to the receiver to unload right away and see that no cars are used for storage purposes.

Such teamwork as this has enabled the railroads to handle the greatest transportation job in history. How much more they can do depends upon the materials they are permitted to get for repair and maintenance, and for additional cars and locomotives.

Whatever that may be, the railroads, the shippers and the receivers—THREE FOR V—will work together to help win this war.

UNITED FOR VICTORY

ASSOCIATION OF
AMERICAN RAILROADS
WASHINGTON, D.C.

Steam at Ft. Eustis

United States Transportation Corps steam locomotives at Ft. Eustis, Virginia were used for training purposes. These photos show the #714 (0-4-0T), #607 (2-8-0) and #612 (2-8-0) on Ft. Eustis trackage, along with a Burro crane. The #612 participated in the 100th Anniversary of the driving of the Golden Spike at Promontory Point, Utah on May 10, 1969. Photos were taken in 1969. *All photos, Don Heimburger collection*

U.S. Navy Whitcomb at Buckeye Yard, Columbus, Ohio, May 28, 1978

U.S. Navy #65-00589 on Chesapeake & Ohio rails near Cass, West Virginia, October 1978

Military Diesels

The Army and Navy owned and operated diesels for freight service, usually at military posts during the war. These photos show a variety of different locomotives from various branches of the military after the conflict. *All photos, Don Heimburger collection*

U.S. Army #2074 and other diesels at Ft. Eustis, Virginia, June 30, 1969

U.S. Navy #65-00536 on C&O near Cass, West Virginia, October 1978

U.S. Army #4021 at Ft. Eustis, Virginia, June 30, 1969

ONE
HUNDRED
YEARS

1846 - 1946

PENNSYLVANIA RAILROAD
Serving the Nation

This is the freight depot of the U. S. Army Consolidating Station, in Chicago, Illinois in April of 1943. *Jack Delano*

Shown at work, Mrs. Dorothy Lucke was employed as a wiper at the Chicago & North-Western Railroad roundhouse in Clinton, Iowa in April of 1943. *Jack Delano*

Multiply him by
1,458,912 --

MULTIPLY him by 1,458,912 and you have the number of passengers who rode The Milwaukee Road's Hiawathas during 1943 — as many people as the population of Milwaukee, St. Paul, Minneapolis and Tacoma combined — the equivalent of the personnel in 97 infantry divisions!

Many of those Hiawatha passengers were men and women in uniform — traveling under orders or on furlough. Many others were civilians on missions vital to war production. And to the credit of Americans, let it be said that trips "just for pleasure" were few and far between.

The nearly a million and a half that the Hiawatha fleet carried last year were swelled by millions of others who rode the Olympian, the Pioneer Limited, the Arrow, the Southwest Limited, the Chippewa, the Marquette, the Sioux and other Milwaukee Road trains.

In addition, hundreds of thousands of men in the armed forces were transported to camps, maneuvers and embarkation ports on special trains via The Milwaukee Road and its connections. Altogether, America's railroads carried over four times as many passengers during 1943 as they did in recent pre-war years.

What form of transportation, other than the railroads, could keep the nation's passenger traffic moving so smoothly under existing war conditions? What other form of transportation could provide such swift, dependable, economical service for the mass movement of a nation of 133,000,000 people?

THE MILWAUKEE
ROAD

SERVING THE SERVICES AND YOU

Milwaukee Road, March 1944

CHAPTER NINE

Women in War

*"Women who stepped up were measured as citizens of the nation, not as women...
this was a people's war."* —Colonel Oveta Culp Hobby, Women's Army Auxiliary Corps

Even before the U.S. entered WWII, what was called a "national emergency" in the country was pretty much a man's world. Men were in charge of the rearmament effort in Washington, management of the nation's plants and factories were in the hands of males, and men were called to serve in the military services. Even the Home Guard enlisted men to fill in behind the departed militia.

Certainly, women were behind the build-up effort, but it was not until fall of 1941 that women's organizations in the U.S. started to visualize a greater role in the defense of the country. Mrs. John L. Whitehurst, president of the General Federation of Women's Clubs, stated that women were being discriminated against "intolerably" in the civilian defense program. Until that time, only seven women were involved in defense policymaking jobs. The August, 1941 issue of *Newsweek* magazine even devoted a story on the subject entitled "U.S. Women Answer Call of National Defense."

More than 150,000 American women served in the Army during WWII. The purpose of the Women's Army Corps (WACs), according to Judith A. Bellafaire in her book *The Women's Army Corps*, was to allow women to help the American war effort directly and individually. The prevailing philosophy, she says, was that women could best support the war effort by performing non-combatant military jobs for which they were already trained. This allowed the Army to make the most efficient use of available labor, and free men to perform essential combat duties, she says.

"The concept of women in uniform was difficult for American society of the 1940s to accept," Bellafaire states.

She goes on to say, "Although women in key leadership roles both within and outside the government realized that American women were indeed capable of contributing substantially to the war effort, even they accepted the prevailing stereotypes which portrayed women as best suited for tasks which demanded precision, repetition and attention to detail. These factors, coupled with the post-Depression fear that women in uniform might take jobs from civilians, limited the initial range of employment for the first wave of women in the Army.

Traditional restrictions on female employment in American society were broken during WWII by the critical labor shortage faced by all sectors of the economy. As "Rosie the Riveter" demonstrated her capabilities in previously male-dominated civilian industries, women in the Army broke the stereotypes which restricted them, moving into positions well outside of traditional roles.

In factories and plants, women were already starting to take on jobs where manual dexterity was required. And Sidney Hillman, associate director general of the Office of Personnel Management, pushed for more women in the defense industries, particularly in aircraft assembly plants. Railroads welcomed women as the war progressed, even hiring them for such rough work as track maintenance. After all, everyone needed to help if the job was to get done.

Southern Pacific MT-4 Class Mountain-type locomotive #4365, one of 21 of this series built between 1925-1929, gets a thorough cleaning by women workers at the railroad's Sacramento, California shops. *Don Hofsommer collection*

On the Nickel Plate Road, which carried 10.4 billion ton-miles of revenue freight during 1946, a 54% increase over 1941, women were employed at engine servicing facilities, seen here in 1943 washing down a steam locomotive tender at Frankfort, Indiana. The NKP employed 131 women in the Mechanical Department. In 1942 the NKP did more with less than any other time in its history. *Jay Williams collection*

Women work the locomotive servicing area at the Chicago & NorthWestern Proviso Yard during the war. *Jack Delano, courtesy Chicago & NorthWestern Historical Society*

A stewardess on a Baltimore & Ohio Railroad passenger train chats with servicemen as they travel on U.S. rails during the war. *Bob Withers*

Molly Pitcher, 1944

Women are doing a big job on the Pennsylvania Railroad

Pennsylvania Railroad

"Molly Pitcher" was a nickname for women who carried water to the troops during the Revolutionary War. The real Molly Pitcher was born in 1754 as Mary Ludwig Hays McCauley, the daughter of a New Jersey dairy farmer. At the age of 13 she married William Hays, a barber who enlisted and became a gunner in the Pennsylvania Artillery. Mary eventually joined her husband in camp during the Philadelphia Campaign (1777-1778) in New Jersey, eventually wintering with the Army at Valley Forge. We all have come to know her as "Molly Pitcher," gaining this title later on at the Battle of Monmouth. In this 1944 Pennsylvania Railroad ad, Molly pitches in with other women to help win the war. *Valley Forge Historical Society*

Baldwin Locomotive Works guard Harry Kettlewood checks the indentification badge of Sophie Cichocki who is employed at the Baldwin's Southwark shop office at Eddystone. *Baldwin magazine, First Quarter, 1944*

Machinist helper Sally Flatley helps tighten a bolt on a B&O steam locomotive dome during the war. *Bob Withers*

United States WAVES, part of a contingent of new recruits, stand at attention on a troop train on the Southern Pacific during WWII. *Don Hofsommer collection*

In 1944, two women work together as engineer and brakeman at the Indiana Ordnance Works at Charleston, Indiana as they perform switching duties with a small 1942-built Plymouth diesel adorned with yellow and black safety stripes. Because of a shortage of men, females were employed at the gunpowder plant that produced 100,000 pounds a day on each of six production lines. *David Myers collection*

Indiana Army Ammunition Plant

The Indiana Army Ammunition Plant, the world's largest smokeless powder factory, was an Army manufacturing facility built in 1941 and located between Charlestown and Jeffersonville, Indiana. It consisted of three areas within two separate but attached manufacturing plants.

Indiana Ordnance Works Plant 1, IOW#1 (3,564.71 acres), made smokeless powder. Indiana Ordnance Works Plant 2, IOW#2 (2,757.49 acres), made rocket propellant. Hoosier Ordnance Plant, HOP (4,326.8 acres), manufactured and loaded propellant charge bags. After Plant 2 was sold, the complex still had 84 miles of trackage and 190 miles of roads.

One of the abandoned power plants on the Indiana site.

Women at Work
for
a Railroad at War

Santa Fe

Another chapter in the story "Working for Victory on the Santa Fe"

America needs millions of women to take over war jobs . . . to stay with those jobs . . . to help speed the day when our fighting men will return victorious!

Santa Fe women are answering this call all along the line.

Right now thousands of Santa Fe women are doing war-vital work to "keep 'em rolling." Many of them are pitching into "unglamorous" jobs . . . greasing engines, operating turntables, wielding a shovel, cleaning roller bearings, working in blacksmith and sheet metal shops. They take pride in their work, too!

Many of them have husbands, sweethearts, brothers or sons in the armed forces. Many came to work to replace a relative who had been called into service. Others took jobs because they knew womanpower must step in when manpower goes to war.

☆ We of the Santa Fe salute these women who know that what they are doing is vital to Victory!

"Back the Attack with War Bonds"

SANTA FE SYSTEM LINES
Serving the Southwest and California
ONE OF AMERICA'S RAILROADS — ALL UNITED FOR VICTORY

Ralph Norton, photographer from the Bloomington, Illinois *Pantagraph*, took this picture of Betty Block, 19-year-old relief operator, as she hands train orders to the fireman of No. 392, the daily freight on the Illinois Central line from Bloomington to Kankakee, Illinois. Miss Block was trained for her work by Agent Charles E. Jackson at Flanagan, Illinois. *Illinois Central magzine, October 1944*

Women And Machines Must
Fill The Labor Gaps

"The ever-expanding military program in which an army of 10 million is now talked of for the end of 1943 can mean only one thing for industry, namely, that women are going to have to be used wherever possible to replace men, and much more extensive mechanization is going to have to be employed in order that the women with their lighter weight and lesser strength may be able to handle many of the jobs formerly performed by men," read an editorial in the December, 1942 issue of *Railway Purchases and Stores*.

HOW WOMEN HELPED

"In the last war, women were extensively used to replace men even in handling materials and sorting scrap. Several railroads are now beginning to use women in storehouses, on the scrap docks and in reclamation plants. But the women of today are not quite the sturdy stock they were of twenty years ago, in that the husky peasant stock, freshly arrived from Europe and hardened to heavy farm labor, has entirely stopped through immigration quotas of the past 20 years. Their daughters today are more accustomed to carrying their handbag with compact and cigarettes than they are to following a plow and swinging a hoe. So those employing women as laborers now are confronted with an entirely different situation from what was experienced 20 years ago.

"Railroads generally have followed the rule of not employing married women, which has automatically eliminated a large number of trained personnel. If that rule were now rescinded, a large number of trained employees, particularly in the clerical group, would become available.

"There has been a natural trend away from employment of women in railroad stores because of the fact that those stores are usually adjacent to railway shops, which in turn are almost always located in out-of-the-way places where it is often unsafe for a woman to go. If women are to be re-employed in connection with railroad stores, special attention will have to be given to insure their safe passage to and from work.

"But the fundamental fact that the female of our species constitutes just 50% of our total population must not be overlooked. In wartime women can do a large percentage of the jobs now performed by men. Women constitute, under present circumstances, the greatest reservoir of labor supply to which industry must turn. Munitions plants have already done so in large measure, but the railroads have been very backward in recognizing the possibilities of filling the gaps in the ranks of labor with women workers. Another condition that makes this more urgent at the present time is the new draft for 18- and 19-year-old boys. In the past year many railroads have pieced out their staffs by the employment of these youngsters, especially during summer months. From now on they will not be available. Therefore, no time should be lost in taking on women workers."

These Women at Willard Do Their Part on the Home Front

From left to right are: Mary Kostoff, Rose Horvath, Rose Stockmaster, Helen Stockmaster, Pauline Stockmaster and Ina Ferguson. Mary Kostoff, Rose Horvath and Helen Stockmaster are packing boxes on freight cars in transportation yards. Rose and Pauline Stockmaster and Ina Ferguson are used on the repair track at Willard Car Shop, Pauline being used as relief box packer in the yards. All are doing an excellent job on the duties assigned to them. *Baltimore & Ohio magazine, March 1944*

Foreign Theaters

"The heroism of our troops...was matched by that of the armed forces of the nations that fought by our side...they absorbed the blows...and they shared to the full the ultimate destruction of the enemy." —President Harry S. Truman

Although U.S. Army transportation organizations and activities in the overseas theaters and bases were solely under the control of theater and base commanders, the Chief of Transportation, Army Service Forces (ASF) had an interest in those organizations and certain direct and indirect responsibilities which were vital to their effectiveness.

The distinctive responsibility of the Chief of Transportation was to carry to overseas commanders the troops and materiel of all services, without which their urgent military missions could not be accomplished.

The Transportation Corps connected the production centers, important supply depots and training camps in the zone of

Doubleheaded Military Railway Service Transportation Corps train, with a 2-8-0 in the lead, moves through a heavily-damaged rail yard in the European Theater. With the yard destruction likely incurred by U.S. or British bombers, it will be a while before anything rolls over these rails. *Bob's Photos*

the interior with the overseas areas where the enemy was located. They constituted an indispensable link in the chain of military efforts which finally came to fruition in combat areas.

Another direct responsibility was the supply of transportation personnel for overseas service. As new theaters were opened, demand for such personnel became heavy, and the Chief of Transportation, ASF, had to relinquish many valuable officers from his own hard-pressed staff, and he recruited many experts from civil life, commissioned and indoctrinated them and sent them to overseas commanders.

He was also responsible for organizing, activating and training many types of troop units which were required overseas in connection with the operation of ports, ships, railways and other transportation functions.

TRANSPORTATION UNITS

During the war, 948 Transportation Corps units, consisting of 11,098 officers and 237,142 enlisted men, served

overseas. Another direct responsibility was to provide the theaters with marine, railway and other types of equipment and supplies, which were required for intra-theater transportation. This involved not only procuring, storing and issuing this material, but adapting its design to meet the peculiar needs of each theater.

During the war approximately 7,500 boats and other units of floating equipment, 90,000 major items of railway equipment, and many other items of supply, were dispatched overseas for the use of the U.S. Army and its allies.

Railroads were limited to a good portion of tonnage of this equipment, being transported as raw materials to factories, and finished goods to ports of embarkation. A less direct and less tangible responsibility was the close contact between the Chief of Transportation, ASF, and the transportation and supply organizations in the overseas commands. Coordination of movements, a realization of each other's problems, and a knowledge of each other's machinery and methods was essential. The effort to attain this mutual understanding

The 729th Railway Operating Battalion is at the French port city of Cherbourg, one of the landing sites of the Normandy invasion; loaded onto passenger cars, the soldiers are off to an unknown destination in 1944. The 729th operated rail lines in support of the First and Ninth armies in Germany, and operated the first liberated train into France. Soldiers of this battalion came to help fight the war from 92 different American railroads. *U.S. Army Transportation Museum*

RIGHT. Paratroopers of the U.S. Army 82nd Airborne, with huge duffel bags full of equipment and gear, load into short box cars in Europe to continue their march to meet the enemy. Note the stack of K ration 43-pound wooden boxes at the right. *82nd Airborne Corps Office of Command Historian*

RIGHT, BELOW. A troop train unloads in Cherbourg, France, bringing the first black troops to their assigned duty post on January 31, 1945. *U.S. Army Transportation Museum*

sprang from both sides and rested with the Chief of Transportation in the zone of interior to keep his organization in an informed and sympathetic relationship to the forces overseas and be responsive to their requirements.

ORGANIZATION IN THEATERS

Viewed as a whole, transportation organization in the overseas theaters suffered from a lack of proper definition in War Department directives, failure to understand the transportation problems involved in conducting offensive campaigns across the Atlantic and the Pacific, and a consequent lack of forethought and planning.

This was largely attributed to the absence of an integrated Army transportation service during peace time. The fact that no War Department directive was issued to correct the situation until almost two years after the U.S. entered the conflict, and that when it was issued it only partly met the requirements, was due to the difficulty of having the need fully appreciated by higher echelons.

The field service regulations on administration in effect when the U.S. entered the war made water transportation and the operation of docks and stevedore service responsibilities of The Quartermaster Corps, railways and inland waterways the responsibility of the Corps of Engineers, motor transport the responsibility of a Motor Transport Service which had no counterpart in the zone of interior, and air transport the responsibility of the Air Corps. Coordination of these services would have been in the theater Supply Division (G-4).

The experiences of WWI and the establishment of a Transportation Service in the zone of interior in March 1942 went a long way in establishing integrated transportation services in the theaters, but the extent of integration, and the form of the organization, was left to theater commanders. The result was a marked lack of uniformity between transportation organizations in the several theaters. Those set up in the early days of WWII were inadequate or unsuitable in certain respects, and numerous changes were necessary.

These differences and fluctuations complicated the task which confronted the Chief of Transportation, ASF, of establishing smooth working relationships with the theaters. WD Circular No. 256, 1943, expressly provided for a Transportation Service in the headquarters of theaters of operation, embracing shipping, railways, highways and inland waterways with the authority to coordinate air transport with the other means of transport. However, this circular left may aspects of theater transportation untouched, and it was not immediately reflected in the transportation organizations in established theaters.

A proposed new manual was to establish the theater Chief of Transportation as Chief of Service, in which capacity he would be the special staff officer for transportation in the theater, concerned with policy and planning. He also would be the traffic manager for the theater and the chief operations officer of the military transportation service. His jurisdiction would include the Military Railway Service, Highway Transport Service, Inland Waterway Service, Intra-theater Shipping Service, ports, staging areas and depots for Transportation Corps supplies.

U.S. Equipment Speeds Aid to U.S.S.R.

Chief of Army's Rail Division Cites Role of American-built Locomotives and Rolling Stock Moving Arms to Russians in Iran

By Col. John A. Appleton, TC

As Chief of the Rail Division, Transportation Corps, Army Service Forces, Col. John A. Appleton is serving with his country's Armed Forces for the second time. During World War I, he saw action as a Captain of Engineers, assigned to railroad duties with the AEF in France. Col. Appleton brings to his important post in World War II a thorough knowledge of railroading gained during his almost 30 years with the Pennsylvania Railroad.

On March 30, 1943 the first all-American train carrying war supplies to Russia steamed into the capital of Iran after a 650-mile journey from the Persian Gulf. Those supplies had been landed by Americans from American ships lying at American-built docks. They had been loaded onto American freight cars hitched to American locomotives, and the train, thus made up, was operated to Teheran by American crews. This performance so impressed Major General A.N. Koroloff, Commander of the Red Army in Iran, that he declared: "We firmly believe that once the Americans start doing something, they do it in the American way. I am glad to say that the impact of United States supplies now is being felt on the whole war front."

PRINCIPLE MISSION

Our principle mission in Iran is to deliver Lend-Lease supplies to the Russians in Teheran, six thousand tons of it to be moved by rail daily. Of course, that is not all the Lend-Lease equipment the Russians are getting, but it is a mighty important part. At Teheran, the Red Army takes over and moves the equipment north and westward to the Russian battlefront. Six thousand tons daily add up to the staggering total of well over 2 million tons per year. We haven't attained that goal yet, but we're spurting towards it. During my own brief stay in Persia last January, the tonnage of our shipments north over the Trans-Iranian Railway was more than doubled.

Before we could move those supplies in such volume, we needed new locomotives and rolling stock. That equipment has been coming through on schedule, and we have every confidence it will continue to do so. To date, more than 150 locomotives have joined the battle of transportation in Iran. Upwards of 3,000 flatcars, tank cars, boxcars and gondolas are rolling through Persia behind them. Even the cabooses which form the rear guard were built in America. When I left Persia last January, American and Iranian crews were setting up one locomotive and 30 cars daily in the machine shops and assembly sheds.

I have seen 1,000 hp. diesel-electrics and 2-8-2 freight locomotives pushing north across the desert above the Persian Gulf. I have seen them traversing the 6,000-foot hills of Luristan and the Elburz Mountains, higher still. Specially-designed cars are now riding the rails through bitter mountain cold and scorching desert temperatures which hit 130 degrees Farenheit in the shade. They're taking every kind of punishment imaginable—and they're holding up splendidly. Nowhere have I seen more inspiring results of American manufacturing skill than in the transportation equipment which is today moving goods across Iran, half-way around the world from the factories where that equipment was produced. *Baldwin magazine, October 1943*

A heavy Baldwin locomotive is lifted off an Allied ship in the Middle East while a soldier with his weapon slung across his shoulder guards the port. *Baldwin magazine, October 1943*

He would also have operational control over all nontactical transportation, except that by air and pipeline, in which cases he would have movement control over nontactical intratheater traffic.

In other words, the proposed manual would give the Chief of Transportation the position in the theater organization and the authority over traffic and the means of transportation, which would enable him to maintain a complete, well-coordinated and effective transportation service.

Military railroads have been a factor in strategy since the middle of the nineteenth century. The military railway operations in WWII far exceeded any earlier operations both in scope and intensity.

CHALLENGES ACCEPTED

The large numbers of troops and the large quantities of freight moved were in themselves a challenge to the Army's railroaders. The great diversity of conditions found in operating on four continents and systematic bombing of railway facilities added obstacles and problems not previously encountered. During the course of the war, military railway operations were carried on by U.S. troops in North Africa, Sicily, Italy, the United Kingdom, France, Belgium, Holland, Germany, Iran, India, Burma, the Philippines, New Caledonia and Alaska.

Altogether, more than 16,000 route miles came under their direct operation, and in addition, many railroads which were permitted to continue under foreign management were supervised. The Transportation Corps was responsible for the procurement of equipment for military railways, the training of railway troop units, maintenance-of-way, maintenance of equipment and the operation of military railway services.

The Corps of Engineers was responsible for laying new track and building new structures. The restoration of damaged or destroyed facilities was shared by the two services according to the needs at the time. The Military Railway Service existed during peacetime as part of the Reserve Corps. The units were sponsored by large railroads, which also provided the personnel, but the interest was not active.

The first step toward placing this service on a more active footing was taken in 1939 by the Chief of Engineers, who had full responsibility for military railways. He appointed two railroad officials as consultants, one to have charge of activities in the field, and the other to be attached to his own office.

RESERVE UNITS ORGANIZED

A general plan of development evolved, and additional reserve units were organized. In the summer of 1941 construction of a short railroad for training purposes was begun in Louisiana and one railway operating battalion was placed on active status. This was substantially the situation on December 1941.

Boarded up and ready for shipment overseas is a Baldwin-made "Austerity" 2-8-2 locomotive. Here it's shown in the Baldwin plant. *Baldwin magazine, October 1943*

"*Even the sudden collapse of Germany would not necessarily bring relief to our railroads, as it would mean the turning of the tide of rail transportation toward the Pacific instead of the Atlantic, with the consequent longer hauls from the production centers of the East. The launching of major operations against Japan while the European campaigns are in full swing, which is now indicated, will involve maximum traffic to both coasts.*" Col. J. Monroe Johnson, director, Office of Defense Transportation

Soldiers stow freight in mocked-up European cars at Camp Lee, Virginia Quartermasters School. *Railway Age, October 30, 1943*

ABOVE. Foot by foot, some 67 miles of cable is unloaded from a freighter to a flatcar by American troops. *Baldwin magazine, October 1943*

A small Baldwin-built plantation tank locomotive switches a railroad yard in Hawaii outside the roundhouse at Waialu Plantation during the war. Scenes like this with U.S. soldiers operating steam across Europe in North Africa and in the Pacific were common, especially once the Allies gained back territory previously lost to the Axis powers. *Baldwin magazine, Second Quarter 1945*

One of the 2-8-2 locomotives built by Baldwin for the U.S. War Department is inspected by Major R. Hart Davies, British Army Staff; Lt. Col. J. S. Seybold, U.S. Army; and Major J. W. Marsh, U.S. Corps of Engineers in 1942 at the Baldwin Locomotive Works plant in Philadelphia. Note the buffers used in foreign service equipment. *Baldwin magazine, June 1942*

With the words "Hail to Victory," Soviet General L.G. Rudenko christens the first of a large lot of Baldwin Decapod locomotives destined for the Soviet Union. At far left is Vasili A. Sergeev, Russian Vice Commissar for Foreign Trade. *Baldwin magazine, First Quarter, 1944*

Palletized cargo was transferred from Liberty Ships to U.S. Army LCM #8222, then floated to the dock and unloaded again by forklift to waiting trains. *U.S. Army Transportation Museum*

Five railway grand divisions, 20 railway operating battalions and three railway shop battalions were then in reserve status. Gradually, as the need for railroad troops developed in 1942, these reserve units were called to active duty, and headquarters were established at Fort Snelling, Minnesota.

In the fall of 1942, railroad troops began leaving the U.S. for overseas service. A detachment was sent to Alaska to bolster operations on the White Pass & Yukon Railroad, and later other troops were assigned to the Alaska Railroad, which was having difficulty meeting wartime requirements.

A number of units went to Iran and others to the United Kingdom. Still other units were assigned to North Africa, where the American and British forces landed on November 8, 1942. It was at this juncture that responsibility for the operation of military railways was transferred to the Transportation Corps.

United States Military Railway units arrived in North Africa, some direct and some via the United Kingdom, within a few days after D-Day. Other units followed shortly. In February the Manager, Military Railway Service, arrived in North Africa with an advance echelon of his headquarters, and soon he was redesignated Director General.

The 1st Military Railway Service, which was set up in North Africa, continued with the victorious Allied Forces into Sicily, Italy and southern France. In all these invasions small detachments of railway troops crossed the beaches with the assault troops to reconnoiter, begin railway operations where possible and prepared plans for the disposition of additional troops and railway equipment which was to follow.

One of the largest battles during WWII was the battle of Monte Cassino, Italy in 1944. German troops occupied an ancient monastery atop Monte Cassino, and the Allied bombing of the monastery was a controversial subject. The battle lasted for five months, and the Allies suffered 25,000 casualties during this time. A pair of hood units from the Military Railway Service pass the Cassino signpost. *Bob's Photos*

Soldiers fill the rear compartment of an Army halftrack with gasoline tanks that have arrived on a railroad train operated by the U.S. Military Railway Service. *David Doyle*

314

In North Africa the 1st Military Railway Service operated about 1,400 miles of standard and meter gauge track, extending from Casablanca to Tunis. For the most part the track and equipment was in fair condition. However, the experience gained in rehabilitating facilities, assembling locomotives and cars received from the U.S., and later working under combat conditions in Tunisia, gave Allied troops valuable experience for the strenuous campaigns in Italy and France, which finally brought some of the units into Germany itself.

NORTH AFRICA

North Africa also gave the United States Military Railway Service experience in working with the British, which was to prove valuable in nearly two years of joint endeavors in Italy. Following action by the Combined Chiefs of Staff, the U.S. Army began taking over operation of the Iranian State Railway from the British in January 1943. As a result of the work of military railway troop units assigned to the Persian Gulf Service Command (later the Persian Gulf Command) and with the aid of American equipment, the 685 miles of track extending from Khorramshahr and Bandar Shahpur to Tehran soon began to handle increased tonnage.

From 47,000 tons which moved northward from the ports in March 1943, the volume increased to 171,000 tons in July 1944. From April 1, 1943 when U.S. troops took full operational control of the line, until June 1, 1945 when their responsibility ceased, the 3d Military Railway Service moved a total of 4,144,000 long tons of northbound freight. Of this amount, 2,749,000 tons was Lend-Lease freight destined to Russia.

AMERICAN TROOPS TO U.K.

American Railway troops and equipment sent to the United Kingdom were intended primarily for use in Europe, but they also served to relieve the manpower and equipment shortages in Britain. The large volume of American military traffic, superimposed upon the abnormally heavy British traffic, placed an unprecedented load upon the British railroads. While being trained for fighting and operating in Europe, American railway troops assembled locomotives and cars, built and operated tracks at and near U.S. Army depots, and learned British railroad organization and methods.

Within a week of the assault on Normandy beaches, advance elements of the 2d Military Railway Service landed in France. Using a jeep equipped with flanged wheels, they reconnoitered the rail lines behind the beachheads as soon as the fighting permitted. On July 3, 1944 an advance detachment of an operating battalion arrived in Cherbourg, and by July 11 it was operating the rail line as far as Carentan.

Restoration of the tracks and other facilities and the importation of cars and locomotives proceeded slowly, but local operations were expanded gradually, and on August 15 numerous trains were loaded on the Cherbourg Peninsula and started rolling toward Paris.

Officers and men of the British Navy attended an intensive course in diesel engine operation and maintenance at the Baldwin Locomotive Works in Philadelphia, Pennsylvania. The course was under the direction of S.W. Moser, front row, right, Baldwin manager of diesel service. *Baldwin magazine, First Quarter 1945*

WAC Corporal Maxine G. Vaught stands in front of a U.S. Army 2-8-0 which she is about to christen *Casey Jones* in honor of the WAC members serving with the Transportation Corps in WWII. The ceremony took place in a Paris railway yard. *Baldwin magazine, First Quarter 1945*

The 729th Railway Operating Battalion moves a trainload of Army tanks, one tank per carload, at Cherbourg, France in 1944. *U.S. Army Transportation Museum*

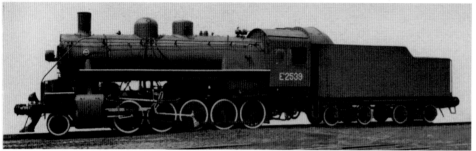

Baldwin built "Russian Decapods" for the war, and although of moderate size as compared to American locomotives of the era, they were large engines as compared to European standards, and were considerably heavier than the British-built "Austerity locomotives" with the same wheel arrangement. They had 25" x 28" cylinders, 52" cross-balanced drivers, a grate area of 64.6 square feet, and a working steam pressure of 180 pounds. Baldwin built 300 of them starting in May, 1943, then 500 more, and later another 138. The locomotives were used in general road service at operating speeds between 40-45 miles an hour. *Baldwin magazine, First Quarter 1945.*

This Decapod required two flatcars for the frame, chassis and boiler, and a low-sided gondola to haul the truck-mounted tender.

316

Soldiers from the 44th Infantry Division arrive in Luneville station from Cherbourg, France on a makeshift troop train consisting of box cars on November 16, 1944. The 44th Division took part in the Seventh Army drive to secure passes in the Vosges Mountains. Within days the 44th was hit by a heavy German counterattack. The Germans eventually lost the battle, and the 44th, along with the 2nd French Armored Division, liberated Strasbourg, situated on the Rhine River. *U.S. Army Transportation Museum*

Military soldiers carefully load ammunition and bombs from a ship into Reichsbahn box cars at an overseas port in 1945. Deutsche Reichsbahn was the state railway during the period of National Socialism. In 1949 the newly-created German Democratic Republic took over the control of the DR on its territory and continued to use the traditional name Deutsche Reichsbahn, while the railway in the new Federal Republic of Germany became the Deutsche Bundesbahn. Since January 1994 the railroad has been called the Deutsche Bahn AG. *U.S. Army Transportation Museum*

A troop train behind steam consisting of short box cars with the Transportation Corps insignia and "U.S.A." stenciled on the sides departs Cherbourg, France in 1944. *U.S. Army Transportation Museum*

Military Railway Service troops operate a small General Electric switch engine #7770 with link and hook couplers and extended buffers in the European Theater battlefront. *Bob's Photos*

The 729th Railway Operating Battalion participated in military campaigns in Normandy, northern France, the Rhineland and central Europe during WWII. Soldiers of this battalion load cylindrical tanks on flatcars in France in 1944. *U.S. Army Transportation Museum*

Thereafter, the railroads followed the advance of the forces across France, and on April 8, 1945 the first train of the 2d Military Railway Service crossed the Rhine at Wesel. Railway equipment moved from the United Kingdom to Europe immediately following the assault and was transported, fully assembled, in LSTs and train ferries, and on the decks of cargo ships. Rails were laid to LST landing sites so that the rolling stock, some of which had been double-decked in the landing craft, could be drawn directly to the shore.

1,500 CONSOLIDATIONS

Including British equipment, 2,016 locomotives were landed in Europe prior to August 1, 1945, of which 1,546 were American-built 2-8-0 steam locomotives and 43,841 freight cars were landed, of which 20,725 were 20-ton box cars and 10,859 were 20-ton gondolas.

In February 1945 the headquarters of the 1st Military Railway Service operating in southern France and the 2d Military Railway Service operating in northern France, were brought under a single general headquarters, and the Director General of the 1st Military Railway Service was placed in command. Prior to that, the Director General of the 1st Military Railway Service reported directly to the Commanding General, Southern Lines of Communication. He had commanded all troop units, controlled the employment of all equipment and stocked all railway supplies.

In contrast, the General Manager of the 2d Military Railway Service had reported to the theater Chief of Transpor-

tation, the base section commanders had commanded the military railway units, and track and bridge materials had been stocked by the Corps of Engineers. Each system had both good and bad features.

The order establishing the general headquarters made the Director General of the two services responsible to the theater Chief of Transportation and provided that he command all military railway service units. It made him responsible for advance planning, development and operation of all railroads required for military purposes, distribution of railway equipment and the stocking of railway supplies. Thus there was a single director for all military railways in Europe, with authority over both railway troops and equipment. Most importantly, the military railways were directly under the authority of the theater Chief of Transportation who was in a position to coordinate operations with other transportation modes in the theater.

CHINA SUPPLY LINE

Following the loss of the Burma Road, the supply line into China was by railway or by a combination of railway and river facilities, from Calcutta to the Ledo area, thence by air (and later by highway) to Kunming.

In order to build up the capacity of the meter gauge portion of the Bengal and Assam Railway, extending 700 miles from Parbatipur to Ledo, this line was placed under Ameri-

319

Members of the 729th Railway Operating Battalion attend services in Railway Chapel Car #1 in France during 1944. Note the flag at the corner of the car displaying a white cross. *U.S. Army Transportation Museum.*

can control in March 1944. A railway Grand Division, five Railway Operating Battalions and one Railway Shop Battalion were superimposed upon the civilian personnel, and American power and rolling stock were introduced.

American equipment to facilitate the transfer of freight from broad gauge to meter gauge at Parbatipur Junction and to improve the car ferry service at Pandu Ferry, also was provided. Flood control projects were undertaken to prevent interruption of services during the monsoon season.

VOLUME INCREASES 300%

A measure of the improvement in service which took place under American direction is seen in that between March 1944 and May 1945, the volume of U.S. freight delivered to the Ledo area by rail increased more than 300%. Although the Manila Railroad was small compared to the systems of Europe and America, it was important to military operations on Luzon, which was to have been the principal base for the assault on Japan.

Railway troops landed at Lingayen Gulf as soon as the beachhead had been secured and began restoring tracks and repairing equipment as the Japanese forces retreated. Other troops were added, and a Railway Grand Division took charge on February 14, 1945. By the end of September there were 164 officers, 2,977 enlisted men and 4,500 native civilians working on the railway lines on Luzon. The Headquarters, 3rd Military Railway Service, which had been stationed in Iran, and certain other units, began arriving in Japan toward the end of August 1945. The plan then placed in effect was to leave the railway system, which was found essentially intact, under the operational control of the Japanese, but to maintain general oversight of the whole, and to schedule trains as necessary to support the U.S. forces of occupation.

During the course of the war, 2,017 locomotives of all types, 51,294 railway cars of various descriptions, as well as

At a Red Cross train stop in Belgium during WWII, the 729th Railway Operating Battalion unloads important supplies for the troops. *U.S. Army Transportation Museum*

other items of railway rolling stock, were sent from the U.S. to military railways overseas. These were exclusive of 3,758 locomotives and 32,789 cars delivered to U.S. allies.

Some locomotives, less than 10%, were shipped in disassembled condition to save ship space and were assembled in the theaters. This equipment was constructed to meet the various gauges, weight limits, bumper and brake styles found in the countries where it was to be used. It was employed to supplement local equipment which was found intact or in repairable condition. Even in a country such as France, where Allied air attacks and enemy forces had done an especially thorough job of destroying railway equipment, large numbers of locomotives and cars were quickly placed in serviceable condition by American railway troops, aided by French civilian workers.

PERSONNEL IN 1945

On June 30, 1945 the total personnel of the Military Railway Service was 1,966 officers and 41,340 enlisted men. Of this total, 1,163 officers and 25,275 enlisted men—more than 60%—were stationed in France, Belgium, Holland and Germany. Of the remainder, 604 officers and 11,390 enlisted men were in other overseas areas, 118 officers and 3,129 enlisted men were being returned to the U.S. for redeployment, and 81 officers and 1,546 enlisted men were in training in the zone of the interior. On the whole, the Military Railway Service was somewhat under authorized enlisted men strength.

The organization of the Military Railway Service followed closely orthodox lines. The Headquarters corresponded to the office of the operating vice president of an American railroad. The Railway Grand Division was set up and functioned similarly to a general superintendent's office. Railway Operating Battalions corresponded to a division superintendent's organization, and the Railway Shop Battalion was in effect a joint locomotive and car shop.

The fact that commissioned officers and enlisted personnel of the units consisted largely of experienced railway men, and that most of the units had been technically trained by large American railroads under actual operating conditions, accounted to a large degree for their proficiency and excellent morale. The results which they achieved overseas won enthusiastic praise from Army commanders under whom they served.

The military railways made the fullest possible use of the services of native railroad officials and workers. Their knowledge of facilities and methods, and their sheer manpower, were of great value. Yet in many instances, when taking over railways in recently-captured areas, American railway troops were forced to rely for a time entirely on their own skill and ingenuity.

The Rail Division in the Office of the Chief of Transportation served as a rear echelon for the organizations overseas. On the basis of information received from the field, it established the military characteristics of railway equipment, determined the organization of military railway units, and collaborated with the Military Training Division in developing appropriate technical training methods. The Rail Division also provided an inspection service to determine the progress and readiness of units in training.

Baldwin magazine, Third Quarter 1944

A 65-ton Whitcomb diesel electric locomotive is camouflaged in this box-like arrangement in Africa to keep it from being bombed by enemy aircraft and artillery. The Whitcombs were used in General Sir Bernard Law Montgomery's victory over the Axis forces in the western desert of North Africa. The locomotives moved material, food and water to Montgomery's fast-moving army, but they also had to escape dive-bombers, and conquer the desert sand and heat. The engines had a low axle rating because of light rails, but also had sufficient power to haul the needed tonnage at a high speed. After the success of the Allies in the African Campaign, the Allies' first major victory of the war, the American Army moved into Italy, and the Whitcomb locomotives traveled right along with them. The first train into the City of Rome, after its liberation by the Allies, was hauled by one of these sturdy veterans of the rails. In June, 1944, came the Normandy invasion and the beginning of the need for dependable rail transportation on the continent of Europe. Whitcombs were shipped across the channel from England by train ferry and were run directly onto the rails ready for service. Thereafter, they played an important part in the rehabilitation of the French Railway System. The first train into liberated Paris, as well as the first supply and hospital trains into Belgium, were drawn by Whitcomb diesels. When General George S. Patton was making his historic drive toward the German border, the need for gasoline for his tanks was acute. On one occasion it necessitated the immediate movement of 38 cars of the precious fuel up to the front line. The Railway Operating Battalion responsible for this movement utilized one of the Whitcomb locomotives, and the tanks received their gasoline on schedule.

Military Railway Service crews operated the first Allied supply trains at Derby, England in 1942. Derby is situated in the East Midlands on the River Derwent, and railroads have served the town since 1840. *U.S. Army Transportation Museum*

A 25-ton U.S. Transportation Corps General Electric diesel switcher grinds its way across a temporary steel bridge replacement in Germany in April of 1945 at the town of Herzogenrath, just north of Aachen. The 1st Platoon, Company B of the 332nd General Service Engineers Regiment rebuilt the bridge; this group served in France, Belgium and Germany during the war, having entered France in 1944. The box car was part of the Belgium railway system. *Bob's Photos*

It's a busy rail yard on the meter gauge Bengal & Assam Railway of India, with flatcars and gondolas loaded with military vehicles and crates. This line was operated by American railway soldiers during the war. The Assam Railway & Trading Company, the Eastern Bengal Railway and the Assam Bengal Railway merged during WWII and was known as the Bengal Assam Railway. In 1948, the Darjeeling-Himalayan Railway also became part of the line and was taken over by the Indian government. *Louis Marre*

LEFT. The caption from the Baldwin magazine, Fourth Quarter 1945, reads, "Crews are not worried when this floating crane tips under the weight of a locomotive being loaded for shipment to France. It is just a routine part of the job." *Baldwin magazine, Fourth Quarter, 1945*

U.S. Army trucks and other vehicles transfer freight from the docks to railway cars at Naples, Italy following restoration of railway service by the Transportation Corps. *Louis Marre*

Baldwin's 70,000th locomotive, built for the U.S. Army, and American Railway Operating Battalion personnel, somewhere in Italy, pose for the camera. *(See pages 45, 171) Baldwin magazine, Fourth Quarter, 1944*

LEFT AND ABOVE. These photos show a diesel locomotive in Rome, Italy in July 1944 with Allied flags adorning the pilot, and a U.S.A. Baldwin-built 2-8-0 waiting patiently in Italy while the Red Cross transfers military wounded to its hospital train. *Baldwin magazine, Third Quarter, 1944*

This was a typical railroad yard scene in Italy after Allied troops advanced further to the front and the Military Railway Service took over. Overturned cars and twisted rails in background give an idea of conditions after German evacuation of the area. *Trains: Gil Reid, used with permission of Kalmbach Publishing Co., all rights reserved.*

In a booklet produced after the war by the U.S. War Department, these two locomotives were pictured as being built for war service. The 2-8-2 above with elephant ears was a 127-ton locomotive built for service in France, and the 2-10-0 Decapod below was a 105-ton engine procured for the Russian railways. During the war the need for locomotive power was acute; the War Production Board was in charge of approving or modifying railroad motive power orders. U. S. locomotives to come from this department's control included the Western Pacific's 4-8-4s; Richmond, Fredericksburg & Potomac 2-8-4s; and Central of Georgia's 4-8-4s. *Louis Marre*

LIMA
LOCOMOTIVES
for France

ON JULY 31 of last year, Lima Locomotive Works, Inc., turned over to the French Supply Mission the first of one hundred eighty 2-8-2 steam locomotives which Lima is building for the rehabilitation of the French railway system.

Here the Belpareil, of Oslo, is ready to leave Weehawken, N. J., for France, completely loaded with a shipment of these especially designed locomotives.

LIMA LOCOMOTIVE WORKS · LIMA LOCOMOTIVE WORKS INCORPORATED · INCORPORATED, LIMA, OHIO

Lima Locomotive Works

U.S. soldiers celebrate their ability to use a railroad pump car instead of walking as part of their assignment in the European theater during WWII. *David Doyle*

English, Russian and American rail workers combine efforts in an engine repair shop where German-made equipment is used to maintain locomotives for the Trans-Iranian Railroad. During World War II, the railway was a vital component of the Persian Corridor supply routes connecting the Persian Gulf to Central Asia and the Soviet Union. The line was of such importance that the Allies imported rolling stock of its own design, including diesel locomotives such as the Alco RSD-1. *Baldwin magazine, October 1943*

325

Whitcomb Locomotives
*Haul the First Train Sent Over the
Famous River by the U.S. Army*

The Whitcombs were scheduled to play a part in a drama more important than any staged during the first drive into Germany. On April 9, 1945, two of them powered the first United States Army train to cross the Rhine River.

Army Engineers, cooperating with the Transportation Corps' Second Military Railway Service, completed the first railroad link across the Rhine, at Wesel, Germany, on April 8, 1945. The connection consisted of a 1,752-foot single-track bridge over the river itself, and a 463-foot bridge spanning a nearby canal. The operation also involved the laying of approximately two miles of connecting track and the re-arrangement of yard facilities at Wesel and Buderich, Germany.

MIRACLE STORY

The story of the building of these bridges is one that has few equals, even in this war abounding in miracles. Starting construction at 6 p.m. on March 29, and working night and day, Army Engineer troops had the main bridge ready for traffic exactly 10 days, 4 hours and 45 minutes later. The short time in which the job was completed is all the more phenomenal in view of the fact that the exact location of the bridge was not known to the Army Engineers until 10 p.m. on March 26. Four possible sites had been under consideration, but rapid military developments made Wesel the logical location.

During the construction period, six diesel locomotives were used to provide day and night service in the approach areas, bringing up and spotting materiel and supplies.

The bridge is a semi-permanent structure of 23 spans mounted on special prefabricated steel pier structures resting on wood pilings. The deck and the railroad track are supported by meter-beams which form the spans between the piers.

Of the total bridge length of 1,752 feet, 1,074 feet are over water and the remainder represents the east and west approaches. Piles, driven to a penetration of 30 feet, were placed in groups of 21 to 24 for each pier. A total of 94 meter-beams were used, exclusive of those required to bridge the adjacent canal.

Early on the morning of April 9, 1945 the first train loaded with rations and other supplies moved over the bridge, into Germany's inner fortress, with one Whitcomb locomotive at the head end and one acting as a pusher at the rear of the train.

GERMANS SURRENDER

One month later, almost to the day, the Germans surrendered, and the actual war duty of the Whitcombs in Europe came to an end. However, there is still plenty of work for them to do, supplying the forces of occupation on which will fall much of the burden of rehabilitating the shattered railway system on the Continent. *Baldwin magazine, Second Quarter 1945*

Bridging the River Rhine in 10 Days

The first railroad link across the Rhine River at Wesel, Germany was completed on April 8, 1945. The operation involved the construction of a single track bridge 1,752 feet long and a 463-foot bridge over an adjacent canal, the rearrangement of approximately two miles of connecting tracks and yard facilities at Wesel and Buderich. The main bridge is a semi-permanent piling supporting a special pre-fabricated steel pier. The superstructure is formed of rolled steel I beams one meter in depth. The upper picture shows pile driving operations being carried on at several locations simultaneously. The picture at the right is a close-up of one of the piers, and the lower picture shows the bridge under construction as seen from the west bank. The demolished highway bridge appears in right background. *Railway Engineering & Maintenance Cyclopedia, 1945*

First French 2-8-2 type locomotive to leave the United States for France is swung on board a waiting ship at Philadelphia. *Baldwin magazine, Fourth Quarter 1945*

Baldwin magazine, Fourth Quarter 1945

Baldwin Locomotive Works shop men prepare to weigh one of the hundreds of Class 141-R 2-8-2's made for France during WWII. The "left-hand" drive locomotives had 23½" x 28" cylinders and 65" drivers and were used as general purpose locomotives that could reach speeds of 65 miles an hour. The engines featured two signal lamps with four locations to classify trains in France, and the smokeboxes were arranged for quick opening with a center clamp and eight dogs spaced around the circumference of the door. The monogram on the front read: "Societe National des Chemins de Fer Francais."

Acclaims Record of U.S. Transport Corps

Some details of the role played by the Army Transportation Corps in the Normandy invasion have just been disclosed by Major General Charles P. Gross, Chief of Transportation, in a report hailing the record of the Corps and marking its second birthday July 31.

General Gross said that the Army was faced with the greatest traffic management job in the world in moving troops and supplies from all over the United Kingdom to the staging areas and to the English Channel ports. To do the job, Major General Frank S. Ross, Chief of Transportation in the European Theater of Operations, set up an elaborate traffic regulating system with the result that troops and their supplies arrived at the exact pier on split-second schedules set for embarkations.

"The work of Transportation Corps shipping specialists began more than a year befor D-Day," he explained. "They had to plan for the shipping requirements for the invasion. Every ship had to be loaded on paper and checked and double-checked with tactical commanders and with the Navy, which was responsible for the safety of vessels at sea. Liberty ships had to be converted to MTV's (Motor Transport Vessels) to carry the thousands of vehicles required for the invasion."

The Military Railway Service is already operating trains out of the port of Cherbourg, General Gross revealed, "and soon they expect to run the 371 kilometer (230-mile) line to Paris." To facilitate the shipment of locomotives and rolling stock to France, rails were laid onto landing craft, he explained. *Railway Age, 1944*

Charles Ludban Sends Home Railroad Pictures From Iran

Charles Ludban, former brakeman and son of Carman Charles Ludban, Willard, Ohio, sent home the above interesting photographs of railroad scenes in Iran, where he is stationed with the army. Photo on left shows a captured German locomotive. To the right is pictured one of the many spans on the Iranian Railroad

Baltimore & Ohio magazine, March 1944

Baldwin Construction Greater Than Ever Before

The Baldwin Locomotive Works has announced that locomotives on order for the U. S. Army and the Lend-Lease Administration in 1944, together with locomotives to be constructed for domestic railroad systems, represent a greater locomotive business than was ever before on company books at one time.

Baldwin built Army tanks as well as locomotives during most of 1943, but in 1944 tank production equipment will be converted entirely to fit the locomotive program, the company said.

Charles E. Binley, chairman of the board, said production of other Baldwin products will not be effected by the stepped-up locomotive schedule. *Buffalo, N. Y. Courier-Express, Nov. 10, 1943*

Boiler and set of connecting rods for one side of the Baldwin "Austerity" 2-8-2 type locomotive built in 1943 for the war effort. *Baldwin magazine, October 1943*

Ralph Kelly, president of the Baldwin Locomotive Works, inspects the 70,000th locomotive which was completed on December 4, 1943. Many of these steam locomotives were shipped overseas. Two days before, the United States brought 15 noted atomic bomb scientists to New Mexico to help build the bomb that ended the war. *Baldwin magazine, First Quarter 1944*

This 65-ton diesel-electric Whitcomb built by the Whitcomb Locomotive Company, a subsidiary of the Baldwin Locomotive Works, was built "for the arduous tasks of war," says an article in Baldwin's magazine of 1944. The supercharged engines were used to provide sufficient power and at the same time permit light axle loading required for foreign service. Continental tunnel clearance dictated the overall height and width of the locomotive and the contour of the cab roof. The first train into Rome was hauled by one of these husky 65-tonners. *Louis Marre*

ABOVE AND BELOW. This is typical of what the U.S. Railway Operating Battalions found when they entered Naples, Italy. Caused by Allied bombing, the tracks, bridges, motive power and rolling stock had to be quickly repaired to help in the continuing war effort. *Louis Marre*

Box Car Finds Haven
France's Post-WWII Gift to State Goes to Museum

A *Merci* box car, a gift from France to Georgia in 1949, has found a new home in Kennesaw. The rail car was moved to the Southern Museum of Civil War and Locomotive History in 2006.

When a $1.1 million education building at the museum opened, the rail car was on public display for the first time in 57 years. The box cars, designed in the late 1800s to hold eight horses or 40 men, carried Allied troops through France in both World Wars.

After World War II, France sent a train of 49 box cars loaded with gifts to New York City as a thank you for American war relief efforts. The wooden box car, about half the size of an American rail car, was decorated with the coats of arms of all the provinces in France.

Each of the 48 states received a car, and one was shared by Washington, D.C., and the territory of Hawaii. *Published in Atlanta Journal, January 8, 2006; photos courtesy Dick Hillman, Southern Museum of Civil War and Locomotive History, Kennesaw, Georgia*

The Transportation Corps used hundreds of U.S.A.-marked cars and locomotives during the war. Some units were for domestic use, some for foreign use, and some were for either one. *All photos, Don Heimburger collection*

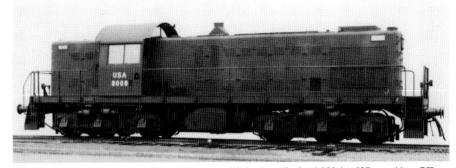

This six-cylinder 1,000-hp 127-ton Alco-GE turbo-charged diesel, built for the U.S. War Department, was constructed for domestic and foreign service.

Identified with "USA," "United States Army" as well as Transportation Corps markings, this 10,800-gallon gasoline tank car was intended for foreign service. Note the spoked wheelsets on this car which was built after the war in 1952.

This U. S. A. 75-ton steam wrecking crane was built to negotiate 60", 63" or 66" gauge track in foreign service. The cab roof can be raised to allow built-up heat to escape.

This six-wheel 80-ton flat car was built for foreign service; note the buffers on each end. The car had a capacity of 180,000 pounds.

This eight-panel rib-sided military 40-ton box car was intended for foreign service.

Soldiers of XIX Corps wave heartily as they bedeck "The Berlin Express" which carried ammunition for use by the 970th Quartermasters Service Company, XIX Corps, U.S. Ninth Army on April 16, 1945. The first U.S. supply train during the war to Berlin operated on July 27, 1945. "Even after six years of war, with accompanying manpower shortages, German railway maintenance was excellent," read a story in the June 30, 1945 issue of *Railway Age*, written by Colonel John W. Wheeler. *U.S. Army Signal Corps, Bob Hall collection*

Two trains—the first to operate on the newly-repaired Naples to Rome line—arrive in Rome at the same time on July 20, 1944. The train on the right carried Secretary of War Henry L. Stimson, and the train on the left carried a load of coal. *U.S. Army Signal Corps, Bob Hall collection*

Oddly enough, the USA 2-8-0 locomotive on the left, brought to France in 1917 and pulled by French locomotive #030-793, was recovered by men of the 729th Railway Operating Battalion during fighting in WWII. The U.S. locomotive was repaired and placed in service moving materiel. Here the locomotive is being turned on July 13, 1944. *Both photos, U.S. Army Signal Corps, Bob Hall collection*

Two U.S. soldiers—John Claridy and Thomas Driscoll—operate a 4-8-0 French locomotive in the yards in North Africa on February 17, 1943. French locomotives provided no seats for the railway crew, and cabooses were often crowded with deadheads, French soldiers, civilians and Arabs. *U.S. Army Signal Corps, Bob Hall collection*

A British London & North Eastern Railway 0-6-0 switch locomotive, called a PUG, moves USA locomotive #2111 at Queens Dock, Glasgow, Scotland in April of 1943. The LNER was one of the Big Four United Kingdom railways, with the second largest trackage, but it was also the poorest railway of the four. *U.S. Army Signal Corps, Bob Hall collection*

Vast quantities of supplies and machinery were stored in the United Kingdom for shipment to continental Europe once the invasion began, including these twin-dome Transportation Corps tank cars at Penrhos Junction, Caerphilly, Wales. This scene was photographed in March of 1944 by the U.S. Army Signal Corps. *Bob Hall collection*

A short freight train with a helper at the rear moves onto the main line from the Canicatti, Sicily railroad yards in 1943. The 727th Railway Operating Battalion landed at Licata, Sicily first on July 12, 1943, three days behind the invasion forces, and the Axis promptly left for Messina. *U.S. Army Signal Corps, Bob Hall collection*

This new 250-ton USA diesel is loaded in England in September of 1944 for trans-channel shipping to France to be used for switching cars in liberated French areas. *U.S. Army Pictorial Service, Bob Hall collection*

At Cherbourg, France, a small Transportation Corps 0-6-0 #1976, with a French crew, switches flatcars loaded with American equipment into the railyards. *U.S. Army Signal Corps, Bob Hall collection*

With Allied troops on the ground in Naples, one job that remained was to protect railroad yards, locomotives, cars and railroad facilities from being bombed further. Here, in December of 1943, men of the 639th and 688th Machine Gun battalions prepare to fire on an approaching enemy reconnaissance plane in the Naples yard. Two of the men at right have binoculars to spot enemy aircraft. *U.S. Army Signal Corps, Bob Hall collection*

Sergeant Oliver Morss of Jasper, Oregon, right, conductor in the 740th Railway Battalion, uses a Belgian railwayman's curved horn to signal the engineer as the brakeman hops aboard a GI supply train in France in October, 1944. *U.S. Army Signal Corps, Bob Hall collection*

A chain hoist lifts a short flatcar at a boxcar assembly line at Oran, North Africa in April of 1943. An Allied plan named *Operation Torch*, which involved concentric attacks, used Oran as one of the landing sites. The total invasion force of all the *Operation Torch* landings comprised more than 400 ships, 1,000 planes and some 107,000 men. During this operation, a battalion of paratroopers made the first U.S. combat jump of the war. *U.S. Army Signal Corps, Bob Hall collection*

A staff sergeant, left, and a corporal guard captured wooden barrels of French wine at St. Leu, Algeria during the latter part of 1942. Note guard shack at end of flat car. *U.S. Army Signal Corps, Bob Hall collection*

Military Railway Service personnel operate a French 2-6-0 steam locomotive with a squarish, flat-top tender in a railway yard in North Africa in February of 1943. *U.S. Army Signal Corps, Bob Hall collection*

An American diesel switcher locomotive, with windows boarded up, is unloaded at Newport News, Virginia shipyard after returning from overseas assignment on January 14, 1946. *Library of Virginia*

CHAPTER ELEVEN

Returning Home from the War

"Among the Baltimore & Ohio's army of 70,000 workers, you will see many of these veterans who have served . . . and have returned to do a splendid job in helping us move the mighty load of war. It is with pride that the B & O salutes America's returning service men and women . . ." —R. B. White, President, Baltimore & Ohio Railroad

Up to the time of the German capitulation, the volume of passenger traffic returning to the United States on Army transports was in a gradually ascending curve, except for periods in 1943 and 1944 when it was swelled by the removal of prisoners of war from North Africa and Europe, respectively.

Prior to V-E Day, the peak month was September 1944, when 146,246 passengers were debarked at home ports.

After V-E Day the curve turned sharply upward, and in November 1945 a total of 744,000 passengers returned from all theaters. The total of Army debarkations from the beginning of the war to November 30, 1945 was 4,860,000 passengers, distributed as follows:

Troops	3,522,000
Patients	487,000
Navy personnel	193,000
Prisoners of war	450,000
Others	208,000
Total	**4,860,000**

The November figure for debarkations (744,000) was approximately 2½ times as great as the highest monthly figure for embarkations in WWI (295,170), and it was exceeded substantially in December. The magnitude of this accomplishment is notable in light of the fact that following WWI the peak month figure for troops landed in the U.S. was only 342,785 (June 1919), although then it was only a matter of shuttling ships back and forth across the Atlantic.

The record number of returning troops was accomplished only by a concentrated effort, planned well in advance. Even before V-E Day, plans had been laid to increase the troop lift radically in order to speed up redeployment from Europe to the Pacific, and the repatriation of troops to the United States.

The immediate program was to convert about 300 freight vessels, which could be spared in view of reduced supply requirements of the European and Mediterranean theaters. In the end, 210 Liberty Ships were fitted to carry 550 passengers each, and 97 Victory Ships to carry 1,500 each. It was arranged also to increase these capacities by about 30% during the summer months by placing cots in certain compartments where this could be done without sacrificing the health of soldiers or sanitary standards.

FOLLOWING V-E DAY

Following V-E Day seven passenger liners which had been in enemy hands were turned over to the U.S. for reconditioning and use as troop ships. It was found, however, that the work on five of them could not be justified, because by the time it would have been completed, the vessels would have become surplus as troop carriers. Consequently, only two of the seven—the *Europa* and the *Vulcania*—were converted and placed in service.

Following V-J Day, many different naval vessels carried returning troops. The Navy already has made available for the joint repatriation operation 178 assault transports, 111 combatant vessels (chiefly aircraft carriers and battleships), and eight hospital ships. Other naval vessels were available in the Pacific as they were transferred from service in connection with the occupation of Japan. Army hospital ships also were used as troop carriers, as they could be spared from the task of bringing back patients. Smaller numbers of troops were repatriated on numerous freight vessels.

Germany Surrenders Unconditionally

On April 25, 1945, Soviet and American troops met at the Elbe River near Torgau, thus cutting Germany in two. Troops of the 69th Infantry Division of the U.S. First Army and the Soviet 58th Guards Division of the 5th Guards Army, were the first of these two Allied countries to link up.

Two days later, Italian dictator Benito Mussolini was captured by Italian partisans and hung. On April 30, as the Battle of Berlin raged, Adolf Hitler committed suicide in his bunker along with Eva Braun, his mistress, whom he had married just a few hours before.

On May 1, German forces in Italy surrendered, and on May 4 German troops in northwest Germany, Denmark and Holland surrendered. On May 6 the Chief-of-Staff of the German High Command, General Alfred Jodl, unconditionally surrendered all German Armed Forces, a half hour after the German troops at Festung Breslau (Fortress Breslau) surrendered to the Soviets.

German surrender documents were signed at 2:41 on the morning of May 7, 1945 at the Supreme Headquarters Allied Expeditionary Force (SHAEF) headquarters in Rheims, France. News of the surrender broke in the West on May 8, now called V-E Day (Victory in Europe). The most devastating world war was over, and now the rebuilding, and the return of troops, began.

B&O timetable, February 18, 1945

On April 30, 1945 troop spaces available on ships in Army service totaled 464,138. By July 31, 1945 the number had increased to 620,355 spaces. On November 30, 1945 spaces on vessels under direct Army control, spaces allocated to the Army on vessels under Navy control and spaces on the one British vessel which continued to carry troops for the United States Army (*Queen Mary*), totaled approximately 1.3 million.

PRIMARY OBJECTIVE

The return of patients with utmost dispatch was made a primary objective. Only a part of this traffic could be handled by hospital ships, and hospital spaces on regular troop ships were used extensively. An attempt was made to remove as many patients as possible from the European and Mediterranean theaters in advance of V-E Day, so that after Germany's capitulation the maximum amount of space could be devoted to returning troops.

All battle casualties had been brought back from those areas within three months of V-E Day, and according to plan such patients would have been removed from the Pacific by the end of 1945.

All ships carrying patients, whether hospital ships or regular troop transports, were provided with complete medical staffs and equipment. Full provision was made for whatever segregation of patients might be necessary, for the continuance of the medical care which had been provided by hospitals in the theaters, and for meeting any emergencies which might arise on the high seas.

The peak month for the return of patients was May 1945, during which 45,562 were landed at United States ports by ships under Army control. At that time, 21 of the 26 hospital ships in the service of the Army were in the Atlantic and were based at the Charleston Port of Embarkation. That port handled little other passenger trafffic, and by concentrating hospital ship operations there, it was possible to give superior attention to the handling of the sick and wounded, as well as the staffing and supplying of the vessels themselves.

DISPOSITION CENTERS

The staging areas at U.S. ports, which had been established to process troops on their way to the theaters, also handled returning troops. Those who were to be separated from the service ordinarily spent about 48 hours in the disposition centers which were set up at the staging areas, while their individual and unit records were being placed in order, and their individual equipment was being inspected.

Then they proceeded to the personnel centers nearest their homes, where final separation took place. Soldiers who were to remain in the Army spent only about 24 hours at the port staging areas before proceeding to personnel centers. The movement between staging areas and personnel centers was carefully organized in order to avoid confusion and preserve discipline. Troop train commanders were assigned to each train, group supervisors were appointed for the groups destined to the respective personnel centers, and a car leader was designated for each car.

From the termination of hostilities in Europe to November 27, 1945—a period of less than 7 months—3,095,813 passengers were returned by the Army from overseas theaters and bases. Of this number, 2,732,348 (88%) were returned by ship, and 363,465 (12%) by air.

The volume of cargo loaded at Army ports of embarkation during the 45 war months totaled 126,787,875 measurement tons. The peak month was March 1945 when 5,926,764 measurement tons were dispatched. After that the obvious weakening of the German position was reflected in a decrease in total shipments.

CARGO DISTRIBUTION

Following the German surrender in May 1945 the decrease in the trans-Atlantic cargo movement more than offset the increase in the trans-Pacific movement. Following V-J Day, total shipments

Another billion dollar highway program

IN thinking about work after the war, don't overlook the 230,000 miles of steel "highways" which the railroads have built and maintain at their own expense. These "highways" provide jobs for more than a quarter of a million men working on construction and maintenance of tracks and roadway — jobs for more than a million other railroad workers — besides still other thousands in the mines, the mills and the forests where roadway materials and supplies are produced.

More than that—the railroads pay real taxes on these "highways," not for their own special benefit, but for the support of schools and other general services, including public highways and streets.

After the last war, between 1920 and 1930, the railroads spent more than four billion dollars for improvements on these "highways," and in addition more than three-and-a-half billion dollars for betterments in equipment. After this war, a similar program will be required.

So there's another highway program which could make a lot of postwar jobs, and which needs no more than a public policy of treating all forms of commercial transportation alike — letting each one pay its own way, which includes the payment of the general taxes upon which governmental services depend.

ASSOCIATION OF AMERICAN RAILROADS
All United for Victory

March 1945

Sit down, Sergeant
Mr. Harvey's Saving this Place for **You**

When Fred Harvey opened his first Harvey House in 1876, he didn't know he was "setting the table" for his sons and grandsons to serve millions of men and women in their country's uniform sixty-nine years later. His idea was to provide early western travelers a good meal—an idea which built a system of hospitality extending thousands of miles over America's main travel routes.

But this system might have been made to order to meet today's war needs! For Fred Harvey restaurants, hotels and dining cars are serving tens of thousands of *extra* meals daily to the Armed Forces. Naturally, these meals take precedence over those for our civilian customers—which

is the reason we may have been unable to serve *you* in our accustomed manner.

But Harvey employees pride themselves, not only in doing their war job well, but also in carrying out the ideals of the original Fred Harvey and his sons and grandsons. That's why, after the war, we want you again to expect of us only the gracious, friendly hospitality traditional with Fred Harvey.

Along the "3000 Miles of Hospitality"

Today the Grand Canyon and its world-famous Harvey Hotel, El Tovar, are being enjoyed mainly by Servicemen on brief stopovers. Tomorrow when you can travel again, plan to visit this grandest of America's beauty spots. Meantime, buy War Bonds!

Fred Harvey

RESTAURANTS · SHOPS · HOTELS · DINING CARS

3000 MILES OF HOSPITALITY—FROM CLEVELAND TO THE PACIFIC COAST

Copyright, Fred Harvey, Chicago, 1945

Life magazine, May 28, 1945

Another great day in railroading was heralded in January, 1888, when the Atlantic Coast Line ran the first de luxe vestibule Pullman train from New York to Jacksonville, Florida.

Today powerful GM Diesel locomotives on the Atlantic Coast Line whisk Florida's fresh fruits and vegetables to major American markets in a matter of hours. This is possible because these locomotives haul heavy trains faster and stay on their job longer with few stops for service.

IT'S A GREAT NEW DAY FOR RAILROADING

ONE thing is certain—Americans will have an entirely new level of transportation, postwar. Two factors will make this inevitable:

The amazing achievements of the railroads under the stress of war.

The new and exciting prewar records for rapidity, regularity of service, safety and comfort the railroads had established with General Motors locomotives.

American railroads are in a favored position to lead in this fine new service because a most vital tool which makes it possible is fully developed and thoroughly proved. Already General Motors Diesel passenger and freight locomotives are operating on more than 100 million miles, annually, of regularly scheduled service. Yes, it's a great new day for railroading—with even greater days ahead.

ON TO
FINAL VICTORY
BUY **MORE**
WAR BONDS

GM GENERAL MOTORS DIESEL POWER

LOCOMOTIVES . . . . . . *ELECTRO-MOTIVE DIVISION*, La Grange, Ill.

ENGINES . . . 150 to 2000 H.P. . . . CLEVELAND DIESEL ENGINE DIVISION, Cleveland 11, Ohio

ENGINES . . . 15 to 250 H.P. . . . DETROIT DIESEL ENGINE DIVISION, Detroit 23, Mich.

February 1945

BALTIMORE & OHIO MAGAZINE

**SOLDIER MEETS DAUGHTER
A TRUE LIFE STORY**

1945

An early Alco-built 4-6-6-4 Challenger uses its considerable muscle to pull a long Union Pacific 17-car troop train through California in 1946 with Chicagoan Seaman First Class George Speir aboard. Speir, enroute from San Diego to the Great Lakes Naval Training Center in Illinois, was about to be discharged. Speir says the train consisted of 14 troop sleepers, two troop kitchen cars and a Harriman rider car for the UP portion of the trip. The train ran over the ATSF, UP, D&RGW, CB&Q, CGW and then the C&NW. Speir used an inexpensive 620 Brownie camera to take the photograph as the train rounded a curve. *George Speir, courtesy of Kalmbach Publishing Co.*

naturally declined sharply. The 45-month total breaks down as follows:

Atlantic:

North and South America	4,559,842
Africa, Mediterranean and Middle East	7,703,582
United Kingdom and Continent	45,300,680
Total Atlantic	77,564,104

Pacific:

North America	6,888,398
Central and South Pacific	17,611,354
Southwest Pacfic	8,356,214
Asia	6,367,805
Total Pacific	49,223,771
Grand Total	126,787,875

It is interesting to review some of the categories of equipment that were shipped overseas; some of this equipment was to be transported back to the United States or its territories after the war. During the war a total of 47,851 aircraft was shipped overseas, some crated and some assembled. This was about 56% of the total number of aircraft sent to the theaters, the remainder having been flown. The technical problems and delays encountered by the theaters in putting together aircraft which had been disassembled and crated for shipment, emphasized the desirability of shipping as many as possible in assembled condition.

Approximately a million wheeled vehicles were shipped overseas during the years 1943 and 1944. Of this total, 68% were boxed and 32% unboxed. Improved methods of nesting and boxing were developed early in the war, but even when boxed, vehicles were light cargo.

On November 24, 1945, happy but tired returning troops board heavyweight passenger cars for the trip back home from the war. The May 28, 1945 issue of *Life* magazine was already promoting the return to normalcy with soldiers coming back: it carried a 25-page spread entitled "A Portfolio of Ideas for Home Planning." *Donald Hofsommer collection*

In this picture, 15,000 battle-weary U.S. troops return from war overseas, arriving in New York City on the 2,139-passenger *RMS Queen Mary.* This scene was repeated over and over again as thousands of military troops came back to American soil and then boarded trains for home or American military posts. The 1,019-foot-long *Queen Mary*, part of the Cunard White Star Line, operated between 1936 and 1967. The *Queen Mary* is now listed on the National Register of Historic Places. *Louis Marre*

Returning U.S. troops board trains at the Oakland, California pier to head home or to their new assignments. The signs read *"Oakland Lark,"* *"San Francisco Challenger"* and *"Oregonian."* One sign reads, "Box lunches, 50 cents." *Donald Hofsommer collection*

A variety of equipment was shipped on deck, in addition to aircraft and vehicles. During 1944 a number of tugs, some weighing up to 200 tons, were carried on the decks of Liberty Ships. Numerous railroad locomotives, weighing up to 127 long tons (such as the RS-1s shipped to Iran), were deck-loaded. Landing craft, barges, railway tank cars, and thousands of armored tanks and half-tracks were shipped this way because they could be made to withstand the weather. Each item of equipment required a particular type of processing to protect it from the elements, and a particular type of blocking and lashing. Special cradles were needed in many cases. The heavier items necessitated shoring up the decks to enable them to withstand the load, and special lifting equipment at both loading and discharge ports had to be provided.

The amount of ammunition and explosives sent overseas was tremendous. During the 45 war months, approximately 9.5 million short tons were shipped to U.S. forces, and about 2 million tons to Allies, making a total of about 11.5 million tons. The highest monthly shipment was 685,000 tons in December 1944, when the invasion of Germany re-

quired extraordinary expenditures of ammunition. Practically all of this cargo, including that for U.S. Allies, was shipped over terminals operated by the Transportation Corps. With few exceptions the terminals were built for that special purpose, and were so designed and operated as to reduce to a minimum the possibility of disasters caused by sabotage or accident.

DISABLED MILITARY PERSONNEL COME FIRST

Tickets for sleeping car accommodations, also for seats in parlor cars and reserved seat coaches, where operated, are sold subject to cancellation prior to or after departure of trains in event space is required to accommodate disabled Military, Naval or Merchant Marine Personnel in accordance with Interstate Commerce Commission Service Order No. 213.

We are sure patrons will cooperate wholeheartedly should occasions of this kind develop in which event every effort will be made to provide substitute space.

J. W. STEVENSON
Passenger Traffic Manager
Chicago 5, Illinois

Illinois Central timetable, July, August, September 1945

Photographed enroute by permission of the War Department

The "Purple Heart Limited"

Its passengers are wounded veterans.

Some, like the three above, compare their souvenirs as an Army doctor looks on. Others read. Or sleep. Or just look out the Pullman window at *America* again.

They are on their way from debarkation ports to General Hospitals near their homes. And Pullman—by providing sleeping cars to supplement the Army's special hospital trains —is privileged to contribute to the comfort

in which they make the trip.

These cars come from the Pullman "pool" of sleeping cars that are in regular passenger service. They may be scattered over several states, serving various railroads, when the Army calls for them. But *centralized control* makes it possible to assemble them to meet almost any demand.

Where they are assembled—when and where they go—cannot be disclosed. But we

can tell you that "Purple Heart Limiteds" are running constantly as part of the program that makes American wounded *the best cared for wounded in the world.*

So please—if you should be unable to get the Pullman space you want exactly when you want it—remember that it may be occupied by wounded veterans.

They come first with us—just as they do with *you!*

PULLMAN
For more than 80 years, the greatest name in passenger transportation

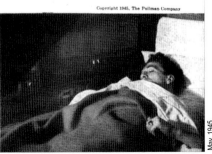

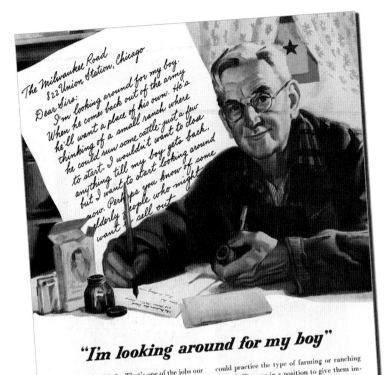

"I'm looking around for my boy"

YOU bet we'll help. That's one of the jobs our Agricultural Development Department is organized for. The Milwaukee Road has no farm land to sell but our agricultural agents are familiar with opportunities in the twelve productive Midwest and Northwest States served by this railroad. Last year, 10,361 home seekers requested our aid in directing them to localities where they could practice the type of farming or ranching desired. We were in a position to give them impartial advice on where they could buy property to suit their needs and finances.

We can and will gladly help *you* too. Your requests for information will be promptly answered. *Address Agricultural and Mineral Development Department, 822 Union Station, Chicago 6, Ill.*

11,000-MILE SUPPLY LINE FOR WAR AND HOME FRONTS

THE MILWAUKEE ROAD

John Kelly collection

Illinois Central timetable, July, August, September 1945

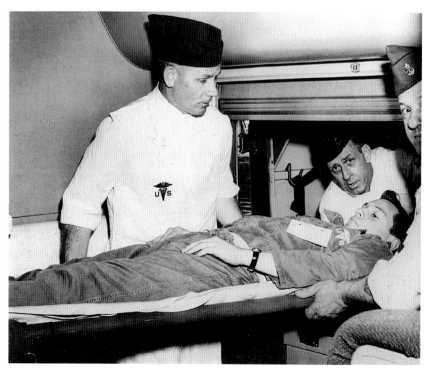

Medical corpsmen demonstrate how wounded soldiers were to be loaded onto medical trains after the war. *Bob Withers*

ABOVE AND BELOW. Wounded U.S. soldiers are put on a military medical train after the war on a stretcher; the medical cars often met troops at the ship dock to receive them for transport to military hospitals. *Both photos, Kalmbach Publishing Company*

Private Brown
HAS LEARNED A LOT OF THINGS

★ From high-school boy to fighting man was quite a jump for Bill Brown. He had never been away from home for more than a few days before he put on khaki. And, for a while, he was confused . . . even more than a little scared.

That was a year ago. Today, Private Brown is a top-notch fighter. He is sure of himself. He has learned to depend on his buddies, on other service branches . . . even other countries . . . to help him do his war job better.

When Private Brown returns, he'll have experience far beyond his years. He'll recognize the value of many business services to aid him in his peacetime work. And he'll use these services fully.

In the Baltimore & Ohio Railroad, with its 70,000 workers and 11,000 miles of track, ex-Private Brown, like millions of other Americans, will find a convenient, economical and speedy means of transportation . . . in business and for pleasure.

B&O timetable, February 18, 1945

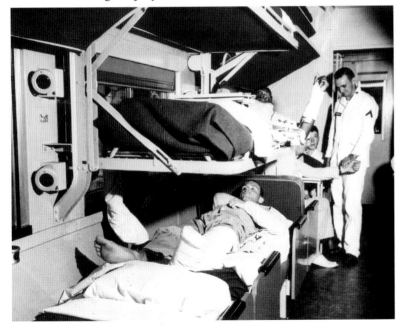

Fare Special for Returning Military

On September 1 the American railroads established a special fare of 1 1/4 cents per mile for members of the Armed Forces who have been released from service. It is open to all former members of the Army, Navy, Marine Corps and Coast Guard who are traveling home or to a place of employment at their own expense. This rate, the same as the special furlough rate, must be applied for within 30 days of discharge. The action will enable service men and women to return to civilian life at the least possible expense to themselves. *Illinois Central magazine, October 1944*

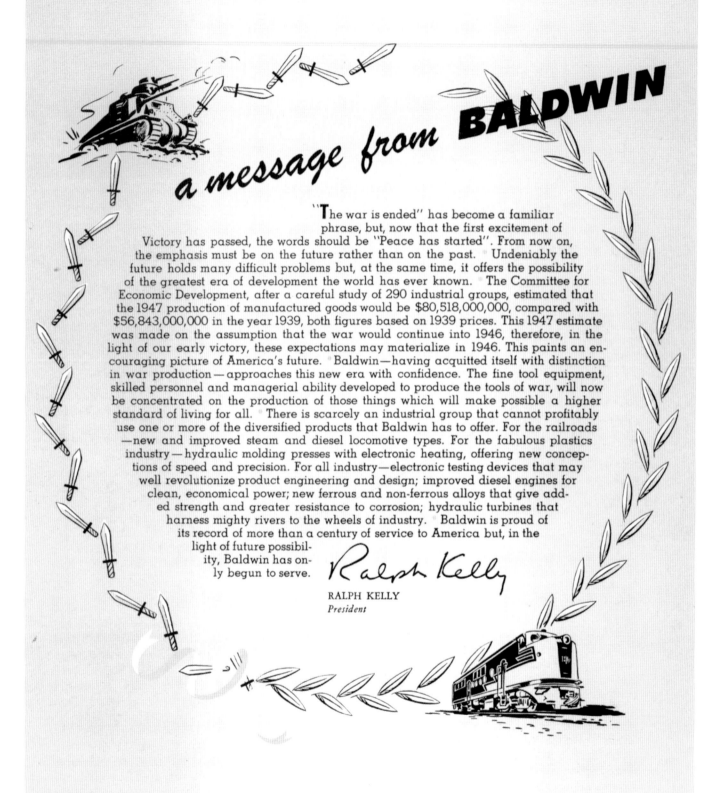

a message from **BALDWIN**

"The war is ended" has become a familiar phrase, but, now that the first excitement of Victory has passed, the words should be "Peace has started". From now on, the emphasis must be on the future rather than on the past. Undeniably the future holds many difficult problems but, at the same time, it offers the possibility of the greatest era of development the world has ever known. The Committee for Economic Development, after a careful study of 290 industrial groups, estimated that the 1947 production of manufactured goods would be $80,518,000,000, compared with $56,843,000,000 in the year 1939, both figures based on 1939 prices. This 1947 estimate was made on the assumption that the war would continue into 1946, therefore, in the light of our early victory, these expectations may materialize in 1946. This paints an encouraging picture of America's future. Baldwin—having acquitted itself with distinction in war production—approaches this new era with confidence. The fine tool equipment, skilled personnel and managerial ability developed to produce the tools of war, will now be concentrated on the production of those things which will make possible a higher standard of living for all. There is scarcely an industrial group that cannot profitably use one or more of the diversified products that Baldwin has to offer. For the railroads —new and improved steam and diesel locomotive types. For the fabulous plastics industry—hydraulic molding presses with electronic heating, offering new conceptions of speed and precision. For all industry—electronic testing devices that may well revolutionize product engineering and design; improved diesel engines for clean, economical power; new ferrous and non-ferrous alloys that give added strength and greater resistance to corrosion; hydraulic turbines that harness mighty rivers to the wheels of industry. Baldwin is proud of its record of more than a century of service to America but, in the light of future possibility, Baldwin has only begun to serve.

Ralph Kelly

RALPH KELLY
President

CHAPTER TWELVE

After the War

"Today the guns are silent. A great tragedy has ended."
—Army General Douglas MacArthur

As soon as the war had ended, and peace was assured, U.S. citizens and people in all countries, wanted to resume a normal lifestyle as soon as possible, but it would take months and years to rebuild what had been damaged and lost.

As Ralph Kelly, president of the Baldwin Locomotive Works, said, "From now on the emphasis must be on the future rather than the past. Undeniably the future holds many difficult problems, but at the same time, it offers the possibility of the greatest era of development the world has ever known."

He couldn't have been more accurate. On U.S. railroads, the time had come to further advance the industry with new, more modern freight and passenger cars, signaling, trackwork and facilities. The future for U.S. rails was *now*.

About a year after the end of WWII hostilities, the men who helped rebuild Chicago & NorthWestern H-l Class #3004 at the Chicago shops, pose for a "dedication" photo. To the right, an official speaks on a platform with a microphone. To his right is an Honor Roll board listing C&NW Railway employees who fought in WWII. U.S. railroads were now on a fast track to improve their stable of motive power, either by building new or rebuilding locomotives. *Don Heimburger collection*

NEXT PAGE. Monster Pennsylvania Railroad diesels, electrics and steam locomotives (6,000-horsepower diesel-electric; the high-speed passenger 4-4-4-4 T-1; the GG-1 electric; and the S2 Class #6200 steam turbine) were featured on the cover of the Second Quarter, 1946 issue of the Baldwin magazine, showcasing what the firm was capable of producing. The steam turbine was introduced to the railroad in 1944, designed and built by the Eddystone plant at Baldwin. *Baldwin magazine, Second Quarter 1946*

BALDWIN

SECOND QUARTER • 1946

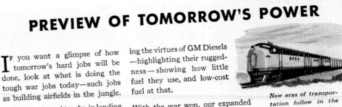

In early 1935 the New York Central retained famed industrial de-signer Henry Dreyfuss to design and coordinate the interior design for the railroad's first streamliner, the *Mercury*. Composed of rebuilt commuter coaches and a couple of 4-6-2 Pacifics, the initial train was nine cars long. The 4-6-4 locomotives were shrouded, bathtub style, and new disk drivers were installed and floodlit at night. With the flashing chrome-vanadium driving rods reciprocating in the glare, the *Mercury* cut a striking image. Here it is in 1945 during WWII on its way to Detriot. *Charlton Kennedy*

All Sleeper Service Restored

Those who are planning trips this summer on trains, will be encouraged to find Pullman accommoda-tions close to normal.

On March 15, the Office of Defense Transportation withdrew its wartime order on sleeping car operation, effective since July 15, 1945. The restrictions and limi-tations on advance reservations in sleeping cars and coaches have already been removed by the majority of the railroads. The order was originally established due to the enormous amount of troop movement and short-age of troop sleepers. Since early February, this has been eased considerably by the completion of most of an order of 1,200 troop sleeping cars, and the Army is now able to handle the brunt of troop travel.

SERVICE RETURNS TO THE PUBLIC

The order saved 895 extra cars for military use. A total of 334 cars were returned to civilian use February 15, another 372 on March 1, and the balance on March 15. Seventy-four Pullman cars were restored to 19 cities on the Pennsylvania Railroad alone on March 1, and ser-vice was fully restored on March 15 involving 13 cities 250 miles, or less, distance. The heavily traveled *Edi-son* between New York and Washington renewed Pull-man car service on March 16 after being absent from public timetables since July. New York, New Haven & Hartford Railroad will also return sleeping cars service to the very popular *Owl* and *Narragansett* which run between New York and Boston.

Most of the established routes under 250 miles that were affected by the Government limit have had their sleeper sevice restored. The days of standing all night in aisles, and sleeping in smoking rooms, are mostly over, but railroad officials are expecting their heaviest summer travel this year. The situation may be quite acute, but it will not reach the wartime stage of conges-tion. *Trains, April 1946*

Standing in front of the 4-6-2 type locomotive built by Baldwin for the Alaska Railroad are William Kinsel, superintendent of motive power, Alaska Railroad; Harry Doubt, master mechanic; and R. E. Bedford, Baldwin Locomotive Works engineer. *Baldwin magazine, First Quarter 1946*

LEFT. "If you ride the trains of the Pennsylvania Railroad between New York and Washington, you have probably noticed this new Baldwin sign which glows with multi-colored neon lights after nightfall," reads the caption for this photo as published in a 1946 issue of the Baldwin magazine.

New trains were put into service after the war. Kansas City Southern's 6,000-hp F-3 diesels (1,500-hp per unit), operated by the Louisiana & Arkansas Railway, were constructed by Electro-Motive and delivered to the railroad in 1948.

New Blue Bird On The Wabash

This is the Wabash Railroad's new Budd-built, all-stainless steel Blue Bird, on its winging flight between St. Louis and Chicago. The Blue Bird will make the round trip daily between these two great terminal cities, adding to the completeness of Wabash service and presenting to its passengers comfort and luxury in rail travel previously unknown.

For the Blue Bird is the latest in the roster of distinguished name trains which Budd has created for the modernization of American railroads. Four of its cars are Vista-Domes, giving passengers an unobstructed view of the rolling prairies, picturesque bluffs and river scenery along the way.

Like all Budd-designed, Budd-built equipment, this train illustrates a principle—that better products are made of ideas as well as steel. This was true of the all-steel automobile body which Budd originated and which has made Budd the largest independent builder of body components in the world. It was true of the steel wheel which Budd developed to take the place of wood. It has been demonstrated in the Budd Disc brake, and in stainless steel highway trailers.

In the railroad field Budd ideas were revolutionary. Ideas that attract passengers by making rail travel more inviting. Ideas that permit faster schedules and yield substantial operating economies. It was Budd vision which led to the whole concept of the modern, stainless steel lightweight streamliner. And Budd today is the only car builder who employs the superior strength of stainless steel to achieve lightweight construction with safety.

The Budd Co., Philadelphia, Detroit

Budd

Welcome Aboard The New Sunset Limited

The Sunset Limited, Southern Pacific's famous streamliner between New Orleans and Los Angeles, has just been completely equipped with new Budd all-stainless steel cars. There are five, fifteen-car trains, altogether, to provide daily service from each terminal. And they are gorgeous.

Interiors range in color from the soft tones of the brooding bayous of Louisiana to the gold of desert sunshine. The brands of pioneer ranches along the route the train traverses are burned right into the leather wall covering in the coffee shop-lounge cars. The Sunset Limited personifies the southwest.

Along with the solid, unmatched strength of their stainless steel structure, these trains provide the greater safety and riding ease of Budd railway disc brakes. Stops are so effortless as to verge on being imperceptible.

The Sunset Limiteds are The Budd Company's most recent contribution to railway progress. They give you a new and compelling reason to experience the pleasure of modern travel by train. The Budd Company, Philadelphia, Detroit.

Budd

LEFT AND ABOVE. Several years after the war, railroads began to introduce new cars and new passenger trains. The Wabash introduced the *Blue Bird* and the Southern Pacific highlighted the *Sunset Limited. Don Heimburger collection*

It's a warm May 1945 afternoon in Ames, Iowa as this 1,000-hp Alco-GE RS-1 road/yard diesel, #1080, built the year before, goes about its yard duties. The war was nearly over, people were going to get back to normal eventually, but U.S. railroads still had a big job to do to help return the soldiers and move materiel where it needed to go. *Don Heimburger collection*

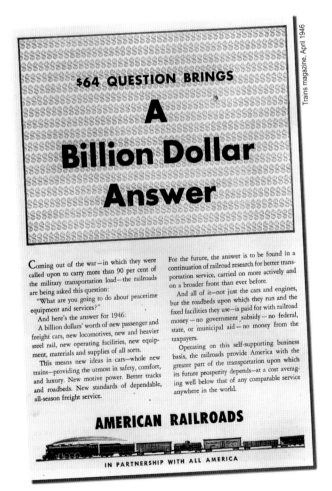

Railways in the Post-War Period

The post-war period regarding which there has been so much talking and planning is rapidly approaching. Apparently the war with Germany will be won within a few months, and Charles E. Wilson, vice chairman of the War Production Board, has estimated that production for war can then be reduced 35%—approximately $35 billion annually. This will release for other use huge volumes of manpower and materials. And the progress being made in the war with Japan indicates that it will not last as long as originally anticipated after the United States, Great Britain and China can turn their entire power against Japan. *Railway Age, 1944*

NEXT PAGE, UPPER RIGHT. The Erie's first FT 1,350-hp diesel road units (A and B units were semi-permanently coupled together) were built by EMD in October of 1944, about a year before the war ended. This was Erie's first use of the yellow-and-black paint scheme. *Don Heimburger collection*

NEXT PAGE, LOWER RIGHT. Chicago, Burlington & Quincy's Class O-5-A #5632 4-8-4 was built in August of 1940 in the West Burlington Shops, with boilers furnished by Baldwin. It had 28 x 30" cylinders, large 74" drivers, steam pressure of 250 psi, a tractive force of 67,500 pounds, power reverse and a Worthington-SA feedwater heater. The O-5-A's were at the Q's zenith of design, and as one fireman put it, "They steamed best under a wide-open throttle." As is noted in *Steam Locomotives of the Burlington Route,* a Class O-5 handled an 82-car train loaded with mail and packages for servicemen overseas on October 17, 1944. Here, #5632 is in charge of a train with at least three troop cars at the headend. *Chris Burritt*

Nine miles of short curves and steep grades through the Ozark Mountains have been tamed by Frisco's Dixon Hill project, at a cost of more than $1,300,000.

Coming 'round the Mountain
...ON NEW TRACK

Along the Frisco Lines, extensive improvements, costing millions of dollars, are being made. Included is such work as relocating right-of-way and track to reduce grades and curves

...improved Centralized Traffic Control...modernizing stations...placing heavier track, reballasting roadbed...and many other forward-looking projects.

This progressive modernization program is enabling Frisco to handle its war traffic more efficiently and will be of inestimable value to the great 9-State Frisco territory after peace.

FRISCO LINES
ST.LOUIS-SAN FRANCISCO RY

A Great Railroad

Trains magazine, June 1945

L&N Postwar Plans

In the immediate postwar era the Louisville & Nashville plans much replacement of old equipment, and as a starter has on order 28 lightweight aluminum passenger cars, costing 2.5 million dollars, and eight 2,000-horsepower diesel road locomotives costing around 1.5 million dollars. Materials for 20 of the passenger cars have already been allocated by the War Production Board. At first opportunity much of the lighter rail on main lines will be replaced with 130-pound. Three new coal branches totaling 14 miles are now under construction and will add to the nation's coal supply in postwar years. *Trains, December 1944*

This Christmas sees us at peace
* * * a permanent peace, we hope,
and certainly one toward which
the railroads have contributed
much. To all railroad men, here
and overseas, **LIMA** extends the
Season's Greetings.

Lima, December 1945

Postwar Passenger Trains
Thousands of new passenger cars

About the only sure thing about postwar passenger service at this time is that thousands of new passenger cars will go into service about as fast as the plants can turn them out.

NEW EQUIPMENT

New York Central has the largest order so far, 300 cars. Canadian Pacific is inquiring for 10 baggage-express, 35 coaches and 5 roomette sleepers. Wabash has ordered a seven-car streamliner, Chicago & North Western has reserved car-building space for an extension of its "400" fleet and replacement with new streamlined cars which have been added during wartime to its present streamliners. The Illinois Central is considering a new streamliner for the Chicago - St. Louis run and the transfer of the *Green Diamond* to Chicago - Waterloo service. Santa Fe has 80 cars on order and will extend streamlined service from Fort Worth to Galveston. The Southern Pacific expects to re-equip the *Cascade*, crack train between San Francisco and Portland. Northern Pacific has reserved car-building space, probably for new *North Coast Limited* cars to compete with the new *Empire Builder*. Louisville & Nashville plans a Cincinnati - New Orleans streamliner. The Rock Island has asked bids for cars to extend its streamlined service, particularly on medium-length daytime runs, and Pere Marquette has reserved car-building space. Rio Grande has ordered 10 cars and Seaboard 25. C&EI plans a Chicago - St. Louis streamliner. In fact, almost every road in the passenger business has plans for some new passenger equipment. *Trains, February 1945*

Quick - what's it pulling, boxcars or berths?

Even a railroad man couldn't tell —until he sees more of the train than the locomotive.

For this particular locomotive—built by American Locomotive and General Electric for the New Haven—is the product of an important development.

You see, for years the railroads have had to bear the terrific expense of buying and maintaining different types of locomotives for freight and passenger service. But today—as a result of American Locomotive's hundred years of experience in railroading—this problem is gradually being licked.

Locomotives are now being built that are *interchangeable* between passenger and freight trains. And they may be Diesel-electric or steam or any modification of either type. It doesn't matter whether they use oil or coal—the important thing is economy of performance.

This development helps reduce the number of locomotives a railroad must buy and maintain. And that's important to you. For it is out of a railroad's *savings* that improvements in service can be offered.

This is just one of many developments that will contribute to finer post-war railroading. And it is significant that it comes from the Company that gave America its first Diesel locomotive, built the world's largest steam locomotive, and has supplied an important share of the locomotives being used for war purposes by the United Nations.

American Locomotive

Alco

THE MARK OF MODERN LOCOMOTION

Black Panther #3000 idles next to K-37 2-8-2 Baldwin #498 at Durango in 1959. *J. Michael Gruber collection*

'Black Panthers' on the Post-War Narrow Gauge

Some of the lessons on railroading learned during WWII were used in future development of Army diesel locomotives. Around 1959, the U.S. Army asked the Denver & Rio Grande Western in Colorado to test experimental multigauge diesel-powered locomotives (Black Panthers) on their tracks. The engines could be adjusted for three-foot, meter or standard gauge. The Army sent the railroad engines 800-hp #3000 (76 tons, General Electric, 1957)) and #4700N, and upon testing between Durango and Alamosa, the engines rocked badly, and it was decided to do testing on the Farmington Branch.

After initial trial runs, the #4700N had more wheel gauge problems than the #3000, and the #4700N was removed from the railroad. Besides derailments with the locomotives, there were frequent mechanical failures, says former D&RGW Assistant Vice President John B. Norwood. "Business was light on the Farmington Branch, and the Rio Grande patriotically suffered and completed the desired testing using Engine #3000. The forces at Durango survived through all the testing."

Myron Henry, left, and "Punk" Blackstone at Ceder Hill, New Mexico in early 1960's when the #3000 diesel broke down. *Doug Harley collection*

This 3-foot-gauge truss-rod U.S. Army flat car #850003, loaded with steel pipes secured by stakes and steel bands, was photographed at Alamosa, Colorado on the Denver & Rio Grande Western in June of 1954. Seven box and flat cars were tested on the D&RGW narrow gauge lines by the military to see how they performed under normal operating conditions. *Mallory Hope Ferrell collection*

Fifteen years after WWII, U.S. Army #4700N was used at Durango, Colorado in experimental tests to see how it operated. The tests were not successful. *Tom Klinger collection*

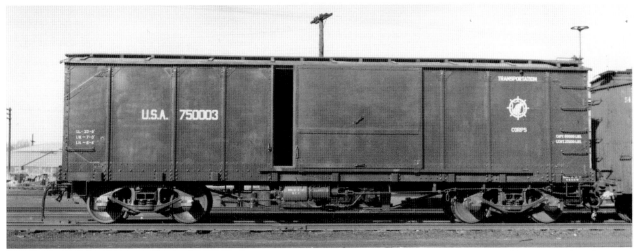

At Aztec, Colorado, U.S. Army #3000 with a freight train rambles down the weed-covered tracks. *John B. Norwood collection*

This boxcar was one of seven various types of freight cars tried out on behalf of the U. S. Army's Transportation Corps on the D&RGW narrow gauge. The cars were designed to be used on various gauges of 42 inches and smaller. Before they could be test run, various safety requirements had to be met, like adding handholds, etc. The cars were assembled from a package of sides, floor and roof. Car #750003 is at Alamosa, Colorado in 1954. *Robert W. Richardson*

There's plenty here you can't see

YOUR TRAIN RIDE of the future may be a more delightful experience because of something you can't see in this picture.

The thing you can't see is the customary gap between the ends of the rails. You can't see it because it isn't there. For the rails, instead of being bolted together, are welded together into lengths of solid metal sometimes a mile long.

This is done by pressure-welding . . . by forcing the rails together at their ends in the heat of oxy-acetylene flames until they become a single, continuous piece, uniform in appearance, structure, and strength.

Pressure-welded track is being used increasingly by railroads because it cuts maintenance costs and provides a smoother, quieter ride for passengers.

Pressure-welding also is used by many other industries. Some use pressure-welding for the construction of overland pipe lines . . . some for the fabrication of machinery parts . . . some for making oil-well tools . . . and some are using pressure-welding to make airplane and automobile parts.

Pressure-welding is a research development of The Linde Air Products Company and The Oxweld Railroad Service Company, Units of UCC.

If you are a bit technically minded or just want to know more about this subject, write for booklet E-5 on Oxy-Acetylene Pressure-Welding.

▼

UNION CARBIDE AND CARBON CORPORATION

30 East 42nd Street, New York 17, N.Y.

─────────── UCC ───────────

Products of Divisions and Units include—
ALLOYS AND METALS • CHEMICALS • PLASTICS
ELECTRODES, CARBONS, AND BATTERIES
INDUSTRIAL GASES AND CARBIDE

May 1946

Railroad Equipment Ordered in First Six Months

Orders for 55,339 freight cars, 752 passenger cars, 298 steam locomotives, 514 Diesel-electric locomotives and one electric locomotive were received by United States equipment manufacturers in the first six months of 1946, according to reports received by *Railway Age*. Of the total of freight cars ordered, 38,167 were for export and 17,172 for domestic service; 13,558 of the latter were ordered by railroads, the rest by car lines and industries. Freight cars for domestic use ordered from contract builders totaled 9,792, while 7,380 were ordered from railway company shops.

The principal purchasers of steam locomotives from American builders in the first half of 1946 were foreign governments and foreign railroads, the export total being 254 compared to 44 steam locomotives bought by American railroads. Domestic orders for Diesel-electric types aggregated 277, while 88 were ordered for export. In addition, there were orders for 149 Diesel-electrics for unidentified purchasers. *Railway Age, July 20, 1946*

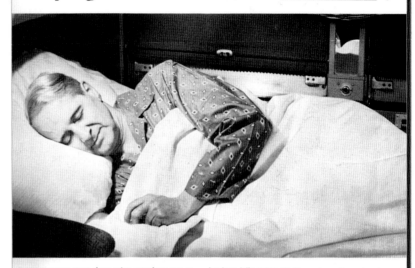

Sleeping Car Restrictions **Removed**!

1. NOW YOU CAN sleep going anywhere you go by train. Sleeping car service on runs of 450 miles or less—banned since last July—has been fully restored.* No need now to waste valuable daytime hours traveling. Reserve a Pullman bed—arrive refreshed by a good night's rest!

2. NOW YOU CAN reserve Pullman space well in advance of your trip—the ban against making reservations more than 14 days ahead is *off*.* No need now to make last-minute travel plans. Make them *early*—make Pullman comfort, safety and service an important part of them!

* Pullman's war job won't be over till the last veteran is home, but future military travel requirements permit the government to lift the ban on the operation of overnight sleeping car lines and to remove the restrictions on advance reservations of accommodations.

Go Pullman

THE SAFEST, MOST COMFORTABLE WAY OF GOING PLACES FAST!

"Welcome Back to Glacier Park!"

"That grin I'm wearing has been a long, long time busting through my whiskers, but blow my horns if I haven't something to grin about!

"They're opening the hotels and chalets in Glacier National Park this summer for folks who've craved for an eyeful of the most eye-filling country in the U.S.A. Come out this summer for a real Western vacation."

• • •

June 15 is the most important date on America's first postwar vacation calendar. It's the opening day of the 1946 summer vacation season in Glacier National Park

on the route of Great Northern's transcontinental Empire Builder.

Up in northwestern Montana, where the American and Canadian Rockies shake hands, Glorious Glacier is the place for the most refreshing vacation of your life—the one you've been wanting and needing.

• • •

A letter or postcard to A. J. Dickinson, Passenger Traffic Manager, Great Northern Railway, St. Paul 1, Minnesota, will bring you complete descriptive material on summer vacation or stop-off tours in Glacier National Park.

GREAT NORTHERN RAILWAY
BETWEEN GREAT LAKES AND PACIFIC

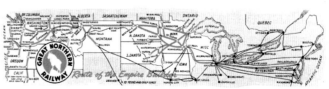

Impressive passenger train-hauling ATSF 4-8-4 #3783, with a collapsible smokestack, gets a fill-up of needed water at Topeka, Kansas on June 5, 1947. *Railway Age* commented that rail passenger traffic in 1946, the first full year after the war, brought the biggest peace-time surge in business in U.S. history. Railroads rolled up 47 billion revenue passenger-miles—less than the 56, 64 and 59 billion records of the comparable portions of the war years 1943 to 1945, but 51% greater than the 31 billion mark of 1942, the first full year of war. Passenger revenues for the first nine months of 1946 totaled $991 million, and passenger train length averaged 10.17 cars. *Don Heimburger collection*

They Succeeded Magnificently

"When victory has been won, Davenport will continue to contribute to the post war progress of an advancing America." —Davenport Locomotive Works

When WWII began, and even prior to that when hostilities seemed imminent, U.S. railroads heard the call for help.

From the Ann Arbor to the Central Vermont, from the Grand Trunk Western to the Green Bay & Western, from the giant, far-reaching Santa Fe to the minuscule 466-mile Virginian and the far-north White Pass & Yukon, railroads formed ranks and pulled their combined weights.

In 1943 the railroads carried 730 billion ton-miles of freight—six times the total of the next largest carrier, the Great Lakes ships. The total was seven times that of pipelines and more than 15 times all inter-city trucks combined. The total was 29 times that of barges and boats on inland waterways other than the Great Lakes.

Between December, 1941 and June, 1944, 23,300,000 troops were carried in organized movements within the U.S., and 97.75% of them traveled by rail. Army freight and express totaled 173 million tons, and all but 8.5% of that was carried by the railroads.

The rails in the U.S. were turned into an iron warpath that was hard to sabotage and hard to stop.

TASK AHEAD DIFFICULT

"All in all, the task with which we are confronted is not an easy one," said Colonel J. Monroe Johnson, Director of the Office of Defense Transportation, in the August 1946 issue of *Railway Purchases and Stores.* "There is much work to be done. During the war period, the railroads of the country performed an outstanding record in transporting the men, munitions and materiel demanded for ultimate victory. The American peope are well acquainted with that record.

"In this peacetime year, they are looking to you and to us to meet the production and distribution demands of our civilian economy. To do that, we will have to excel past performances.

"In spite of the difficulties which I have pointed out and with the full realization of the magnitude of the job, it is a

The next step for the railroads during and after the war was further advancement of motive power, cars, signaling and operating techniques. In the motive power department, Westinghouse-Baldwin tested this new 11,000-volt AC freight and passenger locomotive on the lines of the New Haven, with the NH purchasing five of these 4-6-6-4 types in 1943. One of the new locomotives could pull a 5,000-ton train over a 0.72% grade by momentum, and the increased horsepower of the units allowed raising speeds of a 125-car train from 39 mph to 55 mph, an increase of 41%. *Baldwin magazine, October 1943*

task which must be done. This nation needs now, as never before in peacetime, rail transportation," he continued.

"The war has demonstrated that we cannot live without it. It is no time for faint-heartedness. You in the purchasing and stores departments of the railroads must accept your full responsibilites. You are confronted with diminished budgets and keen competition for the materiel which the money in your budgets will buy. Costs have increased. They may increase futher, but I know of nothing which would be as costly to the American people or the individual railroads as a failure of the railroads to furnish transportation. This nation demands transportation and, whatever the cost, it must be paid."

In S. Kip Farrington, Jr.'s 1944 book *Railroads At War*, he says, "When the war is over, the railroads (will have) performed the transportation miracle of all time. WWII loaded our railways with a job whose hugeness and complexity almost baffles the imagination. Failure could have been fatal. They have succeeded magnificently."

And *indeed* they did.

Estimated International Costs of World War II

Battle deaths 14,904,000
Battle wounded 25,218,000
Civilian deaths 38,573,000
Direct economic costs $1,600,000,000,000

Profile of U. S. Servicemen 1941 - 1945

• 38.8% (6,322,000) of U. S. servicemen and women were volunteers.

• 61.2% (11,535,000) were draftees. Of the 17,955,000 men examined for induction, 35.8% (6,420,000) were rejected as physically or mentally unfit.

• Average duration of service was 33 months.

• Overseas Service: 73% served overseas, with an average of 16.2 months abroad.

• Combat Survivability (out of 1,000): 8.6 were killed in action, 3 died from other causes, and 17.7 received nonmortal combat wounds.

• Noncombat Jobs: 38.8% of the enlisted personnel had rear echelon assignments—administrative, technical, support or manual labor.

50th Anniversary of WWII Commemoration Committee

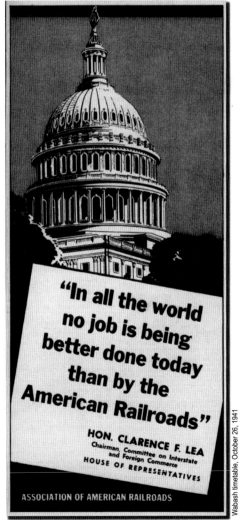

U. S. Active Military Personnel
1939 - 1945
Enlisted Men and Officers

	Army	Navy	Marines	Total
1939	189,839	125,202	19,432	334,473
1940	269,023	160,997	28,345	458,365
1941	1,462,315	284,427	54,359	1,801,101
1942	3,075,608	640,570	142,613	3,858,791
1943	6,994,472	1,741,750	308,523	9,044,745
1944	7,994,750	2,981,365	475,604	11,451,719
1945	8,267,958	3,380,817	474,680	12,123,455

U. S. Armed Forces
Toll of War
1939 - 1945

Killed		Wounded	
Army and Air Force	234,874	Army and Air Force	565,861
Navy	36,950	Navy	37,778
Marines	19,733	Marines	67,207
Coast Guard	574	Coast Guard	432
Total military killed	292,131	Total military killed	671,278

Merchant Marines

Died as POWs	37	Died	5,662
Missing/presumed dead	4,780	Killed at sea	845

50th Anniversary of WWII Commemoration Committee

369

World War II
Chronology of Significant Dates

Prelude 1931-1938

1933
January 30 — Adolf Hitler appointed German Chancellor
October 14 — Hitler announces withdrawal of Germany from the League of Nations

1934
June 30 — "Night of the Long Knives" in Germany
July 25 — Nazis murder Austrian Chancellor Dollfuss

1935
March 16 — Hitler decrees universal military service for Germany
October 3 — Italians invade Ethiopia

1936
March 7 — Germans reoccupy Rhineland

1937
December 12 — Japanese attack U. S. and British gunboats in Yangtze River, sinking *Panay*

1938
March 12 — German Anschluss of Austria

The War 1939-1945

1939
March 15 — Germans enter Prague
March 28 — Madrid falls to Franco forces—end of Spanish Civil War
August 23 — Soviet-German Nonaggression Pact signed
September 1 — Germany invades Poland—World War II begins
November 3 — U. S. Congress passes "cash and carry" amendment to Neutrality Laws

1940
May 14 — Netherlands surrenders
May 26 — Allied evacuation at Dunkirk (to June 4)
May 28 — Belgium capitulates to Germany
June 9 — Norway surrenders
June 10 — Italy enters the war
June 22 — France signs armistice with Germany
July 26 — First U. S. embargo on war trade with Japan
August 27 — U. S. draft law enacted
September 3 — U. S.-British destroyer-cutter-bases deal formulated
September 16 — Mobilization of U. S. National Guard begins (through October '41)

1941
March 11 — U S. Lend-Lease Act signed
April 13 — USSR and Japan sign Neutrality Pact
April 17 — Yugoslavia capitulates
June 22 — Germany invades USSR
July 1 — U. S. forces begin occupying Iceland
August 9 — Roosevelt and Churchill meet in Atlantic Conference (to August 12); Atlantic Charter proclaimed
October 31 — U. S. destroyer *Reuben James* sunk by U-boat
December 7 — Pacific war begins with Japanese attacks on U.S. and British posts (Pearl Harbor and Malaya; December 8 west of International Date Line)
December 8 — United States declares war on Japan
December 10 — Japanese take Guam, make first landings on Luzon
December 11 — Germany and Italy declare war on United States which prompts reciprocal action
December 23 — Wake Island falls; U. S. Army troops arrive in Australia

1942
January 31 — U. S. Army troops arrive in Ireland
February 15 — Singapore surrenders to Japanese
February 22 — Roosevelt orders MacArthur to leave Philippines
April 18 — U. S. (Doolittle) B-25 raid on Japan
May 4 — Battle of the Coral Sea (to May 8)
May 6 — Corregidor surrenders
May 8 — Germany begins summer offensive in USSR
June 3 — Battle of Midway (to June 6)
June 9 — Japanese conquest of Philippines completed
August 7 — U.S. Marines and Army land on Guadalcanal
August 17 — U. S. Eighth Air Force makes first attack on European target (Rouen-Sotteville)

August 24 — Battle of the Eastern Solomons (to August 25)
September 12 — Eisenhower assumes post as Commander-in-Chief Allied Expeditionary Forces (for Northwest Africa)
November 8 — Allied Forces invade North Africa (Operation Torch)
November 12 — Naval battle of Guadalcanal (to November 15)

1943
January 14 — Allied Casablanca Conference begins (to January 23)
March 16 — Convoy battle is climax of Battle of the Atlantic (to March 20)
April 19 — Jewish uprising in Warsaw ghetto
May 11 — U. S. Army lands on Attu
July 10 — Allies invade Sicily
July 22 — Palermo falls to U. S. Seventh Army
July 24 — Allied bombers incinerate Hamburg (to August 3)
September 8 — Eisenhower announces Italian surrender
September 9 — Allies land at Salerno
November 28 — Allied Big Three begin Tehran Conference (to November 30)

1944
January 16 — Eisenhower assumes duties as Supreme Commander, Allied Expeditionary Forces
January 22 — U.S. Army lands at Anzio
February 13 — Combined Chiefs of Staff order intensive bomber offensive against Germany
May 23 — U. S. Army breaks out at Anzio beachhead
June 4 — U.S. Army enters Rome
June 6 — Allies land at Normandy (Operation Overlord)
June 15 — U. S. Marines and Army invade Saipan
June 19 — Battle of the Philippine Sea (Great Marianas "Turkey Shoot"—to June 20)
July 21 — U. S. Marines and Army land on Guam
August 1 — U. S. 12th Army Group becomes operational in France
August 1 — Warsaw uprising begins by Polish Home Army
August 9 — Eisenhower establishes headquarters in France
August 15 — Allies land in southern France (Operation Anvil-Dragoon)
August 25 — Paris liberated
September 17 — First Allied Airborne Army units dropped in Holland (Operation Market-Garden)
October 20 — U. S. Sixth Army lands on Leyte
October 23 — Battle for Leyte Gulf (to October 26)
November 24 — United States begins B-29 raids on Japan
December 16 — Germans attack in Ardennes (Battle of the Bulge)

1945
January 9 — U. S. Army lands on Luzon
January 20 — Hungary signs armistice with Allies
January 30 — Anglo-American talks prior to Yalta Conference begin at Malta
February 3 — U. S. Army reaches Manila
February 4 — Yalta Conference begins (to February 12)
February 19 — U. S. Marines land at Iwo Jima
February 25 — B-29 raid on Tokyo demonstrates effectiveness of incendiary bombs
March 7 — U. S. Army crosses Rhine on bridge at Remagen
April 1 — U. S. forces land on Okinawa
April 7 — U. S. Navy planes sink Japanese battleship *Yamato* in East China Sea
April 9 — Allies begin major attack on Gothic Line (Italy)
April 12 — Roosevelt dies; Harry Truman succeeds him as U. S. President
April 28 — Mussolini is executed by partisans
April 30 — Hitler dies in bunker; Naval Commander Karl Donitz chosen head of state
May 5 — German forces in Netherlands, northwestern Germany and Denmark surrender
May 7 — All German forces surrender unconditionally (2:41 a.m. at Rheims)
May 8 — Proclaimed V-E Day
July 16 — Big Three begin Potsdam Conference (to August 2)
July 16 — Atomic bomb successfully tested at Los Alamos
August 6 — Atomic bomb dropped on Hiroshima
August 9 — Atomic bomb dropped on Nagasaki
August 14 — Japan surrenders, ending World War II
August 30 — U.S. forces begin landing in Japan
September 2 — V-J Day; Japan signs Instrument of Surrender

The bridge over the Elbe River at Torgau, Germany in Saxony, which was blown up by the Nazi, was the spot on the afternoon of April 25, 1945 where an American advance party led by Bill Robertson and the Russian Army came together to cut off the German Army, thus further weakening the German military machine. The castle in the background is the Renaissance Hartenfels Castle which dominates this town of 18,000. Its chapel, built in 1544, was consecrated on October 5, 1544 by Martin Luther. *Courtesy Ursula Heinz*

In a staged photograph after the initial meeting of the American and Russian forces in Torgau, Germany on April 25, 1945, soldiers of both countries shake hands on the damaged bridge over the Elbe River. *Courtesy Ursula Heinz*

A NEW DAY DAWNS IN RAILROADING

War traffic has more than doubled the volume of freight hauled by the Western Pacific Railroad from Salt Lake City to San Francisco. Wherever the going is toughest on this rugged route, General Motors Diesel freight locomotives have kept this vast stream of vital munitions moving steadily.

A crack "Express Train" of 1865 as pictured by Currier & Ives. Four years later an important new era began when the first railroad linked the Atlantic and Pacific.

War building is being rushed ahead with reliable General Motors Diesel power. In the days to come this dependable, economical power will be ready to do the hard jobs of peace.

Throughout history, wars have set up new milestones of transportation progress. And with this war, it is the General Motors Diesel Locomotive that is ushering in the new era. What advances the future will bring are already apparent in the present performance of these locomotives and the way they are helping to meet the abnormal demands upon the railroads today.

KEEP AMERICA STRONG · BUY MORE BONDS

GM GENERAL MOTORS DIESEL POWER	
LOCOMOTIVES	ELECTRO-MOTIVE DIVISION, La Grange, Ill.
ENGINES..150 to 2000 H.P.	CLEVELAND DIESEL ENGINE DIVISION, Cleveland, Ohio
ENGINES.....15 to 250 H.P.	DETROIT DIESEL ENGINE DIVISION, Detroit, Mich.

General Motors, March 1944

The Conductor Was "PUNCH DRUNK"

"I remember we had them jammed in the aisles on that trip. I'd never punched so many tickets in my life. I cracked to one of the train crew that if it kept up, I'd soon be 'punch drunk.'

"When we got to the terminal, I strolled up for a word with Sam, the engineer. He was 'gage-groggy.' They dug that engine of his out of retirement not long ago.

"We chewed it over. Then Sam's fireman came up.

"'Sure, it's tough,' he said. 'But some day we'll look back on this and be proud of the biggest job railroad men ever did.'

"He had the answer. And there *is* one thing that hasn't changed. My Hamilton's as accurate as ever. Gosh, what would I do without that watch!"

Illinois Central magazine, September, 1944

"Maybe you're the guy I'm grateful to!"

"Tough day! Assembly line got all snarled up. Didn't finish till seven o'clock.

"Then came a phone call from Plant 5. They need an engineer. Tomorrow morning. 300 miles away. So it's up to me to climb on my horse—my *iron* horse.

"I tried for a Pullman bed, of course, as soon as I knew I had to go, because a fellow sure does need *sleep* going to *keep* going on a job like mine. But everything was sold. Which didn't surprise me, either, *for I know that half the Pullman fleet is busy moving troops*. And that the *other* half is carrying *more* passengers than the *whole* fleet did in peacetime.

"Anyway, there I was—dead tired—and no bed. I saw myself sitting up all night and getting to that essential job too fagged out to tell a blueprint from a bluepoint.

"But somebody *cancelled* a reservation just in time for me to get this space. Maybe it was *you!* If it was, thanks a million. Boy, will I *sleep* tonight! And will that sleep *pay dividends* tomorrow!"

* * *

You never know how important the Pullman bed that you can't use may be to someone else. So *please* cancel *promptly* when plans change.

That is one of the most helpful contributions you can make to wartime travel, because sleeping cars are loaded to a higher percentage of capacity than ever before. Yet practically every train carrying Pullmans *still* goes out with *wasted space* due to people who either just don't show up or who cancel *too late* for the space to be assigned to others.

And only *your cooperation* can prevent this waste of needed accommodations!

★ LET'S ALL BACK THE ATTACK WITH WAR BONDS! ★

PULLMAN

For more than 80 years, the greatest name in passenger transportation—your assurance of comfort and safety as you go and certainty that you'll get there

General Motors, March 1944

Bibliography

Atkinson, Rick *An Army At Dawn: War In North Africa, 1942 - 1943*. New York, New York, Henry Holt and Company, 2002.

Atkinson, Rick *The Day Of The Battle: The War In Sicily And Italy, 1943-1944*. New York, New York, Henry Holt and Company, 2007.

Ball, Don, Jr., and Whitaker, Rogers E. M. *Decade Of The Trains: the 1940s*. Canada, Little, Brown & Company, 1977.

Cohen, Stan *Rails Across The Tundra*. Missoula, Montana, Pictorial Histories Publishing Company, 1984.

Cohen, Stan *The White Pass And Yukon Route*. Missoula, Montana, Pictorial Histories Publishing Company, 1980.

Classic Trains. Kalmbach Publishing Company, Waukesha, Wisconsin, Winter 2001.

Collias, Joe G. *Mopac Power*. San Diego, California, Howell-North Books, 1980.

Denevi, Don *America's Fighting Railroads*. Missoula, Montana, Pictorial Histories Publishing Company, 1996.

Duke, Donald and Kistler, Stan, *Santa Fe... Steel Rails Through California*. San Marino, California, Golden West Books, 1963.

Dunscomb, Guy L. *A Century Of Southern Pacific Steam Locomotives*. Modesto, California, Guy I. Dunscomb and Son, 1963.

Farrington, S. Kip Jr. *Railroads At War*. New York, New York, Samuel Curl, Inc., 1944.

Greene, Bob *Once Upon A Town*. New York, New York, Harper Collins, 2003.

Greenstein Potter, Janet *Great American Railroad Stations*. New York, New York, John Wiley & Sons, 1996.

Heimburger, Donald J. *Wabash*. Forest Park, Illinois, Heimburger House Publishing Company, 1984.

Hidy, Ralph W., Hidy, Muriel E., and Scott, Roy V. *The Great Northern Railway: A History*, Boston, Massachusetts, Harvard Business School Press, 1988.

Hilton, George W. *Monon Route*. San Diego, California, Howell-North Books, 1980.

Holland, Kevin J. *Classic American Railroad Terminals*. Osceola, Wisconsin, Motorbooks International Publishing Company, 2001.

Humphrey, Robert E. *Once Upon a Time in War: The 99th Division in World War II*. Norman, Oaklahoma, University of Oklahoma Press, 2008.

Nordykel, Phil *All American All The Way*. St. Paul, Minnesota, Zenith Press, 2005.

Rehor, John A. *The Nickel Plate Story*. Milwaukee, Wisconsin, Kalmbach Publishing Company, 1965.

Scribbins, Jim *The Milwaukee Road 1928-1985*. Forest Park, Illinois, Heimburger House Publishing Company, 2001.

Shirer, William L. *The Rise And Fall Of The Third Reich*. New York, New York, Simon and Schuster, Inc., 1960.

Stagner, Lloyd E. *Rock Island Motive Power, 1933-1955*. Boulder, Colorado, Pruett Publishing Company, 1980.

Stagner, Lloyd *Steam Locomotives Of The Frisco Line*. Boulder, Colorado, Pruett Publishing Company, 1976.

Staufer, Alvin F. *New York Central's Early Power*. Medina, Ohio, Alvin F. Staufer, 1967.

Staufer, Alvin F. *Pennsy Power*. Medina, Ohio, Alvin F. Staufer, 1962.

Staufer, Alvin F. *Steam Power Of The New York Central System - Vol. 1*. Medina, Ohio, Alvin F. Staufer, 1961.

Stringham, Paul H. *Illinois Terminal: The Electric Years*. Glendale, California, Interurban Press, 1989.

Turner, Charles W. and Dixon, Thomas W., Jr. *Chessie's Road*. Alderson, West Virginia, Chesapeake & Ohio Historical Society, Inc., 1986.

Voynick, Stephen M. *Climax - The History Of Colorado's Climax Molybdenum Mine*. Missoula, Montana, Mountain Press Publishing Company, 1996.

Wayner, Robert *Diesel Locomotive Rosters*. New York, New York, Wayner Publications, 1975.

Westwood, John *Railways At War*. San Diego, California, Howell-North Books, 1981.

Wilson, Graham *The White Pass And Yukon Route Railway*. Whitehorse, Yukon, Wolf Creek Books, Inc., 1998.

Young, Andrew D. and Provenzo, Eugene F. *The History Of the St. Louis Car Company*. San Diego, California, Howell-North Books, 1978.

Index

A

A.C. Gilbert Company 170
Aachen, Germany 322
Admiral 103
Africa 29
AIR-POM 74
Air Corps 308
Akron and Barberton Belt Railway 212
Alamosa, Colorado 360, 361
Alaska Defense Command 261
Alaska Railroad 100, 260, 262, 264
Alco 261
Alco-Richmond 232
Algeria 97
American Car & Foundry 217, 222, 226
American Locomotive Company 173, 235, 359
Ames, Iowa 356
Anaconda Copper & Brass 273
Anchorage, Alaska 260, 261
Anniston Ordnance Depot 232
Appleton, Colonel John A. 310
Army and Navy Munitions Board 13
Army Engineers 326
Army Liberty Special 41
Arsenal of Democracy 40
Ashtabula, Ohio 106
Association of American Railroads 15, 41, 44, 49, 54, 59, 98,
     111, 116, 123, 139, 150, 175, 191, 217, 291, 341, 367, 369
Atlantic Coast Line 39, 69, 100, 212
Atlantic Coast Transportation Corps 101
Atlantic Seaboard 151
Atlas Car & Mfg. Company 233
ATSF 365
Austerity locomotive 329
Axis 10
Aztec, New Mexico 361

B

Baldwin 26, 45, 47, 48, 49, 51, 56, 167, 168, 171, 197, 199,
     200, 201, 212, 243, 261, 310, 312, 316, 323, 353, 356
Baldwin Locomotive Works 91, 132, 174, 194, 198, 202, 203,
     206, 268, 275, 286, 302, 313, 315, 328, 329, 330, 348,
     349, 351
Baltimore & Ohio Railroad 60, 87, 98, 117, 124, 138, 142,
     168, 177, 237, 265, 301, 305, 338, 339, 347
Battle of the Bulge 14
Bay Village, Ohio 106
Beecher Falls, Virginia 249
Belgium 320, 322
Bellafaire, Judith A. 299

Bell Aircraft 179
Belt Line 106
Bement, Illinois 129
Bengal & Assam Railway 319, 322
Berlin Express 332
Berwick, Pennsylvania 217
Binley, Charles E. 329
Black Panther 360
Block, Betty 304
Blue Bird 354, 355
Blue Cut Hill 26
Boston and Maine Railroad 311
Boston Port of Embarkation 69
Boyce, Louisiana 256
Breeze Corporations 67
British Railways 380
Brooklyn, New York 234
Buckeye Yard, Columbus, Ohio 294
Bucyrus, Ohio 135
Budd, Ralph 10, 27
Budd Company 354, 355
Buderich, Germany 326, 327
Bureau, Illinois 120, 123
Burlington Railroad 6, 88, 134
Burma Road 319
Burpee, Brig. General Clarence L. 380
Burro crane 292

C

Cajon Pass, California 57
Calcutta 319
California Limited 186
Call, Norman 199
Camp Bowie, Texas 236
Camp Chaffee, Arkansas 256
Camp Claiborne, Louisiana 95, 232, 241, 261, 274
Camp Fannin, Texas 259
Camp Haan, California 38
Camp Hoffman, North Carolina 43
Camp Joseph T. Robinson 232
Camp Lee, Virginia 312
Camp Mackall, North Carolina 43
Camp McCoy, Wisconsin 15
Camp Patrick Henry, Virginia 64
Camp Pike, Little Rock, Arkansas 232
Camp Plauche 91, 93, 241
Camp Polk, Louisiana 32, 256, 257
Camp Shelby, Mississippi 92, 99, 182
Canadian Pacific 358
Canicatti, Sicily 334
Carentan, France 315

Carstens, Hal 180
Cass, West Virginia 294
Ceder Hill, New Mexico 360
Centralized Traffic Control (CTC) 15
Central of Georgia Railroad 171, 324
Central Railroad of New Jersey 205
Challenger 181, 342
Charleston, Indiana 303
Charleston Port of Embarkation 340
Cherbourg, France 71, 308, 315, 317, 318, 328, 335
Chesapeake & Ohio 88, 193, 195, 197, 294
Chessie 39, 276
Chicago & Alton Railroad 185
Chicago & Eastern Illinois Railroad 93, 96, 358, 367
Chicago & NorthWestern 37, 68, 88, 115, 141, 171, 181, 197,
    204, 250, 296, 301, 349, 358
Chicago, Burlington & Quincy 10, 356
Chicago, Illinois 103, 118, 119, 125, 127, 129, 141, 142, 143,
    154, 217, 296, 349
Chicago Union Station 128
Chief 117, 123, 144
Chief of Engineers, Transportation Corps 43
Chief of Transportation 41, 103, 111, 133, 306, 307, 308, 311,
    319, 321
China 319
Christie Convertible tanks 257
Cichocki, Sophie 302
City of Salina 11, 173
Claiborne-Polk Railway 90, 92
Claridy, John 334
Cleveland, Ohio 233
Coast Artillary Corps 78
Coast Artillary Replacement Training Center 241
Collias, Joe 206
Cologne, Germany 122
Colorado & Southern Railway 261
Columbus & Greenville 26
Columbus, Mississippi 26
Columbus, Ohio 114
Connor, Lt. Michael 240
Cordic, Regi 184
Corps of Engineers 44, 93, 119, 202, 254, 308, 311, 319
Corsicana, Texas 113
Cotton Belt 113, 248
Covered hoppers 15

D

D-Day 313
Darby Corporation 137
Darjeeling-Himalayan Railway 322
Darlington, Master Sgt. Malcom R. 250
Davenport-Besler Corporation 232
Davenport Locomotive Works 366
Davies, Major R. Hart 313
Dayton Rubber Manufacturing Company 289
Debarkations 339

Decapod 80, 114, 313, 316, 324
Decatur, Illinois 207, 225
Deer Creek, Illinois 148
Delano, Jack 156
Denver & Rio Grande Railroad 262
Denver & Rio Grande Western 39, 171, 206, 261, 360, 361
Denver, Colorado 171
Derby, England 321
Detroit, Toledo & Ironton 196
Deutsche Bundesbahn 317
Deutsche Reichsbahn 317
Dining car 45, 162, 174, 249
Driscoll, Thomas 334
Ducks landing craft 142
Duluth, Missabe & Iron Range 50
Durango, Colorado 361

E

Eastman, Joseph B. 13, 167, 171, 179, 204, 256
East Syracuse, New York 107
East Tennessee & Western North Carolina Railroad 261
Eisenhower, General Dwight D. 65
Elbe River 371
Electro-Motive 131, 353
Elmira Holding and Reconsignment Point 72
Emeryville, California 72
Empire State Express 105
Englewood, Illinois 47
Erie Railroad 356
Eska coal mine 261
Europa passenger liner 339
Explosives piers 77

F

Fairbanks, Alaska 260
Fannin, Colonel James Walker 259
Farrington, S. Kip 367
Fast Mail & Express 186
Feather River Canyon 131
Florida East Coast Railroad 184
Fluckey, Commander Eugene 190, 191
Fort Dix, New Jersey 97
Fort Leonard Wood 237
Fort Mason, California 76
Fort Meade, Maryland 237
Fort Slocum, New York 101
France 313, 320, 322, 324, 333, 335, 336
Frankfort, Indiana 124, 146, 300
Fred Harvey restaurants 186, 341
French Railway System 321
Frisco Lines 146, 182, 198, 358
Fruit Growers Express 235
Ft. Benning, Georgia 135, 236, 239, 257, 259
Ft. Bragg, North Carolina 87
Ft. Eustis, Virginia 231, 240, 241, 242, 243, 244, 245, 246,
    247, 248, 249, 250, 251, 252, 254, 292, 294

Ft. Francis E. Warren, Wyoming 91, 241
Ft. Knox, Kentucky 239

G

Galesburg, Illinois 121, 122
General 103
General American Transportation Corporation 148, 152, 153
General Electric 318, 322
General Federation of Women's Clubs 299
General Motors locomotives 265, 267, 270, 274, 288, 341, 352, 372
Germany 320
Glass, Sgt. Barney E. 248
Gothic heavyweight cars 226
Grand Canyon Limited 122
Grand Central Terminal 161
Grand Junction, Colorado 39
Grant Photo Corporation 42
Gray, Colonel Carl R. Jr. 92
Great Lakes Naval Training Center 223, 342
Great Northern Railway 63, 108, 173, 290, 363
Gross, General C. P. 58, 169, 231, 328
Gulf, Mobile & Ohio Railroad 205, 210
Gutkoska, Technician Third Class J.M. 248

H

H.K. Porter 234
Hamilton Watch Company 185
Hampton Roads, Virginia 69
Hampton Roads Port of Embarkation 64, 66, 88
Harper, Corporal James E. 248
Hartenfels Castle 371
Hatfield, Billy 190
Hattiesburg, Mississippi 96, 97, 99
Hazelton, Ohio 104
Herzogenrath, Germany 322
Hewitt Industrial Hose 149
Hiawatha 128, 297
Hillman, Sidney 299
Hobby, Colonel Oveta Culp 299
Holabird, Maryland 135, 238
Holding and reconsignment points 133
Holland 320
Hospital cars 165, 227
Hospital kitchen cars 136, 222
Hospital ships 339, 340
Hospital train 323
Hospital ward cars 136
Howitzer 24
Howson, Elmer T. 60
Hudgins, Sharon Weldon 183
Hungerford, Clark 92, 93

I

Identification of Organizational Impedimenta (IOI) 74
Illinois Central Railroad 61, 65, 68, 101, 139, 167, 177, 248, 304, 346, 347, 358, 380

Illinois Railroad Museum 221
Illinois Terminal Railroad 118
Illiopolis, Illinois 118
Indiana Army Ammunition Plant 303
Indiana Harbor Belt Railroad. 142
Indiana Ordnance Works 303
International-Great Northern Railroad 51
Iranian State Railway 315
Italy 321

J

Jackson, Charles E. 304
Japan 320
Jefferson Barracks, Missouri 235
Jeffersonville, Indiana 303
Jersey City, New Jersey 222
Johnson, Colonel J. Monroe 312, 366

K

Kansas City Southern Railway 353
Katy Flyer 25, 110
Katy Railroad 183
Kelly, Ralph 329, 348, 349
Kenai Peninsula 260
Kettlewood, Harry 302
Kitchen cars 214, 226, 249
Knight, Colonel W.G. 202
Kunming, China 319

L

La Junta, Colorado 186
Land O'Corn 380
Ledo 319, 320
Lehigh Valley Railroad 171
Le Mans, France 14
Lend-Lease 11, 40, 77, 78, 80, 84, 126, 132, 133, 134, 255, 310, 315, 329
Liberty Ships 11, 344
Licata, Sicily 334
Lightburn Family 109
Lima, Ohio 146
Lima locomotives 25, 84, 193, 194, 195, 196, 209, 243, 252, 323, 325, 358
Lingayen Gulf 320
Little Rock, Arkansas 248
London & North Eastern Railway 334
Los Angeles Union Passenger Terminal 36
Louisiana & Arkansas Railway 11, 353
Louisville & Nashville Railroad 201, 358
Lucke, Mrs. Dorothy 296
Luzon 320

M

M-3 tanks 35, 36, 48, 80
MacArthur, General Douglas 49, 349
MacFadden, Colonel E. F. 202
Mail cars 164

Maine Central Railroad 175
Manila Railroad 320
Mare Island Navy Yard 235
Marietta, Pennsylvania 132
Marietta Holding and Reconsignment Point 98
Markuson, John 190
Marsh, Major J.W. 202, 313
Marshall, General George C. 44
McAlester, Oklahoma Ammunitions Plant 235
McAlester, Oklahoma 183
Medical trains 346, 347
Memphis, Tennessee 83
Meneken, Kansas 29
Merci box car 330
Mercury 181, 352
Meridian, Mississippi 94, 99
Messina, Italy 334
Metal for Victory 11
Meteor 146
Mexican railroad workers 380
Mid-Pacific Railroad 238
Mikado 26, 49, 121
Military Passenger Agreement 111
Military Railway Service 13, 14, 44, 91, 92, 93, 98, 100,
     307, 311, 314, 315, 318, 319, 320, 321, 324, 326,
     337
Milwaukee Road 15, 31, 48, 55, 62, 127, 128, 129, 196, 270,
     274, 276, 280, 297, 346
Mississippi Central Railroad 182
Missouri Pacific Railroad 51, 145, 167, 171, 206, 248
MKT 110
Moberly, Missouri 221
Mohawk 106, 107, 121, 209
Molly Pitcher 301
Monon 227
Monte Cassino, Italy 314
MoPac 206
Morgenthau, Henry 108
Morss, Sgt. Oliver 336
Motor Transport Service 308
Mt. Carmel, Illinois 152
MTL tugboats 32

N

Napa Junction, California 235
Naples, Italy 323, 330, 336
Nashville, Chattangoona & St. Louis 87
National Bearing Metals Corporation 329
National Guard 129
National Guard Extra 127
National Limited 124
Naval Ammunition Depot 235
Navy Supply Depot 230
New Deal 12
New Haven Railroad 13, 214, 366
New Orleans, Louisana 32

Newport News, Virginia 64, 338
New York Central 104, 105, 106, 107, 121, 127, 132, 145,
     148, 150, 151, 152, 158, 160-166, 174, 176, 209, 269,
     276, 352, 358, 368
New York Port of Embarkation 71, 72, 75
Nichols, Missouri 146
Nickel Plate Road 106, 124, 146, 148, 149, 194, 300
Noe, Dave 68
Nolte, Frank 181
Norfolk & Western Railway 30, 82, 117, 118, 153, 174, 197,
     207, 227, 272, 290
Norfolk, Virginia 88, 234
Normandy 308, 315, 319, 321, 328
North Africa 23, 313, 315, 321, 334, 336, 337, 338
Northern Pacific Railroad 85, 215, 230, 358
North Platte, Nebraska 11, 155
North Platte Canteen 11, 155
North Shore Line 33
Northwestern Pacific Railroad 138
Norton, Ralph 304

O

O'Neal, Colonel C. D. 380
Oakland, California 73, 344
Oakland, California Naval Supply Depot 233
Office of Defense Transportation (ODT) 10, 11, 40, 115
Ogden, Utah 188
Ogden Arsenal, Utah 135
Ogden Union Station 188, 189
Oil tankers 145, 146, 150, 151
Okie, Lt. Colonel Fred 96
Oliver Coal Company 208
Omaha, Nebraska 122
Operation Torch 336
Oran, North Africa 336
Ordnance Department 116
Oscawanna, New York 105

P

Pacific Factag Fabrics 271
Pacific Fruit Express 11
Panama Limited 167
Parbatipur Junction 320
Paris, Illinois 152
Parkersburg, West Virginia 124
Pasco, Washington 76, 84, 230, 231
Patton, General George S. 14, 321
Pearl Harbor, Hawaii 10, 43, 77, 133, 242, 251
Pelley, John J. 120, 193
Pennsylvania Railroad 12, 14, 27, 47, 84, 85, 87, 114, 127,
     132, 197, 203, 209, 257, 266, 277, 278, 279, 280, 281,
     283, 284, 287, 288, 296, 301, 349, 353
Pennsylvania Station 102
Penrhos Junction, Caerphilly, Wales 334
Pere Marquette Railway 112, 193, 265, 358
Pershing steam locomotive 259
Peru, Indiana 128
Piggyback trailer trains 15

Pittsburgh & West Virginia 200
Port Johnston, New Jersey 72
Portland, Oregon 78, 80
Port of Embarkation 76, 85
Port of Philadelphia 132
Port of San Francisco 132
Port Traffic Office 132
Port Transportation Division 77
Preparation for Overseas Movement (POM) 74
Prince Rubert, B.C. 77
Proviso Yard 141, 142, 143, 301
PUG 334
Pullman 11, 38, 47, 59, 70, 111, 173, 184, 187, 215, 217, 219, 222, 223, 226, 227, 269, 282, 345, 352, 363, 372, 380

Q

Quartermaster Corps 44, 233, 236, 239, 248, 308
Quartermaster General 43, 125, 133
Queen Mary 340, 343
Queens Dock, Glasgow 334

R

Railroad Museum of Pennsylvania at Strasburg 194
Railroads in Two Wars 49, 59
Railway chapel car 320
Railway Express Agency 41, 62, 136, 175, 195, 225, 276
Railway Grand Division 92, 320, 321
Railway Operating Battalion 92, 95, 96, 97, 99, 101, 240, 248, 319, 320, 321, 323, 333, 334
Railway Shop Battalion 92, 320
Raton Pass, New Mexico 114, 117
Remington Rand, Inc. 118
Reserve Corps 311
Rheims, France 339
Rhineland 319
Rhine River 326
Richmond, Fredericksburg & Potomac 199, 207, 324
Riview, Wyoming 36
Roberts, Dr. Richard C. 188, 190
Rock Island Lines 83, 120, 139, 248
Rome, Italy 321, 323, 330, 332
Roosevelt, Franklin D. 10, 23, 103, 251
Roosevelt, President Franklin D. 108
Rosie the Riveter 12, 299
Ross, Major General Frank S. 380
Russia 310, 315
Russian Decapods 316

S

Sabel, William 182
Sacramento, California 299
Salida, Colorado 262
Sallisaw, Oklahoma 11
San Antonio, Texas 91
San Francisco Port of Embarkation 72, 73, 80, 123
Sangamon Ordnance Plant, Illinois 118
San Luis Obispo, California 22

Santa Fe Railway 11, 12, 13, 24, 30, 34, 36, 42, 46, 62, 108, 114, 116, 117, 120, 121, 122, 123, 126, 140, 144, 154, 202, 211, 269, 290, 304
Schofield Barracks, Oahu, Hawaii 238
Seaboard Air Line Railway 174, 358
Seatrain Texas, transport ship 73
Seattle Port of Embarkation 76, 80
Second Military Railway Service, France 380
Selective Service Act 44
Seybold, Lt. Colonel J.S. 313
Shamokin, Pennsylvania 132
Sheboygan, Wisconsin 204
Sicily, Italy 313
Signal Corps 163
Silverton Northern Railroad 261
Skagway, Alaska 261, 264
Sleeping cars 107
Somervell, Lieut. General Brehon B. 380
South Coffeyville, Oklahoma 110
Southern Museum of Civil War and Locomotive History 330
Southern Pacific Railway 56, 85, 91, 138, 139, 169, 181, 182, 197, 198, 206, 224, 285, 299, 302, 355, 358
Southern Railway 13, 92, 93, 94, 96, 99
Sparks, Nevada 30
Speir, Seaman First Class George 342
Spencer, Delbert 186
Spirit of the Union Pacific 169
St. Leu, Algeria 337
St. Louis-San Francisco Railway 182, 212
St. Louis-Southwestern Railway 113, 280
St. Louis Car Company 78, 79
St. Louis Union Station 56
Standard Stoker Company 13
Stimson, Henry 103, 332
Stores Department 122
Streator, Illinois 122
Streiff, Captain C.J. 235
Sun Shipbuilding & Drydock Company 73
Sunset Limited 355
Sweeney, Colonel Thomas W. 9

T

Tanana River 264
Tank cars 213
Tavener, Ernest O. 115
Techny, Illinois 127
Tehachapi Line 56
Texas 71
Texas & Pacific 182
Thomas Nelson, liberty ship 69
Tolleson, E.E. 96
Topeka, Kansas 365
Torgau, Germany 339, 371
Trac Scouts 35
Traffic Control Division 111, 116, 118
Trans-Iranian Railroad 325

Transit Storage Division 133, 134
Transportation Control Committee 132
Trinidad, Colorado 187
Tripartite Pact 10
Troop kitchen cars 108, 217, 218, 220, 222, 223
Troop sleepers 214, 215, 216, 217, 219, 220, 221, 223, 224,
    225, 226, 352
Troop train consist 222
Truman, Harry S. 306
Tunisia 29, 97

U

U. S. Army Consolidating Station 125, 296
U. S. Army Transportation Corps 13, 40, 41, 43, 44, 64, 65,
    66, 67, 93, 98, 103, 115, 116, 118, 133, 134, 135, 136,
    241, 242, 249, 251, 253, 254, 255, 292, 306, 307, 311,
    313, 315, 318, 322, 326, 328, 331, 335, 344
U. S. military bases 18
U.S. Naval Ammunition Depot, Iona Island, New York 235
U.S. Naval Ammunition Depot, Oahu, Hawaii 233
U.S.S. Barb 190
Union, Illinois 221
Union Carbide and Carbon Corporation 362
Union Pacific Railroad 11, 29, 36, 37, 57, 122, 173, 178, 189,
    269, 270, 274, 342
United Kingdom 315, 319
United Kingdom Crusader tanks 27
United States Railroad Administration (USRA) 8
Unit train 15
Upper Merion & Plymouth 212
USOX 78, 79

V

V-E Day 14, 255, 338, 339, 340
V-J Day 14, 112, 255, 339, 340
Vernon, Ohio 104
Victory Ships 339
Virginian 117

Voorheesville, New York 98, 132
Vosges Mountains 317
Vulcan 252
Vulcania passenger liner 339

W

Wabash, Indiana 149
Wabash Railroad 128, 149, 207, 221, 225, 355, 358
WAC 217, 299, 315
Wagoner, Oklahoma 110, 145
Waialu Plantation 312
War Advertising Council 265
War bonds 12, 54, 108, 169, 187
War Finance Committee 265
War Manpower Commission 380
War Production Board 12, 13, 214
Washington, Idaho & Montana Railroad 232
WAVES 186, 217, 302
Wesel, Germany 319, 326, 327
West Detroit, Michigan 127
Western Pacific Railroad 131, 324
Westinghouse 134
Weston Park, Massachusetts 145
Whellis, Captain Reuben 259
Whitcomb locomotives 202, 204, 233, 234, 259, 321, 326, 330
White, R.B. 338
Whitehorse, Alaska 261
Whitehurst, Mrs. John L. 299
White Pass & Yukon Railroad 260, 261, 262, 313
Whittier Cutoff 260
Wilburn, Illinois 123
Willard car shop 305
Wilson, Charles E. 356
Wilson, William H. 260
Wrecking crane 331

Y

Young, Admiral William B. 59

Roanoke, Virginia Norfolk and Western Railway freight yard, 1944

MILEPOSTS

Illinois Central Magazine, September, 1944

"The train was crowded as trains almost always are these days. The day was hot. The conductor moved slowly up the aisle. For each passenger he had a smile as he took the ticket. He exchanged light conversation with many. Those who asked him, as did the sergeant in front of us, how much service was shown by the decorations on his sleeve, were told that they meant he had been with the railroad for 40 years.

"We handed him our ticket and asked: 'How do you keep your good humor?'

"'I have to,' was his reply. 'It's the only way I can get my work done. If I got crabby, I'd have arguments and I'd never get through the train. Besides, nobody ever did himself or anybody else any good by crabbing.'

"It was a happy contrast to the don-cha-know-there's-a-war-on attitude of too many people who deal with the public. And it was a stroke of good will for the institution with which he has worked for 40 years."—*Editorial entitled "Happy Contrast" by Paul Wollstadt in the Rockford (Ill.) Register-Republic, referring to Thomas J. Cathcart, conductor on No. 13, the Land O'Corn, between Chicago and Rockford*

* * *

"There is a profound lesson in the experience of the railroads, applicable in relations of Government with other industry. The railroads' experience has shown that, given the incentive and opportunity to organize its own voluntary collaboration, industry does not necessarily need to be regimented to insure maximum output even in times of war. The familiar statement that, in such crises, democracy and localized voluntarism have to be superseded by authoritarianism and centralization turns out not to be true."—*New York Times*

* * *

"It is no exaggeration to say that railroads are war roads. For example, half of all the Pullman cars in the United States and one-third of all the coaches are in constant military service. Approximately one and a half million men are transported every month by rail in organized troop movements. In addition, the railroads handle an equal volume of furlough travel. An infantry division, consisting of about

15,000 men, requires about forty trains, while an armored division with all its equipment needs nearly double that number of trains. That the railroads have been able to handle this enormous military traffic on time and with a high degree of comfort is a record of which every American railroader must be proud."—*Lieut. Gen. Brehon B. Somervell, Commanding General, Army Service Forces*

* * *

Railway workers as of the middle of June, 1944, totaled 1,446,860, an increase of 4.6 per cent compared with the corresponding month of 1943. The biggest increase, 7.6 per cent, was in maintenance of way and structures employes.

* * *

Transportation is as truly a weapon as any gun, airplane, tank, or other engine of warfare; because you must get the men, the weapons, and the supplies to the right place at the right time in order to win battles. To beat the enemy we have got to have more and better transportation than he has—just as we must have better soldiers and more and better munitions. *Col. C. D. O'Neal, Transportation Officer, U. S. Army*

* * *

"Railroads have done a splendid job throughout the war and they seem determined to do an equally effective job when peace comes."—*Chicago (Ill.) Tribune*

* * *

"The war has clearly reminded us that the railroads are the jugular arteries of the nation."—*Albion (Mich.) Recorder*

* * *

The first passenger train to be run by the Transportation Corps in France was met by enthusiastic French folks who cheered and tossed flowers to the crew. The trip was to have been made in secret, but the French learned of it through their underground communication system. First passenger included Maj. Gen. Frank S. Ross, chief of transportation in this theater, and Brig. Gen. Clarence L. Burpee, director of the Second Military Railway Service in France.

* * *

Ten thousand Mexican railroad workers are to be brought into the United States as track and maintenance of way workers, the War Manpower Commission announced on July 25. The importation will raise the total number brought in from the

neighboring republic for work on the railroads to approximately 50,000. They are assigned to twenty-nine railroads, and are on contract for six months. The contract is between the worker and the United States Government.

* * *

"Considering the vast haulage chalked up by the railroads of America within the past three years, their record for safety has been remarkable."—*Anderson (S. C.) Independent & Tribune*